INTERNATIONAL RELATIONS

. . .

EDITED BY
SARA PARKER

CHABOT COLLEGE

cognella
San Diego, CA

First published in the United States of America in 2011 by Cognella, a division of University Readers, Inc.

Trademark Notice: Product or corporate names may be trademarks or registered trademarks, and are used only for identification and explanation without intent to infringe.

15 14 13 12 11   1 2 3 4 5

Printed in the United States of America.

ISBN: 978-1-60927-933-2

Front cover: "Globe Encounters"—The size of the glow on a particular city location corresponds to the amount of Internet Protocol (IP) traffic flowing between that place and New York City over a 24-hour period.

Back cover: "World Within New York" shows how different neighborhoods reach out to the rest of the world in a 24-hour period. The widths of the color bars represent the proportion of world regions in contact with each neighborhood.

Published by the New York Talk Exchange. http://senseable.mit.edu/nyte/. Permission to reprint granted by the publisher.

www.cognella.com 800.200.3908

CONTENTS

UNIT 2 • THEORY

UNIT 3 • SECURITY

UNIT 4 • HUMAN RIGHTS

UNIT 5 • INTERNATIONAL POLITICAL ECONOMY AND ENVIRONMENT

Editor's Introduction

SARA PARKER

S cholars of international relations are concerned with understanding the complex relationships of the almost seven billion people on earth. We do so by trying to understand the various ways that humans identify themselves, how they group themselves, how they behave individually and in different types of groups, and the customs, rules, and practices that guide these interactions. An international relations scholar is a jack-of-all-trades—interested in history, the study of humans and societies, economics, communication, diplomacy, geography and philosophy, to name a few. This book is an introduction to topics that fall under the broad subject area that is "international relations" and will provide you with the vocabulary and theories, supported by real-world examples, to help you begin to make sense of an extraordinary international system.

Three central observations about the world guide this particular approach to an introductory study of international relations.

1. We live in a world that is increasingly connected through communication and information, culture, and, of course, economics. In 2008, there were 1.6 billion Internet users, and over 60 percent of the total global population owned a cell phone.[1] There are slightly fewer than 200 countries in the world, and 118 of them have at least one McDonalds.[2] Global trade declined for the first time since World War II in 2009, but is expected to rebound at impressive rates, continuing an almost century-long trend of global economic expansion and integration.[3] A quick survey of the world shows dramatic evidence of idea sharing and development:

    The world's tallest building is in Taipei and will soon be in Dubai. Its largest publicly traded company is in Beijing. Its biggest refinery is being constructed in

India. Its largest passenger airplane is built in Europe. The largest investment fund on the planet is in Abu Dhabi; the biggest movie industry is Bollywood, not Hollywood … The largest Ferris wheel is in Singapore. The largest casino is in Macao, which overtook Las Vegas in gambling revenues last year. America no longer dominates even its favorite sport, shopping. The Mall of America in Minnesota once boasted that it was the largest shopping mall in the world. Today it wouldn't make the top ten.[4]

The catchphrase used to capture such examples is "globalization," which can be defined as developments in technology, communications, travel, and information sharing, as well as increased connectivity and interdependence of global economic markets that have the collective effect of making the world "smaller."

As the world becomes increasingly interconnected, there are bound to be strains on traditional ways of life and age-old cultural practices. For example, it is estimated that nearly half of the estimated 7,000 languages spoken in the world are at risk of extinction. When these languages disappear, "they leave behind no dictionary, no text, no record of the accumulated knowledge and history of a vanished culture."[5] The cumulative effect of global pressures on local communities and longstanding cultural practices is often referred to as a process of "fragmentation."

It is important to acknowledge that globalization can have the effect of both making the world "smaller"(or integrating the world) *and* of "fragmenting" (or pulling the world apart). Furthermore, economic development is inextricably linked with environmental welfare, and the expansion of the former has caused widespread and irreversible damage to the latter. The readings included in this text confront the concept of globalization from a variety of angles—acknowledging that there is no singular interpretation and that overarching conclusions are elusive.

2. The prevention of conflict within and among states is a central concern for members of the global community and for students of international relations. As global trade has increased, global conflict trends have continued to hold steady or have even declined since the collapse of the Soviet Union; "interstate warfare has remained at a relatively low level since the end of the Second World War and the establishment of the United Nations Organization."[6] In 2008, 15 percent of countries experienced major political violence, down from 30 percent in 1992.[7] Interstate wars (war between two or more countries), revolutionary wars, and ethnic wars have all declined from peaks in the mid-1980s to early 1990s.[8]

Yet, our perception is often one that the world is a very dangerous place. With images of terrorists lurking, weapons of mass destruction on alert for launch, and governments constantly attempting to protect their citizens against real and potential threats, it is possible to lose this sense of perspective. The collection of international relations theories presented here asks you to examine conflict at different levels of analysis, to place conflict in historical perspective, and to study *peace* with the same vigilance with which you study war.

Global security threats are absolutely real; however, an overzealous focus on war neglects widespread human suffering in other forms. The world's deadliest conflict since World War II is ongoing in the Democratic Republic of Congo. The vast majority of the 5,400,000 people who have died in that decades-long, protracted conflict have died from nonviolent causes such as malaria, diarrhea, pneumonia, and malnutrition.[9] The readings in this text address traditional security threats such as war, terrorism, and weapons of mass destruction, as well as threats to the basic health and safety of citizens and the planet they inhabit.

3. Rules, norms, and—even in the absence of world government—international law guide the behavior of actors in the international system. As international law scholar Louis Henkin wrote:

> *International relations and foreign policy, then, depend on a legal order, operate in a legal framework, assume a host of legal principles and concepts which shape the policies of nations and limit national behavior. If one doubts the significance of this law, one need only imagine a world from which it were absent ... There would be no security of nations or stability of governments, territory and air-space would not be respected; vessels could navigate only at their constant peril; property—within or without any given territory—would be subject to arbitrary seizure; persons would have no protection of law or diplomacy; agreements would not be made or observed; diplomatic relations would end; international trade would cease; international organizations and arrangements would disappear.[10]*

The compilation of readings in this text begins with the assumption that *patterns of behavior do exist in international relations.* The readings challenge you to identify those patterns, to examine and assess their stability, and to question your own understandings of what constitutes acceptable and appropriate behavior in the international system.

ORGANIZATION OF THE BOOK

The **first unit** of the book introduces you to the concept of globalization and to the players in the international system. We know that landmasses on earth are divided into entities called "countries" or, in international relations terminology, "states." But what are states? How did they get there? Why do they matter? While states have historically been the primary unit of focus in the international system, they are not the only relevant players.

States frequently group together into clubs of states, forming alliances, or partnerships. These organizational units, called Intergovernmental Organizations* (IGOs), such as the United Nations or the European Union, also matter in international relations. Nongovernmental organizations (NGOs), non-profit organizations whose members are united by a cause rather than nationality or geographic borders, also matter in international relations. Some multinational corporations (MNCs) such as Walmart earn more money per year than many states in the world; they also matter in international relations. Last, but certainly not least, the citizenry of the world and those individuals it comprises—known as global civil society—matter as well.

Once you are familiar with the players in the global sphere, the **second unit** will introduce you to international relations theory. Simply knowing the players gives you only a degree of insight as to how they interact with one another. International relations theories attempt to systematize these interactions, to make them understandable, explainable, and even predictable. Both mainstream and so-called "alternative" international relations theories are introduced in unit two.

The **third unit** concentrates on the study of conflict and war, which is, as you will learn in unit 2, a fundamental concern of international relations theory. Is human nature conflict-prone? What are wars' causes, and can we prevent them? Is there such a thing as "just" war? Is Roman philosopher Emperor Marcus Aurelius correct that: "If you've seen the present then you've seen everything—as it's been since the beginning, as it will be forever … The same substance, the same form. All of it"?

While intricately related to the study of conflict, the study of human rights deserves its own category of attention. This topic is examined in **unit four**, alongside the concept of rules and laws in the international system, humanitarian intervention, and consideration of the notion that there is (or should be) a global ethical imperative to uphold universal human rights for all citizens, irrespective of nationality or location.

Unit five returns to the topic of globalization. As previously mentioned, globalization has led to both economic and cultural integration, as well as disproportionate distributions of wealth and cultural fragmentation. Furthermore, human behavior has unavoidable impacts on our planet; environmental concerns that span continents are mutually created and can only be solved through cooperation. This unit raises and seeks to address questions: Why are some countries rich and others poor? What strategies do countries use to develop economically? What role do international institutions play in facilitating economic exchange? What are the most critical environmental crises we face today and how can they be solved?

Each unit includes one or more application articles and/or case studies that will enable you to make connections between the concepts being introduced and real-world situations. The absolute best way one can attempt to make sense of the international system is to learn

---

* Sometimes referred to as an international governmental organization and also abbreviated IGO.

about it! This book will define vocabulary and introduce concepts to start a conversation regarding strands of contemporary thought in international relations scholarship, but you can expand your learning curve exponentially by reading everything that you can about international affairs, past and present.

ENDNOTES

1. The World Factbook. May 27, 2010. Washington DC: Central Intelligence Agency. <https://www.cia.gov/library/publications/the-world-factbook/geos/xx.html> (accessed June 3, 2010).
2. McDonalds, "FAQs for Students." 05/27/2010. <http://www.aboutmcdonalds.com/mcd/students.html> (accessed June 3, 2010).
3. "Trade to Expand by 9.5% in 2010," WTO 2010 Press Releases, March 26, 2010. Geneva, Switzerland: World Trade Organization. <http://www.wto.org/english/news_e/pres10_e/pr598_e.htm> (accessed June 3, 2010).
4. Fareed Zakaria, "The Rise of the Rest," Newsweek, May 3, 2008.
5. John Noble Wilford. "World," New York Times, September 18, 2007.
6. Monty Marshall and Benjamin Cole. "Global Report 2009: Conflict, Governance and State Fragility." Center for Systemic Peace and Center for Global Policy, 2009. <http://www.systemicpeace.org/Global%20Report%202009.pdf> (accessed June 3, 2010); Hereafter cited as Global Report 2009.
7. "Global Conflict Trends." Center for Systemic Peace, March 17, 2010. http://www.systemicpeace.org/conflict.htm (accessed June 7, 2010).
8. Global Report 2009.
9. "Special Report: Congo." Forgotten Crisis. International Rescue Committee, n.d. <http://www.theirc.org/special-reports/special-report-congo-y> (accessed June 3, 2010).
10. Louis Henkin, How Nations Behave Law and Foreign Policy. 2nd ed. (New York: Columbia University Press, 1979), 22.

UNIT 1

✣

ACTORS

Globalization Without End
A Framing

Bruce Mazlish

Let us start with two ways of looking at globalization. The first assumes that globalization is a thread running through all of humanity's past, starting with generations of our hunter-gatherer ancestors, over millennia, gradually migrating across the world. In this sense, there is no set beginning, as well as no foreseeable end. The second involves the fact that globalization in its present-day incarnation is a subject of endless debate as to what it is and where it is going. Taken together, these two ways add up to a kind of "globalization without end," both as discourse and possible reality.

In the Introduction, I essayed a brief definition of globalization. It is well to go a bit further now with this problem. Many who brush up against this definitional problem are aghast at the lack of agreement on what the term means, and often throw up their hands and mutter under their breath "globaloney." This understandable frustration is misguided. Any concept used in regard to large-scale social processes is bound to be vague and contested, for it seeks to aid us in grasping powerful and protean forces, twisting and turning over time, and not easily encompassed by words. So the first thing to recognize, as one scholar tells us, is that "the meaning of some concepts derive [sic] from controversy rather than from any consensus about their meaning."[1]

It is essential to recognize that globalization's meaning or meanings lies in the very arguments brought to bear on the concept. In its simplest form, I will argue, it is a theory about social relations, emphasizing that those relations, whatever their specific form, are becoming more widespread, with the parties to them more and more interconnected and interdependent in various ways. There is always a geographical dimension to this development as greater expansion into the world takes place. Without all parts of the world becoming more and more known, there can only be a limited increase in social relations. In speaking of geography, I should add that today's virtual space is as much a dimension of interconnectivity as was the sixteenth-century circumnavigation of the globe or any number of other, similar transformations of geocultural space.

To give a bit more support to this kind of definition, I will cite the historian C. A. Bayly's view that globalization is "a progressive increase in the scale of social processes from a local or regional to a world level."[2] For him the concept is a heuristic device, one that draws attention to dynamics, while abjuring a description of progressive linear social change. Thus, his definition has the merit of suggesting to us a difference between global, or new global, history and what is called world history; the latter tends to deny or neglect directionality. In contrast, accepting the idea of direction in historical development, the sociologist Sylvia Walby speaks affirmatively of globalization as "a process of increased density and frequency of international or global interactions relative to local or national ones."[3] With these additional definitions, we are on our way to a focused concern with present-day globalization as studied by new global historians.

(1)

Though my emphasis will be on the new globalization, we must constantly bear in mind its antecedents and earlier forms, even at the risk of reciting well-known facts (although they are placed in a new light). Central to the globalization of the past few centuries has been the state, or rather the nation-state. Indeed, as has been frequently noted, the transcending of nation-state boundaries is at the core of one variation on the definition of globalization. Consequently, the coming into being of the modern state is an essential feature as we try to understand globalization past and present.

After the Treaty of Westphalia in 1648, a governmental structure that emphasizes sovereignty becomes more and more important.[4] A brief description suggests that such sovereignty is both political and economic, for the modern state functions increasingly as a single market. Additionally, in theory, such a state is to respect the inviolable sovereignty of other states, but in practice resort is often had to war. Such wars require ever more efficient tax systems, military technologies, improved communications, and a host of similar devices, and thus the further strengthening of the state.[5]

All of these developments can also be found in empires. What was new in the modern states that arose in Europe was their acceptance in principle of other sovereignties, whereas empires, at least according to Martin Van Creveld, cannot accept equals. As he puts it, empires "looking beyond their borders ... saw not other political communities with a right to an independent existence, but barbarians."[6] With nation-states, moreover, we have the possibility of an international system, made up of equal sovereignties along with laws and conventions by which they adjust their relations to each other, and settle differences peacefully. Before the nation as such we cannot really have an international system.

There is a vast literature on the nation-state. I have drawn on it here to make the point that without its emergence what we call globalization today, especially as it plays out in regard to internationalism, would have no meaning. So, too, the European state has been the prime agency in the exploration of the globe, and in its subsequent exploitation. It is the state that introduced the era of global warfare, with the War of the Spanish Succession (1701–14) anticipating the world wars of the twentieth century. It is the nation-state that has been cloned globally (even with only partial success), with over 190 of them now represented in the United Nations. In short, an early phase of globalization was carried out by the very form, the nation-state, which is now under subversion by present-day globalizing forces.

(2)

That is one part of the earlier globalizing story. Another piece is the rise of merchant empires. Their primary aim was to pursue profit, though this might entail the use of violence. In this they differed from the nation-states that stood behind them, which had territorial gain as a direct goal and assumed violence as the necessary means of such acquisition. The two, state and merchant empire, go together, however, for it was the relatively small and rivalrous states, for example, Portugal, Spain, the Italian city states, the Netherlands, England, and France, whence the merchants and their ships came and went, West and East.

It was, as we know, primarily as a result of the new states and the merchant empires that a quantum jump took place in the fifteenth century, and the whole globe swam into view. We need not rehearse the discovery of the "New World," the subsequent circumnavigation of the globe by Magellan in 1517–20 and the later voyages of discovery in the Far East, but merely signal their role in this early phase of globalization. A nice symbolic touch is afforded by the present of a magnificent golden globe whose oceans were made from green enamel by Francis Drake to his Queen, Elizabeth, after being knighted for his circumnavigation of the globe in 1580—the first by an Englishman—and his plundering of the Spanish fleet.

Central to the whole story is the sea. Covering about seven-eighths of the earth's surface, it stood outside the usual empires of history, an uncharted and unconquered realm. When the small nations of the West built fleets that could sail upwind, they could open a new chapter in history and reach all parts of the globe, with the Atlantic and the Pacific oceans linked through the Straits of Magellan. No wonder that "stout Cortez" (actually, Balboa) stood in awe, as Keats tells us, at the sight of the Pacific glimpsed from a peak in Darien!

Numerous advances in astronomy, mapping, surveying and navigating were required for the European vessels to find their way across the largely uncharted seas. As it turned out, navies were expensive, and most empires had neither the will nor the means to harness their resources in this direction. Those states that did profited greatly, though paying a terrible price in lives lost to the watery depths. In any case, the future lay with the European control of the oceans. Spurred on by a religion claiming global dominion—the papal demarcation of most of the known globe between Spain and Portugal was a palpable demonstration though in the event unsuccessful—and by a market-driven economy that knew no geographical limits, the European powers gradually and painfully established a global hegemony. These European nations, becoming imperial, merged the national and the global in one sweeping movement.

The effect of the merchant empires was both material and cultural. As one scholar puts it, "Silks and cottons, coffee and tea, tobacco and opium, tomatoes and potatoes, rice and maize, porcelain and lacquerware—the impact … on European material culture proved profound and permanent. No less striking were the mental changes, beginning with wonder at strange plants, beasts, and men, and culminating in the fruitful cultural relativism that spouted from European encounters with Americans, Africans and Asians."[7] It is not too much to claim that the merchant empires, along with developments in science and philosophy, helped create the conditions in the seventeenth century that led to the early Enlightenment and all that follows from that, including the sense of cosmopolitanism.

Such is the European perspective. In the eye of global history we must also see the impact of the merchant empires not only on their home countries, but also on those whose shores they reached. Japan can serve as one example. In the sixteenth century, Japan and, in this case, Portugal were initially ignorant of one another, as if existing on separate planets. When a vessel carrying a small band of Portuguese merchants was blown off course and three of its men landed in the southwest of Japan, each side was significantly affected by the encounter. The Europeans encountered a culture more civilized than their own, while the Japanese were made aware that "there is another world greater than ours."[8] Such effects were confirmed by the English who arrived in Japan almost 60 years later. Though the Westerners had superior astronomy and knowledge of navigation, they were struck by the sharp swords of the samurai and the cultivated aesthetics of their Japanese hosts. On the Japanese side, muskets and cannon were briefly incorporated by the Shogun into his army, helping him to establish the Tokugawa power that was to persist until the second opening of Japan, with Perry's arrival in 1853, when the Tokugawa was succeeded by the Meiji regime.

These are global effects. They are part of the connections being made by the expansionist powers of Europe through their mastery of the seas. They also mark the beginnings of the gulf of superior development that was to open up between the West and the rest of the world, a development which is conceived of as going forward under the banner of modernity. In this effort, the state and its merchant empires were joined at the hip. The resultant globalization was part of nation-building, in which emerging nations were achieving supremacy over existing empires, or rather substituting ocean-based merchant empires for more traditional land-based ones.

From the beginning, it was trade that played the major role in the great change in awareness that underlay this phase of globalization. It was economic exchange, carried out by the merchant empires, that dramatically affected the conceptualization of space, which, along with time, stands at the heart of one decisive definition of globalization. Of course, there were other causes underlying the great expansion and, paradoxically, contraction of space/time. But the merchant empires are the prime carriers of that change in coordinates. Subsequent history can be told as the story of that ever-increasing contraction and expansion.

It is in this light that we should think of America. America, of course, was supposed to be China when Columbus set sail for the fabled East. Once the new awareness that it was a separate continent took hold, America became the scene of national/imperial expansion in the Southern part, with Spanish conquistadors as agents of the state. In the North we find our familiar merchant empire, embodied in such groups as the Hudson Bay Company and later the Massachusetts Bay Company. Thus, America, as it became known, accidentally being named after Amerigo Vespucci, and with the North subsequently arrogating to itself that name as if South and Central America did not exist, was global in its inspiration, with its discovery affirming the fact that a globe existed, to be circumnavigated shortly thereafter.

Collapsing a long story, I want simply to underline the fact that America became part of an empire, the British one, intimately tied to the merchant empires that traded in slaves, and thus of the entire plantation base of the early modern economy. Henceforth, race would haunt the history of the future USA, a "local" effect of a global movement. So, too, Africa was dragged into the globalization that characterizes this phase of development, though subsequently falling behind Europe and Asia in terms of both nation-building and modernity. In short, as American historians are coming gradually to realize, we cannot understand the USA any more than other sections of the world without placing it from the beginning in the context of globalization.

(3)

I want momentarily to expand our panorama before narrowing our attention to the present and its new globalization. Humanity has sought to give meaning to its existence in time and space through many means, myths and religions being prime examples. With the coming of a form of knowledge known as "history," arising in "scientific" form, i.e., as promulgated by Herodotus and Thucydides in fifth-century Greece, universal or world histories arose. Such visions took the form not only of universal history, but more recently of philosophies of history, world-system analysis, world history, Big History, Global, and now New Global History.[9]

Clearly, there is much debate as to the nature of globalization, its origins, its nodes of existence, how it might be studied, and so forth. One important contribution is the book *Globalization in World History*, edited by A. G. Hopkins, which deals with some of the early stages of global history. A collection of essays, it attacks the illusion that globalization is simply a Western creation, and argues that it is a state of affairs jointly created by all parts of the world. The essays give details about Asia, Islam and other areas and cultures, and their participation in the construction of globalization, though the focus is much on the eighteenth century and the role of the West. In addition, Hopkins sets up a schema in terms of archaic, proto, modern, and postcolonial globalization, best viewed, however, as a "series of over-lapping and interacting sequences rather than as a succession of neat stages."[10] Hopkins' collection and its ideas serve as a useful transition to the New Global History as well as to the discussion of present-day globalization that I am undertaking in this book.

(4)

In undertaking this task, I want to emphasize anew the holistic nature of our enterprise. To do so is to stress that, as one author commented about colonialism, an early factor in modern globalization, it is simultaneously a "process in political economy and culture … indissoluble aspects of the same reality."[11] Or rather, I would argue, globalization is a matter of politics, economics, cultures, and many other factors—reflecting the synthesis and synergy mentioned earlier—a whole that we break into parts because of our inability immediately to grasp it entirely, as well as for disciplinary reasons. That is why, to deal with this problem, New Global History is so insistently interdisciplinary. This is why the sort of analysis involved in the work, say, of Kevin O'Rourke and Jeffrey Williamson, who claim the period 1870–1914 was marked by greater globalization than the present, is so narrow, limited to economics, and resolutely ignoring the larger context in which this one part of globalization exists.[12] It is for this reason that we need a new perspective, embodied in what I am calling New Global History, building as it does on the World and Global histories that have come before it.

In the simplest terms, then, New Global History is dedicated to the study of the new globalization that has emerged some time in the period after WW II. Revealing is the entry of the word "globalization" into the human vocabulary. Some argue that it was coined in the 1960s in the USA or in Latin America, others that it is a neologism introduced in the 1970s by the Japanese. Whichever is correct—and more research is needed on this topic—it represents a profound shift in human consciousness, symbolic recognition and thus self-awareness of what has been taking place in real life. The term speaks of an historically unprecedented development, as part of which the national, regional, and international are supplanted or supplemented by global forces. These are not under the control of any government, and are best spoken of in terms of flows and processes. They present problems that can no longer be dealt with adequately on the local level, but require global efforts.

Not surprisingly, present-day globalization is not only new and emergent, but incomplete and unequal in its effects, good and bad. For scholars it gives rise to what Arjun Appadurai has called "anxiety" about globalization studies. Where, they may ask, are the archives from which to write its story? How can it avoid the pitfalls of self-proclaimed contemporary history (although it is now more than 50 years old) where we are too close to events to understand them? One way to deal with such anxiety is to dismiss the phenomenon completely: it's nothing new, only old wine in new bottles. Another way is to pour scorn on the subject by calling it a mere fashion, soon to pass away. A more dramatic way is to embrace anti-globalization and try to reverse the process itself, whether by protests (such as against the World Trade Organization and World Bank), boycotts (e.g., against Nike), or other demonstrations of hostility.

Closely connected to such scholarly anxiety is the notion of risk. Thus it is the thesis of Ulrich Beck and others that today we are faced with "global, often irreparable damage that can no longer be limited."[13] This can take the form of global warming, ozone holes, disease spread by air travel or acts of human destruction for which no insurance can compensate. Unlike natural disasters, these risks result from "decisions that focus on techno-economic advantages and opportunities and accept hazards as simply the dark side of progress." In a global epoch, of course, these consequences may be both irreversible and catastrophically affect the entire world.

Add to anxiety and risk a host of misperceptions and one can see readily why globalization is such a contested term. As noted earlier, many see present-day globalization as a teleological and deterministic process whose outcome is a homogenized world on the model of America. This flies in the face of the evidence for increasing heterogeneity and the multiculturalism that characterizes many of the developed countries. In similar vein, there is the charge that globalization is simply another word for imperialism. Again, the evidence suggests that, as my historical presentation attempted to show, colonialism and imperialism were partial causes of the earlier globalization that took place before the 1950s, and that present-day globalization may have strong imperial components in it, as the recent discussions about empire suggest, but that a simple equation is ridiculous. In any and all such controversies it helps, too, if we can remember that almost by definition present-day globalization is not just Western but a jointly created process not under any one state's control but made what it is and will be by many agents.

(5)

With these brief comments, I come to a caesura of sorts in my account in this chapter of globalization without end. Of course, each and every factor involved in present-day globalization has antecedents and a genealogy of some kind in back of them. They are involved synergistically and synthetically with one another, and it is the interplay of all the factors that makes for a concept usefully called new globalization. And it is this, in turn, that gives rise to a new global history to study it. What I am suggesting here, however, is that new globalization and its history can only be understood properly in the light of previous surges of globalization and attempts to study their emergence and subsequent trajectories.

It need hardly be remarked that I have scanted or left out completely in my account so far many aspects of the new globalization. (I shall touch on some of these in the Conclusion.) A host of topics requires specific attention. There is, for example, the need for comparison with other such idols of abstraction as cosmopolitanism, colonialism, imperialism, civilizations and empires. As a protean process, globalization can hardly be dealt with without engaging in what seems like unlimited intellectual warfare.

Should we be surprised that such "warfare" has become increasingly global in scope? That almost nothing seems left out of our discussions? That every part of the world is now engaged in a global discourse? That terms like multiculturalism, postmodernism, hybridity, creolization, and so forth flow freely around the world? The fact is that, for better or worse, globalization has become the hegemonic word of our era, inserting itself into all aspects of our lives and our efforts to understand them. Our task, of course, is to break the concept into its parts, and then both to study the parts empirically and to conceptualize them anew into an understandable and manageable whole. It is a seemingly endless task, but one suitable for a globalization that, for the moment at least, seems without end.

Onwards and Outwards
A Kind of Revolution

BRUCE MAZLISH

A s all of us, especially historians, know, there is nothing completely new under the sun. In writing about global history, or rather the new global history, I am aware that I am following a path on which others have taken steps, sometimes giant steps. Let me touch on a few of my predecessors.

I start my tale with Adam Smith and Karl Marx. It was Smith who truly revolutionized economic thinking by emphasizing the division of labor and its promise of almost endlessly increasing production. Its only limit, as he announced in Chapter 3 of *The Wealth of Nations*, was the extent of the market. Building on Smith's perception, Karl Marx, in the *Communist Manifesto*, described how "Modern industry has established the world-market, for which the discovery of America paved the way." His following analysis is uncanny in its anticipation of what is occurring today in the process of globalization (to highlight this fact certain words have been italicized in the quotations from him). Modern industry for Marx, of course, is directed by the bourgeoisie. In sonorous phrase after phrase, Marx hymns the accomplishments of that class in expanding the market. "The need of a constantly expanding market for its products chases the bourgeoisie over the whole surface of the globe. It must nestle everywhere, settle everywhere, *establish connections everywhere*. The bourgeoisie has through its exploitation of the *world-market* given a *cosmopolitan character* to production and consumption in every country." And one more quote: "The bourgeoisie, by the rapid improvement of all instruments of production"—here Marx added technology to Smith's division of labor—"by the immensely facilitated means of communication, draws all, even the most barbarian, nations into *civilisation*."

One forgets too often that Friedrich Engels was the co-author of the *Manifesto*; he has always been in Marx's shadow. However, in preparation for the great document of 1848, Engels had written a year earlier, in his "Principles of Communism," that: "A new machine invented in England deprives millions of Chinese workers of their livelihood within a year's time. In this way, big industry has brought all the people of the earth into contact with each other, has merged all local markets into one world market, has spread civilization and progress everywhere and has thus ensured that whatever happens in civilized countries will have repercussions in all other countries."

One more of the oracular voices must be heard. It is Max Weber's, as when he introduces his *Protestant Ethic and the Spirit of Capitalism* by announcing that "in Western civilization only, cultural phenomena have appeared which (as we like to think) lie in a line of development having *universal* significance and value." Weber then briefly discusses some of these phenomena, including science, and concludes that "the most fateful force in our modern life" is capitalism. Marx had spoken of the capitalist's "werewolf appetite" for profit. In more somber tones, Weber wrote that "capitalism is identical with the pursuit of profit, and forever *renewed* profit." Then he explains its dynamism in less animal-like terms than those used by Marx, stressing its multicausal nature, and especially emphasizing its rational aspect.

It is astonishing how portentous the words of Smith, Marx, Engels, and Weber have turned out to be. They seem to have recognized some of the forces of globalization—science, technology, capitalism—in their early manifestations and sensed their future implications. Even lesser men caught what was in the air, where solid structures were melting. Thus, in the debate over the Napoleonic Code of Commerce in 1803, a proponent of one clause in the Code exclaimed, "The bill of commerce has been invented. In the history of commerce this is an event almost comparable to the discovery of the compass and of America … [I]t has set free movable capital, has facilitated its movements, and has created an immense volume of credit. From that moment on, there had been no limits to the expansion of commerce other than those of the globe itself."

Yet, it is one thing to acknowledge premonitions about globalization, and another to recognize that what is going on around us today transcends these earlier conceptualizations of the phenomenon, though building on them. Before turning back to our own effort to deal with the subject, one last quotation on the particularly economic nature of globalization. It comes from Manuel Castells' *The Rise of the Network Society*. There he announces that: "The informational economy is global. A global economy is a historically new reality, distinct from a world economy. A world economy, that is an economy in which capital accumulation proceeds throughout the world, has existed in the West at least since the sixteenth century, as Fernand Braudel and Immanuel Wallerstein have taught us. *A global economy is something different: it is an economy with the capacity to work as a unit in real time on a planetary scale*" [my emphasis].

(1)

Up to now I have been standing on the shoulders of tall figures, if not giants. It is time to get down and start trudging on the path they have laid out. In doing so, I am, as acknowledged earlier, practicing a form of contemporary history. A further word in defense of my practice. Whether consciously we admit it or not, our writing of history is, overtly or covertly, in part an attempt to situate ourselves correctly in regard to current problems. So it is in regard to our effort to understand globalization today. While employing a multidisciplinary approach, we must comprehend that process in a wide-ranging historical perspective. In doing so, we help create what will become our own past, is now our present, and is unfolding before us as our future.

The fact is that we are entering upon a global epoch. That is the revolutionary development of our present time. Unlike other revolutionary efforts at global reach, such as the communist, the forces of globalization do not have to take on political form. Rather than seizing state power, they are, in fact, often undermining existing state powers. While states do remain major actors in the global epoch, power is shifting increasingly to amorphous forces, such as environmental, or to communications networks, or to new, less fixed sorts of institutions, such as multinational corporations and non-governmental organizations.

This is the major transformation through which we are now living. To signal its importance, we do not need to adopt an apocalyptic tone, nor assume that it will be a linear and completely deterministic development. The "event" itself, occurring as we enter a new millennium, speaks everywhere for itself. What we do need, however, is to raise our awareness—our consciousness—to the level of our situation.

In order to help achieve that sense of new global history and a greater consciousness of our present situation, it is necessary to describe and analyze some of the major features of the emerging global epoch. In this aspiration, I am taking up anew the burden of the classical sociologists, only now on a more extended plane. The classical problem in social theory had been to explain the transition to "modern" society. Marx, preceded by Adam Smith and Hegel, sought both to describe and to analyze the tremendous transformation from "feudal" to "modern," the shift from a society based on personal relations to one largely based on impersonal market forces. Where Marx focused on the economic relations of production, his later compatriot Max Weber emphasized the new rationality. Others stressed cultural factors, and still others highlighted the role of science and political power.

Now the transition to be described and analyzed is not to industrial society as such, but to the globalized society in which increasingly all peoples live. Indeed, the very term "epoch" marks from the first a global perspective. It came into general usage in the early nineteenth century in the field of geology, where the new science was seen as addressing the entire earth.

Geological processes were viewed as worldwide. As William Buckland, one of the pioneers in the new field, remarked, "The field of the Geologist's inquiry is the Globe itself." One spoke, for example, of the Eocene Epoch, marking a new and important period in the earth's development (or, as the change in regard to the earth's flora and fauna would be called after Darwin, evolution). Such an epoch was necessarily global in its dimensions.

Periodization of any kind is central to the human effort to organize time (whether human or geological). We impose boundaries on the otherwise chaotic happenings of the past, seeking to order them by restrictive names. Decades, eras, centuries—these are alternate divisions to that of epochs. Of course, such orderings can, on occasion, mislead rather than guide us through the chaos of events. So, too, can the larger periodizations of Western history: the famous ancient, medieval, modern divisions. We may take for real what is only an illusory reification of time.

This is the test that the phrase "global epoch" will have to undergo. On the assumption that the phrase holds up meaningfully, it offers us an escape from the rather clamorous modern–postmodern debate. With the notion of global epoch, I am suggesting that we have an alternative way of revising, or renewing, our sense of history. In short, the most useful, i.e., illuminating, successor to "modern" history as a periodizing rubric is, I believe, global or "new global history."

(2)

The historical, of course, is simply one way of looking at phenomena. It does have the potential, however, of offering the longer view, and of thus providing a depth of understanding to its object of study that is otherwise unavailable. To recapitulate, globalization can be looked at primarily as an economic development, e.g., as a stage of late capitalism. It can be viewed as a mainly political development, where the nation-state is seen as the prime actor losing vital functions. Or the focus can be on the cultural changes, with a presumed homogenization occurring among peoples. With its holistic approach, of course, New Global History seeks to both integrate and sift through these various ways of looking at the phenomenon.

History's conceptual weakness is that it must deal with all the aspects of a phenomenon—e.g., economic, political, cultural—and the ways they interrelate, yet without an overall, satisfactory theory as to how that interrelation takes place. Yet, its weakness is also its strength, for it is the only one of the human sciences that at least attempts to understand the full, complex reality of human behavior over time, even if under-theorized. To compensate, it must draw heavily on the other human sciences, and their theories and approaches.

History, i.e., historiography, is itself subject to the forces of globalization. For most of human "history," i.e., the 99 percent of the species' past as hunter-gatherers, recorded history, the conscious attempt to know the past "scientifically," did not exist. It is a late development in human evolution. Whether one chooses to start this development with the ancient civilizations of China or India, or wishes to argue for its true beginnings with the Greeks a few thousand years ago, it is clearly of comparatively recent vintage.

Starting perhaps in the seventeenth century, a Western mode of "scientific" history achieved prominence and power. It also achieved hegemony, imposing its Eurocentric version on other peoples. As E. H. Carr innocently expressed the initial stage of this happening, "It is only today that it has become possible for the first time even to imagine a whole world consisting of peoples who have in the fullest sense entered into history and become the concern, no longer of the colonial administrator or the anthropologist, but of the historian." Chinese scholars now look at their past with the same scholarly methodology as found in the West; Indian scholars do the same. In the process, of course, they are changing the Eurocentric myopia, and enlarging all humanity's historical perspective. A new global history, therefore, is possible, though indubitably starting from certain Western preconceptions as to how one conducts such a study.

In short, the practice of history is itself necessarily undergoing globalization. In so doing, it becomes a subject to be studied just as we do other parts of the phenomenon. The very perspective then, the historical, that is used to study globalization is not a static one, but subject to shifting forces and fates. Hence, the lens by which we look at the globalization process becomes itself part of that very process. How exactly this regrinding will occur, only time—and the practice of new global history—will tell.

(3)

In further seeking to understand globalization, especially from an historical perspective, we run into a number of problem areas. A major one concerns the actors to be studied. For the last few hundred years, the writing of history has circled around the activities of the nation-state, its wars, its economic activities, its nationalistic culture, and its political leaders. Profound shifts are underway in this regard. Though, as I have argued, the nation-state will still be a major player in New Global History, its role must be reassessed in terms of the larger process unrolling around it.

At the same time, other players than the nation-state crowd the stage of history. Especially prominent, as we have noted, are multinational corporations (MNCs) and non-governmental organizations (NGOs), both of whose increase in numbers recently has been phenomenal. In a fuller treatment, some of which I will provide in the next section of this book, we would wish to consider their emergence in relation to the notion of civil society, tracing the latter's growth in the soil first laid down in the Enlightenment cultivation of the public sphere and public opinion.

Here, however, I want to focus in a preliminary way on two prominent forms of NGOs, those related to human rights and to the environment. Human rights is a global assertion, rising above the national rights restricted to citizens by earlier democratic movements. Today, although this view is hotly contested in some quarters, one has rights not because one is a German, Frenchman, Iranian, or an American, but because one is a human being. As we all know, however, there are few if any institutionalized "global" courts to enforce these rights (though they are enshrined in a UN Declaration). It is the court of public opinion that mainly gives whatever strength there is to their observation. And that public opinion is shaped and given voice by NGOs, such as Amnesty International, Human Rights Watch and other such organizations. In other words, in our informational/computer age, human rights proponents, in the guise of NGOs, are to a large extent the self-appointed conscience of the globe.

Another proliferating form of NGO relates to the environment. In this area, private, not-for-profit groups mobilize on both a local and a global basis to deal with threats to ecology. It is such groups that prod national governments to take international actions, and advise international agencies how to go about doing this. Using the new informational technology, NGOs such as the Sierra Club, Greenpeace and innumerable others mobilize forces around the world to combat what are clearly global as well as local crises.

Turning now to multinationals, as our other selected actor, they have been traced back two thousand years by classical scholars. This is accurate in the sense that certain trading groups operated across political boundaries. It is anachronistic in that nation-states did not exist at the time, thus giving a different meaning to multinational. When we add the word "corporation," we again must realize that that is a legal term given precise meaning only recently. In any case, modern multinational corporations can be discerned emerging in the seventeenth century and flourishing, for example, in the shape of the Dutch and British East India companies.

Eschewing a continuous history, let us jump to our global present. Today, according to the UN, of the 100 largest possessors of Gross Domestic Product (GDP) over 50 are multinationals. Which means that they are wealthier on that index (which, in fact, can be misleading, confusing value added with GDP; symbolically, however, it is on target) than about 120 to 130 nation-state members of the UN. Another figure: today there are said to be over 60,000 multinationals, a dramatic increase over the numbers existing only a few years previously. And yet another figure: in the past quarter of a century, the list of the top 500 industrial multinationals has shifted from almost entirely American/European to almost two-fifths Japanese/Asian.

How are we to understand what is happening? As a preliminary, we necessarily must define what we mean by a multinational corporation. Then we must describe and analyze the features that we think characterize it: where is it headquartered? Where is its work-force? Where are its sales? Where go its capital flows? etc. Then we must look at these features dynamically, seeing them develop over time. Then we must compare companies with companies and countries with countries, arriving at a global picture.

In fact, an international conference, as part of the New Global History initiative, took place in October 1999 to undertake exactly these tasks. Called "Mapping the Multinational Corporations," the project sought to give visual form to what is happening economically on our globe. To complement the atlases featuring nation-states and their boundaries, it has compiled an atlas, *Global Inc.*, depicting the multinational corporations as they leap across such boundaries.

Increasingly, then, it is the multinational corporations along with the NGOs and an adapting nation-state that are the actors to be studied by the historian or other social scientist. Alongside of these forces, of course, must be placed the UN. A cross between a forum for nations, with their pursuit of national aims by international means, and an institution seeking to transcend its members and their parochial concerns, the UN is still unsure of its mission. That mission, it dimly senses, is a global one, but how to move to fulfill it is clouded in ambiguity and dissent. Justice and Force would seem to be the two key terms in this regard: how to adjudicate local power squabbles in global terms, which must include prevention, and how to enforce UN judgments militarily are the clear challenges. For the student of globalization, the evolution of UN military forces deserves all the attention he or she can give it.

(4)

At this point, we may feel somewhat overwhelmed. There is such a plethora of problems to be found in the seemingly simple notion of globalization. Are we to take everything as our object of study? In one sense, the answer is "yes"; globalization, as I have stressed, must be seen holistically, for each feature is connected to every other. Realistically, however, we can ignore huge swathes of ordinary history and concentrate initially on the factors of globalization, some of which I have tried to enumerate. Doing so, our tasks become limited research projects. Only gradually do we seek to reassemble the pieces, in turn further illuminating our empirical research efforts.

Nevertheless, it is evident that globalization as a real phenomenon threatens to overwhelm us, as does the attempt to conceptualize it. Even the name is contested. Alternative terms for globalization are globalism, glocalization, and globaloney, all of which speak for themselves to one degree or another. Perhaps even more importantly, globalization must be recognized as coming before us not only as an idea, or concept related to a process, but as an ideology, promoted by multinational corporations and by various media, and as an ideal, a new version of the brotherhood and sisterhood of humankind. In short, everything about the subject must be assumed to be a *problematique*.

For by now it must be clear how complicated the subject of globalization is, and how an understanding of the process is so vital to our sense of where we are and how we have come to be there—wherever "there" is. In truth, globalization has redefined, and reoriented, as I have argued, our coordinates of space and time. Here on earth we now have a feeling of a "full earth," in the sense not only of our everywhere encountering other peoples, but in the sense that almost all of the planet's surface and increasingly its depths are becoming known to us. Such knowledge is being matched by our invasion of space, formerly seen as "empty" and "outer." But such "outer" space, in turn, is being increasingly drawn inward, as we reorder our sense of self on earth in terms of the new knowledge we are acquiring.

That knowledge tells us that fundamental economic, political, social, and cultural changes are taking place in a global fashion, in the process we call globalization. Difficult as it is to pin down, and correlated as it is with profound scientific and technological developments, a revolutionary transformation in consciousness, in self-consciousness, and in historical consciousness has been and is taking place. This, in fact, may be the most important consequence of the globalization process. In sum, we are not only transforming the globe but ourselves as well.

The Rise of a New Europe
The History of European Integration, 1945–2007

Antony Best, Jussi M. Hanhimäki, Joseph A. Maiolo and Kirsten E. Schulze

INTRODUCTION

While it is easy to draw a picture of the twentieth century as steeped in blood and conflict, it is important also to see that this period witnessed many different efforts by both states and individuals to overcome national rivalries and to encourage co-operation between countries and peoples. The initial hope in the wake of the First World War was that future peace and prosperity could be guaranteed through the establishment of a universal international organization, the **League of Nations**. This, however, proved to be a false dawn, for this body was compromised from its very inception by the absence of the United States and then proved unequal to the task of co-ordinating 'collective security' in the 1930s. After the defeat of the Tripartite Powers at the end of the Second World War, hope revived again with the formation of the **United Nations (UN)** and its attendant bodies.

> **League of Nations**
>
> An international organization established in 1919 by the peace treaties that ended the First World War. Its purpose was to promote international peace through collective security and to organize conferences on economic and disarmament issues. It was formally dissolved in 1946.
>
> **collective security**
>
> The principle of maintaining peace between states by mobilizing international opinion to condemn aggression. Commonly seen as one of the chief purposes of international organizations such as the League of Nations and the United Nations.

But here too, disillusion soon set in as a result of the fact that the Cold War helped to paralyse the organization and because of the way in which the permanent members of the Security Council used and abused their powers of veto to uphold their national interests.

However, while internationalist dreams of a move towards enlightened world governance were dashed on these rocks, a new path began to emerge in the post-1945 era—the emergence of continental or regional supra-governmental organizations that aimed at the development of economic, social and even political integration. The most successful of these experiments in the pooling of sovereignty took place in Europe with the birth of the **European Economy Community (EEC)** in 1958 and its evolution into, first, the **European Community (EC)** and, finally, the **European Union (EU)**.

The fact that the EEC was able through economic integration to transform war-torn Western Europe into a zone of peace and prosperity not surprisingly inspired statesmen in other parts of the globe to try to follow suit. They were to do so with mixed results. Some regional organizations, such as the **Association of South-East Asian Nations (ASEAN)**, echoed the achievements of the EEC by also bringing economic and political cohesion to previously troubled regions. Others though, such as the largely abortive calls for integration in East Asia, have been less effective. In these cases, however, the reasons for failure, such as the fear of the consequences of pooling sovereignty and the lack of strong political incentives underpinning the integration process, are still important to study, for ironically they help to highlight the causes of success in Europe and South-East Asia.

THE IDEA OF EUROPE

The idea of a united Europe was not an invention of the post-1945 era. Indeed, most of the great conquerors of Europe's long and bloody history—from the Romans to Charles V and from

---

United Nations (UN)
An international organization established after the Second World War to replace the League of Nations. Since its establishment in 1945, its membership has grown to 192 countries.

European Economic Community (EEC)
Established by the Treaty of Rome 1957, the EEC became effective on 1 January 1958. Its initial members were Belgium, France, Italy, Luxembourg, the Netherlands and West Germany (now Germany); it was known informally as the Common Market. The EEC's aim was the eventual economic union of its member nations, ultimately leading to political union. It changed its name to the European Union in 1992.

European Community (EC)
Formed in 1967 with the fusion of the European Economic Community (EEC, founded in 1957), the European Atomic Energy Community (EURATOM, also founded in 1957), and the European Coal and Steel Community (ECSC, founded in 1952). The EC contained many of the functions of the European Union (EU, founded in 1992). Unlike the later EU, the EC consisted primarily of economic agreements between member states.

Napoleon to Hitler—justified their quest in part as a way of bringing stability and order through unity. This idea of a Europe dominated by one hegemonic nation has thus been a constant feature in the annals of European history, but it has little in common with the twenty-first-century understanding of economic and political integration.

The idea of integration based on principles of democratic governance and common markets was new to the post-1945 era. Its impressive appeal was based on a number of factors. The most obvious was that in regard to national security, the West Europeans who championed integration viewed their countries as too weak to stand up against the real or imagined Soviet military threat. At the same time most Western European politicians were not content with a simple abdication of power to American dominance and leadership. The answer therefore was to attempt to create strength through unity, even though this necessarily meant bringing together previously quarrelsome neighbours, such as Germany and France. There was, though, some element of historical continuity in this, for, after all, in previous times Europeans had been more willing to cooperate when they perceived a common external threat. For some parts of Europe, the Soviets were the reincarnation of the Persians, Muslims, Mongols or Turks; they were 'barbarians' at the gates of Europe.

The modern idea of Europe is not, though, based simply on the need to confront an external enemy or on the profitability of common markets, but also looks to the belief that there is a specific European identity. Since the 1940s, when the Italian historian Federico Chabod wrote the first book on the idea of Europe, the argument that 'Europeans' share a common set of values that are rooted in ancient Greece and reached their maturity in the Enlightenment has gained wide acceptance. The notion of a common European identity is, however, controversial because many consider Christianity to be the cornerstone of the continent's value system. Increased immigration from non-Christian parts of the world, as well as the

European Union (EU)
A political and economic community of nations formed in 1992 in Maastricht by the signing of the Treaty on European Union (TEU). In addition to the agreements of the European Community, the EU incorporated two intergovernmental—or supranational—'pillars' that tie the member states of the EU together: one dealing with common foreign and security policy, and the other with legal affairs. The number of member states of the EU has expanded from twelve in 1992 to twenty-seven in 2007.

Association of South-East Asian Nations (ASEAN)
Organization founded in 1967 by Indonesia, Malaysia, the Philippines, Singapore and Thailand to provide a forum for regional economic cooperation. From 1979, and the Third Indochina War, it took on more of a political and security role. Membership increased with the accession of Brunei in 1984, Vietnam in 1995, Burma in 1997 and Cambodia in 1999.

decolonization
The process whereby an imperial power gives up its formal authority over its colonies.

debate over the potential accession of Turkey, a Muslim nation, into the EU, has naturally raised fundamental questions about this interpretation. What is clear, however, is that underpinning the experiment that led to the EEC and EU was a fundamental commitment to liberal democracy and the rule of law.

FROM THE SECOND WORLD WAR TO THE TREATY OF ROME

In the aftermath of the Second World War it was, however, issues of high politics rather than reflections on identity that led West European leaders to consider the necessity of integration, for the problems that faced them were immediate and pressing. The first fact that they had to face was that the experience of the two world wars had shown clearly the catastrophic impact that national ambition and nationalist rivalries could have in the age of modern technology. Put simply, Europe had to take another, more peaceful course or risk destroying itself entirely. The second key factor was that the years of war brought about a relative decline in Europe's influence. Europe's overseas empires were toppling. The colonized peoples in the European empires were demanding greater independence and France, Holland and Britain did not, in the long run, have the will or resources to resist. As the prospect of **decolonization** threatened to translate into a dramatic reduction in the individual European countries' global power and influence, the temptation was to remedy this decline through a pooling of national resources through integration. Moreover, once this process began it had the effect of accelerating decolonization, for the European Powers could only find common cause if they abandoned their imperial rivalries, which included dropping the preferential trade that had existed with their colonies. However, more disturbing than the prospect of imperial decline was that even within their own continent the individual European Powers were now relatively weak compared with the two superpowers, the Soviet Union and the United States. Pooling resources, both economic and military, appeared the only sensible way of redressing this new weakness. In short, integration was the only way in which the nations of Western Europe could avoid becoming mere pawns in the emerging Cold War international system.

Of course, there were plenty of obstacles to the process of integration, for not every European nation had the same interest. Although the former British prime minister Winston Churchill expressed his support for a 'United States of Europe' in 1946, Britain rejected anything that went beyond establishing a free trade area. The initial steps therefore were tentative. The first significant move came in 1949 with the founding of the Council of Europe, which was a pan-European body set up to protect democratic principles and sponsor the integration of legal norms. With its seat in Strasbourg, the Council remains the oldest body that specifically promotes Europe-wide standards and integration. In six decades its membership has risen from ten to forty-seven countries. The European Convention of Human Rights (1950) and the European Court of Human Rights (founded in the same year) remain its most significant achievements.

From early on, though, it was clear that the two key continental Powers, France and Germany, preferred a much 'deeper' form of co-operation that looked beyond the espousal of values to real economic and political integration. For both countries integration was a means of enhancing prosperity and security and thus aiding the massive task of reconstruction. Above all, however, they were faced with the knowledge that their national rivalry, which had contributed so significantly to the calamity of the world wars, could not be allowed to continue and that it could only be tempered through mutually advantageous co-operation. They were not the only ones to realize this, however, for one of the great ironies of European integration was that in the immediate post-war period it received a strong push from the United States. An integral part of the **Marshall Plan** was that it was intended to provide a stimulus for the breaking down of tariff barriers within Europe. In 1947–48, participating countries were required to design a joint plan for recovery, which forced them to work together in the Organization of European Economic Co-operation. In April 1948 the inclusion of West Germany in the

> **Marshall Plan**
> Officially known as the European Recovery Programme (ERP). Initiated by American Secretary of State George C. Marshall's 5 June 1947 speech and administered by the Economic Co-operation Administration (ECA). Under the ERP the participating countries (Austria, Belgium, Denmark, France, Great Britain, Greece, Iceland, Italy, Luxembourg, the Netherlands, Norway, Sweden, Switzerland, Turkey and West Germany) received more than $12 billion between 1948 and 1951.
>
> **European Coal and Steel Community (ECSC)**
> Established by the Treaty of Paris (1952) and also known as the Schuman Plan, after the French foreign minister, Robert Schuman, who proposed it in 1950. The member nations of the ECSC—Belgium, France, Italy, Luxembourg, the Netherlands and West Germany—pledged to pool their coal and steel resources by providing a unified market, lifting restrictions on imports and exports, and creating a unified labour market.
>
> **Federal Republic of Germany (FRG)**
> The German state created in 1949 out of the former American, British and French occupation zones. Also known as West Germany. In 1990 the GDR merged into the FDR, thus ending the post-war partition of Germany.

plan further clarified the American position, indicating that they viewed the economic integration of the former enemy states as a key to Europe's future peace and prosperity.

The United States thus helped to stimulate integration, but it was the Europeans who were behind the first major step. The creation of the **European Coal and Steel Community (ECSC)** in 1951 represented the first milestone. Coal and steel production was not only essential for the reconstruction of countries in Europe, but they were also the economic sectors that had been most important for the production of munitions in the two world wars. Accordingly, even after the foundation of the **Federal Republic of Germany (FRG)** in 1949, France initially maintained its occupation of the main German steel production area, the Saarland region, in order to deny Germany any chance of rearming. However, in 1950 the French foreign minister, Robert Schuman, proposed the creation of a supranational institution that would oversee coal and steel production, thus neutralizing French distrust and German resentment. This proposal was known as the Schuman Declaration, but the man who authored the plan and became the first president of the ECSC's High Authority was Jean Monnet, a former deputy secretary-general of the League of Nations who many consider to be the founding father of European integration. Schuman and Monnet were subsequently able to persuade Belgium, France, the FRG, Italy, Luxembourg and Holland of the benefits of the ECSC, but the attempt to win over Britain failed, and thus the original 'Six' came into being.

Even without the British, the founding countries of the ECSC continued to expand the scope of integration. Not all of their initiatives were successful. Following the ECSC proposal, the French proposed the creation of a European Defence Community (EDC) as a means of nullifying the threat posed by West German rearmament. Ironically, although the treaty was negotiated and signed by the 'Six' in 1952, the French National Assembly then refused to ratify it. Thus, an early opportunity to move towards a common European security policy was missed and instead West German rearmament took place under the umbrella of the **North Atlantic Treaty Organization (NATO)** alliance.

In 1957, however, only three years after the collapse of the EDC, representatives from the six ECSC countries gathered in Rome to consider ambitious plans for deepening economic integration beyond coal and steel production. The result was two treaties: one founded the European Atomic Energy Community (EURATOM), and the other the EEC. Of these the latter was vastly more important, for it created the basic building blocks of modern integrated Europe. Like the future EU, the EEC was forged through a process of compromise that sought to meet the various states' interests. The French, for example, were far more protectionist than the Germans or the Dutch, but accepted the principle of a common market in return for a major role in atomic energy development, the establishment of a Common Agricultural Policy (CAP) and the association of colonial territories with the EEC on favourable terms (Belgium and France were the only ones of the Six that still had substantial colonial holdings in 1957). Meanwhile, the Italians, who were economically in the poorest state, received other incentives,

North Atlantic Treaty Organization (NATO)

Established by the North Atlantic Treaty (4 April 1949) signed by Belgium, Canada, Denmark, France, Great Britain, Iceland, Italy, Luxembourg, the Netherlands, Norway, Portugal and the United States. Greece and Turkey entered the alliance in 1952 and the Federal Republic of Germany in 1955. Spain became a full member in 1982. In 1999 the Czech Republic, Hungary and Poland joined in the first post-Cold War expansion, increasing the membership to nineteen countries.

most importantly free movement of labour and the creation of a European Investment Bank to promote regional development. Although the Rome Treaties were very much a result of a high-level poker game between national politicians, the end result was still impressive. When it entered into force on 1 January 1958, the EEC represented a common market of 167 million people, and its key countries, France and West Germany, had moved from bitter rivalry to the beginning of an integration process that would change European history.

WIDENING AND DEEPENING IN THE SHADOW OF THE COLD WAR

Enlargement is a central part of the story of European economic integration, but it was by no means pre-ordained. For four decades after the Treaty of Rome the Cold War division of Europe set clear parameters as to how 'wide' Europe could become. Meanwhile, different notions about the direction and the nature of European integration, and particularly the degree to which it should be a political as well as an economic process, made a number of states reluctant to join the EEC. That some countries, particularly France, were bent on using the EEC to further their own nationalist agenda, rather than succumb to the loss of national sovereignty that true integration necessitated, cast an additional shadow over European integration in its first decades.

France's president from 1958 to 1969, Charles de Gaulle, symbolized this tendency. Although he disliked the federalist elements of the Rome Treaty, de Gaulle did not challenge it directly. Instead, he sought to use the EEC as a means of advancing French power. EURATOM, for example, was quickly sidelined in favour of France's own nuclear programme. De Gaulle's efforts to portray France as the leader of a continental European bloc did little to further the integration process. Nor did his insistence on the centrality of the CAP, which granted significant subsidies to French farmers, endear him to his fellow Europeans. Eventually his intransigence led in 1965–66 to the 'Empty Chair' crisis, during which France boycotted the meetings of the Council of Ministers—the highest body and executive arm of the EEC—for a six-month period. The solution to what amounted to the first serious internal crisis within the EEC was the so-called Luxembourg Compromise of 1966 which, in essence, gave France a veto right over such key issues as agricultural policy. Following this compromise, the EEC was able to complete a customs union in 1968, earlier than the Rome Treaty had required. This, perhaps more than anything else, signified the emergence of the EEC as an important trading bloc with significant bargaining power on tariff and trade matters vis-à-vis the United States.

De Gaulle's dominance of French politics not only prevented any rapid moves towards further integration, but also acted as an obstacle to EEC enlargement. Concerned at the prospect of Europe's and France's relative loss of power vis-à-vis the United States, de Gaulle was determined to pursue a more independent line in foreign policy, where French political and military power would be supplemented by the vitality of Western European economic growth. Naturally, de Gaulle was jealous of any development that might threaten to undermine France's revival, and it was this that led him to oppose an enlargement that promised a substantial enhancement of the EEC's economic strength but a diminishing of French influence—the accession of Britain.

In the early to mid-1950s, with its empire and associated trade links still largely intact, Britain had been distinctly lukewarm about European integration. It recognized the latter's political potential for solving the German problem, but felt little need to become directly involved. However, by the late 1950s, with decolonization under way in South-East Asia, the Middle East and Africa, Britain looked again at the idea of expanding its trade links with Europe. Its first move was the creation of the European Free Trade Area (EFTA) in 1960. As the name implies, EFTA's purpose was to promote free trade among its member countries without any forging of institutional, systemic or political integration. With seven members (Austria, Denmark, Great Britain, Norway, Portugal, Sweden and Switzerland), EFTA was not inconsequential as a trading zone, but it was handicapped by the fact that less than a year into its existence, the largest EFTA member, Britain, applied for membership of the EEC. For the government of Harold Macmillan, the Outer Seven (as EFTA was called) had always essentially been a bargaining chip that was intended to obtain better conditions for entry into the Inner Six of the EEC.

De Gaulle, however, had no intention of allowing British membership of the EEC. The entry of such a sizeable political, economic and military Power clearly had the potential to clip France's wings. Moreover, de Gaulle was not convinced that Britain was sincere in its sudden conversion to the European ideal, believing that it would merely act as a 'Trojan horse' that would in reality do America's bidding. Thus in 1963 de Gaulle announced that France would veto British entry. In 1967, when the government of Harold Wilson put together a second bid for membership, de Gaulle declared himself still unconvinced and repeated the veto. It was only with de Gaulle gone from the scene that Britain, along with Denmark and Ireland, finally negotiated its way into the EEC in January 1973. Building on the foundations of the customs union established five years earlier, the EEC was now, with its three new members, clearly on its way to becoming a key player in the world economy. Thus, while the Americans may have officially promoted further integration and Britain's entry into the EEC, they were by 1973 beginning to rue the results of their sponsorship. Following the entry of the new members, *Time* magazine marked the event with the headline 'America's new rival', and for the next two years relations between Washington and the Western European capitals went through a difficult patch.

In the subsequent decade and a half the EEC continued its widening and deepening. The 1980s saw southern enlargement as Greece (1981), Portugal and Spain (both in 1986) became members. All three had moved from authoritarian to democratic governments prior to joining; thus the southern enlargements set a precedent: membership of the integrated European community became a means of solidifying democratic rule in new member countries. In the post-Cold War era, a variation of this argument would often be used to justify the entry of the former Soviet bloc countries into the EU.

The latest enlargements were significant, but it was the 'deepening' of European integration that was the truly distinctive feature in the new wave of integration. One important development was the push towards direct democracy. In 1979 the European Parliament (EP), which had started its life in 1952 as the Common Assembly of the ECSC, held its first direct election. Until then, the representatives of the national assemblies had selected the Parliament's members. Since 1979 the EP has grown in size every time new member states have been added. It has also gradually grown in importance by acquiring continent-wide legislative powers and can no longer be described as a mere 'talking shop'. Nevertheless, the EP's significance continues to be hampered by its sheer size (capped at 750 members in the twenty-first century), and the democratic deficit created by the geographical distance of its headquarters in Strasbourg from most voters. Nor does the constant decline in voter participation in EP elections (45 per cent in 2004) augur well for the success of this sort of deepening.

A second important development towards a 'deeper' Europe in the late 1970s was the creation of the European Monetary System (EMS) and the defining of the European Currency Unit (ECU). Although not a new idea, the EMS was pushed forward as a response to the uncertainties in global currency markets in the 1970s following the end of the post-war **Bretton Woods** system. Already in 1972 the EEC countries had agreed not to allow their currencies to fluctuate more than 2.25 per cent against each other and had created a European Monetary Co-operation Fund to help countries stay within this range. The EMS retained this agreement (with Italy being allowed 6 per cent fluctuations) by creating a basket of currencies known as the ECU. The 1979 agreement also created an exchange rate mechanism to help keep fluctuations to the minimum and extended European credit facilities. All this amounted to the first step towards a common currency.

The next important step towards further integration was, undoubtedly, the passing of the Single European Act (SEA) in December 1985– January 1986. This constituted the first major revision of the Rome Treaty and established a single European market. In addition, the SEA also formalized the notion of European Political Co-operation (EPC) by extending the EEC's competencies into the foreign policy arena. Floated in various reports since the early 1970s, the adoption of the EPC, highly contested though it was and remains, signalled another important deepening of the EEC's *raison d'être*.

Bretton Woods
The site of an inter-Allied conference held in 1944 to discuss the post-war international economic order. The conference led to the establishment of the IMF and the World Bank. In the postwar era the links between these two institutions, the establishment of GATT and the convertibility of the dollar into gold were known as the Bretton Woods system. After the dollar's devaluation in 1971 the world moved to a system of floating exchange rates.

Notwithstanding the security and foreign policy aspects of the agreements, the SEA was ultimately a response to a contemporary dilemma. European economies had stagnated in the 1970s and this had given rise to the derogatory term 'euro-sclerosis'. To many, the heart of the problem was the fact that, despite the abolition of tariffs, a number of invisible barriers to internal EEC trade remained intact. Both business and political leaders noted the need to harmonize laws and remove policy discrepancies between the EEC countries; indeed, they listed no fewer than 300 specific issues that needed to be fixed. The basic argument of the French mastermind behind the SEA, Jacques Delors, was that Europe could only improve its competitiveness and escape stagnation by becoming a true common market.

However, only a few years after the passing of the SEA, the future of European integration became far less predictable. In 1989 the Berlin Wall came down, and this and other related events, such as the dissolution of the Soviet bloc and the disintegration of the USSR, inevitably had a profound effect on the path that the EEC would follow in the 1990s.

AN EVER-WIDER EUROPE AND THE CONUNDRUMS OF SUCCESS

The end of the Cold War opened up new possibilities for both the widening and the deepening of European integration. At the time that the Berlin Wall came down, both the German chancellor, Helmut Kohl, and the French president, François Mitterrand, were committed to the cause of integration. Both, in particular, supported the idea that a single European currency was the obvious next step. Needless to say, however, bargaining and self-interest continued to play crucial roles. After 1989, Kohl needed French support to bring about German unification; Mitterrand, much like Robert Schuman with the creation of the ECSC in the early 1950s, wished to anchor an enlarged Germany into an integrated Europe and saw a common currency as a useful way of achieving this goal. The stage was therefore set for another dramatic step forward in the integration process, the Maastricht summit of 1992.

By creating a unique entity, the European Union, the 1992 Maastricht Treaty (or the Treaty on European Union, TEU) laid to rest most concerns about the revival of old national rivalries. It was divided into three so-called pillars: first, the European communities; second, common foreign and security policy; and, third, police and judicial co-operation in criminal matters. Among the most significant outcomes was the harmonization of monetary matters: the TEU provided for the creation of a common currency (the first euro coins and notes would be in circulation ten years after the Maastricht Treaty) and the European Central Bank. The Maastricht Treaty also enhanced the power of various supra-national European institutions (particularly the EP), introduced a social chapter and dropped 'Economic' from the title of the EEC, and thus became the founding contract of today's European Union (EU).

Like any treaty related to European integration, Maastricht was a compromise and it left few of those involved in the negotiations satisfied. The British, even after the staunchly anti-integrationist prime minister Margaret Thatcher had left the premiership in 1990, remained deeply sceptical. Her successor, John Major, insisted that Britain would not join the common currency and during the tough negotiations his continental counterparts eventually accepted this decision (Denmark followed Britain in also refusing to join the euro). In the end the treaty was ratified by all twelve member states of the EC, but the Danes had to hold a second referendum to reach that point, while French voters gave the treaty only a slim majority. In Britain, politicians did not dare to ask the public's view. Ratification was instead pushed through the House of Commons (the final vote in May 1993 was 292–112 in favour). In other key countries, such as Germany, there was little opposition in the legislature but much scepticism in the press.

Historic but unsatisfactory and unpopular, the Maastricht Treaty was followed by several further attempts to deepen European unity. In 1997 EU member states negotiated the Amsterdam Treaty, which stressed the need for a Europe-wide employment policy as well as a true common foreign and security policy. Perhaps most tellingly, the Amsterdam Treaty, which entered into force in 1999, aimed to enhance individual rights and freedoms while strengthening the powers of the European Parliament. Equally significant, the Treaty of Nice (signed in 2001 and in force two years later) fixed the relative voting powers of individual countries in the Council of the European Union, the highest decision-making body of the EU. It also enlarged the number of seats in the EP to reflect the forthcoming enlargement of the EU. These initiatives all reflected the biggest dilemma and irony for the EU as the twentieth century drew to a close. Never before had democracy been so widely accepted in Europe, but the citizens participating in that historic experiment felt increasingly alienated from the faceless institutional hybrid that the EU had become. Perhaps because of this, the role of national parliaments and national politics retained their significance and popularity (voting percentages were customarily much higher in national elections than European ones).

The scepticism of the multitude did not, however, stop the rapid widening of the EU. After the end of the Cold War Europe saw three significant enlargements: in 1995 (three countries), 2004 (ten) and 2007 (two). As a result, six decades after the Rome Treaty, in 2007 the EU consisted of twenty-seven member states. The Franco-German dominance that had characterized much of the history of the EEC was thus increasingly challenged by influential newcomers like Poland, while the EU's geographical balance shifted towards the east. In terms of population growth, the six nations that concluded the Rome Treaty in 1957 had a total combined population of 167 million. In 2007 the EU's population was 493 million, of which 'only' 215 million lived in the 'original Six'. Unlike in traditional states like China or India where population rises with a decrease in mortality rates, the EU's rapid population growth was mainly due to the external expansion that had taken place since the end of the Cold War. But in contrast to most cases of expansion in

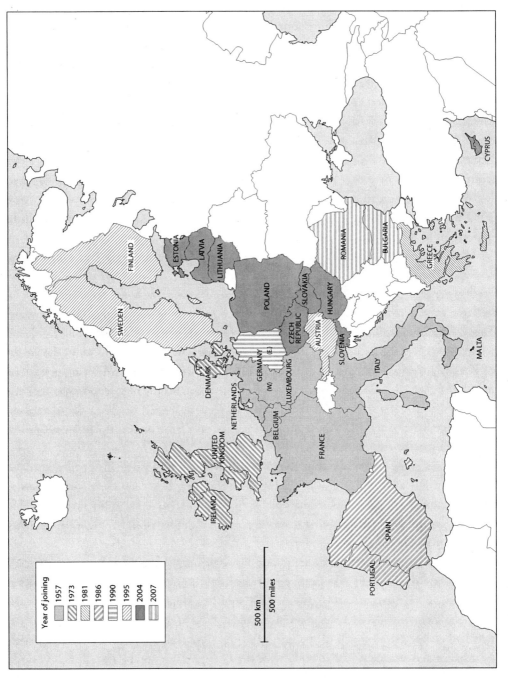

Map 21.1 EEC/EU enlargements

European history, the unique feature of EU expansion was its peaceful nature. Nations had voluntarily joined this new realm, and when doing so they accepted a number of economic, political and social contracts.

This presented no real problem during the first post-Cold War enlargement. The entry of Austria, Finland and Sweden into the EU in 1995 simply meant the arrival of three 'like-minded' countries (liberal democracies for several generations), whose citizens, in fact, enjoyed income levels above the average of the original twelve EU nations. In EU parlance, this meant that the three countries met the three so-called Copenhagen criteria for enlargement: that is, first, stability of democratic institutions; second, a functioning and competitive market economy; and, third, an ability and willingness to adapt to the obligations of EU membership. In fact, the refusal of such countries as Norway and Switzerland to join was in large part based on fears that membership would translate into a net economic loss, as well as a potential loss of national identity. However, while the Cold War neutrality that had kept Austria, Finland and Sweden out until 1989 no longer presented an obstacle to membership in 'Europe', issues of national and economic suitability were soon to be at the forefront in the debates related to enlargement into Eastern Europe.

In 2004, in the largest wave of expansion yet, ten countries, Cyprus, the Czech Republic, Estonia, Hungary, Latvia, Lithuania, Malta, Poland, Slovakia and Slovenia, joined the EU. The bulk of these new members were from the former Soviet bloc, with limited experience in democratic governance, and most possessed emerging economies. The average per capita income of the ten accession countries in 2004 was just over €9,000, while the figure for the existing members was more than €20,000. The contrast with the two 2007 entrants was even starker. While EU per capita GDP had actually increased to €26,000 by this date, the combined figure for Bulgaria and Romania, which were also not great beacons of democracy in the eyes of most West Europeans, was less than €9,000.

Why was there such a rush to join the EU? Why did the wealthy countries accept the poorer countries of Eastern and Central Europe into their midst? Where will enlargement end? Such big questions require complex answers. Different countries had different motivations when submitting their applications for accession to the EU, but it seems that the overriding rationale among applicants was twofold: EU membership provided access to a large, wealthy market and assurances against future intervention into their internal affairs from abroad. The last point was particularly significant to the countries that had lived under Soviet domination throughout the Cold War and had proved eager to join NATO in the 1990s. Concerns within these nations about the loss of their newly gained freedom to a faceless EU bureaucracy were outweighed by the assumed benefits of belonging to one of the world's wealthiest and most stable clubs.

The explanation for the willingness of the prosperous West Europeans to accept poor cousins from the East also has its economic and security components. To most of the former, the EU represents an island of democratic stability and a well-functioning market economy, but EU leaders also had their own collective threat perceptions, ones that were dramatically increased during the wars in the former Yugoslavia. In this sense, EU enlargement provided a way of removing instability on the outskirts of 'Europe' by holding the prize of membership as a carrot for 'good behaviour'. The wealthier Western Europeans (or at least their representatives) were also willing to pay the economic price for such a policy:

the initial bill for the 2004 enlargement, such as new subsidies to the accession countries, was estimated at more than €40 billion for the 2004–06 period. Further billions of euros will be transferred through the EU's so-called structural funds in forthcoming years.

There was also another side to this particular equation. As noted above, the countries that joined the European Union in the new millennium were responsible for the rapid expansion of the EU's population. Equally significantly, however, the new entrants clearly gave a boost to the 'new' Europe of the early twenty-first century. In 2007, for example, Poland and the Czech Republic, two of the top performers of the 'class of 2004', enjoyed annual growth rates of approximately 6 per cent, which was double the EU's average. In addition, the accession of the new states provided some older members with access to a new labour force that contributed to economic growth, with Britain and Ireland in particular benefiting from the arrival of East European migrant workers.

This expansion of the EU into Eastern Europe, did not, however, do much to overcome one of the EU's central problems, its ability to take on a global role in the post-Cold War world. Perhaps the biggest challenge for the EU remains the need for a well-defined and commonly accepted interpretation of its Common Foreign and Security Policy (CFSP). Defined in the 1992 Maastricht Treaty as one of the three pillars of the EU, the CFSP has never worked well. The inability of the twelve, fifteen, twenty-five and now twenty-seven countries to co-ordinate their foreign policies is a well-documented fact. The French and the British, for example, continue to bicker over transatlantic relations as much as they did in the 1960s during the presidency of Charles de Gaulle. And it is difficult to imagine how states such as Finland and Portugal, or Malta and Denmark, could have similar security interests.

To be sure, there has intermittently been successful co-ordination, but it has tended to be confined to the economic arena. The EU countries have been increasingly successful in harmonizing their approach over issues of tariffs and trade, for example forming a cohesive group in the negotiations at the World Trade Organization. The EU is also the world's biggest donor of development aid. Originally concentrating on Africa, the EU has developed comprehensive policies for virtually all continents (save North America). In addition, the EU's external relations are characterized by a focus on humanitarian aid and the promotion of human rights. In the autumn of 2007, for example, the EU was quick to condemn human rights abuses and institute economic sanctions after the brutal crackdown by Burma's ruling military junta against widespread pro-democracy protests.

The EU does, however, lack unity and effectiveness when it comes to some of the most pressing international issues of the twenty-first century. It has worked closely with other countries and international organizations on issues like the environment, terrorism, international crime, drug trafficking and illegal immigration, but it lacks the type of collective capacity that may be needed to carry out military operations, an issue that has been on the table ever since the failure of the EDC in the early 1950s. As a result, on most large-scale security issues, such as the intervention in Kosovo in 1999 or Afghanistan after 2001, the

EU has yielded to NATO; this, in turn, has naturally prolonged the European countries' reliance upon the United States in the security field.

An added, perhaps the most fundamental, problem is the sheer confusion about where the power lies when it comes to foreign and security policy. Since 1999 the EU has had a high representative for foreign and security policy, but there is also a commissioner for external relations, a Council of Foreign Ministers (in which all twenty-seven member states' foreign ministers meet regularly), as well as a large number of committees. Each country, naturally, has its own specific needs and interests, which further complicates the process of unified decision-making. In fact, although EU leaders agreed in 2004 to create the post of EU foreign minister, the plan remains on hold owing to the rejection by French and Dutch voters of the EU Constitutional Treaty in 2005.

In short, in the international arena the EU has yet to replace the dwindling influence of individual European Powers with something more substantial. National differences and bureaucratic confusion play a major role in explaining the paradox that one of the world's richest regions remains—sixty years after the Treaty of Rome that created the EEC—a virtual dwarf when it comes to global political influence.

THE EEC/EU AS INSPIRATION: INTEGRATION IN ASIA AND THE AMERICAS

The success of European integration is not just evident in the fact that most of the former members of the Warsaw Pact aspired to membership after the end of the Cold War, for the EU's achievements have also inspired politicians and intellectuals outside Europe. As with the countries of Central and European Europe, what has interested its extra-European admirers has been the ability of integration to bring both political stability and economic growth. With decolonization and superpower rivalry in the Cold War having created profound and long-lasting instability, the potential of regional integration to deliver a respite from territorial disputes and from an unhealthy reliance on the superpowers for trade and security is undoubtedly beguiling.

The first indication that another region might step along the same road came in 1967 with the formation of ASEAN. The idea that South-East Asia might benefit from economic integration was not, however, new. As early as 1945 the British had used their paramount influence in the region to push for a multi-national approach towards post-war reconstruction. This culminated in 1950 with the establishment of the Colombo Plan, in which the British Commonwealth and the United States offered economic aid to the newly independent states and colonies of South and South-East Asia. However, contrary to the pattern in Western Europe, where the Marshall Plan proved an important stimulus to economic integration, the Colombo Plan did little to encourage co-operation between the newly independent states. Moreover, integration was impossible in the light of the fact that the region was deeply divided about how to react to the Cold War. Indonesia and Burma, which had both experienced a turbulent journey to independence, were jealous of their newly acquired sovereignty and mistrustful of the West, and thus became enthusiastic advocates of neutralism. Meanwhile, the Philippines, with its close ties to Washington, and Thailand, with its fear of communist control of Indochina, became in 1954 members of the American-dominated **South-East Asian Treaty Organization (SEATO).**

The first indigenous step towards economic integration came in July 1963 when Malaya, the Philippines and Thailand formed the Association of South-East Asia (ASA). Any further efforts to build on this platform were, however, soon frustrated by the controversy later that year over the creation of Malaysia, which was opposed by the Philippines diplomatically and Indonesia militarily. Two events in 1965–66 helped to break the logjam. First, the United States, in the face of the escalating war in Vietnam, tried to stabilize the region and isolate the communist bacillus by sponsoring the cause of regional economic development and encouraging Japanese capital investment. Second, the South-East Asian states suddenly found themselves in a position to take advantage of this encouragement because the most destabilizing and divisive politician in the region, President Sukarno of Indonesia, was removed from power. Sukarno's ousting and the rise to prominence of General Suharto provided a catalyst for profound change, for Indonesia now emerged as an anti-communist state that was willing to accept Malaysia's existence and to play a decisive part in developing the region. Accordingly, in August 1967 ASA metamorphosed into ASEAN, consisting of Malaysia, Singapore, Thailand, Indonesia and the Philippines.

At first ASEAN was a rather loose organization, which concentrated entirely on economic, social and cultural matters. Before too long, however, it was forced to extend its remit into the political field. The stimulus for this was the steady American de-escalation of its presence in South Vietnam. Fearing that this might encourage Soviet and Chinese machinations, in November 1971 the ASEAN states adopted the idea of regional neutralization and declared that South-East Asia was 'a zone of peace, freedom and neutrality'. ASEAN's move towards greater cohesion was then further cemented later in the decade by the Vietnamese invasion of Cambodia in 1978–79, which raised the prospect of a threat to Thai security. ASEAN's ability to talk for the region, its moves to encourage Western capital investment and its average annual economic growth rates of 6–9 per cent meant that it soon found international sponsors. The United States, with its animus towards Vietnam still running high, was willing after 1978 to support the organization's political pretensions, while Japan emerged at this point as its major trading partner and source of international aid, as well as the inspiration for the individual states' development of export-orientated economies.

However, while the organization did much to encourage trade and investment, it differed from the EEC in that it lacked any solid institutional base or any outright commitment to the ideal of greater integration and the formal pooling of sovereignty. It was only in 1994 that it finally launched the ASEAN Free Trade Area and it has never followed the EEC/EU's example in regulating agricultural production, allowing for the free movement of labour and introducing a parliament to oversee legislation. Moreover, while it began in the 1990s to espouse the cause of democracy, it has found it difficult to live up to this rhetoric owing to the arrival of new members such as Brunei Darussalam in 1984, Vietnam in 1995, the Lao People's Democratic Republic and Burma in 1997, and Cambodia in 1999.

Moving into the twenty-first century, ASEAN faced two key challenges: first, formulating a security response to the threat emanating from Jemaah Islamiyya (JI), a regional *jihadist* network with links to **al-Qaeda** (see Chapter 22); and second, Burma's lack of progress towards democracy. The authoritarian nature of Burma's military government became the focus of ASEAN discussions as Burma's turn to chair ASEAN in 2006 approached. Burma's military government and its poor human rights record were seen as detrimental to ASEAN interests. It was feared that under Burmese chairmanship ASEAN would lose vital trade and economic relations with Western

> **South-East Asia Treaty Organization (SEATO)**
> An alliance organized in 1954 by Australia, France, Great Britain, New Zealand, Pakistan, the Philippines, Thailand and the United States. SEATO was created after the Geneva conference on Indochina to prevent further communist gains in the region. However, it proved of little use in the Vietnam War and was disbanded in 1977.

countries which had levied sanctions against Burma's military regime. This would have damaged ASEAN's 'Vision 2020', which saw the organization playing a pivotal role in the international community. In an almost unprecedented fashion, given ASEAN's principle of non-interference in the domestic affairs of its member states, legislators from Malaysia, the Philippines and Singapore urged Burma to withdraw from the chairmanship. At the same time, in an attempt to keep this an 'internal issue', they rejected Western calls to suspend Burma's ASEAN membership. The chairmanship crisis was resolved in July 2005 when Burma's foreign minister requested a postponement so that Burma could focus on national reconciliation. Reconciliation, however, has remained elusive. In September and again in November 2007, pro-democracy demonstrators and Buddhist monks were brutally suppressed as they took to the streets in what was called the 'Saffron Revolution'. While ASEAN condemned the Burmese military government's crackdown and pressed for the release of pro-democracy leaders, it failed to take concrete steps to deal with Burma.

Thus ASEAN has remained rather limited in scope. However, its success both in the political and in the economic field has enabled it to provide a useful foundation for other attempts to develop new international fora. For instance, in the field of security, the rise of China under Deng Xiaoping's leadership led in 1993 to ASEAN seeking to reduce potential international tension by sponsoring the development of an ASEAN Regional Forum (ARF). This organization brings together the main Powers with interests in the region in the hope that a consensus on security issues can be found. In addition, from 1996 biennial conferences were established between the EU and ASEAN. Another regional development came in the economic field with the foundation in 1989 of an organization called Asia-Pacific Economic Co-operation (APEC), which was an Australian initiative with significant American and Japanese support. Again the organization existed primarily as a force that was designed to pave the way for greater trade liberalization, but, as it included the United States, the PRC, Russia and Japan, it also proved another useful forum for consultation and dialogue.

There has also been talk of ambitious plans to move beyond the establishment of regular ASEAN, ARF and APEC summit conferences and to attempt more directly to emulate the work of Schuman, Monnet and Delors. Most notably in December 2005 a summit meeting of Asian-Pacific Powers was held in Kuala Lumpur to investigate the possibility of moving towards the formation of an Asian Community. After a year in which PRC–Japanese relations had fallen to their lowest ebb since relations were opened in 1972, the idea of a move towards an EU-type organization that would overcome past hostilities echoing the reduction of Franco-German rivalry held great attraction. However, the diversity of political ideologies and practices in Asia, to say nothing of the strategic rivalries and huge discrepancies in economic power, made progress extremely difficult to achieve.

In the 1990s the Western Hemisphere also saw a movement towards free trade and regional integration, which were considered by many as the best long-term solutions to Latin America's economic difficulties. The principal and most ambitious attempt to bring about hemispheric integration was the **North American Free Trade Agreement (NAFTA).** Signed in October 1992, NAFTA brought together the United States, Canada and Mexico into a trading bloc of 370 million people. The three countries pledged to eliminate trade barriers, duties and tariffs over the subsequent fifteen

> **al-Qaeda (Arabic: Base)**
> Islamist umbrella organization established by Osama Bin Laden drawing upon the network of international *jihadists* established during the Afghan War to support the *mujahedeen*. Founded as early as 1988, al-Qaeda emerged into the public eye in 1990.

years. Its most substantial impact was on Mexico, for NAFTA opened up the country to American (and Canadian) investment. However, it also raised the spectre of companies moving south to take advantage of cheaper labour, and understandably, American and Canadian labour unions were NAFTA's most persistent foes. In the end, NAFTA did boost the growth of regional trade (American–Mexican trade, for example, doubled between 1993 and 1997, from $83 billion to $157 billion).

NAFTA was, in fact, probably most significant for Mexico. It allowed President Carlos Salinas to push through aggressive economic reforms of privatization and liberalization and, so it was hoped, to move away from the semi-authoritarian rule of the Institutional Revolutionary Party (PRI). Unfortunately for those dreaming of Mexico's 'democratization', Salinas was faced with a sudden explosion of guerrilla warfare when the Zapatista movement in the poor Chiapas region denounced and, in 1994, forcefully opposed both NAFTA and Salinas. The following year Mexico faced a currency crisis that could only be solved with an American-backed IMF bailout of $50 billion. Suddenly, Mexico looked like a Third World country in the midst of a political and economic crisis, rather than a fast-developing democratic partner in the NAFTA bloc. Yet by 1997 the internal stability as well as the economic state of Mexico began to improve, in large part as a result of the boost in the American economy. By the end of the century Mexico, Canada and the United States shared, albeit in differing degrees, in the boom of the late Clinton years. Yet it is worth noting that underneath the façade of prosperity lay a deep undercurrent of poverty: in Mexico, an estimated one-third of the population lived below the poverty line at the end of the millennium. In large part owing to continued discontent within Mexico, the July 2000 elections resulted in the final end of Mexico's one party rule as the PRI, after seventy-one years, lost the presidency to Vicente Fox Quesada's centre-right National Action Party (PAN).

In the 1990s there was also much talk about extending NAFTA eventually to incorporate all of the Western Hemisphere (generally called WHFTA, the Western Hemisphere Free Trade Area). Many, including President Clinton, spoke of NAFTA as a mere starting point. With many economic analysts predicting a boom in the Latin American economies, the hopes of a hemispheric trading bloc dwarfing that of the European Union were high. Yet, by the end of the decade, there was neither a WHFTA nor an expansion of NAFTA. A number of political and economic obstacles help explain this. First, the Latin American countries, perhaps most significantly Brazil, were concerned that WHFTA might endanger their attempts to diversify their trade portfolios and lead to increased political dependency on the North. Second, NAFTA, unlike the European Union, had little to offer beyond removing trade barriers. There were no provisions for the free movement of people and no political superstructure. This point linked closely with the question of the nature of regimes to be allowed to join a prospective WHFTA. Should membership in a prospective WHFTA be based on political criteria (in the same way as in the EU)? If so, what should one make of Mexico's early membership, for as a *de facto* one-party state it hardly constituted a democracy. Last, one needs to stress the continued American reluctance to submit to any sort of supra-governmental authority. Thus, by the end of the 1990s, the talks about WHFTA (or the alternative Free Trade Area of the Americas, FTAA) were in deadlock, a situation made worse by an emerging economic crisis in Latin America that would soon plunge such countries as Argentina into a serious recession. Instead, the concrete results of the free trade movement in the Western Hemisphere were (in addition to NAFTA) limited to such smaller-scale regional free trade zones as the **Mercosur**, the Common Market of the South that linked Argentina, Brazil, Uruguay and Paraguay in 1991.

> **North American Free Trade Agreement (NAFTA)**
>
> A 1992 accord between Canada, Mexico and the United States establishing a free-trade zone in North America from 1 January 1994. NAFTA immediately lifted tariffs on the majority of goods produced by the signatory nations. It also calls for the gradual elimination of barriers to cross-border investment and to the movement of goods and services between the three countries.

Where scholars disagree: realists, liberal inter-governmentalists, functionalists and federalists

The basic debate about European integration focuses on a simple question: how to explain the emergence of the EEC and EU? There are two broad ways of answering the question: by emphasizing the role of member (nation-)states or by stressing the impact of supra-national institutions. The answers reflect the cleavage between those who think that the creation of the common market has been the central outcome of the integration process and those who believe that it is the shared institutions, customs and laws that truly define the 'new Europe'.

Those who maintain that nation-states have and will remain the main movers of the process of integration are, in general, referred to as realists or neo-realists. Their key argument is that the decades of integration have not fundamentally changed the role of the nation-state as the prime actor in European international relations. States are simply pursuing their national interests in a changed context, as maintained by such authors as Kenneth Waltz and John Mearsheimer. Relatively close to the 'realists' are those scholars labelled as 'liberal inter-governmentalists'. Like the realists, they stress the role of individual states, but they also tend to emphasize the domestic political setting in EEC and EU member states as the key determinants of how these nations act within the inter-governmental playing field. A key practitioner of this school of thought is Andrew Moravcsik.

A third broad approach to explaining European integration is usually called functionalism or neo-functionalism. Building upon the theories of Ernst Haas and Leon Lindberg, such scholars explain the integration from the early 1950s to the present as a gradual spillover process. While the original ECSC was limited to two industrial sectors, the functionalists argue, various interest groups and political parties responded to problems in related sectors by pushing to enhance the competence and scope of the Community and the Union. The 'deepening' of integration, such as the move from a common market to a common currency, is often cited as a more recent case that 'proves' the neo-functionalists' argument. Among its most prominent representatives is Stanley Hoffman.

Lastly, there are the federalists. Authors like John Pinder generally maintain that the deepening of integration was not due to some spillover effect but was rather a reflection of the inability of individual governments to deal with a growing number of transnational issues—security, trade, environment—without close co-operation. The federalists also stress the idealistic aspects of the process of European integration, namely the fact that democratic governance is at the heart of the integration experience. Perhaps more than the analysts in other groups, the federalists are concerned about the so-called democratic deficit within the European Union. This seems like a legitimate concern, for if European integration is simply a modern expression of nationalism it is based upon shaky ground.

CONCLUSION

'Europe will not be made all at once, or according to a single plan'; these words from Robert Schuman's famous declaration that in May 1950 launched the ECSC are symbolic of the nature of post-war European integration. Almost six decades later, building 'Europe' remains a work in process, lacking a clear single-minded direction. Nevertheless the emergence of the EU is an impressive achievement. By 2007 a grouping of previously antagonistic countries had somehow managed to form an entity that, in the end, did represent an island of stability in a perilous and rapidly changing world. The twenty-seven countries of the EU had previously often fought against each other, and even in the Cold War had formed such military (offensive or defensive) alliances as NATO and the Warsaw Pact. By 2007 they were co-operating, belonging to a community that accounted for about a fifth of the world's exports and imports, and more than 30 per cent of the global gross domestic product. While the future of the EU remains uncertain, further enlargements (to Croatia and possibly to Turkey) appeared more or less a certainty. Furthermore, the deepening of integration is similarly on the cards, despite the often negative attitude of the citizens of EU states. While lacking in the global clout reserved for more traditional nation-states like the United States, Russia or China, the EU is clearly an integral part of the global community in the early twenty-first century. Moreover, outside Europe the success of the EU has acted as an inspiration to politicians who have sought greater strength for their countries both economically and politically through regional unity and the pooling of sovereignty. These extra-European institutions have, however, achieved relatively limited success, which only helps to underline the impression that the EU has benefited from a number of distinct advantages that are difficult for others to emulate. The 'European experiment' rested, after all, on the need to overcome the trauma created by two disastrous wars and the threat posed by the Soviet Union. Moreover, it had the advantage that all of its members were committed to liberal democracy and the rule of law, as well as sharing a common culture. Built on these solid foundations, the EU has been able to widen and deepen in a continuous process of evolution, while its imitators, lacking the same base for consensus building, have not made much progress.

Mercosur

Or the Southern Cone Common Market. A Latin American trade organization established in 1991 to increase economic co-operation in the eastern part of South America. Full members include Argentina, Brazil, Paraguay and Uruguay. Bolivia and Chile are associate members. Mercosur's goals include the gradual elimination of tariffs between member states and harmonization of external duties.

RECOMMENDED READING

Much has been written about European integration, but a great deal of it remains too detailed for a general audience. Perhaps the best general overviews are John Gillingham, *European Integration 1950–2003: Superstate or New Market Economy?* (Cambridge, 2003), John Pinder, *The European Union: A Very Short Introduction* (Oxford, 2007) and Pinder, *The Building of the European Union* (Oxford, 1999). Derek Urwin, *The Community of Europe: A History of European Integration since 1945* (London, 1994) offers a slightly dated survey of the history of integration, while Ben Rosamond (ed.), *Theories of European Integration* (London, 2000) offers an interesting contrast of the various ways in which scholars have explained the phenomenon of integration. For a magisterial account of Europe's post-war history, including integration, see Tony Judt, *Postwar: A History of Europe since 1945* (New York, 2005). Further examples of overviews include James Dean, *Ending Europe's Wars* (New York, 1994), James E. Goodby, *Europe Undivided* (Washington, DC, 1998), M. Emerson, *Redrawing the Map of Europe* (New York, 1998), Michael J. Brenner, *Multilateralism and Western Security* (New York, 1995),

F. Cameron, *The Foreign and Security Policy of the European Union* (London, 1999), A. Mayhew, *Recreating Europe* (New York, 1998), Tom Buchanan, *Europe's Troubled Peace, 1945–2000* (Oxford, 2006) and M. A. Smith and G. Timmins, *Building a Bigger Europe* (Aldershot, 2000). A comprehensive collection of essays discussing the various aspects of the European Union is Helen Wallace and William Wallace (eds), *Policy Making in the European Union* (Oxford, 2000).

For the controversies over British entry into the EEC see N. Piers Ludlow, *Dealing with Britain: The Six and the First UK Application to the EEC* (Cambridge, 1997), James Ellison, *Threatening Europe: Britain and the Creation of the European Community, 1955–1958* (London, 2000) and Helen Parr, *British Policy towards the European Community: Harold Wilson and Britain's World Role, 1964–1967* (Aldershot, 2005). For the 'Empty Chair' crisis, see N. Piers Ludlow, *The European Community and the Crises of the 1960s: Negotiating the Gaullist Challenge.* (London, 2006). For the Maastricht Treaty see Cole Mazzucelli, *France and Germany at Maastricht: Politics and Negotiations to Create the European Union* (London, 1999).

The most detailed analyses of the EU's foreign policy include Paolo Foradori, *Managing a Multilevel Foreign Policy: The EU in International Affairs* (Lanham, MD, 2007), Cameron Fraser, *An Introduction to European Foreign Policy* (London, 2007), Neil Winn and Christopher Lord, *EU Foreign Policy beyond the Nation-State* (London, 2001) and Simon Nuttall, *European Foreign Policy* (Oxford, 2000). European integration in a global context is discussed in a number of books. See, for example, David Calleo, *Rethinking Europe's Future* (Princeton, NJ, 2001) and Gregory Treverton, *America, Germany, and the Future of Europe* (Princeton, NJ, 1992). There is no shortage of works on the development and impact of European integration. For an account exploring America's role in this development, see Geir Lundestad, *'Empire' by Integration* (New York, 1997). For an influential perspective on the transatlantic relationship, see Thomas Risse-Kappen, *Cooperation among Democracies: The European Influence on US Foreign Policy* (Princeton, NJ, 1995).

For studies of ASEAN see Jurgen Haacke, *ASEAN's Diplomatic and Security Culture: Origins, Developments and Prospects* (London, 2003), David Jones, *ASEAN and East Asian International Relations: Regional Delusion* (Northampton, MA, 2006) and Shaun Narine, *Explaining ASEAN: Regionalism in Southeast Asia* (Boulder, CO, 2002). In regard to ASEAN's relations with Japan, see Sueo Sudo, *The Fukuda Doctrine and ASEAN* (Singapore, 1992). See also P. Korhonen, *Japan and Asia Pacific Integration: Pacific Romances 1968–1996* (London, 1998). On NAFTA and free trade see George Grayson, *The North American Free Trade Agreement* (Lanham, MD, 1995), Barry Bosworth *et al.*, *Coming Together? Mexico–US Relations* (Washington, DC, 1997) and Silvia Saborio, *The Premise and the Promise: Free Trade in the Americas* (New Brunswick, NJ, 1992).

Collective Security Revived
The Formation of the United Nations

NORRIE MacQUEEN

Whatever the fate of the League as an institution, the *idea* of a global international organization with responsibility for the regulation of international security had become firmly lodged in political and popular consciousness by the time of the Second World War. Even as the League of Nations disintegrated in the later 1930s and another world war loomed, there was a general expectation that the experiment would be rerun, though in different terms, when conditions in the international system allowed.

THE SECOND WORLD WAR AND THE ORIGINS OF THE UNITED NATIONS

Two years after the outbreak of the Second World War in Europe and just months before the United States was drawn in to it after the Japanese attack on Pearl Harbor, an Anglo-American commitment was made to the construction of a new organization when the war was finished. The Atlantic Charter was signed in August 1941 during a meeting between the British prime minister Winston Churchill and the American president, Franklin D. Roosevelt held on a warship off the Canadian coast. Collective security was back on the agenda, despite the experience of the League. After the war the signatories intended 'to see established a peace which (would) afford to all nations the means of dwelling in safety within their own boundaries'. To this end, all nations 'for realistic as well as spiritual reasons must come to the abandonment of the use of force'. This would involve the establishment of 'a … permanent system of general security', and pending this, 'nations which threaten, or may threaten aggression outside of their frontiers' would be disarmed. The first use of

Norrie MacQueen, "Collective Security Revived: The Formation of the United Nations," from *Peacekeeping and the International System*, pp. 43–60. Copyright © 2006 by Taylor & Francis Group. Permission to reprint granted by the publisher.

the term 'United Nations' came the following year when it was adopted by the twenty-six states fighting the Axis powers.

American state department officials had, in fact, been working on an outline of a new organization as early as 1940. After the United States entered the war, however, plans for the permanent 'general security' system envisaged in the Atlantic Charter began to take firmer shape. The process accelerated as an allied victory looked increasingly likely. In 1943 the American secretary of state, Cordell Hull, signed up his Soviet and British counterparts—commissar for foreign affairs Vyacheslav Molotov and foreign secretary Anthony Eden—to a declaration committing them to the creation of 'a general international organization based on the principles of the sovereign equality of all peace loving states and open to membership by all such states, large and small for the maintenance of international peace and security'.

Detailed planning of the new organization was, of course, constrained by the overarching priority of winning the war. Human and material resources for this were in short supply and perhaps, too, at some level of consciousness, excessive planning of the post-war system was felt to invite hubris. For President Roosevelt, who among the major wartime leaders was the most enthusiastic for a post-war security organization, there was a particular concern. He was keenly aware of the fate of the American relationship with the League. For all the moral energy of Woodrow Wilson, his fellow Democrat predecessor, the reaction in Congress had still been against continued leadership of the post-war system. It was necessary, therefore, to move ahead cautiously and to design a system in which American power would be enhanced and preserved rather than dissipated and diminished.

The tripartite commitment to a new organization secured by Cordell Hull was made public during the Tehran Conference of allied leaders in November 1943. In the run-up to this, some fundamental differences in national preferences had been revealed. The American view favoured the regulation of international security collectively by the major powers in the system. In real terms, following an allied victory in the war, this would mean the United States itself, the Soviet Union and Britain. The key decision-making processes around the maintenance of international security would be controlled by the big powers. To this end, the American planners argued, there could be no return to the requirement for unanimity that the League had imposed on its members. The burdens and dangers of this big-power role, it was proposed, should be eased by a stage-by-stage process of disarmament among the other states in the international system.

The British view was less radical, and in some respects still informed by the old nineteenth-century concert system. Churchill's view, in other words, was more 'realist' than Roosevelt's in that he did not share American confidence in the transforming power of collective security. States would still look first and last to their own capacities to guarantee their security, Churchill believed. For Britain, the lesson of the League was that the construct of sovereignty would continue to dominate the behaviour of states and could not be negotiated away simply by the creation of a new institution with a new constitution. The participation or otherwise of the United States in the new organization would not alter that fundamental fact. Small and medium-sized powers would not willingly subordinate themselves to the control of big powers, however well intentioned. And, from the other side of the power spectrum, the commitment of the big powers to a consistent effort across all parts of the system was questionable in the British view. With the League's experience over Manchuria and Abyssinia in mind, Britain was sceptical about the extent of big-power commitment to expensive and burdensome involvement in areas of the world that they did not regard as vital to their own national interests. Security cooperation would be best pursued on a regional rather than a global basis, which would focus collective concerns on areas and issues of direct national interest. Britain therefore would be concerned with western Europe, while the United States would be responsible for the western hemisphere. Constructed in this way the United Nations would provide an organizational umbrella with little direct responsibility for security on the ground. The new organization should therefore have a 'council of Europe', a 'council of Asia' and so on. Above these regional bodies there would be a 'high court', which would be a development on the existing Permanent Court of International Justice, which was established under the League.

The Soviet leader Joseph Stalin was initially suspicious of the American plan for the concentration of power in so few—and predominantly capitalist—hands. To begin with he seemed to favour the British position, which in some respects would have legitimized Soviet domination of eastern Europe, at least in terms of the control of regional security. Eventually, however, the American model came to be more favoured in Moscow when the possibility of US rejection of any system other than Roosevelt's was made clear. A repeat of America's rejection of the League could not be contemplated. From Stalin's perspective the most important thing was that any system should be dominated by the major powers and that the USSR should be at the centre of it. The Soviet Union had been excluded from the League until 1934, by which time the institution's authority was already fatally undermined, and Stalin was determined that this history would not be repeated.

Roosevelt's vision of the United Nations prevailed, therefore, just as Wilson's had for the League. In both cases this was no more than a reflection of the 'realist reality' of the international system at each historical juncture. The United States had emerged from both world wars not only as a victor but as the one most able, by virtue of its resilient national power, to dictate the terms of the post-war disposition.

THE NEW ORGANIZATION EMERGES:
FROM DUMBARTON OAKS TO SAN FRANCISCO

Concrete planning for the new organization began the year following the commitment by the powers at Tehran. A crucial sequence of meetings took place in August 1944 at Dumbarton Oaks, an estate outside Washington. Here the Soviet and British ambassadors to the United States, Andrei Gromyko (who was later to be Soviet foreign minister during much of the cold war era) and Sir Alexander Cadogan, were closeted with the American assistant secretary of state, Edward Stettinius. China, at this time still nominally under the control of Chiang Kai-shek's nationalists, was also represented. These states were to comprise Roosevelt's 'four policemen', who would preside at the centre of the new security organization. The purpose of the Dumbarton Oaks meeting was to convert the general thinking already undertaken by the leading allies into a solid set of proposals that could then be presented to the broader anti-Axis alliance now close to winning the war. There was little disagreement about the general architecture the United Nations should be built upon. This was dictated by much the same logic involved in the design of League of Nations, which, as we saw, had resulted in something analogous to a modern state.

Where the League had a Council composed of the major powers, the United Nations would have a Security Council, which again corresponded roughly to a national executive or cabinet. The Security Council would have eleven members (increased in 1966 to fifteen). There would be two classes of Security Council membership. The permanent members comprised the four states represented at Dumbarton Oaks (the US, USSR, Britain and China) and later France, which was still under German occupation at the time of the meeting and did not participate. The biggest of the victorious war allies therefore would be Roosevelt's 'policemen', who would take the lead responsibility for the management of collective security. The legal basis of this role, which we will explore in due course, would eventually be laid out in Chapter VII of the United Nations Charter, the organization's constitution and descendant of the League Covenant.

The special role of the permanent members brought with it the power of veto over actions proposed by other members of the Security Council. In this way, the traditional national interests and prerogatives of the biggest powers in the system would be preserved while decisive action would not, in theory, be constrained by the need for unanimity as it was in the League. While many have criticized the whole principle of the veto, it was designed as a means of acknowledging the reality of power in, and the special national interests of, the biggest states in the system, while still permitting the possibility of work-able collective security. While the League required all of the states on the Council to give their positive support to a decision, in the new organization a permanent member might abstain or absent itself from a vote on a resolution without nullifying it.

The six (later ten) non-permanent members of the Security Council would serve for two-year periods. To ensure continuity, half of them would be elected to the Security Council each year by their regional groupings in the General Assembly. This General Assembly was the successor to the League Assembly. Like its predecessor it could be seen as in some senses corresponding to a national parliament. All UN members would have a seat and a vote in the General Assembly. The approach to UN membership agreed at Dumbarton Oaks was essentially a universalist one; admission would, in principle, be open to all. As we have seen, the effectiveness and authority of the League had been vitiated not only by the non-participation of the United States but by the initial exclusion of Germany and the Soviet Union. This had two negative effects. First, it created an impression of the League as an alliance of First World War victors. Second, it fostered a culture in which membership and non-membership were equally valid foreign policy options for states. This became evident when the future Axis powers, Germany, Italy and Japan, withdrew from the organization one by one in the 1930s. This was a fatal flaw in an institution charged with the management of collective security in the international system as a whole. It was agreed at Dumbarton Oaks therefore (and later embodied in the Charter itself) that membership of the United Nations would be open to all 'peace-loving states'. There were difficulties in applying this formula in the first decade of the United Nations when the Soviet Union used its veto on membership applications to control the growth of the then western majority in the General Assembly. But from the mid-1950s, with a very few significant qualifications that we will discuss in due course, the United Nations General Assembly was a genuinely universalist body.

Unexpectedly, perhaps, the first serious signs of east–west division emerged at Dumbarton Oaks over the arrangements for the General Assembly rather than the Security Council. While the Soviet Union's interests seemed to be guaranteed in the Council by its right of veto, the weakness of communist power in the system as a whole was sharply exposed in the more 'democratic' forum of the General Assembly. While playing a crucial part in the allies' final war effort, in a sense the USSR still stood alone in 1944. It remained the only communist state in the system. As the negotiators sat down at Dumbarton Oaks the future of what would become the satellite states of the eastern bloc was still far from certain, though there was an assumption that liberation from German occupation would lead to democratic self-determination. Although the nationalists in China were gradually falling before Mao Zedong's apparently unstoppable communist advance, they still represented Chinese interests at Dumbarton Oaks. They would also, controversially, represent China in the United Nations until 1971. Moscow therefore felt vulnerable in the new forum.

The issue also went beyond the nascent ideological division between east and west. The idea of sovereign equality among members on which the General Assembly was built was a venerable Westphalian principle. It also had a certain emotional appeal in a system that was in the final phase of a war fought against large powers that had trampled on the rights of small ones. But none of this could quite disguise the anomaly that saw a state such as the Soviet Union, with its huge population, given precisely the same power in the General Assembly as, say, a small Latin American country representing perhaps less than a million people. The Soviet attempt to redress this situation involved an inventive piece of multiple counting. Gromyko proposed that all sixteen republics of the Soviet Union should have separate membership of the General Assembly. The other delegates, aware that whatever the rhetoric of the Soviet constitution the USSR was in reality a ruthlessly centralized state, dismissed the proposal out of hand and the matter remained unresolved at Dumbarton Oaks.

Despite this and a number of other issues such as arguments over limitations on the use of the veto being left pending after Dumbarton Oaks, the meeting had been successful overall in reaching agreement on the framework for the new organization. The next phase in its development took place during the conference of allied leaders at Yalta on the Russian Black Sea in February 1945. Here the precise terms of the Security Council veto were agreed, with the Soviet Union accepting that it should not apply to attempts at 'peaceful settlement' of disputes. The issue of General Assembly representation was also settled—though to no one's real satisfaction—when the USSR accepted two further seats for Ukraine and Byelorussia. The squabble was an early portent of emerging cold war divisions within the organization.

The formal establishment of the United Nations took place in San Francisco in April 1945 on the eve of allied victory in Europe but still several months from the end of the war in Asia. The meeting took place less than two weeks after the death of President Roosevelt, who had been succeeded by his vice president, Harry Truman. The new president, although from a different, less patrician, Democrat tradition, nevertheless shared his predecessor's commitment to the new organization. Early fears that there might be a repeat of the League experience, with America (despite its leading role in the construction of the organization) rejecting membership of it, proved misplaced. Roosevelt had been careful to build a bipartisan consensus and Republican support for the new body had been carefully secured. The cross-party commitment to the UN was symbolized by the participation of leading Republicans in the San Francisco ceremonies.

Fifty-one states gathered to sign the new Charter. All were members of the anti-Axis alliance, though some only recently so. The wartime status of the signatories may have suggested on one level that the UN was to be an alliance of victors, an image that had undermined the moral authority of the League, as we have observed. But the sheer numbers of signatories pointed in another direction—towards a universality of membership that the League never attained. The document to which they put their nations' signatures represented the second attempt in the twentieth century to codify a system of collective security as an alternative to national defence.

THE 'PACIFIC SETTLEMENT OF DISPUTES' AND 'ACTION WITH RESPECT TO ACTS OF AGGRESSION'

Two sections of the United Nations Charter, Chapters VI and VII, deal with the specifics of international security and set out the role of the organization in guaranteeing it. As we will see, the term peacekeeping does not appear in the United Nations Charter and it is doubtful that such activity was ever contemplated by those drafting its articles in 1944 and 1945. Peacekeeping therefore has no specific identity in international law. This has not deterred scholars and practitioners from attempting to locate it by association with some part of the Charter. In the absence of a clear articulation, peacekeeping has in the past been referred to as a 'Chapter six-and-a-half' activity. This is a legally meaningless term but it nevertheless says something about the nature of peacekeeping. It is, in this view, poised between Chapter VI, which is concerned with the 'Pacific Settlement of Disputes', and Chapter VII, which is the central statement of collective security and deals with 'Action with Respect to Threats to the Peace, Breaches of the Peace, and Acts of Aggression'.

The approach of Chapter VI is essentially 'voluntarist' in that the processes and measures outlined in the Chapter do not involve enforcement by the UN. In this sense it represents an attempt at collective security before the deployment of international military force. The Chapter begins with Article 33 of the Charter, which sets out an extensive menu of procedures to be followed by parties to a dispute, 'the continuance of which is likely to endanger the maintenance of international peace and security'. They are to 'seek a solution by negotiation, enquiry, mediation, conciliation, arbitration, judicial settlement, resort to regional agencies or arrangement, or other peaceful means of their own choice'. Article 34 empowers the Security Council, if it chooses to do so, to determine whether a dispute is likely to pose a threat to peace and security, and Article 36 permits it to 'recommend appropriate procedures or methods of adjustment'. In the event of the parties failing to reach a means of resolving their dispute, Article 37 requires them to refer the matter to the Security Council. At this stage it is open to the Security Council to propose mechanisms of settlement. As this might, implicitly, involve the deployment of peacekeepers there is at least an argument that a legal basis for peacekeeping can be inferred from this part of the Charter.

Alternatively, the Council might view the dispute and the threat it could pose to broader international security as sufficiently serious to be considered under Chapter VII of the Charter. This chapter is in many ways the most significant part of the whole document. It was certainly the most difficult to find agreement on at Dumbarton Oaks. It represented, simply, an attempt to impose on the international system mechanisms of collective security that would succeed where the earlier League experiment had failed. To this end it required far-reaching and burdensome commitments from all Charter signatories. Here once again perhaps we can discern the influence of the legalistic culture of the United States that we touched on when we explored the League Covenant. The lesson to be taken from the failure of the collective security under the League, it seemed, was not that the basic project was flawed, but that its legal structures were insufficiently strong. This second attempt, therefore, would impose clear and unavoidable obligations. The result was a constitution that, potentially, demanded a major qualification of state sovereignty. A measure of the extent of this commitment and the unease it originally generated was Switzerland's decision not to join the United Nations, a position it reversed only in 2002. Despite being widely admired for its good international citizenship (illustrated, for example, by its hosting of the League of Nations headquarters in Geneva), Switzerland viewed the Charter as a treaty commitment that would have compromised its historical neutrality. And, in truth, had the powers given to it under Chapter VII ever been fully exercised by the Security Council, Switzerland's concerns would have been fully justified.

Article 39, with which Chapter VII opens, empowers the Security Council to 'determine the existence of any threat to the peace, breach of the peace, or act of aggression' and to 'decide what measures shall be taken … to maintain or restore' peace and security. The range of these measures is presented in Articles 41 and 42. The first of these Articles is concerned with pressures short of military force: economic sanctions, transport and communications blockades and the severance of diplomatic relations. However, Article 42 determined that should 'the Security Council consider that measures provided for in Article 41 would be inadequate or have proved to be inadequate, it may take such action by air, sea, or land forces as may be necessary …' Although the League Covenant did not explicitly rule out military action to enforce collective security, it had little to say on the subject and placed no obligations on members. Now, however, Article 43 of the UN Charter required that all members 'in order to contribute to the maintenance of international peace and security, undertake to make available to the Security Council, on its call … armed forces, assistance and facilities … necessary for the purpose of maintaining international peace and security'.

These arrangements would effectively have created a UN army that could be raised on need. At an early stage of the planning of the Charter the possibility of an actual standing army was in fact raised. The idea was eventually dropped, but on practical rather than political grounds, which gives a sense of the extent of the ambitions of the wartime planning behind the United Nations. As it was, UN forces would be under the command of a joint staff composed of the military leaders of the permanent members of the Security Council. This was the Military Staff Committee (MSC), which is covered by Article 47. The MSC would be directed by the five chiefs of staff of the permanent members and would be 'responsible under the Security Council for the strategic direction of any armed forces placed at the disposal of the Security Council'.

Article 51, the final part of Chapter VII, appears at first reading to represent an opt-out clause from the far-reaching arrangements that the preceding articles had outlined. The 'inherent right of individual or collective self-defence' was recognized as a legitimate recourse for states under direct assault. In fact, it describes an emergency situation in which a surprise attack may be resisted only 'until the Security Council has taken measures necessary to maintain international peace and security'. In other words, it is not an alternative to Security Council action, merely a preliminary to it. Similarly, the following section of the Charter, Chapter VIII, which deals with 'Regional Arrangements' and which acknowledged the role of local agencies in the maintenance of peace and security, was also only a limited qualification of Security Council control. Article 53 confirmed that the Security Council might utilize regional bodies for enforcement action, but only 'under its authority'. In other words, collective security action might be franchised out, but it could not be undertaken by a competing focus of international authority.

The collective security arrangement of the Charter reflected the concern of its American planners that the history of the League should not be allowed to repeat itself. Urgent decision-making should not be made impossible by unclear and diffuse lines of authority and initiative. The power vested in the permanent members of the Security Council was simply the constitutional embodiment of Roosevelt's idea of a select group of powerful world policemen. It was not an arrangement that was attractive to all of the rank and file membership of the UN, however. At San Francisco some of the more established smaller states opposed this concentration of power, arguing that it was incompatible with the democratic principle of sovereign equality. Australia and New Zealand sought a larger role for the General Assembly in security matters than the Dumbarton Oaks plan had envisaged. A proposal was put by them that the Assembly should approve any enforcement action planned by the Council. But the United States remained adamant that there should be no debilitating seepage of authority. The other permanent members of the Security Council were, of course, happy to agree.

Like the League, the United Nations would be served by a secretariat composed of permanent international civil servants. These would owe their primary loyalty to the organization rather than to their states of origin. At the head of this secretariat, as in the League, there would be a secretary-general. There was, however, a feature of the UN Charter—absent in the League Covenant—that emphasized the UN's determination to make collective security work. The office of secretary-general was to be more than simply an administrative position. The head of the secretariat was to have a personal proactive role in the maintenance of international security. Article 99 of the Charter empowered the secretary-general to 'bring to the attention of the Security Council any matter which in his [sic] opinion may threaten the maintenance of international peace and security'. In 1945, before the international system became polarized by the cold war, this was a significant but not a particularly controversial innovation. One potential conflict in the arrangements for the secretary-general was avoided when the United States backed down from its proposal that he or she should be appointed by the General Assembly. Aware of its vulnerability in a forum in which it would be outnumbered by western states, the Soviet Union objected. It was therefore agreed that the responsibility would lie with the Security Council, whose decisions were, of course, subject to veto.

At San Francisco the discussions about who should be appointed as the first secretary-general of the organization underlined the sensitivity of the post. The United States proposed the Canadian foreign minister, Lester Pearson, who was rejected by the Soviet Union as too 'western'. Moscow's own suggestion, the foreign minister of Yugoslavia, was ruled out by the western powers for being too close to the Soviet camp. Eventually it was agreed that Trygve Lie, the foreign minister of Norway, would be a suitable choice. This selection process was a portent of future difficulties. In 1945 Norway was still regarded as largely neutral between east and west; four years later, however, it was a founding member of the North Atlantic Treaty Organisation (NATO) and Lie's position became much more controversial. As the UN divided between opposing camps in the 1950s and 1960s, the neutrality of the secretary-general would become a major area of dispute, particularly in issues relating to the organization's security and peacekeeping functions, as we will see.

Like its predecessor, the new UN was to have a permanent headquarters. San Francisco was a one-off venue (the founding session of the UN there was held in the Opera House). There was no clear agreement or, for that matter, very strong disagreement among the major powers about where the UN should call home. The old League headquarters, the Palais des Nations in Geneva, was not suitable for a number of reasons. For one thing, Switzerland, as we have seen, had opted not to join the United Nations and it would hardly have been appropriate for a non-member to host the general headquarters. But the Geneva building was also inescapably linked with the perceived failure of the earlier institution, and the UN was determined to present itself as a fundamentally new beginning in international cooperation. In addition to the objections to Geneva in particular, there was a wider resistance to the idea of the UN being based in Europe at all. An American location was widely favoured, and not just by the friends and allies of the United States. Many of the smaller member countries felt it would strike a blow against the Eurocentrism that had characterized international relations for centuries past. And, states of the western hemisphere made up a considerable proportion of the UN's initial membership in the years before European decolonization brought an influx of Afro-Asian members. The matter was settled when the American millionaire philanthropist, John D. Rockefeller, bought and presented to the UN a site on New York's East River.

The general consensus over the location of the headquarters building could not, however, disguise the widening rents in the political fabric of the UN. These would have fundamental implications for its role in international security. By definition collective security requires as its starting point a collective will. If it was just about reasonable in 1945 to suppose that this might persist in the post-war system, events soon suggested that it would not. As global bipolarity deepened in the later 1940s and 1950s, it became clear that the hopeful assumptions of the charter-makers at Dumbarton Oaks, and the later optimism of their political masters, were profoundly misplaced. In fairness it must be acknowledged that in the peculiar circumstances of the time—on the path towards final victory in a war of unprecedented scale and ferocity—the commitment of the allies to continued cooperation in the post-war system was to an extent taken for granted. And, of course, in the previous century and a half, major wars had given rise to workable systems of regulation based on cooperation among the victors. We have already discussed the European concert system that followed the French Revolutionary and Napoleonic Wars in 1815. More recently there had been the experience of the League, which had loomed large in the planning of the UN. In both, the wartime allies had maintained reasonably high levels of post-war cooperation. In 1945 the League's major disability appeared to have been the non-participation of the United States, and this was a problem that would not arise in the new institution.

Moreover, the technological basis of the impending cold war was not at all apparent when the Charter was being drafted. In 1945 few if any had an inkling of the profound political impact nuclear weapons would have on international politics and the extent to which their existence would shape the post-war system. The Charter was signed at San Francisco several months before the first use of atomic bombs on Hiroshima and Nagasaki, and the Dumbarton Oaks meeting had taken place more than a year earlier. There had been an awareness that some level of east–west competition was likely after the war, even as the allies were advancing on Germany in 1944 from their respective points of the compass. The general agreement on the importance of having a veto arrangement in the Security Council was an indication of this. But the notion that this competition could create a situation in which two superpowers with unprecedented destructive capacity would confront each other over virtually every conflict anywhere on the globe would have seemed fantastic.

This, however, was what the future held in store. The result was that the Charter's plans for collective security would in effect be irrelevant before they had ever been properly tested. In an elementally divided system all international conflict would inevitably be seen through different, ideologically constructed prisms by each side. Consensus on the rights and wrongs of any crisis would be impossible to achieve. The identity of the aggressor would depend on the political character of any conflict and the broader loyalties of the antagonists. Although the word 'aggression' is used freely in Chapter VII of the Charter, no definition is offered. In reality, though, even if one had been, it is unlikely that it would have made any significant difference. The political judgements of the big powers would not have been subordinated to legal terminology. In the realm of ideology 'aggression' could never be an objective concept. And, of course, without the capacity to agree on the rights and wrongs of an international conflict, the Charter, however legally comprehensive, was an empty vessel as far as collective security was concerned. The veto became not an obstruction to collective security, as some later suggested, but a means of assuring that even a United Nations without enforcement capacities could at least continue to exist.

COLLECTIVE SECURITY TESTED: THE KOREAN WAR

The only occasion during the cold war that the UN's collective security powers were invoked—and then rhetorically rather than constitutionally—came in 1950 with the crisis over Korea. By this time the shape of the post-1945 international system was already emerging. During the winter of 1947–48 there was a major east–west confrontation over Berlin, which had been divided into different zones of occupation between the allies at the end of the war. Berlin lay within East Germany, which was now effectively a Soviet satellite, and Russia now sought to complete its control by making the western presence in the city unviable. Land access to Berlin from the west was blocked and the western allies responded with a complex and expensive airlift into their zones. The crisis—in which the UN had only a minimal role—eventually subsided, but the battle lines of the cold war had been clearly marked. Elsewhere, in the parts of eastern Europe from which the German occupiers had been expelled by the Red Army, it was becoming clear that the

Soviet presence, asserted through the establishment of local communist regimes, was to be a permanent one.

A parallel situation existed in parts of Asia as well. Korea had been annexed by Japan in 1910 after a troubled history of relations between the two countries stretching far back into history. Although the original act of expansionism little troubled the western powers, during the war against Japan the allies had set the independence of Korea as one of their war aims. However, by the end of the war the situation had become complicated. Like Germany, different halves of Korea had been occupied by the west and the Soviet Union respectively. Moscow had committed forces to the Asian theatre only belatedly in the summer of 1945. This involvement would have been unfeasible while the Red Army was forcing its way westwards towards Germany, but after the Nazi surrender Stalin was able to stake a claim to a place in the Asian settlement by declaring war on an already fatally weakened Japan. At the end of the fighting, therefore, Soviet forces occupied the northern part of the Korean peninsula and American forces the southern part. Korea therefore was divided into two de facto states each ruled by regimes that reflected the ideologies of their occupiers. The delivery of the allies' commitment to creating an independent post-war Korea was not going to be easy in these circumstances.

In the north the Soviets had put in power the local communist leader Kim Il Sung, while in the south the American protégé was Syngman Rhee, who, after elections in 1948, led a pro-western nationalist administration. The new government in the south seemed to see the unification of Korea as best achieved by its absorption of the north. North Korea, for its part, aspired towards the creation of a single communist state as the proper outcome of unification. In both parts of the peninsula local military forces had been built up by the two external patron powers, though Soviet and American troops were withdrawn from Korea in 1948 and 1949 respectively. On the eve of the new decade a fierce war of words developed between two well-armed Koreas confident in their external support, with each insisting on its right to extend its authority over the other.

The overwhelming western majority in the General Assembly meant that the United Nations as an institution favoured the claims of the south and recognized Syngman Rhee's regime as the legitimate representative of 'Korea'. But the Soviet veto in the Security Council prevented the admission of that 'Korea' to the UN. Meanwhile tensions continued to build, and by the beginning of 1950 spasmodic but violent incidents were taking place on the border between north and south. This frontier ran along the 38th parallel of the world map, and this was a geographical term that would become a powerfully evocative political expression in the coming years.

The crisis was considered by the Security Council in unusual circumstances. There was no Soviet delegation present. The USSR was boycotting the Council in 1950 in protest over the continued representation of China at the UN by Chiang Kai-shek's nationalists. The previous year the communists had finally extended their control over all of mainland China and the remnants of the pro-US nationalist regime had escaped to the island of

Formosa (later known as Taiwan). Here, too, the large western majority in the General Assembly guaranteed that membership issues would be resolved in favour of the United States' clients and supporters. Although the nationalists had effective control over only a tiny fragment of China's territory and population, it retained the UN seat. Moreover, as China had been considered to be a great power when the Charter was being drawn up, the small group of nationalists on Formosa also occupied a permanent seat on the Security Council with all the associated powers and privileges. Moscow's then ally Mao Zedong now controlled mainland China and its huge population but was denied any recognition whatsoever by the United Nations. The Soviet Union was understandably angered by a situation that seemed to fully justify its early concern over the imbalance of power between east and west in the UN. This situation over the representation of China at the UN persisted until 1971 when a general accommodation was reached between Washington and Beijing, though in the meantime relations between the USSR and Communist China had broken down catastrophically. In 1950, however, the two communist giants were closely allied against the west. The effect of Soviet action in support of Communist China's claims to UN membership, however, was that the Security Council that discussed the Korean crisis was composed entirely of western or pro-western states. And, of course, its decisions were not subject to Soviet veto.

As a result of this, when forces from the north pushed across the 38th parallel in large numbers on 25 June, the Security Council was able to demand their withdrawal back across the border. This was ignored by North Korea, which, it had become clear, was engaged in a wholesale invasion. Still unconstrained by the Soviet veto, the Security Council now called on UN members to assist South Korea against the northern invasion. Significantly, however, this resolution made no reference to Chapter VII of the Charter and was couched in terms of 'recommendation' rather than 'decision'. Even free of the threat of veto, it seemed, the western powers were cautious about attempting to deploy the full battery of the UN's collective security powers. In parallel, the United States had begun to mobilize on its own behalf, moving naval forces into the waters between mainland China and Korea. American forces also conducted sea- and air-launched attacks against northern military formations. Finally, at the end of June, American ground forces from bases in Japan (where there was still a large occupying army) were deployed in support of the South Korean army. America's allies in the region—Britain (which still had considerable imperial interests in Asia), Australia and New Zealand—announced their intention to intervene as well. Meanwhile Washington justified its action in the terms of the UN Charter, invoking Article 51, which, it will be recalled, acknowledged the right to collective self-defence. The Korean War was now under way and attention became increasingly focused on the response of the United Nations.

This response was to be a resolutely pro-western one. Still with a free hand in the Security Council, the western powers now set about creating a Unified Command among the forces fighting against North Korea. This multinational army would be legitimized by the UN and would fight under the UN flag. The Unified Command was put under the control of the commander of American forces in Asia, the hawkish and politically ambitious General Douglas MacArthur. The Unified Command would 'report' to the Security Council rather than be directed by it. The Security Council was not, of course, in a position to provide this direction. Under the terms of Article 47 of the Charter any Security Council command responsibility would have been assigned to the MSC. This was unthinkable, as the chief of staff of the Red Army would have been a key participant.

The arrangement put in place appeared to provide the western coalition (which would grow to involve seventeen states) with United Nations legitimacy as a collective security force. It would not, however, involve risking the politically fatal consequences of attempting to invoke Chapter VII of the Charter. To conform to the procedure established by the Charter the force would, anyway, have to have been formed in the first place with reference to Article 43, which placed military obligations on all UN members. The reality was that the American-led Unified Command was effectively a military alliance engaged in a war against the forces of an opposing alliance. This was a considerable distance from anything foreseen in Chapter VII. As this Chapter represented the beginning and end of the entire collective security system of the United Nations, the western manoeuvre inadvertently pointed up the indelible flaw at the centre of the UN project. Collective security as envisaged by the authors of the UN's constitution was fundamentally unworkable in a bipolar system.

On the ground the western 'UN' forces (two-thirds of which were American) enjoyed considerable success, at least at the beginning. Although the northern forces exploited the shock of their original invasion to push deep into South Korea, in September 1950 a massive western assault from a beachhead at Inchon near the capital, Seoul, stopped the advance. The invaders were now pushed back towards the 38th parallel. But military success for the United States created a major dilemma for the United Nations. With the northern forces once again confined behind their own border, the objective of the UN action had surely been achieved. From an American strategic perspective, however, there was now an opportunity to defeat North Korea and resolve the Korean problem permanently in the interests of the west. Any remaining credibility in the claim that the action was based on multilateral 'collective security' would now disappear and the character of the war as an old-fashioned struggle for domination would be fully revealed.

By this stage the west's free rein over the Security Council had ended. At the beginning of August 1950, faced with what it saw as a western rampage at the UN, the Soviet Union thought better of its pro-Beijing gesture and returned to the Security Council. It did so, moreover, as president of the Council, a position that had passed to it by rota during the summer. Now, with the Soviet veto poised above the table, it was clear that any attempt by the American-led forces in Korea to press their military and political advantage would not be directly supported by the Security Council. The western powers now explored two complementary ways to retain UN legitimacy. First, earlier Security Council resolutions, passed in the absence of the Soviet Union, could be presented as legitimizing continued military action. Second, the west could attempt to move the issue away from the Security Council altogether. In the more favourable forum of the General Assembly there would be no Soviet veto to obstruct western war aims in Korea. There would, instead, be a huge pro-western majority there. Accordingly, in October 1950, the General Assembly was persuaded to adopt a resolution calling on the UN to take control of security 'throughout Korea'. The legal basis of this resolution was questionable. The General Assembly had the right under Articles 10 and 11 of the Charter to discuss issues of international security. It could then make recommendations to the Security Council. But it certainly had no power to authorize military action. For the United States, however, the General Assembly vote was sufficient to sanction the advance of Unified Command forces north of the 38th parallel.

This precipitated a critical change in the nature of the war. As the North Korean forces were being pushed back towards the border, China quickly discerned the risk of a counter-invasion of the north. It duly pronounced this a threat to its own security. But unimpressed by vague threats from a potential enemy that he judged to be exhausted and ill-equipped after decades of revolution, civil war and foreign occupation, MacArthur pressed ahead. In response, Chinese communist 'volunteers' began to cross into North Korea from the Chinese province of Manchuria. The human waves that they now threw against the western forces that had crossed into North Korea reversed the flow of the war once again. The 'UN' forces were now those forced back across a border they had recently crossed in triumph.

Now on the defensive on the battlefield, the United States worked to shore up its position in the UN. It did so by attempting to bring the General Assembly even further into the security arena. America now sought to shift fundamentally the goalposts through which the legitimization of UN military action had to pass. This involved a fundamental departure from Roosevelt's original vision of a UN in which authority for collective security and enforcement were to be concentrated in the hands of the big policemen of the Security Council. In effect, the Charter was now revised to pass power to the General Assembly in the event of Security Council action being stalled by disagreement. In November 1950, at the behest of the American delegation, the General Assembly passed the so-called 'Uniting for Peace' resolution. This permitted the transfer—in certain circumstances—of discussion and decision-making in matters of international security from the Security Council to the General Assembly. The conditions under which this could happen would arise when:

> the Security Council because of lack of unanimity of the permanent members, fails to exercise its primary responsibility for the maintenance of international peace and security in any case where there appears to be a threat to the peace, breach of the peace or act of aggression. [In these circumstances] the General Assembly [would] consider the matter immediately with a view to making

appropriate recommendations to Members for collective measures, including
… the use of armed force where necessary.

The use in the resolution of the exact language of Chapter VII was not accidental; this was no less than an attempt to move collective security power away from the Security Council. The use of the Uniting for Peace procedure did not, as events developed, prove as fatal to the UN's credibility as it might have done. Over the coming years the composition of the Assembly changed radically. New states, many of them former colonies that did not automatically identify with western interests, changed the political landscape in a way that made the procedure much less attractive to those who had designed it. In November 1950, however, it threatened to subvert the entire purpose of the UN as originally conceived.

On the ground in Korea the war continued, with fighting concentrated around the 38th parallel and without any decisive breakthrough by either side. There was a growing concern among the western allies about the nature of the American command. Specifically, General MacArthur's intentions and their implications for the conduct of the war caused considerable suspicion. Increasingly, his gung-ho approach to the conduct of the war grated with both allies and other American military leaders and politicians. His general demeanour was also uncomfortable to many who had a more sober view of how a 'UN commander' should conduct himself. Western leaders in general were becoming more circumspect about the whole undertaking in Korea as the prospect of a quick and triumphant outcome retreated at the beginning of 1951. Finally, in April 1951 after some intemperate remarks that contradicted official American policy, MacArthur was summarily dismissed by President Truman. This proved to be something of a watershed for the western effort in Korea and, belatedly, for the image of the United Nations as an impartial world body. The reunification of Korea under the control of the South, which had been MacArthur's key war aim, was no longer at the top of the public agenda. As a result the war was no longer quite as damaging as it had been to perceptions of the UN's political identity. Long and mistrustful negotiations led in July 1953 to an armistice between the sides in the war that merely reconfirmed the 38th parallel as a de facto international frontier. This was some way short of a peace agreement, and no long-term settlement was ever agreed. In the face of the immensely complex local circumstances where common ground was virtually impossible to locate, this may not have been surprising. But it nevertheless represented a failure for the peacemaking capacity of the United Nations.

The war achieved nothing for the Korean people, North or South. It was a wholly destructive event, unmitigated by any political progress. How did it leave the United Nations? The UN emerged from Korea with an image in the world that fell far short of the hopes of its founders. It had come to look dangerously like a mere western alliance. It may have appeared to its more internationalist-minded supporters that the price of American involvement—supposedly the crucial advance on the League of Nations—had come at a self-defeating price. Not only, it seemed, was the dream of a functional collective security system unrealizable, but the mechanisms that were supposed to realize it were dangerously vulnerable to political exploitation. This was not, it must be said, a widely held perception in western public opinion. The early 1950s was not a notably liberal era. Assumptions about Korea were shaped by the pervasive anti-communism of the time and a considerable degree of racial and cultural prejudice. This meant that western—that is 'UN'—efforts in Korea were not subject to the same critical scrutiny they would be in later conflicts, most obviously that in Vietnam. But beyond the west, among those open to communist propaganda and those nationalists in the European empires who were poised to take control of their new states as decolonization approached, the image of the UN had been badly damaged. Would the United Nations now follow the League into irrelevance and worse, or would it merely formalize itself into the western alliance that many now assumed it to be? Or was there a way forward, an adjustment of role and identity that could give the United Nations a new, genuinely multilateralist role even amid the bipolarity of the cold war? Could the organization find a military purpose that would enable it to lessen cold war conflict rather than contribute to it as had happened in Korea?

The United Nations System

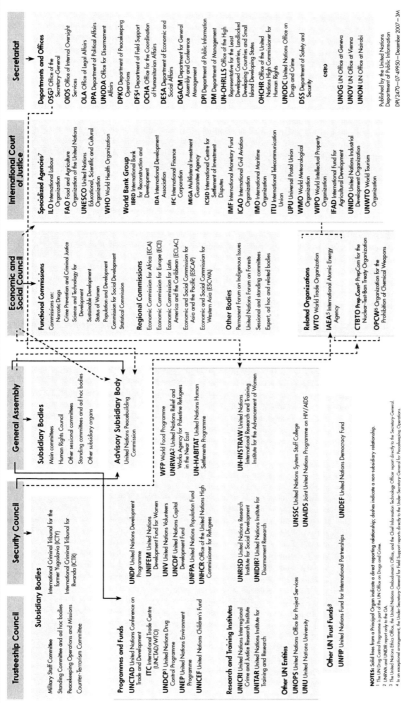

The Multinational Corporations
Ruling the Globe?

The Cold War is a segment of recent history, usually treated in traditional fashion by historians as an episode in international relations; I have suggested that the Cold War also deserves treatment as a context for the rise of globalization. The appearance in the course of present-day globalization of two major new actors, the multinational corporations (MNCs) and the non-governmental organizations (NGOs), requires a somewhat different treatment. They are actors in the process of globalization, rather more than, as with the Cold War, the complex context in which globalization made its appearance. Needless to say, they did not emerge full-blown from Clio's forehead in the post-WW II period. Both had an existence before present-day globalization in various shapes and forms. Only after 1945, however, do they become preeminent players on the global scale.

As such, they share the stage with nation-states, which continue to be the central actors even in the global epoch. Some commentators see the MNCs as displacing the state in importance. I think it more useful to look at the evolving relationship between the two, and to study the MNCs in their own right (reserving the study of the NGOs for the next chapter). There is, of course, an enormous literature on them, starting with the definitional problem—what is an MNC?—and advancing to the questions of their change over time, their shift in terms of geographical place, their transformation during the process of globalization, and so forth. For example, there seems to be a general shift from trading companies to resource extraction, then to manufacturing, and then to service and financial service companies as the dominating types of MNCs, a shift which is gradual and in which the earlier forms do not disappear but persist as part of a larger whole.

My aim is not to tackle the MNCs per se, but to bring to bear on them the perspective of New Global History. And even here only in terms of a limited optic, more to show how the perspective works than to give a total picture. Specifically, I will treat the MNCs as much more than mere economic actors; their actions have profound impacts on and implications for the rest of society. Even here, however, I will not focus on MNCs in their entirety, which could range from the environment to consumerism and all points in between, but rather on the MNCs in regard to the problem of governance. For they are the new Leviathans of our time, and consequently have great political as well as economic power; indeed, in the eyes of some, as noted, they can claim to rule the world.

I will seek entrance to the realm of MNCs, therefore, by first asking the question: who rules the globe? A simple and clear answer exists to this rather simple-minded question: no one state, party, person (although for the religious minded the answer might be God). This conclusion is especially true in what we are labeling a global epoch or an Age of Globalization. Here we are confronted increasingly with flows and processes, difficult to control or even to understand. These amorphous entities seem to escape the power and authority of existing institutions, and to transcend their restraining boundaries. (Indeed, we can perceive that these amorphous flows and processes pose challenges to the national state as well as to the international system.)

In the fictional universe of the sci-fi writer Isaac Asimov, for example, in his book *I Robot*, a couple of corporations do, in fact, take on the role of ruling the globe. For our part, we need not go to that extreme, but simply examine the actual way in which MNCs have increasingly come to dominate our societies. They are clearly one of the ruling forces in our world, challenging, supplanting, or collaborating with more established institutions, such as the nation-state. As the name multinational suggests, they are still connected to nations, though the nature of the connection has been rapidly changing. In this setting, we need to recognize the MNCs, as suggested earlier, as Leviathans—using the term in imitation of the sovereign state treated by Hobbes in an earlier time—now taking on, potentially or in practice, the power and authority of more traditional structures.

(1)

The importance of MNCs was made dramatically evident in the UN statement, noted above in Chapter 2, that of the 100 largest possessors of GDP over 50 were corporations. In this view, these MNCs are wealthier and thus potentially more powerful than 120 to 130 of the nation-states. Though this measure is, in fact, as previously noted, misleading—the figures given in regard to the MNCs are based on revenue rather than value added, i.e., the way in which GNP is measured—it symbolizes an important truth: when the corporate revenues of a company such as Exxon-Mobil or Wal-Mart are greater than the GDP of a country such as Austria, for example, our traditional conceptions of who rules the world must be closely reexamined.

The simplest definition of an MNC, sometimes also called a transnational enterprise, is a firm that controls income-generating assets in more than one country at a time. A more complicated and meaningful definition would add that an MNC has productive facilities in several countries on at least two continents with employees stationed worldwide and financial investments scattered across the globe.

Taking 1600 as our starting point, we found the English East India Company and its Dutch counterpart, plus a small number of others, as our early examples. Plotting a curve, we see very slow, almost flat, growth through the decades until 1914, when we can number about 3,000. Growth subsequently occurs very gradually until in 1969 we can count 7,258, and then there is an explosion with the curve rising to 18,500 in 1988, 30,400 in 1992, 53,100 in 1987, 59,902 in 1999, and 63,000 at the turn of the century!

Aided by technology—improved communication via satellites and other devices, faster transportation, and so forth—the MNCs have grown by leaps and bounds in the process we call globalization. Large and small, coming into and going out of existence with some rapidity, these business enterprises have rushed past national boundaries and transcended existing power relations. While they vary in type—some are state related, for example—most are on the model of the American private corporation. This certainly is so on principle; in fact, of course, there are all kinds of mixed modes. Still, overwhelmingly, they are not public entities, though grounded in public and national law. As many of their CEOs have declared, the primary loyalties are to globalized companies rather than to the countries in which they are headquartered.

The phenomenal growth of the MNCs is marked by increasing concentration at the top, characterized by mergers and acquisitions resulting in huge corporations. We seem to be in a sort of post-Westphalian stage: in the seventeenth and eighteenth centuries this stage was marked by the absorption and disappearance of various political state bodies, i.e., principalities, provinces, and so forth; today a similar process is taking place only now in regard to our new economic Leviathans. Thus, of the Fortune 500 list of a few decades ago, 33 percent no longer existed in their own right ten years later. Fifteen years later, in 1995, another 40 percent were gone. What stands out, however, is the steady persistence of the growth in MNCs and their power.

At this point, we have a relatively nuanced and calculable picture of MNCs and their historical development. Although still sketchy, this picture allows us to return better informed to the question of whether and in what ways the MNCs, with their werewolf appetite for expansion, to use Marx's phrase, are able to translate their economic power into other forms—cultural, political, social—as well. It is to this question that we now turn directly.

(2)

In the broadest sense, the MNCs have an impact on almost every sphere of modern life, ranging from issues of personal identity to issues of community, from policymaking on the environment to international security, and from the future of work to the future of the nation-state, and beyond the state to regional and international bodies and alliances. Impact, however, is not the same thing as controlling power.

The first thing to be said is that MNCs are corporations, that is, legal entities created by the state. In theory at least, the state controls the corporations, can subject them to taxes, and can entangle them in regulations and restrictions. In practice, however, as a result of globalization and its market arrangements, the MNC can often escape these bonds by "rigging" the state, that is, using the corporations' financial strength to "buy" the government apparatus through corruption and campaign contributions. More fundamentally, in its search for low labor costs and favorable tax codes, the global corporation can move its operations in order to escape onerous state controls. In this sense, it is rootless and so amorphous that it cannot be captured by national state institutions. In turn, its currency and market manipulations fall into a vacuum, where no international body has authority. In a word, the MNCs are masterless.

Now it should be clear that this last statement is somewhat hyperbolic; yet it points in the right direction. With this said, however, masterless does not equate with masterful. Indeed, the case can be made that the MNCs are the beneficiaries of a system of institutions such as the IMF and the World Bank that has been set up by states, and specifically the United States. The international financial regime encapsulated in the terms of the Bretton Woods system is, in this view, a prerequisite for the economic and political power exercised by the MNCs as, under the regime's umbrella, they shape the process of globalization. On such a reading, the state and MNCs reign together.

MNCs can influence the state in particular instances, for example, affecting and perhaps determining government policy in regard to nationalistic takeovers, such as Venezuela. Influence is obviously exercised when CEOs shuttle in and out of governments, most egregiously in the USA in terms of the military/industrial complex. Again, however, we must emphasize how general and difficult to grasp firmly such versions of "rule" necessarily are. By themselves, MNCs "rule" only in the most shadowy of fashions. It is as part of a system that they exercise what powers they have. And that system is both a national one and a global one. It is especially, I would argue, in the latter realm that our new Leviathans are most powerful.

Opposition to them also often takes a global form. Worldwide protests and anti-globalization movements are the counterweights to the powers of the MNCs. After all, MNCs sometimes undermine national government efforts to control their own economies, may use foreign investments to dictate dependent governments' actions, can promote consumerism in ways deleterious to the health and welfare of the client nation, and so forth. MNCs can also be accused of tilting the North/South scales further in favor of the former. Operating on a global scale, MNCs are opposed by global anti-globalists, often with the aid of various international non-governmental organizations (INGOs) and NGOs.

Such opposition is made stronger by the very nature of the MNCs. They are non-representative and non-accountable, or, if they are, only so to their shareholders. As participants in ruling the globe they are not seen as legitimate in part for the reason just given. While themselves sovereign, in the sense of being relatively free from external control, they are hardly transparent as governments are supposed to be. Questions of democratic governance abound. If, in fact, MNCs exercise partial rule in our global society, must they be held to account for their policies and actions, and these be made known to world opinion?

In the strange ways of history, the MNCs have been heavily invested in creating the NGOs, and beyond them the global civil society of which they are a part, and which together hold the MNCs accountable and call their legitimacy into question. In the eighteenth century, economics and trade were seen as constituent parts of civil society. Now, in the view of most theorists, they stand outside that circle. In fact, however, it is the MNCs that have provided the satellites that permit and foster global communication and the computer websites that facilitate the spread of the NGOs and their messages. The devil, as it is seen by many people, must be given its dues, and recognized as providing the antidote, at least potentially, to its possible poisonous effects.

Among these poisonous effects are the polluting of the atmosphere by unregulated MNCs. Here again, however, the negative must be placed against the positive encouragement of global environmental groups that result from the MNCs' fostering of the communication revolution. As yet, the negative effects of the Bhopals and Exxon Valdeses badly outweigh the positive, but it can be argued that the global world which the MNCs are helping to construct, even if in unintended fashion, carries the seeds of better things to come.

Whatever power MNCs exercise, they cannot command armies (except, perhaps, in the shape of private security forces), they cannot levy taxes on a population, and they are unable to pass laws in a legislative body, as the state is able to do. Thus it is difficult to measure the MNCs power in the usual terms. To borrow a phrase from Joseph Nye, who speaks of the "soft power" of the USA, i.e., its spread of its culture and authority, which permeates society, perhaps we can speak of MNCs as exercising their rule through soft power.

Whatever effective dominion is exerted by MNCs is largely tied to their role in the process of globalization. The latter's persistence is itself tenuous, in the sense that a nuclear explosion by a terrorist organization (for example, acquiring the weapon on the black market and transporting it in the hold of a container ship) or a breakdown of the worldwide computer system engineered by hackers or hostile powers could cause much of globalization to come to a sudden stop. Thus, the rule of MNCs, such as it is, requires the failure of such efforts, as well as of anti-globalization sentiment, to derail the globalization effort that undergirds the corporate regime.

(3)

Putting aside doomsday scenarios (and excluding anti-globalization from this category), we must take the world as it is and return to the question: who currently rules that world? Let us approach this question now with MNCs in mind by taking a slightly different tack. I want to ask: is there a global elite in which the corporations are a/the core element? While there may not be a ruling class, as Marx and others had it, there can be little doubt that traditional economic and political elites have existed in the past, as depicted by various studies. In general, these elites have taken the form of national elites. With globalization transcending national sovereignty in many ways, is the emergence of a global elite a new addition?

On the assumption that such an elite is coming into existence, we need to ask who comprises it, and how they exercise their power and for what purposes. Is such an elite homogeneous, though we know it to be made up of different segments—such as business, media, military—and how do these segments relate to one another? Do the MNCs and their executives play a dominant role? In attempting to answer these questions, we must remember that, needless to say, the nation-state has not been disappearing, or even withering away, and we need to inquire into the ways national and then regional elites form part of a global elite.

A few comments can be hazarded. The first is that the existence of English as the new *lingua franca* enables members of the global elite to communicate with one another easily. Thus they inhabit roughly the same linguistic world. Next, and without question, this elite is overwhelmingly male. Females do exist in the global elite, but they do not play a major role, and certainly do not lead. Gradual change may be ahead, but even that is problematic.

One reason why change is possible, however, is that members of the global elite go to more or less the same schools. And today's business and legal schools are increasingly "manned" by women students. This potential, however, generally runs up against what is called the glass ceiling. Another choke point is in the meeting places of the elites, such as golf clubs and other supposedly recreational settings. The exclusion of women is not just a matter of rights but of power. A glance at the attendees of other venues of power, such as the Trilateral Commission or Davos, shows the same preponderance of men.

An Asian counterpart of Davos is BOAO Forum for Asia CEO Summit, whose meeting in 2005 was held in Hainan, PR China. Here, too, the attendees were almost all men. What is of further interest is how little overlap between the members of Davos and of BOAO there seemed to be. A conscious effort was certainly made to keep the meeting Asian in focus, with the USA, for example, excluded. A quick glance at the invitees, however, suggests that the same sort of interests are represented at the Hainan meeting as at Davos, with equally impressive backgrounds in the corporate world. In both settings, the business and governmental world meet and exchange views as to how national and global policies are to be formulated and to go forward, both in their regional domains and more globally.

Whichever part of the world they live in, members of the global elite have similar lifestyles. There are even periodicals that tell them where to stay, what clothes to wear, what restaurants to patronize, and whom to know. Though as yet there is no manual of the CEO à la the manuals of the courtier of an earlier age, the equivalent is available. The result is a cosmopolitan leadership, easily recognizing one another in the corridors of power. Businessmen, lawyers, accountants, management consultants all speak the same language and wear the same suits.

To make the global elite more concrete, a colleague, Elliott Morss, advanced the hypothesis that there is not one but four global elites. He argued that the first derives its status from social and family backgrounds; the second from its power to develop and implement profit-making ideas, e.g., Microsoft; the third from a top position in a state, e.g., president of France, or a global organization, such as the World Bank; and the fourth from its role as managers of global organizations.

Yet there is no conspiracy among these members of the global elite to rule the world. The result, however, when we add in military leaders, is in fact a hand covered in velvet influencing and guiding our global society. It is not particularly a visible hand. This fact accords with the nature of globalization as a matter of flows and processes, where power is not located in fixed institutions, other than as they foster globalization itself. It is instead a kind of "virtual" power, growing naturally out of the information revolution of our time. Here, it would seem, we finally have an answer to our question of who rules the world.

(4)

I want to conclude by reiterating my argument that MNCs do not rule the world as such, or at least not by themselves. While they make up a large part of the global elite, they are not alone in its composition. Instead, MNCs are in a ceaseless though not inevitable competition and cooperation with other factors, creating the globalization that sets the conditions of rule. If I am right about our present-day version of the invisible hand, the problems of our time may not be so much located in the rulers of our world but in the fact that there is no "ruler" as such.

Even when MNC leaders are linked to military leaders—the famous military-industrial complex that President Eisenhower warned against—as well as the other sets of leaders mentioned, the result is not a world simply driven by them and the institutions they head. In an Age of Globalization it appears that a headless rider is in the saddle, with great power but little control. It is a scary thought, but one in accord with many of the facts to be found in the course of other work in New Global History.

The NGOs Movement

Nation-states, national forces, and, as we have seen in the previous chapter, MNCs are all leading actors on the international and global stage. Another increasingly important actor is the non-governmental organization (NGO) (under whose heading is also included international non-governmental organizations), an entity which is best treated as being part of a gathering social movement. Thus, one observer declares that: "The role of NGOs in the twenty-first century will be as significant as the role of the nation state in the twentieth." Another speaks of a "global associational revolution," and refers to NGOs as a "fifth estate." However hyperbolic such statements may be, there is little doubt that they point in a significant direction.

In Chapter 2 I gave NGOs a preliminary glance. Now I wish to put a spotlight on them at center stage. In doing so, I want to emphasize that we need to look upon them as both cause and effect of globalization. In their multitudinous forms, NGOs spread especially the juridical and cultural messages of the global perspective. Of equal importance, they step into the breach unoccupied by the nation-state and the MNCs in regard to governance structures. In taking on these tasks, the NGOs form what we can regard as a profound social movement. On the other side of the causal equation, NGOs have been arising like the proverbial mushrooms in the rain as a result of the actions, or inactions, of other actors in the globalization process; as I shall argue, they act frequently as the counterpart of the MNCs, as the handmaidens of ill-equipped nation-states, and as the carriers of racial, ethnic and economic minority hopes, not to mention the hopes of the whole of humanity.

Bruce Mazlish, "The NGOs Movement," from *The New Global History*, pp. 42–52. Copyright ©
2006 by Taylor & Francis Group. Permission to reprint granted by the publisher.

The NGOs Movement | 71

Given their importance, potential and present, it is extraordinary how difficult it is to get a firm grip on NGOs, in terms of definition, numbers, range, type, etc. In the chapter on MNCs I mentioned the project that mapped them. That project was unusually successful in its immediate aims. As noted, both an historical atlas and a volume of essays resulted as planned. In producing them, an acceptable definition of what is meant by an MNC was easily arrived at, and, with much effort, the empirical data concerning the origin, spread, power, etc. of these new Leviathans were accumulated and visually represented. It is not clear as yet, however, to what extent the long-range aim, to change the way in which large numbers of people see the globalizing world, has been realized. That realization will depend on the spread of the idea.

A similar project, to map the NGOs, is encountering much greater initial difficulty. The definitional problem is horrendous, the data collection mind-boggling, the relation of NGOs to civil society daunting. All this in spite of an enormous collection of first-rate literature on the subject(s). The challenge is matched only by the need to meet it, for it is imperative today to see the globe, as with the MNC, in its true globalizing colors. In one sense, the present chapter might serve as a prolegomena to a possible mapping project, an example of how empirical research might be combined with theoretical speculations.

(1)

As with all other aspects of NGOs, their definition is much contested. Most observers would agree that they are not set up or run by states or governments, but arise as voluntary and not-for-profit organizations, hence NGOs. At this point, contention arises over which organizations are to be included. Should those that promote commerce or are business oriented be put in this category? (My tendency is to do so.) Should churches and church-related institutions fit in? Ought we to distinguish, say, between the Catholic Church and Catholic Relief or Catholics for Free Choice (my own view is that the first does not belong among NGOs, and the latter two do). Simply to mention these few examples is to demonstrate the different opinions on the subject that can readily be found.

What further complicates the matter is that many of our potential cases are ambiguous. As George Thomas points out, many NGOs receive money from governments, and often administer substantial percentages of state aid monies. Lines are not firmly drawn between governments and NGOs; yet to exclude some of the latter on the grounds that they are therefore not really non-governmental is to miss seeing that states are "outsourcing" some of their work to these new organizations. So, too, it would mean ignoring the fact that the image of NGOs as pure, clean activist groups is just that, an image, and the reality is a messy one in which they become implicated with other actors in other sectors, and have mixed intentions and results.

Even the question of what we are talking about is not simple. There is a spectrum of sorts running from IGOs (international governmental organizations), to INGOs, to

NGOs, again with many crossovers. Terminology can vary: QUANGOs, or quasi non-governmental organizations, is a preferred non-American term for NGOs, thereby reflecting the ambiguities referred to above (see the *OED*, 1997 Additions). The question of tax status can be another crude measure. For example, in the USA one could assert that an NGO is an organization that has 501 C status. For purposes such as ours, however, of seeking to understand NGOs in terms of a global perspective, this last definition appears to limit the inquiry rather than to further it. Again, I prefer a more inclusive definition.

As it happens, the first usage in English of the phrase NGO, according to the *OED*, is in 1946. As we know, of course, what have come to be called NGOs existed before the word. Again we face the Molière problem, as when the French playwright has his bourgeois character, enlightened by a tutor as to the difference between poetry and prose, declare in astonishment, "Oh, so I have been speaking prose all my life!" The lesson we bring from the play is that behavior may exist long before consciousness of that behavior. That consciousness, then, becomes as much a fact about NGOs as their first entrance on the stage of history.

Thus, though it is both important and essential to go back to earlier forms of NGOs—perhaps Islamic charities, anti-slavery movements, women suffragettes, and so forth—we must maintain the awareness that something different entered the post-WW II world. Extent, intensity, level of penetration of society, and consciousness of the development, these are all constituent of the NGO as a profound cause and consequence of globalization as it is presently developing. Most importantly, the NGO takes on new attributes, especially as it exists in a context of globalization (which itself is being newly understood).

To push this thought a bit further, an example emphasizing the word "organization" might help. Thus, nineteenth-century anti-slavery societies were organized in a manner very different from the way they would be today. Though slavery was seen as an international problem, pressure was largely brought upon legislators in a mainly (but not exclusively) national context. Literary texts were a prime means, the printing press a prime weapon. The anti-slavery movement (and one notes the word) was primarily a matter of elite opinion, influenced by a loose set of organizations. Contrast this with such a society today. It would be global in its reach, recruiting members and organizing them into a computer network. It would undoubtedly seek to work in conjunction with the UN. Its ability to bring the matter before a global audience would be great. In short, it would be a global organization. And in this way it would be part of an overall NGO movement.

With all this said, we must also realize that the global NGO social movement has tended to be Western in its origins and to have a Western definition. In the eyes of many it certainly pushes Western values and is probably a part of imperialism, overt or covert. Blatant in the nineteenth century in the case of the Salvation Army, it may take more subtle form in numerous twentieth-century NGOs, especially of the INGO variety. So, too, many non-Westerners object to the individualistic assumptions of so many NGOs in contrast to their own societies' emphasis on communitarian impulses. In the eyes of some,

Western and non-Western, NGOs are simply an expression of a bourgeois society and its values (we will see the same problem arise with the concept of civil society).

(2)

In mapping the MNCs, reported on in the previous chapter, the growth in their numbers from their beginnings in the 1600s, as expressed visually, took on the appearance of a J-shaped curve. These numbers were relatively easy to establish. The task is much more demanding in regard to NGOs. Hard numbers are incredibly difficult to come by. The compilation of the list of NGOs at particular points of time and in particular locales is a work in progress. Fortunately, for our purposes here, pending the further work of the mapping project, we need only recognize the general direction in the growth of NGOs.

If we restrict ourselves to INGOs, much easier to identify and count, we can see how they have proliferated. As John Boli and George Thomas, for example, tell us, "they have done so spectacularly, from about 200 active organizations in 1900 to about 800 in 1930, to over 2,000 in 1960, and nearly 4,000 in 1980." The two authors reported this development in 1999, and clearly more data have accumulated since then. Operating, however, with the data available up to 1980, we can see that if we were to map them as we did earlier with the MNCs, a similar J-shaped curve would emerge. This should not surprise us, for, as we suggested earlier, the rise of NGOs and MNCs appears to be correlated, with the former being called forth by some of the actions of the latter. Needless to say, the INGO curve starts later in time, and has fewer entries up to now than the MNCs.

INGOs are of many types: scientific, technical, professional, medical, and business-related ones account for the greatest number. They generally tend to operate below the radar of public notice except in special moments, and it is INGOs such as Amnesty International or Doctors without Borders that attract our attention. Yet globalization is fostered as much by the setting of technical standards and the establishing of communications infrastructure as by the moral/political activities of the better known INGOs. There is no need to derogate one at the expense of the other. They are engaged in the same social movement, along with the sports organizations that sprang up in pre-1991 Eastern Europe, all operating outside the formal state apparatuses and regimes.

Unfortunately, the figures I have been offering are Western in orientation. The Japan NGO Center for International Cooperation (JANIC), itself a non-profit networking NGO founded in 1987, offers a list of 116 Japanese NGOs whose activities are directed to overseas good causes. Here, too, we see how the conversation is bedeviled by the confused language of INGOs and NGOs. Comparable figures are needed from other areas of the globe, such as Latin America, the Middle East, and the whole of Asia. The Caucasus has its own NGOs with overlaps to INGOs, as does Africa. In short, a comprehensive effort to map the number of NGOs, their growth curves (or declines if this were in fact the case), their range, their membership, etc. is vital if we are to look toward a fuller understanding of globalization in this sector.

(3)

Of all the INGOs, those devoted to human rights are central. As INGOs, of course, organizations such as Amnesty International and Human Rights Watch escape the tight hand of the state; being devoted to human rights, they also transcend the boundaries of tribal, ethnic, religious, and national affiliations. Thus, they epitomize the globalizing tendencies of our present world.

Human rights is an historical construction, both as idea and partial reality. As idea, it is espoused by philosophers such as Immanuel Kant, and attached by affinity to the additional idea of cosmopolitanism. Paul Gordon Lauren prefers to treat the idea as a series of visions, whose inspiration and emerging reality he treats in his excellent book *The Evolution of International Human Rights*, showing how human rights were conceived and then achieved parturition in various parts of the world but particularly in the Western societies of the eighteenth century and thenceforward. Coming to the end of his story, he offers a quote to the effect that "human rights became 'the single most magnetic political idea of the contemporary time'."

This is certainly a striking claim. In more mundane terms we may see that, as another author puts it, "After World War I, concern focused on guaranteeing rights by treaty for certain racial, religious and linguistic minorities in the defeated states. … World War II finally convinced states that human rights is a global issue." Thus, we are confronted with the same sort of "history" that I sought to sketch earlier: one effort to expand rights, e.g., to slaves, leads to others of various kinds, until with the war of 1939–45 we find the effort extended to all humanity.

The midwife in this case is the UN and the NGOs attached to it. The story of the UN Declarations has already been touched on in Chapter 3. Here we need to remind ourselves that the UN may be thought of as a birth of Siamese twins, where one is attached to the fervent belief in national sovereignty and the other to a different "sovereign," peoples and their rights, not states. At the very beginning, in this context, to change metaphors, NGOs were a general force operating in society, spreading the notion of human rights, existing in the air so to speak. Very quickly, however, they were accorded formal consultative status. As William Korey informs us in one of the earliest and best accounts of the development, "A recent study offers the following data: only 41 NGOs held consultative status with the UN Economic and Social Council in 1948; 20 years later, in 1968, the total reached nearly 500; 25 years later, by 1992, the figure surpassed 1,000."

Neither NGOs nor human rights had it all their own way. Quite the opposite. Fervid opposition was offered in the UN by countries afraid that the various Declarations and the attempts to carry them out would expose their own potential violations. Often willing to approve in principle, numerous states were quick to make sure that principle did not become practice, vitiating any attempts to set up effective enforcement mechanisms. Then at the UN's beginning and now, repressive states keenly recognized the UN/NGO connection and blocked or shut down the work of the latter in their home countries. Two of the most recent repressions and curtailments have occurred in Vladimir Putin's Russia and in monarchist Nepal.

Nevertheless, human rights and their practice were placed front and center on the global agenda. That agenda, however, is open to vigorous argument. The idea itself is attacked, in the name of local rights and traditions, say, by China or various Islamic countries. It is challenged as emphasizing individual over community rights, political above economic and social rights. Its universalistic premise is sharply questioned, and proponents of Asian values, in an inversion of the charge of Orientalism, appear to press for a part of the world to be seen as "inhuman." (Of course, the retort is to claim that humanity is not all alike, but that this hardly adds up to inhumanity.)

Human rights, and the NGOs and other forces that fight for them, make many people anxious and defensive. In the French Revolution, rights were opposed to privileges. The same is true today. Different privileges—power, gender, and property, for example—come readily to mind, and few people like to give up privilege of any sort. An even more fundamental challenge embedded in human rights is its privileging of "humanity" as the constituency to be borne in mind when debating about such matters as climate control, nuclear regulations, the arms trade, and a host of other surging global problems. Such a constituency displaces the state, or religion or ethnicity, etc. as the reference for legislative and executive action. No wonder its adherents hail human rights in semi-religious terms and its opponents see in it the hand of the devil. In all of these fights, NGOs are at the forefront. They claim to be the self-appointed conscience of humanity.

(4)

It will not have escaped the reader that NGOs are involved in many fights on many fronts. Of primary significance is their role in regard to governance. Governance is not government—NGOs, after all, are non-governmental. Rather, as P.J. Simmons and Chantal de Jonge Oudratt remind us, the term governance "signifies a diverse range of cooperative problem-solving arrangements, state and nonstate, to manage collective affairs." A vacuum, or no man's land, is created by the flows and processes of globalization, and into this space step NGOs when governments falter. For problems that transcend the usual geographical and institutional boundaries, new means of, so to speak, going with the flow have had to be devised.

Let me give one example, showing how state governments, the UN, and NGOs conspired to produce a judicial body, an international criminal court, in order to handle on a permanent basis crimes against humanity. Its origins, of course, lie in earlier attempts to handle charges of genocide: the failed Constantinople trials circa 1919 to deal with the murder of over one million Armenians by the Ottoman Turks in 1915 (a raging battle has reawakened over whether this is to be called genocide or a massacre); the more successful Nuremberg trials of WW II (not to mention the often overlooked trials of a similar nature for the Far East, to deal with Japan), where the term genocide was introduced along with the more general concept of crimes against humanity; and the subsequent international courts called into being to deal with the Yugoslav and Rwandan mass killings. At the end of this line is a permanent International Criminal Court (ICC), hardly a completely new idea, but marking a quantum jump of an "old" idea.

What is new is that it is a permanent international tribunal with global jurisdiction. Thus it forms part of an emerging global governance structure. The ICC took shape in a conference convened in Rome in 1998. Here 160 states, seventeen inter-governmental organizations, fourteen specialized agencies of the UN, and representatives of 250 accredited NGOs took part in the final drafting of the statute. The Rome meeting did not come out of nowhere. In 1994, for example, more than 800 NGOs formed a coalition for an ICC. Other NGOs advocated the new court in other venues. As one legal scholar sums it up, "The non-governmental groups mobilized political support and worked to advance the principles of accountability and redress for victims," victims who otherwise had no one to speak for them.

The ICC was set up in the face of strong opposition from a number of countries. China, Russia, and the USA all viewed it as an infringement of their national sovereignty, and ultimately refused to sign the agreement, which nevertheless went into effect without them. Here, I believe, we have a crucial test of the two parts of the UN—the one pointing in the direction of national sovereignty and the other to peoples' rights—and their ability to work together on a global scale. Adherence to the ICC serves as a kind of litmus test of intentions. Yet even without intention one can see a movement over more than half a century toward a global governance structure to deal with problems that can no longer be handled capably and alone on a local, i.e., national, level. It is hardly to be wondered at that those whose privileges are threatened by this drift of affairs are strongly opposed to what is happening—and to the NGOs that are playing so large a role in this development.

Opposition to NGOs can take place on other, more substantial grounds. In speaking of NGOs and governance we must not only take account of their effect externally, but also turn the question back on the NGOs. They claim to speak for those who have no other voice. But who has authorized them to do so? Nobody has elected them. What is the nature of governance within their own ranks? The issues of accountability and transparency arise as much with NGOs as with the MNCs. If NGOs are to participate in governing the world, on what basis can they claim to do so?

These are hardly unexamined issues. For example, a Global Accountability Project offers a guide to raising and dealing with such questions (see http://www.oneworldtrust. org). Periodicals such as the *Economist* periodically report on how, for example, NGOs that lobby an organization, such as the EU, use the very same money granted to them to lobby for further funds. Frequently NGOs engaged in the same effort fight one another as much as their presumed targets, and so forth. In short, the reality of NGOs and their activities is often far removed from their shining ideals. For these carriers of governance, then, *Realpolitik* all too frequently trumps their vaunted moral purity. In this, they are all too like the states whose efforts they seek to supplement.

More intellectual challenges to the governance claims of NGOs come from other quarters. One scholar, for example, analyzes them in the same marketing terms as those used in the case of MNCs. His intent is to show that the "brand name" NGOs, such as Amnesty International, pick and choose the local NGOs they will support with a close eye on how it will play on the international stage. Will it increase their own visibility, their own ability to raise funds? Just as INGOs clamor for support from the UN and other agencies (including the public), so lesser NGOs clamor for support from the INGOs which alone can give them the visibility they so desperately need. Only if the given NGO can "market" itself in a way to make it stand out from all the other worthy NGOs does it have a real chance to succeed. In short, both INGOs and NGOs have what may be seen as a seedier side to their noble claims to be the conscience of humankind.

In a more philosophical vein are attempts to examine the fundamental underpinnings of NGOs and what they stand for. I shall offer two instances to stand for many. One calls into question the belief that increased inter-dependence, along with a conviction about increased dialogue, will lead to more equity. The first author argues, instead, that asymmetry characterizes the dialogue, fostered and masked by the rhetoric of interdependence, as if all voices were equal, and thus does not lead to more justice. Another argues that a speed-up of society—or what we might call increased time/space compression—at first enabled and supported democratization, but past a certain point a reverse effect occurs. This second author does not make the application to NGOs, but we can certainly do so.

Seen from these lights, our "associational revolution," as embodied in NGOs, is a very complicated and debatable matter. They can be seen to be as much a problem in global governance as a solution. Even beyond, in regard to all the other functions they seek to perform, the same judgment might be made. This is not my view. Stumbling, fumbling, fudging, and nudging, NGOs as a social movement are a major, almost dominant factor in present-day globalization. As someone said of religion, if it didn't exist, we might have to invent it. NGOs in their expanded nature are as much an "invention" of the global epoch as the satellites and computer networks that make much of their work possible. That NGOs trail clouds of dark "glory" cannot obscure their contributions to our globalizing world. Only perfectionists would demand the unblemished ideal.

(5)

I do not wish to leave the topic of NGOs without placing them, finally, in the context in which they belong: civil society. NGOs are not the same as civil society, but they are a part of it, and we need at least to glimpse that whole. In antiquity, the idea of civil society was equivalent to the state or political society. This equation was broken in the seventeenth to eighteenth centuries in Western Europe, when civil society arose in opposition to the absolutist state. We must pause and note that the development of the nation-state turns out to have been requisite for the emergence of the modern civil society. At this time civil society at first meant the realm of economics, whose "free" markets stood separate from though protected by the state. Toward the end of the century of Enlightenment, it came to mean public opinion, a counter-weight to the secrets of raison d'état. In this realm, marked institutionally by the salons, the cafes, the Masonic lodges, and the academies of the time, the critical, rational spirit was presumed free to roam without restrictions other than civility.

Briefly, then, this is the heritage of civil society. As a concern it seems to have faded in the second half of the nineteenth century. It takes on new life in the second half of the next century. Then the context was not the absolutist state but totalitarianism, specifically that of the Soviet Union. Thus in Eastern Europe the only form in which opposition could effectively take shape was in terms of voluntary associations (many of them sporting ones). Solidarity in Poland, or Vaclav Havel's dissident group Charter 77, are more impressive examples. Their success made civil society a hot subject, linked closely to the likelihood of liberal democracy.

Before going further, a few attempts at abstract rather than historical definition. It is useful to follow up on the historical origins of the concept, noting that civil society is "a political space, or arena, where voluntary associations seek to shape the rules that govern one or the other aspect of social life." Another try, somewhat more abstract, informs us that it "is the sum of institutions, organizations and individuals located between the family, the state and the market in which people associate voluntarily to advance common interests." An even more philosophical approach, taken by Jürgen Habermas, tells us that "civil society is made up of more or less spontaneously created associations, organizations and movements that find, take up, condense and amplify the resonance of social problems in private life, and pass it on to the political realm or public sphere."

As can be seen, all emphasize the manner in which civil society stands in regard to state power—a kind of unspoken challenge to national sovereignty—while necessarily cooperating and working alongside that power. While most definitions and discussions seek to align civil society associations with liberal democracy, this is by no means a necessary connection. Such associations flourished under absolute monarchy in the seventeenth century, in fact were called forth by its existence. In the late twentieth century, although such associations may have aimed at some form of democracy, the fact is that they existed for a decade or more in Eastern Europe under a non-democratic system.

If this fact is accepted, then one can seek to extend the conceptual reach of civil society into non-Western societies. Thus, scholars examine the possibility of its existence in the Muslim world, for example, in terms of taking particular Islamic forms, such as the *waqf*, or charitable trusts (the counter-part of foundations in the Western world), or seek to show how Islamic traditions can co-exist with this aspect of modernity. Defining civil society as a mélange of associations, clubs, guilds, etc. coming together to provide a buffer between state and citizen, some Islamic scholars argue for its co-existence with their religion and particular state systems. The same consideration can be found in Chinese studies, which in general are pessimistic about the space available for civil society in Chinese traditions and the present-day Chinese communist state system.

What holds our interest in these discussions is the place available for NGOs in the globalizing world. As I am suggesting, NGOs are a part of, not a proxy for, civil society. Thus, at the same time as we are told of the difficulties of establishing civil society in the Arab world, we noted that there the number of NGOs grew from about 20,000 in the mid-1960s to over 70,000 late in the 1980s. They are one means of expressing the civility and the aspiration for participation in the governing process that can be found in all sorts of societies. When these organizations link in various ways with other NGOs and INGOs around the world, they become part of a social movement.

As such, they join with other forces that are working toward a new form of civil society: global civil society. We are talking about an attempted whole, in which international criminal courts, innumerable agencies of the UN (directed at problems, for example, of the environment, nuclear regulation, security, diasporas, and refugee population movements), and a host of other institutional efforts to deal with issues that transcend traditional boundaries are in dialogue or conflict with national sovereignty. In focusing on NGOs, I am seeking to view them in the context of this larger whole, a new global civil society. By their very definition, NGOs allow us to think beyond the existing bounds of nationhood, ethnicity, religion, while sometimes fostering their aims, and permit us to imagine and work toward other, larger bonds.

(6)

Fostered by the gaps in governance created by globalization, and facilitated by the computer revolution, NGOs of all kinds, dealing with a whole host of issues, large and small, move in a momentous social movement. Sometimes in conjunction with government bodies, sometimes in opposition to them, they have become an indispensable part of the globalization process. Able to escape or circumvent the control of communications by states, standing in an often awkward aloofness from existing political parties (though, as the Greens show, sometimes being aligned with them), they need to be approached as both an ideal animating humanity and a reality that is "human-all-too-human".

Politics of the People
The Other Side of the Oil Pipeline

PAMELA L. MARTIN

Most people dream of flying over the Andes to the Amazon, or the Oriente, as they call it in Ecuador, to marvel at the natural miracles in the lush rainforest of South America. But this October 2006 trip, hosted by the nongovernmental organization (NGO) Acción Ecológica, was one that viewed utter devastation.

The trip began with a flight from Quito, Ecuador's capital, to Lago Agrio, an Amazonian city on the Colombian border originally developed by Texaco when it began oil extraction in 1972. Lago Agrio and its inhabitants, both colonists and indigenous peoples, have been battling the consequences of oil development since a 1993 lawsuit against Texaco, which is still being heard in a court in Loja, Ecuador. In some estimations (such as those by lawyer and researcher Judith Kimerling in her 1991 book *Amazon Crude*), the oil spills and contamination of this region of Ecuador equal or supersede those of the 1989 Alaskan Exxon Valdez oil spill.

The vistas from an airplane window were of carpeted Andean mountain slopes with varying shades of green peeking through the clouds. The plane passed over various volcanic lakes of vibrant blue and the thermal bath and spa region of Papallacta, which now has the new oleoduct (OCP) running through it—literally, the pipe crosses over the road arriving to the hotel. In Lago Agrio, common visions of the tropics faded to large industrial hangers and bare land. Before the group of about forty activists loaded onto buses, they were warned that the Colombian and Ecuadorian military work in tandem in this region and that they have a history of unfriendliness (and even violence) to those who view petroleum extraction sites. This area is also one of great contention between the two countries, as

Pamela Martin, "Politics of the People: The Other Side of the Oil Pipeline," pp. 1–10. Copyright © 2010 by Institute for the Study of Diplomacy. Permission to reprint granted by the publisher.

Politics of the People | 81

Colombian FARC (Fuerzas Armadas Revolucionarias de Colombia) guerrilla members have been reported to operate and train in this area, and Colombian refugees escaping the FARC have settled in this region as well. In addition, Colombia, in coordination with a U.S. military base in Ecuador's coastal city of Manta, fumigates coca plantations on this border. Colombia has recently renewed its fumigation activities despite concerns from President Rafael Correa and other Ecuadorian political leaders.[1] Therefore, the Oilwatch toxitour not only included visits to extraction sites and the peoples who live in their midst but also perceived a serious air of violence and tension on this once peaceful border.

The tour passed by secondary oil tubes that carried lighter crude and melded with the verdant flora of the rainforest floor. In total, four oil extraction sites were visited—Campo Libertador, Campo Parahuaco, Campo Shushuqui, and Campo Secoya. Campo Parahuaco and its neighbor site, Atacapi, were opened by Texaco in 1968. Campo Libertador and Campo Secoya were the first Texaco sites to be operated by the national Ecuadorian company Petroecuador in 1992.[2] The names derive from the indigenous languages of the region. The CONAIE (the national indigenous confederation of Ecuador) and CONFENIAE (the regional indigenous confederation of the Amazon) protested against the use of indigenous names by oil companies throughout the early 1990s, and now oil fields and refineries may not use such names on their sites. The most startling vision when one sees an oil extraction location up close is the large flames that soar through the sky, creating an immense heat and loud, searing noises.

> At Campo Libertador, a local farmer told his story of losing cattle, other live-stock, and crops, and of illnesses that affected his family members and neighbors. When asked if this affected his livelihood, he said, "Yes, we have no animals left on which to live or fish to eat."[3]

> At Campo Shushuqui, one woman cried, "The children in my family are sick, and I can no longer raise cattle because I cannot find clean water for them to drink."[4] She was sobbing when she told the group that she was destitute and without help from the government and Texaco and now without help from the state oil company Petroecuador.

> Finally, a local farmer took the group behind his newly constructed house, which had been destroyed by a pipeline explosion, to a stream where petroleum flowed freely and mixed with the water.

Shockingly, as the group strode toward a smaller oil pump in the middle of a deforested area, a cow drank right out of the contaminated liquid. The ever more depressing tour continued until the last site, Secoya, where massive explosions of fire from the Ecuador Poverty Percentages by City and Region, 1995–2006 oil refineries burst into the air. At each site, there were lakes of crude oil sitting around the extraction areas, with some that had been covered by flora. One could throw a rock on top of the lake only to see it stay there, not even seeping into the black depths of the crude oil. According to the tour guide and president of the NGO Acción Ecológica, Alexandra Almeida, "When an oil leak is reported, oil companies [until 1992 this was Texaco; now Petroecuador manages operations in these areas] would gather all of the crude oil and affected vegetation in a septic tank and bury it underground. Over the years, these tanks leak and enter the water system."[5] These sad circumstances silenced all forty members of the tour by the end of the day.

Ecuador Poverty Percentages by City and Region 1995–2006

City or Region	1995	1998	1999	2006
Quito	27.3	19.9	29.1	20.9
Guayaquil	34.6	40.2	47.9	36
Coast	51.6	58.4	62.8	52.4
Highland	52.4	53	59.3	43.6
Amazon	**71.5**	**63.2**		**66.8**
Rural	76.5	77.9	81.6	72.7
Urban	36.3	40.6	47	35.6
National Total	52.6	56.3	61.1	49.1

Source: Carlos Larrea, Ana Isabel Larrea, and Ana Lucia Bravo, "Petróleo, sustentabilidad y desarrollo en la Amazonia Norte de Ecuador: Dilemas para una transición hacia una sociedad post-petrolera," (Quito: FLACSO: unpublished manuscript, 2008). See also, Instituto Nacional de Estadisticas y Censos, *Encuesta de Condiciones de Vida, 1995, 1998, 1999, 2006,* at www.inec.gov.ec.

By the time the tour ended in Coca, an Amazonian city on the River Coca below Lago Agrio, other members of the local communities had gathered to march into the town center and protest against further destruction of their lands. There were actors dressed in local costumes singing songs and rhymes about oil and transnational companies, and parents and children with balloons and holding banners, saying, "Get out U.S. Military Base in Manta," "No more Destruction of our Land," "A March for Our Dignity," "Marching for Justice until Texaco Cleans and Restores our Land." There was a sense of hope among the people and relief that such a tour had come to their small Amazonian city to recognize their struggle.

BACKGROUND

Nearly half of Ecuador's territory is Amazonian, covering 130,000 km2, or 2 percent of the entire Amazonian region in South America. Five percent of the country's population lives in the area, which has experienced rapid growth, from 263,797 people in 1982 to 372,563 in 1990 and then to 613,339 people in 2000.[6] While settlers were encouraged by the government, as in other Amazonian countries, to conquer this region and develop

Economic Indicators for Ecuador, 2009

Amazon Crude Oil Price	$70.87 (October 2009)
Gross Domestic Product	$24 Billion
External Debt	$7.493 Billion (public)
	$6.375 Billion (private)
Total Exports August 2009	$1.318 Billion
Total Petroleum Exports August 2009	$799.3 Million

Source: http://www.inec.gov.ed/web/guest/inicio

it throughout the 1960s and 1970s, prosperity has not favored them. Instead, they rank among the poorest members of their society. While 54.5 percent of Ecuadorians from the highlands, or sierra, rank among the poor, 79.2 percent of their Amazonian neighbors are classified as poor, according to Ecuador's National Institute of Statistics.[7] The percentage of people living in poverty in the provinces most severely impacted by oil development is even higher, at 82.42 percent in Sucumbios and 80.2 percent in Orellana. Additionally, literacy rates are far lower in this part of the country, and clean drinking water is provided to only 13 percent and 14 percent (in Sucumbios and Orellana, respectively) of the population of this area as compared to the national average of 48 percent.[8]

In terms of oil reserves, Ecuador ranks fourth in Latin America and has thirty-two petroleum blocks with approximately 5.6 billion barrels of oil. It is number fourteen on the list of countries that export oil to the United States, down from number six only two years ago due to conflicts with U.S. oil companies and state licensing agreements, plus decreased production (EIA 2009). Oil production constitutes 43 percent of the country's exports and has been the principal source of state income since 1973. The Ishpingo-Tambococha-Tiputini (ITT) petroleum block is estimated to have 846 million barrels of recoverable petroleum, which is heavy crude—about 14.7 API (American Petroleum Institute gravity)[9]. The daily production of oil is estimated at approximately 107,000 barrels for thirteen years, with a continual declining production for twelve more years. Independent reports conducted for Petroproducción Ecuador indicate that proven reserves are 944 million barrels of heavy crude and that there may be up to another 1,530 billion barrels of reserves.[10]

THE PUZZLE—WHAT'S A LEADER TO DO?

Ecuador is no stranger to battles with oil companies. In May 2006, it booted out Occidental Oil Company (Oxy), claiming that Oxy had illegally sold interests in its fields in 2000 to a Canadian firm, EnCana. In 2005, the Ecuadorian government determined such action was illegal. By 2006, the interim president, Alfredo Palacio, who replaced ousted President Lucio Gutiérrez, was feeling pressure by social movement activists to reject a free trade agreement with the United States. This anti-free-trade movement, led by indigenous activists under the national organization CONAIE, also called for better compensation from transnational companies to the Ecuadorian people.[11] With anti-free-trade sentiments circling the Andes from their neighbors in Venezuela and Bolivia and a call for nationalizing the resources of the country, the Ecuadorian legislature voted for an increase on the profit tax of transnational oil companies from 30 percent to 60 percent. In response to Oxy's refusal to pay the increase in taxes, the Ecuadorian Hydrocarbons Law was revised in April 2006, and the Ecuadorian government decided to terminate Oxy's contract and assume its holdings in block 15 of Yasuni National Park in the Amazon. This oil field takeover caused the U.S. government to discontinue free trade agreement talks with Ecuador, thus highlighting an interesting connection between foreign trade policy concerning countries and private oil company disputes.[12] All in all, activists in block 15, including the Quichua, Secoya, Siona, and Shuar indigenous peoples, declared victory against Oxy and what they said were its destructive measures in their sacred lands.[13] In addition, the cessation of free trade talks with the United States signified a giant leap forward for those who called for social justice and antiglobalization.

To complicate this geopolitical dilemma, President Correa of Ecuador announced in January 2007 that he would consider a plan to export Ecuadorian crude oil to Venezuela in exchange for Venezuelan derivative refining, a technology that Ecuador does not have. The refining was typically done by U.S. and other multinational corporations. Such a deal would provide an estimated $60 million annually to Ecuador's ailing coffers and eliminate foreign refinery intermediaries. The ecological dilemma is that increased refining and crude oil would likely come from Ecuador's precious and internationally protected Yasuni National Park in the Amazon from the ITT block—a block where, in addition to natural biodiversity, uncontacted indigenous Huaorani communities (primarily Tagaeri, Taromenane, and Oñamenane peoples) live and have had a history of violently resisting outside involvement. This contested area, a UNESCO World Biosphere Reserve, has been hailed as one of the most biodiverse on the planet, containing more fish, flora, and fauna species than in all of North America.

In response to a call for a moratorium on petroleum extraction in this area by ecological and environmental international and national NGOs, including Amazon Alliance, Rainforest Action Network, Amazon Watch, and Acción Ecológica, among others, President Correa in March 2007 gave international NGOs an eight-to-ten month time period to provide $350 million annually to the Ecuadorian government to preserve this rainforest ecosystem.

"If we don't get the money, we'll exploit ITT," said Correa in a press conference.[14]

Thus, the international nongovernmental community, in addition to state organizations and multinational corporations, has become embroiled in the rich rainforest dilemma.

While Venezuela, Bolivia, Mexico, and Chad have histories of such ousters of foreign companies, Ecuador has always put forth a relatively friendly face in the world of petroleum concessions. This new turn in its history and its leadership threatens not only Ecuador's economic gains from its top taxpayer but also its geopolitical relationship with a long-time ally in the United States. Ecuadorian President Correa, a U.S.-trained economist who rejects the free trade agreement with the United States, also calls for renegotiations with increased favor for Ecuador concerning foreign oil companies, including more nationalist policies and closure of the U.S. military base in Manta on Ecuador's coast. His demands confront geopolitical and security issues that Ecuador has with U.S. southern neighbors and allies.[15] Given Ecuador's large international debt and high unemployment rate (nearly 10 percent with underemployment at 51 percent),[16] free trade markets and increased returns for the high price of crude oil would seem beneficial for the country and its geopolitical relationship with its largest economic partner, the United States.[17] So why would its citizens then be cheering for the ouster of an oil company that provided employment and supporting a moratorium on oil production from its largest reserve (20 percent of all reserves in the country)?

ENTER THE NGOs

A Forum on Oil, Human Rights, and Environmental Reparation from the South

To provide perspective on the dangers of exploitation of the Amazon, Oilwatch.org, a coordinating nongovernmental organization of various other organizations in the lesser developed world (or South) that are affected by oil, hosted the *Forum on Oil, Human Rights, and Environmental Reparation*[18] in Coca, Ecuador, in October 2006. Acción Ecológica, a very vibrant and politically active Ecuadorian nongovernmental ecological organization, was the national coordinator and host of the conference. The forum did not include heads of state or oil company executives. Rather, it consisted of the voices of the people—women, men, children, community activists and leaders, teachers, and farmers—who had been impacted by oil development in their lands. It was the reverse image of what is in the press and seen on television—the actual words of those who drank polluted waters and suffered cancer from petroleum's dreaded byproducts and toxins.

The Forum on Oil, Human Rights, and Environmental Reparation hosted a confluence of leaders and people from all over the world in the rainforest to take a toxitour of the rainforest's devastation and to exchange their plights, strategies, and hopes for a better future as well as to celebrate ten years of Oilwatch's international mobilization on behalf of rainforests in the South of the globe. The forum began with a tour of contaminated sites in the Amazon, followed by a march for human rights and the dignity of the peoples who live in affected areas. It culminated in an exchange of experiences from peoples all over the global South. Alaskan Eyak, Nigerian, East Timorese, Nicaraguan Miskito, and Congolese people, among others, told their stories to and shared their experiences with Shuar, Cofan, Secoya, Huaorani, Quichua and other indigenous groups and affected peoples of Ecuador.

What Is Oilwatch?

Oilwatch defines itself as a principled movement against resource extraction with a common identity from the global South and common political goals and mobilizing strategies. Its transnational networks began in February 1996, in Quito, Ecuador with the participation of fifteen organizations from Brazil, Cameroon, Colombia, East Timor, Gabon, Guatemala, Mexico, Nigeria, Peru, South Africa, Sri Lanka, and Thailand. Currently, the network has members in more than fifty countries. It states that it is a

> network that builds solidarity and fosters a common identity among peoples of the South. Oilwatch understands similarities in the current pattern of resource exploitation in countries of the South, which reflects a historical legacy of disempowerment of peoples and considers the recognition of the right of peoples to self-determination as primary in the resolution of environmental problems.[19]

Oilwatch's principled network supports the following political aims:

a. To stop the expansion of socially destructive and environmentally damaging oil activity in the tropics and other parts of the global South;

b. To support communities in the global South that resist the destructive activities of oil companies;

c. To create consciousness of a model of development that is not based on destructive energy sources and respects sovereignty, justice, dignity, and human rights;

d. To forge a network of national and regional organizations that act at the local level so that they can intervene in a united way at the international level to protect the lives and livelihood of local peoples; and

e. To link the environmental impacts with that of the social impacts of the hydrocarbon activities, from a southern prospective.[20]

Unlike some claims that NGOs and local peoples seek funding in an economic market of supply and demand, Oilwatch and its national and local partners seek funding from "like-minded" sources, not just those that will supply funding.[21] The coordinating director of Oilwatch International, Esperanza Martinez, stated that "Oilwatch and Acción Ecológica have differences of opinion from some larger, international NGOs. They have become very neoliberal in their approach."[22]

In a recent discussion with the Ecuadorian NGO director of Jatun Sacha, Michael McColm, McColm also noted a distinct difference between larger, international NGOs and smaller local and national ones. He said that once the government of Ecuador, in this case, can claim to have the support of more visible NGOs, such as The Nature Conservancy or others, this gives it legitimacy for its actions, even if the government counters the local and national desires of the people and environmental standards.[23]

Thus, the Forum on Oil, Human Rights, and Environmental Reparation in Coca was sponsored by international NGOs, including Hivos Holland, Action Aid International, Oxfam International, Bread for the World Germany, Broederlijk Delen Holland, Global Greengrants Funds, and the Basque and Barcelona governments of Spain, among others.[24] All of their mission statements include themes of the global South and their right for self-sustainability and development, which concurs with the Oilwatch mission. In this case, Oilwatch is a global movement that does seek resources in the supply and demand market but tempers that search with principles and common norms and values. That being said, at the forum in Coca, it was clear that the sponsors carried more weight in meetings and certainly had more access to local peoples and forum organizers. This may be the result of repeated visits and close relationships, or a search for future funding, or a combination of the two. In any event, at each session of the forum and with each speech, it was clear that the values among its participants were focused on the common issues of the South and the petroleum extractive industries.

Stories from Abroad

The rest of the forum consisted of testimonial after testimonial of the experiences of indigenous and local peoples in the areas of petroleum extraction. Their lands were different and their peoples were different, but the stories were all the same, which they, too, recognized.

Willman Jimenez of Red de Lideres Angel Shingri, Ecuador, spoke of the discovery of an oil leak and a protest of local peoples that turned violent when police and military members carted him off to the Anglo-French company's, Perenco's, extraction site. He and a colleague, Alfonso Cango, went as observers of the Human Rights Committee of Coca, Ecuador, to view the high-temperature water pipes of the Perenco oil site that had burned community members and their livestock. The military and police told the local protesters to retreat. Once the protesters were outside the company installations, they peacefully remained, opposing the contamination of their lands. Jimenez noted that once the police saw that the people would not retreat, "they shot tear gas at the protesters and arrested Mr. Jimenez." After destroying Jimenez's camera and regularly maltreating him, according to his account, he was set free after sixteen days of imprisonment.

Jimenez commented, "Who is going to pay for the tragic moments that I lived, for the injuries from the bullets shot at me by the military, for the psychological distress, the damage to my family, and the unfounded accusations by Perenco?"[25]

The representative from Congo told a similarly tragic story. Jean Aimé Brice Mackosso of Justice et Paix in Congo explained that he was also imprisoned for three weeks for protesting oil exploration and extraction in his country. He noted that "war came with petroleum." Congo experienced wars in 1957, 1989, and 2000. Mackosso lamented that the "arms were paid for with petroleum … then they asked us to pay the international debt with our money from petroleum." Congo, a country of three million people, began oil exportation in 1969, and today 70 percent of its population still lives on under $1 per day. Finally, Mackosso stated that the ecological disasters of Ecuador were similar to those of Congo. He called for "solidarity in these issues, as many peoples, particularly those from Congo, could not protest openly against this violence and ecological devastation."[26]

Santina Soares of La'o Hamutuk, an organization from East Timor, spoke of the independence of her country from Indonesia in 2002 and their fight with Australia over undersea oil and gas mining rights. She argued that East Timor remains poor and unable to manage its own national sovereignty due to Australia's stronghold on its national resources. Her organization protests the profit-sharing from maritime drilling for petroleum in the Timor Sea and calls for profits from petroleum to be used to decrease poverty and increase social services for the Timorese people. In tears, she described the pitiful living situations of women and children in refugee camps in their capital city, citing the horrific human rights violations, including rapes that occur on a daily basis. Her solution to this nightmare is an active civil society to "build strong national and global networks." At the end of her comments, she thanked the local peoples of Ecuador for sharing their experience, both in words and action, as a form of global fraternity through common struggles.[27]

Like the previous speakers, Keania Karikpo of Oilwatch Africa, based in Nigeria, told the story of his people's struggle with multinational oil companies and government military forces, from the horrific hanging of Ken Saro Wiwa and eight Ogoni activists in November 1995 through the 2001 protests of the Nigerian peoples. He spoke of brutal killings and rapes in the communities of Kaiama, Umuechem, and Choba, where Shell, Agip, and Wilbros oil companies operate, respectively. He described oil companies' influence as "a complex mix of events that have had the combined effect of destroying resource rich communities." He concurred with his colleagues that police and military violence had stirred local resentment and increased violence, as well as caused environmental destruction and abominable health circumstances.[28]

The Ecuadorian Shuar and Quichua and Colombian U'wa indigenous leaders and peoples shared their stories of protest against the Argentinian Compania Generale de Combustibles, S.A. (CGC), and Occidental Oil Company. Each group spoke of their human rights, their rights as ancestral peoples of the land, and their continued fight against intrusion until there is a moratorium against extractive activities. Patricia Gualinga of the Shuar community said that a major component of the success of her community in making its struggle visible was "allies like Greenpeace, Amazon Watch, and Oilwatch."[29]

Among other indigenous and local leaders, Alaskan leader Dune Lankhart spoke of the Exxon Valdez case and his move to use the compensation funds to buy the lands that were spoiled to preserve them for future generations of indigenous peoples in this territory along Alaska's coastline. He referred to this as "compassionate capitalism,"[30] or a system that recognizes the market but infuses it with community values and goals. This goal provides a striking contrast to the general economic principle of supply and demand consumerism in the global market. Lankhart suggested that affected peoples of the South should join together to form economic cooperatives to purchase lands and to establish profitable businesses to support community efforts and local/ indigenous cultures and to protect ancestral lands.

THE DAVID AND GOLIATH TRIBUNAL

As part of the forum's protest of the abuses of multinational oil companies and the frustration of the thirty thousand indigenous peoples of the northern Amazonian region of Ecuador who filed a claim against Texaco, now Chevron Corporation, for environmental destruction of their lands in 1993, an Ethical Tribunal and Popular Judgement of the Chevron Corporation was conducted. Representatives from the plaintiffs (indigenous and campesino members of the Lago Agrio region) and from the defendants, Chevron Corporation, presented their arguments in the case. The case is currently being heard in Lago Agrio, Ecuador, and seeks compensation for damages to the water and soil of the plaintiffs' regions in the amount of over $6 billion. This case has a more-than-sixteen-year history, having been filed in New York City (then Texaco's headquarters), only later to be deemed out of jurisdiction. The U.S. Court of Appeals ruled that Chevron Corporation had to accept the jurisdiction of the Ecuadorian courts and their judgment, thus reenforcing the control of the Ecuadorian legal system in this case.[31] In October 2003, the plaintiffs refiled the case in Lago Agrio, Ecuador, where it is currently being heard and has been ordered to be completed by 2009.[32]

Texaco-Chevron Corporation

The lawsuit has been termed "the David and Goliath" of its time and holds significance for other local communities worldwide as well as for the multinational resource extraction industries. Chevron Corporation claims that the "plaintiffs' attorneys are doing a grave disservice to their clients by refusing to pursue any claims against the proper party, state-owned oil company Petroecuador. As the exclusive owner and operator of the oil fields for over 15 years, Petroecuador has not only failed to honor its legal obligations to remediate oil field sites, but its disastrous record of pollution and environmental mismanagement over these many years is a fact that plaintiffs' attorneys choose to ignore."[33] Texaco, the operating company in charge of exploration, design, construction, and production, shared profits with Petroecuador, the state-run company, since 1976 (62.5 percent Petroecuador). From 1990 through 1992, Texaco transitioned its holdings and the sites to Petroecuador. Petroecuador has been the sole owner and operator of these fields since 1992, when Texpet ended its minority interest.

At the forum, Chevron's attorney argued that the local communities should blame their own government for the pollution of their homes and water systems, as it has maintained a majority share or sole proprietorship of these more than 340 locations for over thirty years. In addition, Chevron argued that Texpet completed a $40 million remediation plan in 1998, which the Ecuadorian government acknowledged. Texpet claimed to have "remediated" its 37.5 percent of the locations (nearly 160 in total) that were said to be contaminated.[34] Chevron stated that there has been "no credible scientific evidence to support their claims. Laboratory analysis of soil and water samples taken from the oil fields clearly shows that no petroleum-related health or environmental risks exist at areas formerly remediated by Texpet."[35] Therefore, Chevron denied responsibility for the cleanup of the affected areas.

The Plaintiffs

The tribunal took place before more than five hundred people, and its purpose was to consider not only environmental damage claims but also the violations to the human rights of those who live in the impacted areas. One man who lives in the area said, "No, no, I lived here then. This oil was dumped in 1982 by Texaco—I remember. And later it was supposed to be cleaned up. They came in here and said they cleaned it up, but all they did was shove dirt on top. So you see, why are you talking about Petroecuador? It was Texaco all along."[36]

The findings of the multinational tribunal were that Chevron-Texaco violated international conventions on human rights by not guaranteeing the Siona, Secoya, Waorani, and Cofan peoples' right to health and a safe environment. Testimonies of increased rates of cancer in affected areas were given in addition to the disappearance of an indigenous group, the Tetete. In addition to asking the global community to abstain from purchasing Chevron-Texaco products, the tribunal demanded that Chevron-Texaco remediate all affected areas of its former operations and to continue to be responsible for future environmental impacts, as its operations will have long-term consequences.[37]

Pablo Fajardo, lead attorney for the plaintiffs said, "One of the problems with modern society is that it places more importance on things that have a price than on things that have a value. Breathing clean air, for instance, or having clean water in the rivers, or having legal rights—these are things that don't have a price but have a value. Oil does have a price, but its value is much less. And sometimes we make the mistake."[38]

THE RESULTS AND THE FUTURE

What are the results of the Forum on Oil, Human Rights, and Environmental Reparation, post-October 2006? Esperanza Martinez, the former director of the Oilwatch international secretariat, helped coordinate the transition of the secretariat in Nigeria for Oilwatch Africa and organized a forum on the postpetroleum state for the World Social Forum in Nigeria in January 2007.[39] As the forum's stated political goals are consciousness-raising and network-building to form part of a global resistance at the local level, the forum did increase networks and raise awareness among its partners about the struggles of others around the globe. Given its decentralized organizational structure, it is difficult to pinpoint local and national policy outcomes due directly to Oilwatch coordination activities. This is certainly not the unified and hierarchical international nongovernmental organization to which scholars refer when writing about a global civil society. However, it is a global mechanism for normative change infused with political goals and strategies for local peoples.

Back to the question of why thousands would protest in the streets of Ecuador against a free trade agreement with the United States, or boot Occidental Petroleum Corporation from its long-time Amazonian station, or oppose multinational extractive industries. From above, Thomas Friedman tells the story of the effects of the oil industry in "The First Law of Petropolitics": "The rising price of oil clearly has a negative impact on the pace of freedom in many countries, and when you get enough countries with enough negative impacts, you start to poison global politics."[40] From below, the story is told by the forum in the Ecuadorian Amazon and by the struggles of peoples throughout the globe concerning the oil industry's effects on those who do not have voices loud enough to be heard or pockets deep enough to be seen on the evening news.

However, decisions for Ecuador on this difficult issue are not over yet. President Correa is still considering the opportunity to expand into the Yasuni National Park, Ecuador's most coveted protected area. While local, national, and international NGOs call for a moratorium on the ITT region, Brazilian Petrobras, Venezuela's Pdvsa, and China's oil companies are vying for entrance and lucrative profit-sharing programs with the ailing Ecuadorian state. Can Ecuador afford NOT to exploit the ITT block for more oil to pay off its debts and fund social programs for its peoples? Are multinational extractive industries to blame for the consumer demand for petroleum?

The October 20–22, 2006, Forum on Oil, Human Rights, and Environmental Reparation in Coca, Ecuador, illustrated the challenges that global civil society faces in confronting globalization and resource extraction. Is such a forum part of the broader, democratizing effect of globalization and transnational networks among citizens of the world? Does such a form of mobilization create new opportunities for democracy on a global scale or limit the ability of states to resolve their sovereign issues?

NOTES

6. *El Comercio*, "La fumigación con glifosato si causa daños en Sucumbíos," December 28, 2006.

7. Alexandra Almeida, "Foro Internacional Petróleo, Derechos Humanos y Reparación: Toxitour," October 20, 2006.

8. Interview by author, Coca, Ecuador, October 20, 2006.

9. Interview by author, Coca, Ecuador, October 20, 2006.

10. Interview by author, Coca, Ecuador, October 20, 2006.

11. Guillaume Fontaine and Ivan Narváez, eds., "Yasuní en el Siglo XXI: El Estado Ecuatoriano y la Conservación de la Amazonía," *ICONOS* 30 (2007) (Quito: Facultad Latinoamericana de Ciencias Sociales [FLACSO]): p. 255.

12. Ibid., p. 55.

13. Esperanza Martínez, "De Kyoto a Quito," *Llacta! Acción Ecológica* (May 9, 2007), at http://www.llacta.org/organiz/coms/2007/com0096.htm.

14. This information is from an independent report from the Beicip Franlab (2004) as contracted by Petroproducción. Esperanza Martínez, *Yasuní: Más de 100 Buenas Razones para NO Sacar el Petróleo* (Quito, Ecuador: Amazonia por la Vida, November 2008); Carlos Larrea et al., "Yasuní-ITT [Ishpingo-Tambococha-Tiputini] initiative a big idea from a small country," July 2009, p. 12, http://www.yasuni-itt.gov.ec/download/Yasuni-ITT-Jul09-eng-lish.pdf.

15. Larrea et al., "Yasuní-ITT initiative," p. 12.

16. *El Comercio*, "200 pobladores de Orellana y Sucumbios protestan en Quito," May 9, 2006, at http://elcomercio.terra.com.ec/solo_texto_search.asp?id_noticia=26373&anio=2006&mes=5&dia=9; *El Comercio*, "CONAIE Amenaza hoy con movilizaciones por caso Oxy," May 4, 2006, at http://elcomercio.terra.com.ec/solo_texto_search.asp?id_noticia=25858&anio=2006&mes=5&dia=4; "La Marcha Ant-Oxy Llega hoy a la Capital," *El Comercio* May 9, 2006: at http://elcomercio.terra.com.ec/solo_texto_search.asp?id_noticia=26345&anio=2006&mes=5&dia=9; *El Comercio*, "El Gobierno Declara la Caducidad con Oxy," May 16, 2006, at http://elcomercio.terra.com.ec/solo_texto_search.asp?id_noticia=27156&anio=2006&mes=5&dia=16.

17. *El Comercio*, "TLC [Tratado de Libre Comercio]: La Negociación Entró en Limbo," May 17, 2006, at http://elcomercio.terra.com.ec/solo_texto_search.asp?id_noticia=27276&anio=2006&mes=5&dia=17.

18. *Acción Ecológica*, "Justicia Ambiental Con Occidental Fuera," June 5, 2006, at http://www.accionecologica.org/webae/index.php?option=com_content&task=view&id=621&Itemid=39.

19. *El Comercio*, "Correa revisará los contratos petroleros," March 15, 2007, at http://contaminacionpercent20amazonia/concesionespercent20ypercent20correapercent20marpercent2015percent202007.htm.

20. Rafael Correa, "Plan del Gobierno del Movimiento del Pais 2007–2011: Un Primer Gran Paso para la Transformación Radical del Ecuador," 2006, at http://www.rafaelcorrea.com/docs/Plan_de_Gobierno_Alianza_PAIS.pdf.

21. Instituto Nacional de Estadisticas y Censos, at http://www.inec.gov.ec/web/guest/inicio.

22. Ecuador's unemployment rate is 10.7 percent officially but underemployment is 47 percent (2005 estimate), at http://indexmundi.com/ecuador/unemployment_rate.html. Ecuador's international debt is estimated at $10 billion, on which President Correa has threatened a default. Lester Pimentel, "Funds: Ecuador Heeds Advice

on Default," *International Herald Tribune*, March 15, 2007, at http://www.iht.com/articles/2007/03/14/bloomberg/bxfund.php.

23. Oilwatch, Forum on Oil, Human Rights, and Environmental Reparation, October 20–22, 2006, at http://www.oilwatch.org/index.php?option=com_content&task=view &id=555&Itemid=1&lang=en.

24. Oilwatch principles, at http://www.oilwatch.org/index.php?option=com_content&tas k=view&id=5&Itemid=6&lang=en.

25. Oilwatch political aims, at http://www.oilwatch.org/index.php?option=com_content& task=view&id=5&itemid=6&lang=en.

26. Bob Clifford, "Merchants of Morality: Globalization at Work," *Foreign Policy* (March 2002): p. 36; Bob Clifford, *The Marketing of Rebellion: Insurgents, Media, and International Activism* (New York: Cambridge University Press, 2005).

27. Esperanza Martinez (director, the Oilwatch Secretariat), interview by author, Quito, Ecuador, May 22, 2006.

28. Michael McColm (director, Jatun Sacha), interview by author, Quito, Ecuador, October 23, 2006.

29. Sponsors for the *Forum on Oil, Human Rights, and Environmental Reparation*, Oilwatch, at http://www.oilwatch.org/index.php?option=com_content&task=view&id=5&Itemi d=6&lang=en.

30. Testimony by Willman Jimenez, Red de Lideres Angel Shingri, Ecuador; Coca, Ecuador, October 20, 2006.

31. Testimony by Jean Aimé Brice Mackosso (Justice et Paix, Congo), Coca, Ecuador, October 20, 2006.

32. Testimony by Santina Soares (La'o Hamutuk, East Timor), Coca, Ecuador, October 20, 2006.

33. Testimony by Keania Karikpo (Oilwatch Africa, Nigeria), Coca, Ecuador, October 20, 2006.

34. Testimony by Patricia Gualinga (Pueblo Originario Kichwa de Sarayacu, Ecuador), Coca, Ecuador, October 20, 2006.

35. Interview by author with Dune Lankhart, Coca, Ecuador, October 21, 2006.

36. William Langewwieshce, "Jungle Law," *Vanity Fair*, May 2007, at http://www.vanity-fair.com/politics/features/2007/05/texaco200705.

37. *Amazon Watch*, "Ecuador Court Speeds Up Chevron's $6Billion Amazon Trial Over Rainforest Contamination," March 20, 2003, at http://www.amazonwatch.org/view_news.php?id=1353.

38. Texaco in Ecuador, at http://www.texaco.com/sitelets/ecuador/en/plaintiffs_myths.asp.

39. Ibid.

40. Ibid.

41. Quoted in Langewwieshce, "Jungle Law."

42. *Tribunal Etico y Popular de Juzgamiento a la Empresa Chevron-Texaco*, October 22, 2006, Coca, Ecuador, at http://www.oilwatch.org/reparacion/index.php?option=com_cont ent&task=view&id=82&Itemid=44&PHPSESSID=e4fle91051ecc2b6c41e0272cde la321.

43. Quoted in Langewwieshce, "Jungle Law."

44. Martinez interview, January 4, 2007.

45. Thomas L. Friedman, "The First Law of Petropolitics," *Foreign Policy*, (May-June 2006)

UNIT 2

✝

THEORY

Theories of World Politics

CHARLES W. KEGLEY, JR. AND GREGORY A. RAYMOND

> There is an inescapable link between the abstract world of theory and the real world of policy. We need theories to make sense of the blizzard of information that bombards us daily. Even policymakers who are contemptuous of "theory" must rely on their own (often unstated) ideas about how the world works in order to decide what to do … Everyone uses theories—whether he or she knows it or not.
>
> Stephen M. Walt

Although the academic study of international relations is relatively new, attempts to theorize about state behavior date back to antiquity. Perhaps the best example can be found in Thucydides, the Greek historian who analyzed the Peloponnesian War (431–404 BCE) between ancient Sparta and Athens. Thucydides believed "knowledge of the past" would be "an aid to the interpretation of the future" and therefore wrote a history of the war "not to win the applause of the moment, but as a possession for all time." Examining the hostilities like a physician diagnosing a patient, his detailed clinical observations were recorded as a case study that described the symptoms of war-prone periods and offered a prognosis of the probable consequences of different foreign policy actions.

Greece in Thucydides's day was not unified; it contained a welter of small, autonomous city-states scattered throughout the Balkan Peninsula, the Aegean Archipelago, and what is today western Turkey. Sparta and Athens were the strongest of these fiercely independent

Charles W. Kegley, Jr. and Gregory A. Raymond, "Theories of World Politics," from *The Global Future: A Brief Introduction to World Politics*, pp. 27–53. Published by Wadsworth Publishing, 2010. Copyright © by Cengage Learning, Inc. Permission to reprint granted by the rights holder.

states. The former was a cautious, conservative land power; the latter, a bold, innovative sea power. Relations between them were contentious. When their rivalry eventually escalated to war in 431 BCE, they became trapped in a long, debilitating military stalemate.

Stung by mounting losses during a decade of fruitless combat, in 421 BCE Sparta and Athens agreed to a cessation of hostilities. Neither side expected it to last, however. The two rivals refrained from attacking one another over the next few years, but each side maneuvered to gain an advantage over the other in anticipation of the next round of fighting. A strong, reliable network of allies, the Athenians thought, might provide a decisive edge when the war resumed. To consolidate their position among Greeks living on islands throughout the Aegean Sea, in 416 BCE Athens sent an expedition of thirty-eight ships and approximately three thousand soldiers to Melos, a city-state that wished to remain nonaligned during the war. The Athenians declared that if Melos did not agree to become their ally, it would be obliterated. The Melians argued that such a brutal attack would be unjust since they had not harmed Athens. Moreover, it was in Athens's self-interest to show restraint: destroying Melos would drive other neutral city-states into the Spartan camp. Finally, the Melians pointed out that it would be unreasonable to surrender while there was still hope of being rescued by the Spartans. Scornful of these appeals to justice, expedience, and reasonableness, the Athenians proclaimed that in interstate relations "the strong do what they can and the weak suffer what they must." Regardless of the merits of the Melian argument, Athens had the strength to subjugate Melos if it so desired. Resistance was futile; nevertheless, the Melians refused to submit. The Athenian troops promptly besieged the city, forcing it to capitulate shortly thereafter. Following the city's surrender, they killed all adult men and sold the women and children into slavery.

The Athenian practice of raw power politics raises timeless questions about world affairs. How can states achieve security in an anarchic international system? In the absence of a central authority to resolve the disputes among states, are there limits to the use of military power? What role should ethical considerations play in the conduct of foreign policy? This chapter will focus on the three schools of thought that have most influenced how policymakers and scholars think about these kinds of questions: realism, liberalism, and constructivism.

CONTENDING THEORIES OF WORLD POLITICS

Imagine yourself the newly elected president of the United States. You are scheduled to deliver the State of the Union address on your views of the current world situation. Your task is to identify those international issues most worthy of attention and explain how you plan to deal with them. To convince citizens these issues are important, you must present them as part of a larger picture of the world, showing how the situation you face may be part of a pattern. You must, in short, think *theoretically*. The success of your effort to explain the causes of current problems, predict their long-term consequences, and persuade others that you have a viable policy to address them will hinge on how well you understand the way the world works.

When leaders face these kinds of intellectual challenges, they fortunately benefit from the existence of several theories of world politics from which they can draw guidance. **A theory** is a set of statements that purports to explain a particular phenomenon. In essence, it provides a map, or frame of reference, that makes the complex, puzzling world around us intelligible. Choosing which theory to heed is an important decision, because each rests on different assumptions about the nature of international politics, each advances different causal claims, and each offers a different set of foreign policy recommendations. Our aim in this chapter is to compare the assumptions, causal claims, and policy prescriptions of realism, liberalism, and constructivism, the most common theoretical perspectives policymakers and scholars use to interpret international relations. We begin with realism, the oldest of these contending schools of thought.

REALIST THEORY

Political realism has a long, distinguished history that dates back to the writings of Thucydides about the Peloponnesian War. Other influential figures that contributed to realist thought include the sixteenth-century Italian philosopher Niccolò Machiavelli and the seventeenth-century English philosopher Thomas Hobbes. Realism deserves careful examination because its worldview continues to guide much thought about international politics.

The Realist Worldview

Realism, as applied to contemporary international politics, views the nation-state as the most important actor on the world stage since it answers to no higher political authority. States are sovereign: they have supreme power over their territory and populace, and no one stands above them wielding the legitimacy and coercive capability to govern the international system. Given the absence of a higher authority to which states can turn to for protection and to resolve disputes, realists depict world politics as a ceaseless, repetitive struggle for **power** where, like in the Melian episode described by Thucydides, the strong dominate the weak. Because each state is ultimately responsible for its own survival and feels uncertain about its neighbors' intentions, realism claims that prudent political leaders seek arms and allies to enhance national security. In other words, the anarchic structure of the international system leads even well-intentioned leaders to practice **self-help**, increasing military strength and aligning with others to deter potential threats. Realist theory does not preclude the possibility that rival powers will cooperate on arms control or on other security issues of common interest. Rather it asserts that cooperation will be rare because states worry about the distribution of **relative gains** emanating from cooperation and the possibility that the other side will cheat on agreements.

Realists, with their emphasis on the ruthless nature of international life, tend to be skeptical about the role of ethical considerations in foreign policy deliberations. As they see it, some policies are driven by strategic imperatives that may require national leaders to contravene moral norms. Embedded in this "philosophy of necessity" is a distinction between private morality, which guides the behavior of ordinary people in their daily lives, and reason of state (*raison d'état*), which governs the conduct of leaders responsible for the security and survival of the state. Whatever actions that are in the interest of state security must be carried out no matter how repugnant they might seem in the light of private morality. "Ignoring one's interests, squandering one's resources in fits of altruism," so this line of argument goes, "is the fastest road to national disaster." For a national leader, "thinking with one's heart is a serious offense. Foreign policy is not social work" (Krauthammer 1993).

The Evolution of Realist Thought

We have seen how the intellectual roots of political realism reach back to ancient Greece. They also extend beyond the western world to India and China. Discussions of "power politics" abound in the *Arthashastra*, an Indian treatise on statecraft written during the fourth century BCE by Kautilya, as well as in works written by Han Fei and Shang Yang in ancient China.

Modern realism emerged on the eve of the Second World War, when the prevailing belief in a natural harmony of interests among nations came under attack. Just a decade earlier, this belief had led numerous countries to sign the 1928 Kellogg-Briand Pact, which renounced war as an instrument of national policy. Now, with Nazi Germany, Fascist Italy, and Imperial Japan all violating the treaty, British historian and diplomat E. H. Carr (1939) complained that the assumption of a universal interest in peace had allowed too many people to "evade the unpalatable fact of a fundamental divergence of interest between nations desirous of maintaining the *status quo* and nations desirous of changing it."

In an effort to counter what they saw as a utopian, legalistic approach to foreign affairs, Reinhold Niebuhr (1947), Hans J. Morgenthau (1948), and other realists articulated a pessimistic view of human nature. Echoing the seventeenth-century philosopher Baruch Spinoza, many of them pointed to an innate conflict between passion and reason; furthermore, in the tradition of St. Augustine, they stressed that material appetites enabled passion to overwhelm reason. For them, the human condition was such that the forces of light and darkness would perpetually vie for control.

The realists' picture of international life appeared particularly persuasive after World War II. The onset of rivalry between the United States and the Soviet Union, the expansion of the Cold War into a wider struggle between East and West, and the periodic crises that threatened to erupt into global violence all supported the realists' emphasis on the inevitability of conflict, the poor prospects for cooperation, and the divergence of national interests among incorrigibly selfish, power-seeking states.

Whereas these so-called "classical" realists sought to explain state behavior by drawing upon explanatory factors located at the individual level of analysis, *neorealism* (sometimes labeled structural realism), the next wave of realist theorizing, emphasized the systemic level of analysis. Kenneth Waltz (1979), the leading proponent of what has come to be called "defensive" realism, proposed that international anarchy—not some allegedly evil side of human nature—explained why states were locked in fierce competition with one another. The absence of a central arbiter was the defining structural feature of the international system. Vulnerable and insecure, states behaved defensively by forming alliances against looming threats. According to Waltz, balances of power form automatically in anarchic environments. Even when they are disrupted, they are soon restored.

The most recent variant of realist theory also resides at the systemic level of analysis, but asserts that the ultimate goal of states is to achieve military supremacy, not merely a balance of power. For John Mearsheimer (2001) and other exponents of "offensive" realism, the anarchic structure of the international system encourages states to maximize their share of world power in order to improve the odds of surviving the competition for relative advantage. A state with an edge over everyone else has insurance against the possibility that a predatory state might someday pose a grave threat. To quote the old cliché: The best defense is a good offense.

The Limitations of Realism

However persuasive the realists' image of the essential properties of international politics, their policy recommendations suffered from a lack of precision in the way they used such key terms as *power* and *national interest*. Thus, once analysis moved beyond the assertion that national leaders should acquire power to serve the national interest, important questions remained: What were the key elements of national power? What uses of power best served the national interest? Did arms furnish protection or provoke costly arms races? Did alliances enhance one's defenses or encourage threatening counteralliances? From the perspective of realism's critics, seeking security by amassing power was self-defeating. The quest for absolute security by one state would be perceived as creating absolute insecurity for other members of the system, with the result that everyone would become locked in an upward spiral of countermeasures that jeopardized the security of all (Vasquez 1998; 1993).

Because much of realist theorizing was vague, it began to be questioned. Realism offered no criteria for determining what historical data were significant in evaluating its claims and what epistemological rules to follow when interpreting relevant information (Vasquez and Elman 2003). Even the policy recommendations that purportedly flowed from its logic were often divergent. Realists themselves, for example, were sharply divided as to whether U.S. intervention in Vietnam served American national interests and whether nuclear weapons contributed to international security. Similarly, whereas some observers used realism to explain the 2003 U.S. invasion of Iraq (Gvosdev 2005), others drew upon realist arguments to criticize the invasion (Mansfield and Snyder 2005; Mearsheimer and Walt 2003).

A growing number of critics also pointed out that realism did not account for significant developments in world politics. For instance, it could not explain the creation of new commercial and political institutions in Western Europe in the 1950s and 1960s, where the cooperative pursuit of mutual advantage led Europeans away from the unbridled power politics that brought them incessant warfare since the birth of the nation-state some three centuries earlier. Other critics began to worry about realism's tendency to disregard ethical principles and about the material and social costs that some of its policy prescriptions seemed to impose, such as retarded economic growth resulting from unrestrained military expenditures.

Despite realism's shortcomings, many people continue to think about world politics in the language constructed by realists, especially in times of global tension. A recent example can be found in the comments by former British adviser Michael Gerson (2006, 59–60) about how the United States should deal with Iran's nuclear ambitions. Arguing from the realist assumption that "peace is not a natural state," he has called for a robust American response based on a steely-eyed focus on the country's national security interest in preventing the proliferation of weapons of mass destruction in the Middle East. "There must be someone in the world capable of drawing a line—someone who says, 'This much and no further.'" Peace, he concludes, cannot be achieved by "a timid foreign policy that allows terrible threats to emerge." Unless those who threaten others pay a price, "aggression will be universal."

LIBERAL THEORY

Liberalism has been called the "strongest contemporary challenge to realism" (Caporaso 1993). Like realism, it has a distinguished pedigree, with philosophical roots extending back to the political thought of John Locke, Immanuel Kant, and Adam Smith. Liberalism warrants our attention because it speaks to issues realism disregards, including the impact of domestic politics on state behavior, the implications of economic interdependence, and the role of international norms and institutions in facilitating international cooperation.

The Liberal Worldview

There are several distinct schools of thought within the liberal tradition. Drawing broad conclusions from such a diverse body of theory risks misrepresenting the position of any given author. Nevertheless, there are sufficient commonalities to abstract some general themes.

Liberals differ from realists in several important ways. At the core of liberalism is a belief in reason and the possibility of progress. Liberals view the individual as the seat of moral value and assert that human beings should be treated as ends rather than means. Whereas realists counsel decision makers to seek the lesser evil rather than the absolute good, liberals emphasize ethical principle over the pursuit of power, and institutions over military capabilities (see Doyle 1997; Howard 1978; Zacher and Matthew 1995). Politics at the international level is more of a struggle for consensus and mutual gain than a struggle for power and prestige.

Instead of blaming international conflict on an inherent lust for power, liberals fault the conditions that people live under. Reforming those conditions, they argue, will enhance the prospects for peace. The first element common to various strands of liberal thought is an emphasis undertaking political reforms to establish stable democracies. Woodrow Wilson, for example, proclaimed that "democratic government will make wars less likely." Franklin Roosevelt later reflected this view when he asserted "the continued maintenance and improvement of democracy constitute the most important guarantee of international peace." Based on tolerance, accommodation, and procedural rights, democratic political cultures are said to shun lethal force as a means of settling disagreements. Politics is not seen as a **zero-sum game**, so that the use of persuasion rather than coercion, and a reliance on judicial avenues to settle rival claims are the primary means of dealing with conflict.

According to liberal theory, conflict resolution practices used at home are also employed when dealing with international disputes. Leaders socialized within democratic cultures share a common outlook. Viewing international politics as an extension of domestic politics, they externalize their norms of regulated competition. Disputes with kindred governments rarely escalate to war because each side accepts the other's legitimacy and expects it to rely on peaceful means of conflict resolution. These expectations are reinforced by the transparent nature of democracies. The inner workings of open polities can be scrutinized by anyone; hence, it is difficult to demonize them as scheming adversaries.

The second thrust common to liberal theorizing is an emphasis on free trade. The idea that commerce helps promote conflict resolution has roots in the work of Montesquieu, Adam Smith, and various Enlightenment thinkers. "Nothing is more favourable to the rise of politeness and learning," noted the philosopher David Hume (1817), "than a number of neighboring and independent states, connected by commerce." This view was later embraced by the Manchester School of political economy and formed the basis for Norman Angell's (1910) famous rebuttal of the assertion that military conquest yields economic prosperity.

The doctrine that unfettered trade helps prevent disputes from escalating to wars rests on several propositions. First, commercial intercourse creates a material incentive to resolve disputes peacefully: War reduces profits by interrupting vital economic exchanges.

Second, cosmopolitan business elites who benefit most from these exchanges comprise a powerful transnational interest group with a stake in promoting amicable solutions to festering disagreements. Finally, the web of trade between nations increases communication, erodes parochialism, and encourages both sides to avoid ruinous clashes. In the words of Richard Cobden, an opponent of the protectionist Corn Laws that once regulated British international grain trade: "Free Trade! What is it? Why, breaking down the barriers that separate nations; those barriers, behind which nestle the feelings of pride, revenge, hatred, and jealousy, which every now and then bunt their bounds, and deluge whole countries with blood" (cited in Wolfers and Martin 1956).

Finally, the third commonality in liberal theorizing is an advocacy of international institutions. Liberals recommend replacing cut-throat, balance-of-power politics with organizations based on the principle that a threat to peace anywhere is a common concern to everyone. They see foreign policy as unfolding in a nascent global society populated by actors who recognize the cost of conflict, share significant interests, and can realize those interests by using institutions to mediate disputes whenever misconceptions, wounded sensibilities, or aroused national passions threaten their relations.

The Evolution of Liberal Thought

Contemporary liberal theory rose to prominence in the wake of the First World War. Not only had the war involved more participants over a wider geographic area than any previous war, but modern science and technology made it a war of machinery: Old weapons were improved and produced in great quantities, new and far more deadly weapons were rapidly developed and deployed. By the time the carnage was over, nearly twenty million people were dead.

For liberals like U.S. President Woodrow Wilson, World War I was "the war to end all wars." Convinced that another horrific war would erupt if states resumed practicing power politics, liberals set out to reform the international system. These "idealists," as they were called by hard-boiled realists, generally fell into one of three groups (Herz 1951). The first group advocated creating international institutions to mitigate the raw struggle for power between egoistic, mutually suspicious states. The League of Nations was the embodiment of this strain of liberal thought. Its founders hoped to prevent future wars by organizing a system of **collective security** that would mobilize the entire international community against would-be aggressors. The League's founders declared that peace was indivisible: An attack on one member of the League would be considered an attack on all. Since no state was more powerful than the combination of all other states, aggressors would be deterred and war averted.

A second group called for the use of legal procedures to adjudicate disputes before they escalated to armed conflict. Adjudication is a judicial procedure for resolving conflicts by referring them to a standing court for a binding decision. Immediately after the war, several governments drafted a statute to establish a Permanent Court of International Justice (PCIJ). Hailed by Bernard C. J. Loder, the court's first president, as the harbinger of a new era of civilization, the PCIJ held its inaugural public meeting in early 1922 and rendered its first judgment on a contentious case the following year. Liberal champions of the court insisted that the PCIJ would replace military retaliation with a judicial body capable of bringing the facts of a dispute to light and issuing a just verdict.

A third group of liberal thinkers followed the biblical injunction that states should beat their swords into plowshares and sought disarmament as a means of avoiding war. Their efforts were exemplified between 1921 and 1922 by the Washington naval conference, which tried to curtail maritime competition among the United States, Great Britain, Japan, France, and Italy by placing limits on battleships. The ultimate goal of this group was to reduce international tensions by promoting general disarmament, which led them to convene the Geneva Disarmament Conference in 1932.

Although a tone of idealism dominated policy rhetoric and academic discussions during the interwar period, little of the liberal reform program was ever seriously attempted, and even less of it was achieved. The League of Nations failed to prevent the Japanese invasion of Manchuria (1931) or the Italian invasion of Ethiopia (1935); major disputes were rarely submitted to the Permanent Court of International Justice; and the 1932 Geneva Disarmament Conference ended in failure. When the threat of war began gathering over Europe and Asia in the late 1930s, enthusiasm for liberal idealism receded.

The next surge in liberal theorizing arose decades later in response to realism's neglect of **transnational relations** (see Keohane and Nye 1971). Although realists continued to focus on the state, the events surrounding the 1973 oil crisis revealed that nonstate actors could affect the course of international events, and occasionally compete with states. This insight led to the realization that **complex interdependence** (Keohane and Nye 1977) sometimes offered a better description of world politics than realism, especially on international economic and environmental matters. Rather than contacts between countries being limited to high-level governmental officials, multiple communication channels connected societies. Rather than security dominating foreign policy considerations, issues on national agendas did not always have a fixed priority. Rather than military force serving as the primary instrument of statecraft, other means frequently were more effective when bargaining occurred between economically interconnected nations. In short, the realist preoccupation with government-to-government relations ignored the complex network of public and private exchanges crisscrossing national boundaries. States were becoming increasingly interdependent; that is, mutually dependent on, sensitive about, and vulnerable to one another in ways that were not captured by realist theory.

While interdependence was not new, its growth during the last quarter of the twentieth century led many liberal theorists to challenge the realist conception of anarchy. Although agreeing that the international system was anarchic, they suggested that it was more properly conceptualized as an "ordered" anarchy because most states followed commonly acknowledged normative standards, even in the absence of hierarchical enforcement. When a body of norms fosters shared expectations that guide a regularized pattern of co-operation on a specific issue, we call it an **international regime** (see Hansenclever, Mayer, and Rittberger 1996). Various types of regimes have been devised to govern behavior in trade and monetary affairs, as well as to manage access to common resources like fisheries and river water. By the turn of the century, as pressing economic and environmental issues crowded national agendas, a large body of liberal scholarship delved into how regimes developed and what led states to follow their injunctions.

Fueled by a belief that increased interdependence can lead to higher levels of coopera-tion, this new wave of liberal theorizing, known as *neoliberalism* (also called neoliberal institutionalism), mounted a serious challenge to realism and neorealism during the last decade of the twentieth century. Neoliberals argued that states attempt to maximize **abso-lute gains** by cooperating to advance mutual interests, and that international institutions provide a mechanism for coordinating multilateral action and reducing the odds of anyone reneging on their commitments. On the one hand, institutions strengthen cooperative arrangements by providing information on the preferences of others; on the other, they dampen the incentive to cheat by monitoring compliance with agreements.

More recently, neoliberals have explored **moral hazard** dilemmas that can arise when states behave in ways that exacerbate a pressing problem because they expect international institutions to bail them out. For example, a country that is unable to make payments on its outstanding debts may continue borrowing under the assumption that an institution such as the International Monetary Fund will provide it with financial backing (Martin 2007, 118–124). Research into dilemmas of this kind have led neoliberals to gain insights into how international institutions occasionally carve out enough autonomy to pursue their own agendas despite pressure to respond to the desires of their most powerful members.

The Limitations of Liberalism

Liberal theorists share an interest in probing the conditions under which the convergent and overlapping interests among otherwise sovereign political actors may result in coop-eration. Taking heart in the international prohibition, through community consensus, of such previously entrenched practices as slavery, piracy, dueling, and colonialism, they emphasize the prospects for progress through institutional reform. Studies of European integration during the 1950s and 1960s paved the way for the liberal institutionalist theories that emerged in the 1990s. The expansion of trade, communication, information, technology, and immigrant labor propelled Europeans to sacrifice portions of their sover-eign independence to create a new political and economic union out of previously separate units. These developments were outside of realism's worldview, creating conditions that made the call for a theory grounded in the liberal tradition convincing to many who had previously questioned realism. In the words of former U.S. president Bill Clinton, "In a world where freedom, not tyranny, is on the march, the cynical calculus of pure power politics simply does not compute. It is ill-suited to the new era."

Yet as compelling as contemporary liberal institutionalism may seem at the onset of the twenty-first century, many realists complain that it has not transcended its idealist heritage (see Application: Steel and Good Intentions). They charge that just like the League of Nations and the Permanent Court of International Justice, institutions today exert minimal influence on state behavior. International organizations cannot stop states from behaving according to balance-of-power logic, calculating how each move they make affects their relative position in a world of relentless competition (Mearsheimer 1994/1995; 1995).

Critics of liberalism further contend that most studies supportive of international institutions appear in the **low politics** arena of commercial, financial, and environmental affairs, not in the **high politics** arena of national defense. While it may be difficult to draw a clear line between economic and security issues, some scholars note that different institutional arrangements exist in each realm, with the prospects for cooperation among self-interested states greater in the former than the latter (Lipson 1984). National survival hinges on the effective management of security issues, insist realists. Collective security organizations naively assume that all members perceive threats in the same way, and are willing to run the risks and pay the costs of countering those threats (Kissinger 1992). Because avaricious states are unlikely to see their vital interests in this light, international institutions cannot provide timely, muscular responses to aggression. On security issues, conclude realists, states will trust in their own power, not in the promises of international institutions.

A final realist complaint lodged against liberalism is an alleged tendency to turn foreign policy into a moral crusade. Whereas realists claim that heads of state are driven by strategic necessities, many liberals believe moral necessities impose categorical imperatives on leaders. Consider the 1999 war in Kosovo, which pitted the North Atlantic Treaty Organization (NATO) against the Federal Republic of Yugoslavia. Pointing to Yugoslav leader Slobodan Milosevic's repression of ethnic Albanians living in the province of Kosovo, NATO Secretary General Javier Solana, British Prime Minister Tony Blair, and U.S. President Bill Clinton all argued that humanitarian intervention was a moral imperative. Although nonintervention into the internal affairs of other states had long been a cardinal principle of international law, they saw military action against Yugoslavia as a duty because human rights were an international entitlement and governments that violated them forfeited the protection of international law. Sovereignty, according to many liberal thinkers, is not sacrosanct. The international community has an obligation to use armed force to stop flagrant violations of human rights.

To sum up, realists remain skeptical about liberal claims of moral necessity. On the one hand, they deny the universal applicability of any single moral standard in a culturally pluralistic world. On the other hand, they worry that adopting such a standard will breed a self-righteous, messianic foreign policy. Realists embrace **consequentialism**. If there are

---

APPLICATION: Steel and Good Intentions

Political realists frequently refer to those who believe that international morality can contribute to fostering peaceful relations among states as "idealists" or "Utopians." Asking us to look at the world with candor, they insist that politics is a struggle for power that cannot be eliminated from the international scene. In the words of Otto von Bismarck, German chancellor during the late nineteenth century and the foremost realist of his day, conducting foreign policy with moral principles would be like walking along a narrow forest path while carrying a long pole in one's mouth.

Although the prevailing caricature of realists depicts them as ruthless practitioners of guileful tactics, many policymakers who subscribe to realism aver that prudence requires raw power to be restrained by moral limitations. In the passage that follows, Margaret Thatcher, who served as prime minister of the United Kingdom from 1979 to 1990, discusses how realist prescriptions about the use of power as well as moral principles informed her foreign policy decisions.

> Above all, foreign; and security policy is about the use of power in order to achieve a state's goals in its relations with other states. As a conservative, I have no squeamishness about stating this. I leave it to others to try to achieve the results they seek in international affairs without reference to power. They always fail. And their failures often lead to outcomes more damaging than pursuit of national interest through the normal means of the balance of power and resolute defense would ever have done.
>
> It is sometimes suggested, or at least implied, that the only alternative ... [to idealism] is the total abandonment of moral standards. ... Yet I am not one of those who believe that statecraft should concern power without principle. For a start, pure *Realpolitik*—that is, foreign policy based on calculations of power and the national interest—is a concept which blurs at the edges the more-closely it is examined ... [T]he pursuit of statecraft without regard for moral principles is all but impossible, and it makes little sense for even the most hardnosed statesman to ignore this fact
>
> ... For my part, I favor an approach to statecraft that embraces principles, as long as it is not stifled by them; and I prefer such principles to be accompanied by steel along with good intentions (Thatcher 2002, xix–xxii).

For Thatcher, who dealt with issues ranging from confrontations with the Soviet Union to war with Argentina during her tenure in office, moral posturing was no substitute for a muscular foreign policy. However, effective policy required a moral vision.

no universal standards covering the many situations in which moral choice must occur, then policy decisions can only be judged in terms of their consequences in particular circumstances. Prudent leaders recognize that competing moral values may be at stake in any given situation, and they must weigh the trade-offs among these values, as well as how pursuing them might impinge on national security and other important interests. As the former U.S. diplomat and celebrated realist scholar George Kennan (1985) once put it, the primary obligation of government "is to the *interests* of the national society it represents, not to the moral impulses that individual elements of that society may experience."

CONSTRUCTIVIST THEORY

Since the end of the Cold War, many students of international relations have turned to social constructivism in order to understand world politics. In contrast to realism and liberalism, which emphasize how material factors such as military power and economic wealth affect the relations among states, constructivism focuses on the impact of ideas. As discussed in the previous chapter, international reality is defined by our images of the world. Constructivists emphasize the inter-subjective quality of these images. We are all influenced by collective conceptions of world politics that are reinforced by social pressures from the reference groups to which we belong. Awareness of how our understandings of the world are socially constructed, and of how prevailing ideas mold our beliefs about what is immutable and what can be reformed, allow us to see world politics in a new, critical light.

The Constructivist Worldview

As shown in Table 2.1, constructivists differ from realists and liberals most fundamentally by insisting that world politics is socially constructed. That is to say, material resources, such as those contributing to brute military and economic power, only acquire meaning for human action through the structure of shared knowledge in which they are embedded. The social structure of a system makes actions possible by constituting actors with certain identities and interests, and material capabilities with certain meanings (see Hopf 1998; S. Smith 1997; Onuf 1989). Hence the meaning of a concept such as "anarchy" depends on the underlying structure of shared knowledge. An anarchy among allies, for example, entails a different meaning for the states in question than an anarchy composed of bitter rivals. Thus, British nuclear weapons are less threatening to the United States than the same weapons in North Korean hands, because shared Anglo-American expectations about one another differ from those between Washington and Pyongyang. The nature of international life within an anarchy, in other words, is not a given. Anarchy, as well as other socially constructed concepts like "sovereignty" and "power," are simply what states make of them (Wendt 1995).

The Evolution of Constructivist Thought

The intellectual roots of constructivism extend from the work of the early twentieth-century Frankfurt School of critical social theory to more recent research by Peter Berger and Thomas Luckmann (1967) on the sociology of knowledge and by Anthony Giddens (1984) on the relationship between agency and social structure. Sometimes described as more of a philosophically informed perspective than a fully fledged general theory (Ruggie 1998), contstructivism includes a diverse group of scholars who by and large agree that the international institutions most people take for granted as the natural and inevitable result of world politics need not exist (see Hacking 1999). Like the institution of slavery, they are social constructs that depend upon human agreement for their existence and are therefore changeable.

The unraveling of the Warsaw Pact and subsequent disintegration of the Soviet Union stimulated scholarly interest during the 1990s in constructivist interpretations of world politics. Neither realism nor liberalism foresaw the peaceful end to the Cold War and both theories had difficulty explaining why it occurred when it did. Constructivists pointed to the challenge that Mikhail Gorbechev's "new thinking" posed to traditional ideas about national security (Koslowski and Kratochwil 1994). New thinking, they suggested, led to the rise of new **norms** governing the relations between Moscow and Washington.

Norms can be the sources of action in three ways: they may be *constitutive* in the sense that they define what counts as a certain activity; they may be *constraining* in that they enjoin an actor from behaving in a particular way; or they may be *enabling* by allowing specific actions (Raymond 1997). In American football, for instance, there are constitutive rules that give meaning to action on the field by defining what counts as a touchdown, a field goal, or a safety. There also are two kinds of regulative rules that guide play: constraining rules prohibit things like clipping and holding, while enabling rules permit players to throw laterals and forward passes. Similarly, in the modern world system, constitutive norms of sovereignty define what counts as statehood, while regulative norms that either constrain or enable specify how sovereign states ought to conduct themselves. Rather than simply following a *logic of consequences*, where the anticipatory costs and benefits of alternative actions are weighed to ascertain what will maximize one's interests, states take into account a *logic of appropriateness*, where the norms that define what consists of legitimate conduct guide behavior.

For constructivists, the game of power in international relations revolves around actors' abilities through debate about values to persuade others to accept their ideas. People and groups become powerful when their efforts to proselytize succeed in winning converts to those ideas and norms they advocate, and a culture of shared understandings emerges. The capacity of some activist transnational nongovernmental organizations, such as Human Rights Watch or Greenpeace, to promote global change by convincing many people to accept their ideas about political liberties and environmental protection are examples of how shared conceptions of moral and legal norms can change the world. Shared understandings of interests, identities, and images of the world—how people think of themselves,

Table 2.1 A Comparison of Realist, Liberal, and Constructivist Theories

Feature	Realism	Liberalism	Constructivism
Core concern	How vulnerable, self-interested states survive in an environment where they are uncertain about the intentions and capabilities of others	How rational egoists coordinate their behavior through rules and organizations in order to achieve collective gains	How ideas and identities shape world politics
Key actors	States	States, international institutions, global corporations	Individuals, nongovernmental organizations, transnational networks
Central concepts	Anarchy, self-help, national interest, relative gains, balance of power	Collective security, international regimes, complex interdependence, transnational relations	Ideas, shared knowledge, identities, discourses
Approach to peace	Protect sovereign autonomy and deter rivals through military preparedness	Democratization, open markets, and international law and organization	Activists who promote progressive ideas and encourage states to adhere to norms of appropriate behavior
Global outlook	Pessimistic: great powers locked in relentless security competition	Optimistic: cooperative view of human nature and a belief in progress	Agnostic: global prospect hinges on the content of prevailing ideas and values

who they are, and what others in the world are like—demonstrably can alter the world when these social constructions of international realties change (Barnet 2005; Adler 2002; Onuf 2002).

The Limitations of Constructivism

The most common criticism of constructivism concerns its explanation of change. If changes in ideas and discourses lead to behavioral changes within the state system, what accounts for the rise and fall of different ideas and discourses over time? How, when, and why do social structures of shared knowledge emerge? "Constructivists are good at describing change," writes political scientist Jack Snyder (2004, 61), "but they are weak on the material and institutional circumstances necessary to support the emergence of consensus about new values and ideas." Moreover, even if new values and ideas are not reflections of developments in the material world, critics charge that constructivists remain unclear about what nonmaterial factors lead certain ideas and discourses to become dominant while others fall by the wayside (Mearsheimer 1994/95, 42–43). In particular, they "downplay the individual psychological needs" that "shape the social construction of identities" (Levy 2003b, 273). "What is crucial," asserts Robert Jervis (2005, 18), "is not people's thinking, but the factors that drive it." Constructivists, he continues, have excessive faith in the ability of ideas that seem self-evident today to replicate and sustain themselves; however, future generations who live under different circumstances and who may think differently could easily reject these ideas. For constructivists, socially accepted ideas, norms, and values are linked to collective identities—stable, role-specific understandings and expectations about self (Wendt 1994). Although constructivists recognize that shared identities are not pre-given and can change over time, critics submit that constructivists cannot explain why and when they dissolve.

A related concern about constructivism is that it overemphasizes the role of social structures at the expense of the purposeful agents whose practices help create and change these structures (Checkel 1998, 340–342). According to Cynthia Weber (2001, 76–78), constructivism as exemplified in the work of Alexander Wendt (1999) reifies states as the authors or producers of international life; that is, it treats them as objects that already exist and says little about the "practices that produce states as producers." Although Wendtian constructivism calls our attention to the importance of the intersubjectively constituted structure of identities and interests that influence how states see themselves and behave, it does not offer an account of the practices that construct states themselves as producers of international anarchy and other features of world politics.

Despite these criticisms, constructivism remains a popular approach to the study of world politics. By highlighting the influence that socially constructed images of the world have on our interpretations of international events, and by making us aware of their inherent subjectivity, constructivism reminds us of the contingent nature of all knowledge and the inability of any theory of world politics to fully capture global complexities.

WHAT'S MISSING IN THEORIES OF WORLD POLITICS?

Although realism, liberalism, and constructivism dominate thinking about international relations in today's academic and policy communities, these schools of thought have been challenged. Two of the most significant critiques have come from radicalism and feminism.

The Radical Critique

For much of the twentieth century, socialism was the primary radical alternative to mainstream international relations theorizing. Although there are many strands of socialist thought, most have been influenced by Karl Marx's (1818–1883) argument that explaining events in contemporary world affairs requires understanding capitalism as a global phenomenon. Whereas realists emphasize state security, liberals accentuate individual freedom, and constructivists highlight ideas and identities, socialists focus on class conflict and the material interests embodied by each class (Doyle 1997).

"The history of all hitherto existing society," proclaim Marx and his coauthor Frièdrich Engels (1820–1895) in the *Communist Manifesto,* "is the history of class struggles." Capitalism, they argue, has given rise to two antagonistic classes: a ruling class (bourgeoisie) that owns the means of production, and a subordinate class (proletariat) that sells its labor, but receives little compensation. According to Marx and Engels, "The need of a constantly expanding market for its products chases the bourgeoisie over the whole surface of the globe." By expanding worldwide, the bourgeoisie gives "a cosmopolitan character to production and consumption in every country."

Vladimir Ilyich Lenin (1870–1924) extended Marx's analysis to the study of imperialism, which he interpreted as a stage in the development of capitalism where monopolies supplant free-market competition. Drawing from the work of British economist John Hobson (1858–1940), Lenin maintained that advanced capitalist states eventually face the twin problems of overproduction and under-consumption. They respond by seeking foreign markets and investments for their surplus goods and capital, and by dividing the world into spheres of influence that they can exploit. While his assertions have been heavily criticized on conceptual and empirical grounds (see Dougherty and Pfaltzgraff 2001, 437–442), the attention given to social classes and uneven development engendered several new waves of theorizing about capitalism as a global phenomenon.

One prominent example is dependency theory. As expressed in the writings of André Gunder Frank (1969), Amir Samin (1976), and others (see Dos Santos 1970; Cardoso and Faletto 1979), dependency theorists claimed that much of the poverty in Asia, Africa, and Latin America stemmed from the exploitative structure of the capitalist world economy. As they saw it, the economies of less-developed countries had become dependent upon exporting inexpensive raw materials and agricultural commodities to advanced industrial states, while simultaneously importing expensive manufactured goods from them. Raúl Prebisch, an Argentinian economist who directed the United Nations Economic Commission for Latin America, feared that these producers of primary products would find it difficult to develop, because the price of their products would fall over time relative to the price of manufactured goods. Dependency theory was criticized for recommending withdrawal from the world economy (T. Shannon 1989; also Packenham 1992), and was eventually superseded by efforts to trace the economic ascent and decline of individual countries as part of long-run, system-wide change.

World-system theory, which was influenced by both Marxist and dependency theorists, represents the most recent effort to interpret world politics in terms of an integrated capitalist division of labor (see Wallerstein 2005 and 1988; Chase-Dunn and Anderson 2005; Chase-Dunn 1989). The capitalist world economy, which emerged in sixteenth-century

Europe and ultimately expanded to encompass the entire globe, is viewed as containing three structural positions: a *core* (strong, well-integrated states whose economic activities are diversified and capital-intensive), a *periphery* (areas lacking strong state machinery and engaged in producing relatively few unfinished goods by unskilled, low-wage labor), and a *semi-periphery* (states embodying elements of both core and peripheral production). Within the core, a state may gain economic primacy by achieving productive, commercial, and financial superiority over its rivals. Primacy is difficult to sustain, however. The diffusion of technological innovations and the flow of capital to competitors, plus the massive costs of maintaining global order, all erode the dominant state's economic advantage. Thus in addition to underscoring the exploitation of the periphery by the core, world-system theory calls attention to the cyclical rise and fall of hegemonic core powers.

Whereas the various radical challenges to mainstream theorizing enhance our understanding of world politics by highlighting the roles played by corporations, transnational movements, and other nonstate actors, they overemphasize economic interpretations of international events and consequently omit other potentially important explanatory factors. According to feminist theorists, one such factor is gender.

The Feminist Critique

During the last quarter of the twentieth century, feminism began challenging conventional international relations theory. In particular, feminist theory attacked the exclusion of women in discussions about international affairs as well as the injustice and unequal treatment of women this prejudice caused. The mainstream literature on world politics dismissed the plight and contributions of women, treating differences in men's and women's status, beliefs, and behaviors as unimportant. As feminist theory evolved over time, it moved away from focusing on a history of discrimination and began to explore how gender identity shapes foreign policy decision making and how gendered hierarchies reinforced practices that perpetuated inequalities between men and women (see Tickner 2005 and 2002; Enloe 2004; Beckman and D'Amico 1994; Peterson and Runyan 1993).

Rather than conceiving of gender as the biological differences between men and women, feminists see gender as socially defined expectations regarding what it means to be masculine or feminine. Even though not all men and women fit these expectations, feminists assert that higher value is attributed in the political sphere to idealized masculine characteristics like domination, autonomy, and competition, which are then erroneously depicted as reflecting objective laws rooted in human nature (Tickner 1988). By treating this idealization as if it were grounded in universal laws of behavior, feminists insist that conventional international relations theories provide only a partial understanding of world politics.

Although all feminists stress the importance of gender in studying international relations, there are several contending schools of thought within feminist scholarship. Some feminists assert that on average there are no significant differences in the capabilities of men and women; others claim differences exist, with each gender being more capable than the other in certain endeavors; still others insist that the meaning ascribed to a person's gender is an arbitrary cultural construct that varies from one time or place to another (Goldstein 2002). Regardless of the position taken on the issue of gender differences, feminist scholars emphasize the relevance of women's experiences in international affairs and the contributions they have made. More than simply acknowledging the impact of female leaders such as Margaret Thatcher of Great Britain, Megawati Sukarnoputri of Indonesia, Golda Meir of Israel, Corazón Aquino of the Philippines, Angela Merkel of Germany, Christina Fernández de Kirchner of Argentina, or Michelle Bachelet of Chile, they urge us to examine events from the personal perspectives of the countless women who have been involved in international affairs as caregivers, grassroots activists, and participants in the informal labor force. "Women have never been *absent* in world politics," writes Franke Wilmer (2000). They have, for the most part, remained *"invisible* within the discourse conducted by men" about world politics.

One result of the feminist critique of conventional international relations theorizing has been a surge in research that uses gender as an explanatory variable when analyzing world politics. For example, recent studies have found that high levels of gender equality within countries are associated with low levels of interstate and intrastate armed conflict (Caprioli 2005; Melander 2005; Regan and Pasevicute 2003; Caprioli and Boyer 2001). Pointing to the results from these and other studies, feminists recommend that everyone who studies international politics "ask gender questions and be more aware of the gendered implications of global politics" (Tickner and Sjoberg 2007, 199).

FORECASTING THE GLOBAL FUTURE WITH THEORIES OF WORLD POLITICS

As we seek to understand the global future, we must recognize the limitations of our knowledge of world politics. The world is complex, and our understanding of its workings remains incomplete (see Controversy: Can Behavioral Science Advance the Study of World Politics?). As one scholar suggests, comprehending world politics is like trying to make sense of a disassembled jigsaw puzzle (Puchala 1994). Each piece shows a part of the whole picture, but it's unclear how they fit together. Some pieces depict a struggle for power among self-interested states; others reveal countries pooling their sovereignty to create a supranational union. Some pieces portray wrenching ethnonationalist conflicts; others reveal an absence of war between democracies. Some pieces show an upsurge in parochialism; others describe an emerging global civil society. As discussed in the pervious chapter, one of the difficulties of forecasting the global future is that disintegrative trends are splintering the political landscape at the very time that integrative trends are shrinking the planet. "Whereas some countries seem mired in a dog-eat-dog world of international anarchy and self-help, others appear to live in a world of international institutions and interdependence.

Theories are like maps. They guide us in fitting the seemingly incompatible pieces of complex puzzles together to reveal the complete picture. But just as some maps are more accurate than others, some theories are more useful than others. "There is nothing so practical as a good theory," psychologist Kurt Lewin once remarked. But what makes a "good" theory? The following are some of the criteria that social scientists use when judging the quality of a theory (see Van Evera 1997):

- *Clarity.* A good theory is clearly framed: Its concepts are precisely defined, cause and effect relationships governing observed patterns are adequately specified, and the argument underpinning those hypothesized relationships is logically coherent.
- *Parsimony.* A good theory simplifies reality: It focuses on an important phenomenon and contains all of the factors relevant for explaining it without becoming excessively complex.
- *Explanatory power.* A good theory has empirical support: It deepens our understanding of a phenomenon, and explains things about it that are not accounted for by rival theories.
- *Prescriptive richness.* A good theory provides policy recommendations: It describes how problems can be avoided or mitigated through timely countermeasures.
- *Falsifiability.* A good theory can be proven wrong: It indicates what evidence would refute its claims.

Although realism, liberalism, and constructivism are the dominant ways of thinking about world politics today, none of these theories completely satisfies all of the criteria listed above. Recall that realism is frequently criticized for relying upon ambiguous concepts, liberalism is often derided for making naive policy recommendations based on idealistic assumptions, and constructivism is charged with an inability to explain change. Moreover, as the challenges mounted by radicalism and feminism suggest, these three mainstream theories overlook seemingly important aspects of world politics, which limits their explanatory power.

Despite these drawbacks, each has strengths in highlighting certain kinds of international events and foreign policy behaviors. As international relations scholar and former U.S. policymaker Joseph Nye (2005, 8) notes, "When I was working in Washington and helping formulate American foreign policies as an assistant secretary in the State Department and the Pentagon, I found myself borrowing from all three types of thinking: realism, liberalism, and constructivism. I found them all helpful, though in different ways and in different circumstances." Because we lack a single overarching theory able to account for all facets of world politics, we will draw on realist, liberal, and constructivist thought in subsequent chapters. Moreover, we will supplement them with insights from radicalism and feminism, where these theoretical traditions can best help to interpret the topic covered.

CHAPTER SUMMARY

- A theory is a set of interrelated propositions that explains why certain events occurred. Three overarching theories have dominated the study of world politics: realism, liberalism, and constructivism.

- Several strains of realist theory exist. At the risk of oversimplification, the realist worldview can be summarized as follows:

  1. People are by nature selfish, competitive, and domineering. Changing human nature is a Utopian aspiration.

  2. The international system is anarchic. Without the support and protection of a higher authority, states strive for autarchy and engage in self-help.

  3. Under such conditions, international politics is a struggle for power, "a war of all against all," as the sixteenth-century English philosopher Thomas Hobbes put it. The primary obligation of every state in this environment—the goal to which all other objectives should be subordinated—is to follow its "national interest" defined in terms of acquiring power.

  4. Security is a function of power, and power is a function of military capability. States should procure the military capability to deter or subdue any potential rival. They should not entrust their security to the good will of allies or to the promises of international law and organizations.

  5. International stability results from maintaining a balance of power among contending states.

- Various forms of liberal theory also exist. The liberal worldview can be summarized as follows:

  1. People are capable of collaboration and mutual aid. Malicious behavior is the product of an environment that encourages people to act selfishly. Reason enables people to change the conditions they live under, and therefore makes progress possible.

  2. The first important change needed to reduce the probability of war is to promote national self-determination and democratic governance. The domestic characteristics of states vary, and these variations affect state behavior. Democracies are more peaceful than autocratic governments.

  3. The second important change is to promote international commerce. Economic interdependence leads states to develop mechanisms to resolve conflict, which reinforces the material incentive to avoid wars that inhibit business opportunities.

  4. The third change is to replace secret diplomacy and the shifting, rival military alliances characteristic of balance-of-power politics with international institutions based on collective security. Competitive, self-interested behavior need not be arbitrary and disorderly. By encouraging reciprocity, reducing

CONTROVERSY: Can Behavioral Science Advance the Study of World Politics?

How should scholars analyze world politics? Unfortunately, there is no simple answer to this question. The field of international relations is torn between differing conceptions of what the study of world politics should encompass and how its subject matter should be investigated. Traditionally, scholars tried to understand some unique political event or sequence of events by submerging themselves in archival records, legal documents, or field work related to the phenomenon under investigation. Relying on experience and wisdom to evaluate this material, they typically presented their insights in a narrative that asserted: "Based on *my judgment* of the information that I have examined, I conclude X, Y, and Z."

Dissatisfied with the reliability of a research methodology that depended so heavily on the personal judgment and intuitive information-gathering procedures of a single individual, various scholars in the 1960s promoted a movement known as **behavioralism**, which had as its goals the application of the scientific method and rigorous quantitative techniques to the study of world politics (see J. Singer 1968). In brief, behavioralists assumed that a world exists independent of our minds; this world has an order that is open to human understanding; recurring patterns within it can be discovered; and reproducible evidence about these patterns can be acquired by carefully formulating and stringently testing **hypotheses** inferred from theories devised to explain how the world works. What made behavioralism innovative was its systematic, empirical approach to the process of inquiry, replacing ad hoc, idiosyncratic procedures for information gathering with explicit, replicable procedures for data making, and supplanting the appeal to the "expert" opinion of authorities with a deliberate, controlled method of data analysis. Behavioralism attempted to overcome the tendency of many traditional researchers to select historical facts and cases to fit their preexisting conceptions about international behavior. Instead, all available data were examined. By being as clear and precise as possible, behavioralists asserted that other researchers could determine how a given study was conducted, evaluate the significance of its findings, and gradually build a cumulative body of intersubjectively transmissible knowledge.

A variety of criticisms have been leveled against behavioralism over the past few decades. One of the most common draws from the work of the German sociologist Max Weber (1864–1920), who believed that the mode of explanation used in the social sciences was different from that in the physical sciences. Many people influenced by Weber contend that unlike physicists who do not analyze sentient beings engaged in purposeful behavior, social scientists face perplexing questions about why their subjects *chose* to act in a certain way and what meaning they ascribed to their actions. Not burdened with the need to consider how molecules may or may not choose to respond to external stimuli, physicists appeal to causal laws that hold true across time and space in order to explain such things as why gasses become liquids at certain temperatures. But to explain things like why a national leader chooses to respond in a particular way to some external stimulus, social scientists must understand the reasons behind the actions that were taken. This difference between the physical and social sciences, so the argument goes, makes it difficult for the student of world politics to emulate the physicist when conducting empirical research. Instead of using quantitative techniques to search for law-like regularities that span the universe of international phenomena, this school of thought urges the social scientist to employ qualitative, interpretative methods to figure out the intentions of particular actors at specific moments in time.

Another prominent criticism of applying the scientific method to world politics comes from postmodernism, a label commonly given to a diverse group of thinkers influenced by French philosophers Jean-Francois Lyotard (1924–1998), Michel Foucault (1926–1984), and Jacques Derrida (1930–2004), among others. Premised on the belief that knowledge is only true relative to some situation or historical condition, postmodernists contend that it is impossible to analyze world politics from an objective, value-free point of view. Because no one can discover transcendent truths, scholars are exhorted to unmask the hidden meanings in prevailing texts and discourses, question the adequacy of the worldviews they espouse, and examine how these accounts of world politics are able to dominate and silence others.

Most scholars today remain motivated by the quest to build theories of world politics that can be used to describe, explain, and predict occurrences in world politics. What do you think about how they should go about this task? Is the scientific analysis of international behavior a reasonable undertaking? If so, can the research techniques of the physical sciences be applied to the study of world politics? Or do the social sciences require a different approach to inquiry that gives more weight to the intentions of human agents? Alternatively, are both causal and interpretative explanations of world politics impossible? Do you concur with postmodernists who argue that any attempt to apply the scientific method to international behavior is misguided because there is no singular, objective reality to study?

uncertainty, and shaping expectations, international institutions help states coordinate their behavior and achieve collective gains.

5. World politics is increasingly shaped by transnational networks, in which states are enmeshed in complex webs that include multinational corporations, international organizations, and nongovernmental organizations.

- Constructivist theories of world politics are united by a common focus on the importance of ideas and discourse. Their worldview can be summarized as follows:

1. The fundamental structures of world politics are social; they acquire meaning through shared human understandings and expectations, and are sustained by recurrent social practices.

2. These collective, intersubjective structures define the identities of international actors.

3. Social identities constitute actors' interests and shape their actions by stipulating what behavior is appropriate in a given situation

4. International actors acquire agency through language; rules and other forms of discourse make the world what it is.
5. Agents and structures are mutually constituted: Agents shape society, and society shapes agents through reciprocal interaction.

- The explanation of world politics cannot be reduced to any one simple yet compelling account. While realism, liberalism, and constructivism each explain certain types of international phenomena well, none of them adequately captures all facets of world politics. As a result, rival interpretations of world politics have periodically challenged these mainstream theories. In recent years, theorists belonging to the radical and feminist schools of thought have voiced some of the most prominent criticisms of conventional international relations theory.

KEY TERMS

absolute gains	high politics	power
behavioralism	hypotheses	relative gains
collective security	international regime	self-help
complex	low politics	theory
interdependence	moral hazard	transnational relations
consequentialism	norms	zero-sum game

SUGGESTED READINGS

Baldwin, David A. *Theories of International Relations*. Burlington, VT: Ashgate, 2008.

Chernoff, Fred, *Theory and Metatheory in International Relations: Concepts and Contending Accounts*. New York: Palgrave-Macmillan, 2007.

Dougherty, James E., and Robert L. Pfaltzgraff, Jr., *Contending Theories of International Relations*, 5th ed. New York: Addison Wesley-Longman, 2001.

Dunne, Tim, Milja Kurki, and Steve Smith, eds. *International Relations Theories: Discipline and Diversity*. Oxford: Oxford University Press, 2007.

Elman, Colin, and Miriam Fendius Elman, eds., *Progress in International Relations Theory: Appraising the Field*. Cambridge, MA: MIT Press, 2003.

CRITICAL THINKING QUESTIONS

A vigorous debate between neorealists and neoliberals has dominated mainstream international relations scholarship for the past twenty-five years (Lamy 2008). The issues dividing the two camps center on the different assumptions they make about the following topics (Baldwin 1993, 4–8):

- *The Nature and Consequences of Anarchy.* Whereas everyone recognizes that the international system is anarchical because effective institutions for global governance are lacking, neorealists argue that anarchy may be preferable to the restraints of world government. Neoliberals see anarchy as a big problem that can be reformed through the creation of strong global institutions.
- *International Cooperation.* Although neorealists and neoliberals agree that cooperation is possible, neorealists think it is difficult to sustain while neoliberals believe it can be expected because collaboration yields rewards that reduce the temptation to compete.
- *Relative versus Absolute Gains.* Neorealists believe that the desire to get ahead of competitors by obtaining relative gains is the primary motive behind state behavior, whereas neoliberals believe states are motivated by the search for opportunities that will produce absolute gains for all parties.
- *Priority of State Goals.* Neorealists stress national security as the most important goal pursued by states. Neoliberals think states place a greater priority on economic welfare.
- *Intentions versus Capabilities.* Neorealists maintain that the distribution of states' capabilities is the primary determinant of their behavior and international outcomes. Neoliberals maintain that states' intentions, information, and ideals are more influential than the distribution of capabilities.
- *Institutions and Regimes.* Neorealists argue that institutions such as the United Nations are arenas where states carry out their competition for influence. Neoliberals believe that international institutions create norms that are binding, on their members and that change patterns of international politics.

How significant are these differences between neorealists and neoliberals? Which assumptions do you think are the most accurate for interpreting twenty-first-century world politics? Are there any important issues that are left out of this debate?

The End of History?

FRANCIS FUKUYAMA

The triumph of the West, of the Western idea, is evident first of all in the total exhaustion of viable systematic alternatives to Western liberalism. In the past decade, there have been unmistakable changes in the intellectual climate of the world's two largest communist countries, and the beginnings of significant reform movements in both. But this phenomenon extends beyond high politics and it can be seen also in the ineluctable spread of consumerist Western culture in such diverse contexts as the peasants' markets and color television sets now omnipresent throughout China, the cooperative restaurants and clothing stores opened in the past year in Moscow, the Beethoven piped into Japanese department stores, and the rock music enjoyed alike in Prague, Rangoon, and Tehran.

What we may be witnessing is not just the end of the Cold War, or the passing of a particular period of post-war history, but the end of history as such: that is, the end point of mankind's ideological evolution and the universalization of Western liberal democracy as the final form of human government.

Have we in fact reached the end of history? Are there, in other words, any fundamental "contradictions" in human life that cannot be resolved in the context of modern liberalism, that would be resolvable by an alternative political-economic structure? If we accept the idealist premises laid out above, we must seek an answer to this question in the realm of ideology and consciousness. Our task is not to answer exhaustively the challenges to liberalism promoted by every crackpot messiah around the world, but only those that are embodied in important social or political forces and movements, and which are therefore part of world history. For our purposes, it matters very little what strange thoughts occur to people in Albania or Burkina Faso, for we are interested in what one could in some sense call the common ideological heritage of mankind.

In the past century, there have been two major challenges to liberalism, those of fascism and of communism. The former saw the political weakness, materialism, anomie, and lack of community of the West as fundamental contradictions in liberal societies that could only be resolved by a strong state that forged a new "people" on the basis of national excessiveness. Fascism was destroyed as a living ideology by World War II. This was a defeat, of course, on a very material level, but it amounted to a defeat of the idea as well. What destroyed fascism as an idea was not universal moral revulsion against it, since plenty of people were willing to endorse the idea as long as it seemed the wave of the future, but its lack of success. After the war, it seemed to most people that German fascism as well as its other European and Asian variants were bound to self-destruct. There was no material reason why new fascist movements could not have sprung up again after the war in other locales, but for the fact that expansionist ultranationalism, with its promise of unending conflict leading to disastrous military defeat, had completely lost its appeal. The ruins of the Reich chancellory as well as the atomic bombs dropped on Hiroshima and Nagasaki killed this ideology on the level of consciousness as well as materially, and all of the proto-fascist movements spawned by the German and Japanese examples like the Peronist movement in Argentina or Subhas Chandra Bose's Indian National Army withered after the war.

The ideological challenge mounted by the other great alternative to liberalism, communism, was far more serious. The appeal of communism in the developed Western world, it is safe to say, is lower today than any time since the end of the First World War. This can be measured in any number of ways: in the declining membership and electoral pull of the major European communist parties, and their overtly revisionist programs; in the corresponding electoral success of conservative parties from Britain and Germany to the United States and Japan which are unabashedly pro-market and antistatist; and in an intellectual climate whose most "advanced" members no longer believe that bourgeois society is something that ultimately needs to be overcome. This is to say that the opinions of progressive intellectuals in Western countries are not deeply pathological in any number of ways. But those who believe that the future must inevitably be socialist tend to be very old, or very marginal to the real political discourse of their societies.

One may argue that the socialist alternative was never terribly plausible for the North Atlantic world, and was sustained for the last several decades primarily by its success outside of this region. But it is precisely in the non-European world that one is not struck by the occurrence of major ideological transformations. Surely the most remarkable changes have occurred in Asia. Due to the strength and adaptability of the indigenous cultures there, Asia became a battleground for a variety of imported Western ideologies early in this century. Liberalism in Asia was a very weak reed in the period after World War I; it is easy today to forget how gloomy Asia's political future looked as recently as ten or fifteen years ago. It is easy to forget as well how momentous the outcome of Asian ideological struggles seemed for world political development as a whole.

The first Asian alternative to liberalism to be decisively defeated was the fascist one represented by Imperial Japan. Japanese fascism (like its German version) was defeated by the force of American arms in the Pacific war, and liberal democracy was imposed on Japan by a victorious United States. Western capitalism and political liberalism when transplanted to Japan were adapted and transformed by the Japanese in such a way as to be scarcely recognizable. Many Americans are now aware that Japanese industrial organization is very different from that prevailing in the United States or Europe, and it is questionable what relationship the factional maneuvering that takes place with the governing Liberal Democratic Party bears to democracy. Nonetheless, the very fact that the essential elements of economic and political liberalism have been so successfully grafted onto uniquely Japanese traditions and institutions guarantees their survival in the long run. More important is the contribution that Japan has become both a symbol and an underpinning of the universal homogenous state. V.S. Naipaul traveling in Khomeini's Iran shortly after the revolution noted the omnipresent signs advertising the products of Sony, Hitachi, and JVC, whose appeal remained virtually irresistible and gave the lie to the regime's pretensions of restoring a state based on the rule of the *Shariah*. Desire for access to the consumer culture, created in large measure by Japan, has played a crucial role in fostering the spread of economic liberalism throughout Asia, and hence in promoting political liberalism as well.

The economic success of the other newly industrializing countries (NICs) in Asia following on the example of Japan is by now a familiar story. What is important from a Hegelian standpoint is that political liberalism has been following economic liberalism, more slowly than many had hoped but with seeming inevitability. Here again we see the victory of the idea of the universal homogenous state. South Korea had developed into a modern, urbanized society with an increasingly large and well-educated middle class that could not possibly be isolated from the larger democratic trends around them. Under these circumstances it seemed intolerable to a large part of this population that it should be ruled by an anachronistic military regime while Japan, only a decade or so ahead in economic terms, had parliamentary institutions for over forty years. Even the former socialist regime in Burma, which for so many decades existed in dismal isolation from the larger trends dominating Asia, was buffeted in the past year by pressures to liberalize both its economy and political system. It is said that unhappiness with strongman Ne Win began when a senior Burmese officer went to Singapore for medical treatment and broke down crying when he saw how far socialist Burma had been left behind by its Asian neighbors.

But the power of the liberal idea would seem much less impressive if it had not infected the largest and oldest culture in Asia, China. The simple existence of communist China created an alternative pole of ideological attraction, and as such constituted a threat to liberalism. But the past fifteen years have seen an almost total discrediting of Marxism-Leninism as an economic system. Beginning with the famous third plenum of the Tenth Central Committee in 1978, the Chinese Communist party set about decollectivizing agriculture for the 800 million Chinese who still lived in the country-side. The role of the state in agriculture was reduced to that of a tax collector, while production of consumer goods was sharply increased in order to give peasants a taste of the universal homogenous state and thereby an incentive to work. The reform doubled Chinese grain output in only five years, and in the process created for Deng Xiao-ping a solid political base from which he was able to extend the reform to other parts of the economy. Economic statistics do not begin to describe the dynamism, initiative, and openness evident in China since the reform began.

China could not now be described in any way as a liberal democracy. At present, no more than 20 percent of its economy has been marketed, and most importantly it continues to be ruled by a self-appointed Communist party which has given no hint of wanting to devolve power. Deng has made none of Gorbachev's promises regarding democratization of the political system and there is no Chinese equivalent of *glasnost*. The Chinese leadership has in fact been much more circumspect in criticizing Mao and Maoism than Gorbachev with respect to Brezhnev and Stalin, and the regime continues to pay lip service to Marxism-Leninism as its ideological underpinning. But anyone familiar with the outlook and behavior of the new technocratic elite now governing China knows the Marxism and ideological principle have become virtually irrelevant as guides to policy, and that bourgeois consumerism has a real meaning in that country for the first time since the revolution. The various slowdowns in the pace of reform, the campaigns against "spiritual pollution" and crackdowns on political dissent are more properly seen as tactical adjustments made in the process of managing what is an extraordinarily difficult political transition. By ducking the question of political reform while putting the economy on a new footing, Deng has managed to avoid the breakdown of authority that has accompanied Gorbachev's *perestroika*. Yet the pull of the liberal idea continues to be very strong as economic power devolves and the economy becomes more open to the outside world. There are currently over 20,000 Chinese students studying in the U.S. and other Western countries, almost all of them of children of the Chinese elite. It is hard to believe that when they return home to run the country they will be content for China to be the only country in Asia unaffected by the larger democratizing threat. The student demonstrations in Beijing that broke out first in December 1986 and recurred recently on the occasion of Hu Yao-bang's death were only the beginning of what will inevitably be mounting pressure for change in the political system as well.

What is important about China from the standpoint of world history is not the present state of the reform or even its future prospects. The central issue is the fact that the People's Republic of China can no longer act as a beacon for illiberal forces around the world, whether they be guerrillas in some Asian jungle or middle class students in Paris. Maoism, rather than being the pattern for Asia's future, became an anachronism, and it was the mainland Chinese who in fact were decisively influenced by the prosperity and dynamism of their overseas co-ethnics—the ironic ultimate victory of Taiwan. [...]

What has happened in the four years since Gorbachev's coming to power is a revolutionary assault on the most fundamental institutions and principles of Stalinism, and their replacement by other principles which do not amount to liberalism *per se* but whose only connecting thread is liberalism. This is most evident in the economic sphere, where the reform economists around Gorbachev have become steadily more radical in their support for free markets, to the point where some like Nikolai Shmelev do not mind being compared in public to Milton Friedman. There is a virtual consensus among the currently dominant school of Soviet economists now that central planning and the command system of allocation are the root cause of economic inefficiency, and that if the Soviet system is ever to heal itself, it must permit free and decentralized decision-making with respect to investment, labor, and prices. After a couple of initial years of ideological confusion, theses principles have finally been incorporated into policy with the promulgation of new laws on enterprise autonomy, cooperatives, and finally in 1988 on lease arrangements and family farming.

In the political sphere, the proposed changes to the Soviet constitution, legal system, and party rules amount to much less than the establishment of a liberal state. Gorbachev has spoken of democratization primarily in the sphere of internal party affairs, and has shown little intention of ending the Communist party's monopoly of power; indeed, the political reform seeks to legitimize and therefore strengthen the CPSU's rule. Nonetheless, the general principles underlying many of the reforms—that the "people" should be truly responsible for their own affairs, that higher political bodies should be answerable to lower ones, and not vice versa, that the rule of law should prevail over arbitrary police actions, with separation of powers and an independent judiciary, that there should be legal protection for property rights, the need for open discussion of public issues and the right of public dissent, the empowering of the Soviets as a forum in which the whole Soviet people can participate, and of a political culture that is more tolerant and pluralistic—come from a source fundamentally alien to the USSR's Marxist-Leninist tradition, even if they are incompletely articulated and poorly implemented in practice. [...]

The Soviet Union could in no way be described as a liberal or democratic country now, nor do I think that it is terribly likely that *perestroika* will succeed such that the label will be thinkable any time in the near future. But at the end of history it is not necessary that all societies become successful liberal societies, merely that they end their ideological pretensions of representing different and higher forms of human society. And in this respect I believe that something very important has happened in the Soviet Union in the past few years: the criticisms of the Soviet system sanctioned by Gorbachev have been so thorough and devastating that there is very little chance of going back to either Stalinism or Brezhnevism, in any simple way. Gorbachev has finally permitted people to say what they had privately understood for many years, namely, that the magical incantation of Marxism-Leninism were nonsense, that Soviet socialism was not superior to the West in any respect but was in fact a monumental failure. The conservative opposition in the USSR, consisting both of simple workers afraid of unemployment and inflation and of party officials fearful of losing their jobs and privileges, is outspoken and may be strong enough to force Gorbachev's ouster in the next few years. But what both groups desire is tradition, order, and authority; they manifest no deep commitment to Marxism-Leninism, except insofar as they have invested much of their own lives in it. For authority to be restored in the Soviet Union after Gorbachev's demolition work, it must be on the basis of some new and vigorous ideology which has not yet appeared on the horizon.

If we admit for the moment that the fascist and communist challenges to liberalism are dead, are there any other ideological competitors left? Or put another way, are there contradictions in liberal society beyond that of class that are not resolvable? Two possibilities suggest themselves, those of religion and nationalism.

The rise of religious fundamentalism in recent years within the Christian, Jewish, and Muslim traditions has been widely noted. One is inclined to say that the revival of religion in some way attests to a broad unhappiness with the impersonality and spiritual vacuity of liberal consumerist societies. Yet while the emptiness at the core of ideology—indeed, a flaw that one does not need the perspective of religion to recognize—it is not at all clear that it is remediable through politics. Modern liberalism itself was historically a consequence of the weakness of religiously-based societies which, failing to agree on the nature of the good life, could not provide even the minimal preconditions of peace and stability. In the contemporary world only Islam has offered a theocratic state as a political alternative to both liberalism and communism. But the doctrine has little appeal for non-Muslims, and it is hard to believe that the movement will take on any universal significance. Other less organized religious impulses have been successfully satisfied within the sphere of personal life that is permitted in liberal societies.

The other major "contradiction" potentially unresolvable by liberalism is the one posed by nationalism and other forms of racial and ethic consciousness. It is certainly true that a very large degree of conflict since the Battle of Jena has had its roots in nationalism. Two cataclysmic world wars in this century have been spawned by the nationalism of the developed world in various guises, and if those passions have been muted to a certain extent in postwar Europe, they are still extremely powerful in the Third World. Nationalism has been a threat to liberalism historically in Germany, and continues to be one in isolated parts of "post-historical" Europe like Northern Ireland.

But it is not clear that nationalism represents an irreconcilable contradiction in the heart of liberalism. In the first place, nationalism is not one single phenomenon but several, ranging from mild cultural nostalgia to the highly organized and elaborately articulated doctrine of National Socialism. Only systematic nationalism of the latter sort can qualify as a formal ideology on the level of liberalism or communism. The vast majority of the world's nationalist movements do not have a political program beyond the negative desire of independence from some other group or people, and do not offer anything like a comprehensive agenda for socioeconomic organization. As such, they are compatible with doctrines and ideologies that do offer such agendas. While they may constitute a source of conflict for liberal societies, this conflict does not arise from liberalism itself so much as from the fact that the liberalism in question is incomplete. Certainly a great deal of the world's ethnic and nationalist tension can be explained in terms of peoples who are forced to live in unrepresentative political systems that they have not chosen.

While it is impossible to rule out the sudden appearance of new ideologies or previously unrecognized in liberal societies, then, the present world seems to confirm that the fundamental principles of sociopolitical organization have not advanced terribly far since 1806. Many of the wars and revolutions fought since that time have been undertaken in the name of ideologies which claimed to be more advanced than liberalism, but whose pretensions were ultimately unmasked by history. In the meantime, they have helped to spread the universal homogenous state to the point where it could have a significant effect on the overall character of international relations. [...]

This does not by any means imply the end of international conflict *per se*. For the world at that point would be divided between a part that was historical and a part that was post historical. Conflict between states still in history, and between those states and those at the end of history, would still be possible. There would still be a high and perhaps rising level of ethnic and nationalist violence, since those are impulses incompletely played out, even in parts of the post historical world. Palestinians and Kurds, Sikhs and Tamils, Irish Catholics and Walloons, Armenians and Azeris, will continue to have their unresolved grievances. This implies that terrorism and wars of national liberation will continue to be an important item on the international agenda. But large-scale conflict must involve large states still caught in the grip of history, and they are what appear to be passing from the scene.

The end of history will be a very sad time. The struggle for recognition, the willingness to risk one's life for a purely abstract goal, the worldwide ideological struggle that called forth daring, courage, imagination, and idealism, will be replaced by economic calculation, the endless solving of technical problems, environmental concerns, and the satisfaction of sophisticated consumer demands. In the post historical period there will be neither art nor philosophy, just the perpetual caretaking of the museum of human history. I can feel in myself, and see in others around me, a powerful nostalgia for the time when history existed. Such nostalgia, in fact, will continue to fuel competition and conflict even in the post historical world for some time to come. Even though I recognize its inevitability, I have the most ambivalent feelings for the civilization that has been created in Europe since 1945, with its north Atlantic and Asian offshoots. Perhaps this very prospect of centuries of boredom at the end of history will serve to get history started once again.

Chinese-American Hegemonic Competition in East Asia

A New Cold War or Into the Arms of America?[1]

KEVIN COONEY

INTRODUCTION

The primary task of this chapter will be to examine the hegemonic competition between the United States and China in East Asia. While the United States and the Soviet Union strived to keep their distance (economically and militarily) from each other during the Cold War, the hegemonic competition between the United States and China is remarkable for its all-out economic engagement between the two. At the same time these two nations are preparing their militaries for conflict with each other. When thinking about the Sino-American relationship one could easily get the picture of two men hugging each other in "friendship" with knives poised at each other's back waiting for the other to make a wrong move. Each side needs the other; neither trusts the other.

Examining this intricate engagement between rivals will be no simple task as nothing ever happens in a vacuum, and the bilateral Sino-American relationship is no exception. The relationship is very complex with numerous variables outside the control of either nation. The politics, geography, resources (and the lack thereof), economics, and history of the nations of East Asia all play a role in shaping the policy decisions of Beijing and Washington toward each other. Furthermore, the overall global geopolitical situation provides both opportunities and constraints for both nations.

Before beginning with the analysis an explanation of some of the fundamental assumptions in this chapter is needed. The first and most important is the rejection of the conventional wisdom that the United States is in decline especially vis-á-vis China. This

Kevin J. Cooney, "Chinese–American Hegemonic Competition in East Asia: A New Cold War or Into the Arms of America?," from *The Rise of China and International Security*, pp. 38–58. Copyright © 2009 by Taylor & Francis Group. Permission to reprint granted by the publisher.

Chinese-American Hegemonic Competition in East Asia | 133

notion is flat out rejected as having no empirical basis in fact when one examines the data in the overall global geopolitical and economic contexts. Furthermore, the data would indicate that overall American military power along with its economic power are not only not in decline, but rather that they are still in ascendancy. The global discourse about the "rise of China" (whether one views it positively or negatively) results in a false impression that a hegemonic shift is about to take place. It is not. This hegemonic shift argument fails to account for the overall global political and economic context.[2] This chapter will present the case that a hegemonic shift is not likely in the near future and that it is only likely in the long term (100 plus years). Evelyn Goh in the next chapter takes the middle range approach by seeing it as a being at least 50-plus years into the future.

This is not to imply that China is not rising; it is in fact rising at a spectacular rate. China is narrowing the gap between itself and the rest of the world. The problem for those that see a hegemonic shift in the process is that neither American military nor economic power are in decline. As will be shown in detail throughout the chapter China's rise will continue but not necessarily at the expense of American economic or military power. Moreover, the rise of China is likely to fuel American ascendancy rather than hasten its decline. This argument for American ascendancy will run parallel to the argument on the rise of China throughout the chapter.

The organization of the chapter will take the following form. First we will examine the "Great China Question" as to the actions and intentions of China toward the United States, East Asia, and globally. This will be followed by an examination of United States policy toward China. The final section will briefly look at how the nations of Asia, both American allies and non-allies alike, are hedging their bets by engaging China economically, while retaining the option of running "into the arms of America"[3] should China prove to be an aggressor nation.

The Great China question

There is a cartoon with Uncle Sam on stage and a hook reaching out to remove him while China waits to the side for its time on stage. The caption reads, "Your 15 minutes are almost up Sammy." China is seen as a nation waiting in the wings to succeed the United States as the dominant global hegemon. If China is a potential threat to American global domination then the fundamental questions of Asian Security (and of global security in general) are:

- What are China's true intentions?
- Is China a growing hegemon that will return the world to a bipolar system?
- Will China be an aggressor nation balanced against United States hyper power?
- Will China be seen as a threat by and to Asia as well as America and its principal ally in the region, Japan?

- Or is China simply a developing nation, as it claims, that is peacefully expanding its power base to protect its own interests?

For American foreign and security policymakers, there is currently no greater question that needs to be answered.

The current war on terror is a known factor for American policy. Terrorism is a clear and present danger to America and its allies; however, China is a possible future threat to America. Prudence and realism would dictate that the United States prepares for an aggressor China. Idealism on the other hand, suggests that the United States (and the region) should work with China and try to engage China politically and economically in order to encourage the peaceful growth of China politically, militarily, and economically. So what is the United States doing? In many ways it is doing both, under the current administration of George W. Bush. It is prioritizing the more prudent and cautious realist hard line quietly while encouraging the engagement of China economically and to a lesser extent diplomatically. The problem with this policy is that it leads to schizophrenic perceptions of American policy which are justified. The United States is economically heavily investing itself in China as rapidly as possible. This economic investment ties China's future success to the United States and vice versa.

At the same time, America is politically engaging China in disputes over the trade imbalance, the value of the Yuan, and other economic issues in a protectionist way. It is also continuing to challenge China on its human rights record. Concurrently, the American military is preparing for a future where China is the enemy. In its latest report to Congress on the Military Power of the People's Republic of China 2006,[4] the Department of Defense questions China's intentions. It notes that China's leaders have "failed to explain" in an "adequate" way the rationale behind their many recent arms purchases that appear to be targeting the United States military.[5] This report to Congress is then used to justify American military expenditures to counter the growing "China Threat" to American security.

When one looks at all of these policies individually the schizophrenia of American policy is obvious. It would seem to be that the American Treasury, Commerce, Defense, and State Departments are all reading from different scripts or are at least not on the same page. The critics of the George W. Bush Administration (of which there are legions) see this as one further example of his incompetence. However, when one looks at the Administration's policy from the macro point of view, one can see a level of coherence that is not evident at first when looking at the individual policies. The Bush Administration is protecting American interests at all levels. It is engaging China in such a way that China will have a hard time separating itself from American interests. If China's interests are America's interests and vice versa, the chances of conflict are greatly reduced. However, it is not in America's interests to be politically or economically bullied or to be challenged militarily.

The Bush Administration is in many ways continuing the policies of the administrations of his father and Bill Clinton which was to keep China guessing as to American intentions. American policy, it would seem, is to "walk softly, but carry a big stick" as Teddy Roosevelt once said. In many ways the current Bush Administration is letting the market decide China's future intentions—the market being the global capitalist economic system that China has invested itself so heavily in. President Bush's policy is thus to engage China politically and economically while continuing to protect American interests in both economic and military hegemony. In sum, current American policy is hoping that China will have too much at stake to become an aggressor nation.

Only time will tell whether this is the best policy or not, however the policy does have some very real risks. The next section will look at these risks for both the United States and China.

Strategically speaking

Strategic theory dictates that a nation never wants to put itself in a position of making itself a tempting target for an aggressor state. There are two ways to make a state a tempting target. The first and more obvious one is to unilaterally disarm to the point of weakness. An aggressor state would see the weak state as a tempting target or a target of opportunity for expansion, domination, or pre-emptive neutralization. The second way a state can make itself a target of aggression is to grow its military capabilities to a level that make it a potential threat to the more powerful state, thus potentially causing the more powerful state to pre-emptively attack it out of its own security concerns. Examples of this currently are China and North Korea, with Japan and the United States being the more powerful states. The East Asian military status quo is currently acceptable to the United States and its principle ally in the region, Japan. However, the military build-up in China could alter the balance of power and will likely cause Japan and the United States to pursue a more aggressive policy toward China with the possible (though unlikely) result being conventional or (in worst case) nuclear conflict.

China is in many ways counting on American greed for cheap products to avoid a new cold war while it builds the People's Liberation Army (PLA) into a modern military force that can compete with the US military at least regionally if not eventually globally. China is hoping to build up its military capacity to the point of advantage or parity with the United States while continuing to trade with the United States at a large surplus partially helped by its artificially weak currency. China hopes to put the United States in a position where the latter cannot afford militarily or economically to defend Taiwan, Japan, or any other imperial aspirations the former has in East Asia.

The United States on the other hand is hoping to keep China engaged economically to the point that the latter is economically too dependent on the Western markets to risk economic sanctions and the resulting collapse of its economy by invading Taiwan or taking a military action in any other state in Asia. In many ways the United States is counting on China's greed for more profits and growth to keep it from becoming more aggressive. However, China appears to be crossing the line to being a true threat to both America and the region, as the political leadership of both major political parties in Washington see China as a growing threat. China seems to be announcing to the world through its actions (not words) that it is planning to engage the United States militarily in the future. Probably not in the near future, but someday in the future China plans to be America's military enemy and is preparing its military for that day. As former CIA Director R. James Woolsey put it, "China is pursuing a national strategy of domination of the energy markets and strategic dominance of the western Pacific."[6] Cragg Hines in an editorial for the Houston Chronicle described the problem based on a conversation he had with a former American policymaker:

> It's the "notion of tectonic plates shifting" the geopolitics of the region and the world, said Randy Schriver, who until recently was deputy assistant secretary of State for East Asia and Pacific affairs. We are in danger of a steady but discernible drift into a strategic rivalry.[7]

China's military modernization is not a recent phenomenon. The Chinese military and political establishments were truly shocked during the First Gulf War when the United States so quickly and easily defeated Saddam Hussein's battle-tested Iraqi Army including the Republican Guard. Only after the war did China come to recognize that the most recent Revolution in Military Affairs (RMA) had occurred and that China needed its own military modernization and internal RMA. This recognition can be seen throughout Chinese military journals in the few years following the 1991 Persian Gulf War. Previously China had counted on its own sheer numerical superiority in manpower to challenge and intimidate the United States from any hostile action including defending Taiwan. The First Gulf War taught China that numerical superiority alone would not tip the balance against the United States military. Only technological equality/superiority and numerical advantage combined would make China a true challenger to the American hegemony.[8]

Challenging America

Since the wake-up-call of the Gulf War in the early 1990s, China has embarked on a rapid military modernization and overall numerical downsizing program with the United States armed forces in mind as the potential enemy. China recognizes that while they do have a need for overall numerical superiority over the United States military, they do not need the massive numerical superiority that Mao envisioned and used effectively during the Korean War. The emphasis is now on quality over sheer quantity. The numerical downsizing of China's army is seen as a practical necessity in order to free up resources to build a more professional and well-trained army while remaining numerically superior. This restructuring of China's military is an ongoing process, as the Xinhua News reported on July 13, 2005, under a headline, "Chinese Military to be Restructured." The article stated that:

> According to a statement issued by the Headquarters of the General Staff of the PRC People's Liberation Army (PLA), the PLA is expected to shift its traditional structure by adding new battle units and cutting outdated ones in an effort to create new combat effectiveness. The PLA program is attempting to change the structure of the PLA by cutting its divisions and increasing brigades, reported the Liberation Army Daily, the traditional mouthpiece of the Chinese armed forces.[9]

In order to modernize quickly China has pursued both internal military development and external purchases. China has purchased the latest weaponry and technology from Russia, Israel,[10] and also the European Union[11] as much as it has been able to under post Tiananmen Square sanctions. It has also begun to build up its own technological military industrial complex in order to be less dependent on foreign sources of arms. An example of the recent Chinese development is the J-10 all-weather fighter plane. The J-10 is very similar to the now canceled Israeli Lavi program and is widely acknowledged to be based on technology purchased from Israel, given the similarities between the two aircraft.

A further example of China's military build-up is its pursuit of cruise missile technology in order to offset the power of the United States Navy and its growing anti-ballistic missile systems. China is particularly interested in obtaining/developing supersonic cruise missile technology in order to force the American carrier battle groups to stay further out to sea in order to protect the asset.[12] It has also purchased four Sovremenny destroyers from Russia. These ships were specifically designed to attack aircraft carriers and carry Russian Moskit anti-carrier missiles (SS-N-22 Sunburn) that can be armed with conventional or nuclear warheads.[13]

China is also engaging the United States in cyber warfare or computer-based spying. Through the internet, China has an ongoing program of hacking American military, government, and private commercial computers in order to acquire technology and military secrets along with private commercial technology. This new cyber-based threat could be enhanced in time of crisis to bring down the American economy which has become so technologically dependant.[14] The United States government has code named this effort by the Chinese "Titan Rain."[15]

China is also intent on demonstrating its technological advancements through its space program. On October 15, 2003, China became just the third nation to independently send a man into space and return him successfully to earth when Lieutenant Colonel Yang Liwei became China's first astronaut (or Taikonaut in Chinese). Almost two years later on October 12, 2005, China repeated the feat by sending two men into space for almost a week. The Chinese have had a space program since the 1970s. However, much of its recent success is due to its close working relationship with the Russian space program. Collaboration with the Russians permitted China to leapfrog over many technological hurdles that otherwise might have delayed China's independent space program.[16] China has a stated goal of putting a man on the moon by the year 2020, something only America has done previously (and currently is trying to repeat by 2018).

Of much greater concern to the United States was China's test of an anti-satellite missile on January 11, 2007. The test missile shot down an aging Chinese weather satellite over 500 miles above the earth's surface. This makes China only the third nation after the United States and the former Soviet Union to successfully test an anti-satellite weapon. The United States owns 53 percent of all satellites currently orbiting the earth. This test was seen by commentators and governments around the globe as a direct challenge to the United States and its heavy dependence on high technology, communications, and imaging-based defensive systems. China seems to be signaling to the world that it does not intend to use space in a peaceful way only. An example of the worldwide condemnation of China's action can be seen in the comments by Japanese Foreign Minister Taro Aso, responding to the test, in a news conference, "We told China that we doubt if we could call this a peaceful use (of space)."[17] This militarization of space by China could signal a new cold war: this time between the United States and China.

The United States is well aware of China's military build-up. Voice of America reports that Admiral William Fallon, commander of the combined United States forces command in the Pacific, on a visit to China suggested that the PRC's ongoing military build-up might be too extensive for a country not facing any outside threats. He stated:

> I'm not about to sit here and determine what percentage of GDP or how many Yuan or whatever ought to be devoted, but my sense is that I don't see a particular threat to China, so military capabilities expansion, [it] seems to me, ought to be commensurate with the growth and development of a country.[18]

The point Admiral Fallon was making was that the United States is not a threat to China and that China was wasting money on military development that could be better used to help develop China. Implicit in the admiral's comment was that if America were planning to attack China (for whatever reason), it would have done so already when China was in a much weaker position than it is today. China's "city buster" nuclear deterrent is more than adequate reason for America to keep conflicts with China under control including any efforts by Taiwan to declare independence.[19] However, even if a conflict could be limited to the conventional (if both sides feared using nuclear weapons or using them first), a conventional conflict with China is not in America's or China's interests as it could wreak economic havoc on both nations.

However, China in spite of statements to the contrary does seem to be keeping a "first use" policy on the table as an option. On July 14, 2005, the Financial Times reported from Beijing that Zhu Chenghu, a major general in the People's Liberation Army who is also a professor at China's National Defense University said that China is prepared to use nuclear weapons against the United States if it is attacked by Washington during a confrontation over Taiwan.[20] Zhu Chenghu is quoted as saying: "If the Americans draw their missiles and position-guided ammunition on to the target zone on China's territory, I think we will have to respond with nuclear weapons." He added that China's definition of its territory includes warships and aircraft.[21]

A Wall Street Journal reporter is quoted as saying:

> [R]ecent warnings about Beijing's military buildup took on a very real signifi-cance, when Chinese Maj. Gen. Zhu Chenghu of the People's Liberation Army warned last week that US military "interference" in a conflict over Taiwan could lead to a Chinese nuclear attack on the US, and he reinforced every worst fear of a "China threat." "… it was clear to those of us who witnessed last Thursday's warning that it was no accidental outburst."[22]

China seems confident and willing to play a game of nuclear brinkmanship with the United States. This is of concern not only to the United States, but also its main ally in the region, Japan. China's new-found confidence to challenge the United States is not limited to military acquisitions; China is also looking for economic domination by glob-ally securing access to raw materials. China is basically taking a play out of America's Cold War playbook by adopting the policy of encirclement. During the early days of the Cold War, the United States had a policy of encircling its rival, the Soviet Union, by making allies on all of its sides. Besides the North Atlantic Treaty Organization in the West, there were the US–Japan Security treaty in the east, the Southeast Asian Treaty Organization in the Pacific, and the Middle East Treaty Organization (later renamed Central Treaty Organization) in the Middle East.

What the United States did through military alliances, China has been doing through economic alliances. China has been aggressively pursuing economic/resource alliances in Africa, Latin America, Central Asia, and even Europe. China has been taking advantage of the American distraction with the war on terror and the occupation of Iraq to secure resources, trading rights, and investments with regimes that are hostile to America or have spotty human rights records in places such as Sudan, Zimbabwe, and Venezuela. China is using its new-found wealth to buy friends and allies around the world. China, unlike the United States, is willing to ignore corruption and human rights abuses in exchange for raw materials and economic opportunity. China hopes that by securing resources from politically corrupt regimes they can buy loyalty in its battle for hegemony with America, and China is very confident in its ability to do this.[23]

Much of China's new-found confidence comes from not only its surging economy, which in purchasing power parity terms has already passed Japan and reached the second largest in the world, but also in a general perception that the current hegemon—the United States—is in decline. However, unlike in major EU countries where such a perception of American decline is common, American ascendancy is widely recognized within Asia capitals. Japan in particular seems to recognize this in its choice to continue its alliance with the United States. Nevertheless, China, it seems, is preparing for a long drawn-out challenge to American power that could be over 100 years in the making. Of course this is in the absence of currently unknown intervening variables that might cause a rapid decline in American power.

Japan's role in America's China strategy: utilities and limits

This brings us to our next important area of inquest, China's challenge to Japan, America's most important ally in the region. This is very important because of the enhanced security role that Japan plays in overall American policy. The inclusion of Japan in our study of America's reaction to China's rise is very important in that Japan, it would appear through successive Prime Ministers and governments, has and is willing to bet its future in Asia and thus globally on continued American global hegemony. China's growing expansionism and hegemonism were begun by Jiang Zemin and succeeded by Hu Jintao. More than anything else except the threat of North Korea, the threat of China is propelling Japan forward with its efforts to alter its constitution. The United States welcomes the revision of Japan's constitution as American policy desires a more fully capable Japan to support American policy in Asia. China has been called a sleeping dragon, but in reality Japan is the real sleeping dragon, which China may be taunting recklessly. In fact, Deng Xiaoping is said to have warned his successors about Japan by telling them to "let sleeping dogs lie," but they have been loath or unable to follow his advice. Japan's constitution has truly limited Japan in its military development and its ability to project power. However, if the threat of China ever causes Japan to abandon its constitutional limitations, China might regret its recent bullying of Japan.

An example of China overplaying its hand occurred on September 9, 2005, just two days before national elections in Japan. China, in what appeared to be an effort to intimidate Japanese voters the way it intimidates voters in Taiwan, sent warships to patrol an area surrounding disputed islands and natural gas fields in the East China Sea. If it was meant to intimidate Japanese voters then it had the opposite effect when the right-wing and more nationalistic Junichiro Koizumi and the LDP won re-election in an overwhelming landslide victory over a more pacifist orientated opposition.

This was not an isolated incident. In recent years and months, China has gotten bolder about fomenting anti-Japanese nationalism within China. This includes riots and street demonstrations outside of Japanese consulates and business assets within China. Many of these protests are triggered by Japanese actions like visits to Yasukuni Shrine (where several class "A" war criminals have been enshrined) by Japanese leaders and the publication of revisionist textbooks approved by the Japanese Ministry of Education that whitewash Japanese atrocities during World War II. In the past, these events have sparked official protests by China (and Korea), but what is different now is that the Chinese government and Communist Party seem to have given sanction to the street protests.[24] However, the Chinese street protests have had the unintended result of awakening the average Japanese citizen to the challenge and potential threat that China is to Japan.

It would appear that China was hoping to marginalize and intimidate Japan so that it is a less effective ally of the United States. This marginalization seems to be having the opposite effect. The problem for China in the long run is that in awakening large-scale anti-Japanese sentiment among its general population it may find it politically impossible in the future to repair relations with Japan when it needs to. This can lead to generational hatreds like the world witnessed in the former Yugoslavia. However, the current state of relations is not solely China's fault in that Japan could have done more in the last 60 years to heal the Sino/Japanese relationship by demonstrating greater sensitivity to Chinese suffering under its rule and offering a more sincere apology for its actions that China could accept. The United States could also have encouraged this process along. Nevertheless, the current state of relations between the two great powers in Asia does not bode well for the future.

Historically since World War II, Japan has been very circumvent about naming threats to Japan. The 1997 Guidelines signed between the United States and Japan simply referred to "situations in the areas surrounding Japan" as the threat. However, Japan is beginning to openly voice its concerns about China's growing military power. In its annual 2004 Defense White Paper it noted China's increasingly bold maritime ambitions. The defense paper, which echoes concerns expressed about China's military build-up in the United States Defense Department, said Japan's public was "exceedingly concerned" about the intrusion of Chinese vessels, including a nuclear submarine, into Japanese waters. "Regarding the pick-up in China's maritime activity, the trends need to be watched," it said. "It has been pointed out that the Chinese navy is aiming to become a so-called 'blue-water navy,'" it added, referring to development of a deep-water fleet.[25] This trend continued in 2005 with a new defense white paper that argued that Japan needed to start to respond to Chinese military spending.[26] This could mark the beginnings of an arms race in East Asia and pull Japan further away from Article Nine and toward constitutional revision and normalcy.

It is important to note that China really has nothing to fear from Japan militarily. Japan no longer has the imperial capability (or desire) that it once had due to an aging and declining population and a changed world. Each nation has the capacity to harass the other, but neither can really invade or conquer each other. This current status quo should be good enough to allay any Chinese fears about a resurgent imperial Japan, but China does not seem to be satisfied with the status quo. On the other hand, China's internal anti-Japan message has been very successful at raising a generation of anti-Japanese Chinese with the unintended consequence of growing nationalism within Japan as well. Faced with growing and potent hostility from China, the Japanese have become more patriotic and open to a militarily stronger and more assertive Japan and thus a much more valuable ally of American policy in the region. This more assertive Japan is something that the United States sees as a very desirable counter to growing Chinese military influence and assertiveness in the region.

China's Achilles' heel

China's new-found assertiveness is not without risks to itself. China's new economy is energy dependant. Oil is China's great weakness or rather the lack of adequate oil reserves to fuel its industrial appetite. China is not like the United States which has greater oil reserves than Saudi Arabia (the problem for the United States is that the cost of extracting the oil is cost prohibitive even at $70 a barrel, but not technically or fiscally impossible if needed). China needs new energy sources to feed its growing new industries and continuing access to its current imports. Brownouts are frequent and common in some major cities of China. Many Chinese factories need to keep generators on standby just to keep the factories running. Evidence of China's energy problem can be seen in this Associated Press report from July 19, 2005:

BEIJING POWER CRUNCH PROMPTS SHUT DOWN (2005–07–19)

(It was) reported that workers at thousands of Beijing companies are about to get an unscheduled vacation thanks to the scorching summer heat. Beginning this week, 4,689 businesses will take mandatory weeklong breaks on rotation to cut down on energy use in the PRC capital and avoid pushing up already rapidly climbing power prices, the official Xinhua News Agency said Tuesday.[27]

It is important to note that China is still a developing economy and that its energy needs are growing with it. China is rushing to develop hydroelectric power at the cost of massive environmental upheaval and population displacement. The Three Gorges Dam on the Yangtze River is but one example of this.

China has also lobbied furiously with Russia for a pipeline from the Siberian oilfields to Manchuria. Japan, on the other hand, lobbied just as furiously for the pipeline to be built to the Siberian coast as not to be dependent on China for the free flow of oil. Both nations got part of what they wanted in that the pipeline will split and go to both Manchuria and the Siberian coast as Russia wants China to be a major market for its oil but does not want to be dependent on China's control of the spigot to market its oil to international customers. The problem will now be to build this new pipeline in a politically and economically volatile Russia.

While Japan and China share the common need for a secure energy supply, Japan as America's ally is approaching the issue from a much different perspective. Japan sees the United States as an ally that it can depend on so it works with the United States to secure its energy needs. China, on the other hand, sees the United States as a potential rival and does not like its dependence on the United States Navy's Seventh Fleet for securing safe passage for its energy supplies from the Middle East to its coastal ports in southeastern China.

China's energy needs have risen as spectacularly as its economy. China has gone from a net exporter of oil in 1992 to the world's second largest importer of oil behind the United States. China is very aware of its oil problem and is doing everything it can to secure energy resources on the open market. Its recent attempt to buy the American Oil giant UNOCAL (Union Oil Corporation of California) and its August 2005 purchase of PetroKazakhstan are evidence of this effort to secure the oil reserves through these companies. If China were ever to attack Taiwan, it would likely lose its access to Middle Eastern oil through combined maritime interdictions from the United States Navy's Seventh Fleet, Japan's Maritime Self Defense Force, Royal Australian Navy, and possibly the Indian Navy. This could force China into a desperate attempt to militarily seize the Russian oil fields (particularly those that are owned, in whole or in part, by Chinese oil companies) bringing Russia into a conflict between the United States and China on the side of the United States. This would result in a two-front war for China of which its probabilities of a positive outcome would be almost zero. It could only use its nuclear weapons to ensure that there is no winner, only losers. China's dependence on energy in the form of Middle East oil is the Achilles heel of its military ambitions in East Asia.

With this weakness in mind, China has been working to obtain new sources of oil and natural gas in order to diversify its suppliers. Chief among these efforts have been China's diplomatic efforts in Africa, especially in Sudan and Nigeria. It is also making efforts in America's own backyard among Latin American nations, such as Venezuela and Ecuador, in clear conflict with the Monroe Doctrine.

Energy is not China's only Achilles heel. The environment in China is also an important threat to Chinese power. China's virtually unregulated industrial expansion has produced an environmental disaster of biblical proportions. Reports of untreated toxic waste flowing freely into rivers, workers and children growing up with near toxic levels of air pollution, and a near total breakdown in preventative public health services as evidenced by the growth of "snail fever"[28] and the SARS outbreak of 2004 have led to almost daily reports of riots in rural China by peasants demanding that the government protect them. The government in China has been doing very little to curb or control pollution, and in the absence of government control, the peasants are taking the law into their own hands and shutting the offenders down.[29] The cost of cleanup will be prohibitive when China is finally forced to deal with the problem.

China's third Achilles heel: its new-found wealth or in reality the lack thereof. China is accumulating wealth at an unprecedented rate due to its trade surpluses with the United States and Europe. However, China is hoarding this wealth rather than investing it in itself. While it is spending (almost recklessly) on the PLA, it is neglecting its own infrastructure, people, the environment, and its future stability. China's current domestic policy is like a person who takes a cash advance from his credit card, puts it in the bank, and declares himself rich. The problem is that the interest and payments will eventually destroy him. China, in the same way, by investing in its military and by neglecting its people and domestic needs will eventually pay a price that it cannot afford to pay.

A fourth and final Achilles heel of China: China's position in the world system. China represents an opportunity for the world economy, but it is not currently an essential element. China produces goods cheaply, but the goods that it produces are for the most part not essential commodities for the West. This is why in a conflict over Taiwan the United States and its allies could embargo oil going into China and not be threatened by the loss of Chinese goods being exported. There is nothing that China currently produces that cannot be produced elsewhere if needed. There would be a temporary loss of supply, but the long-term result would be the relocation of the industries. The world basically does not depend on China, China depends on the world. It is for this reason that the world and the United States are willing to continue their engagement of China while being aware of the military threat it poses the region. They see China as the eventual loser of any conflict because the world can turn its back on China, but China cannot turn its back on the world. The next section will briefly look at American ascendancy.

American ascendancy

While many scholars may lament (or rejoice depending on one's perspective) in the seeming decline of American power, there is no conclusive empirical evidence of American hegemonic decline. The only evidence of imminent American decline is anecdotal. Rather the empirical evidence would indicate that American power is still in overall ascendancy. The American economy is currently the largest in the world (with the exception of the combined nations of the European Union). It is currently growing at 4.9 percent for the year 2007. This means that the American economy will grow by nearly $700 billion by 2007. China on the other hand is growing at the rate of 9–12 percent annually. Using the larger figure of 12 percent the Chinese economy will grow by $310 billion in 2007. Using an average growth rate of 4 percent for the United States and 10 percent for China, China will pass the United States in the year 2036. This can be seen in Figure 3.1.

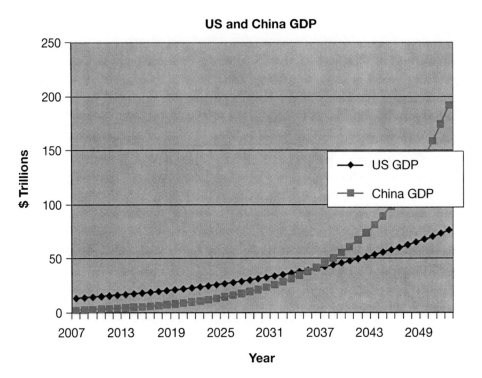

Figure 3.1. *American and Chinese linear GDP growth projections based on 4% and 10% annual growth rates respectively over 45 years starting in 2008*

The major problem with this type of economic projection is that it is linear. The real world is not linear; there are economic ups and downs and constantly changing variables. Historically there has never been a correct 50-year linear projection of GDP for any nation. Linear assumptions assume that such things as population, size of workforce, productivity, investments in infrastructure, and military spending all remain constant over time. In the real world they do not. This is especially true in rapidly developing nations such as China which are constantly in a state of change. More developed economies such as the United States and the Member States of the European Union tend to have more stable growth rates with less radical changes in GDP over time. To illustrate this, if the United States economy were to grow at a steady 3.5 percent (the average GDP growth rate of the United States over the last 30 years) over the next 100 years and China was to continue to grow at 12 percent for the next 5 years (2008–2012), and then continue to grow at 10 percent over the following 5 years (2013–2017), and then slow to a solid 6 percent over the next 10 years (2018–2027), and finally settle to a steady and stable growth rate of 4 percent of a developed, mature economy over the next 80 years, there would still be a $97 trillion gap in GDP between the two nations in the United States' favor. This can be seen in Figure 3.2.

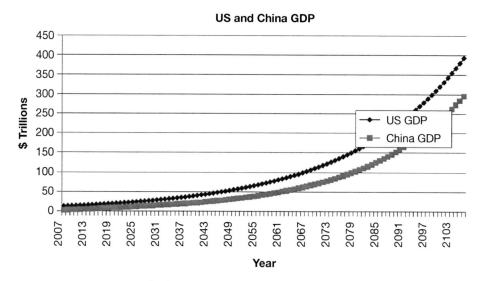

Figure 3.2. *American and Chinese linear GDP growth projections based on 3.5% annual GDP growth rate for the United States and 12% (2008–2012), 10% (2013–2017), 6% (2018–2027), and 4% (2028–2106) growth rates for China*

China's growth in the last 20 years has been nothing short of spectacular; however the problem for China in its quest to pass up the United States is America's overall lead in terms of GDP and overall economic wealth. The United States economy grows as much each year as some economies are in size. Gerard Baker described it well in *The Times of London*:

> Given that the United States is a $12 trillion (£6,700 billion) economy, the new data mean that in the first quarter the US added to the global output an amount that, if sustained at that pace for a year, would be about $600 billion—roughly the equivalent of adding one whole new Brazil or Australia to global economic activity every year, just from the incremental extra sweat and heave and click of 300 million Americans.
>
> Think of it another way. In an era in which China embodies the hopes and fears of much of the developed world, the US with a growth rate of half that of China's, is adding roughly twice as much in absolute terms to the global output as the Middle Kingdom, with its GDP (depending on how you measure it) of between $2 trillion and $4 trillion and its growth of about 10 percent.[30]

David Brooks of the *New York Times* furthers this argument of America not being in decline by examining the economic competitiveness rankings and he finds that in regard to American decline:

... that's just not true. In the first place, despite the ups and downs of the business cycle, the United States still possesses the most potent economy on earth. Recently the World Economic Forum and the International Institute for Management Development produced global competitiveness indexes, and once again they both ranked the United States first in the world.

In the World Economic Forum survey, the US comes in just ahead of Switzerland, Denmark, Sweden and Germany (China is 34th). The US gets poor marks for macroeconomic stability (the long-term federal debt), for its tax structure and for the low savings rate. But it leads the world in a range of categories: higher education and training, labor market flexibility, the ability to attract global talent, the availability of venture capital, the quality of corporate management and the capacity to innovate.[31]

This is not to say that there could not be currently unknown intervening variables that would change this equation and America's fortunes; this is merely to emphasize the sheer size of the gap between American and Chinese wealth and economic power. To put this in a different perspective, if you were offered 5 percent of a million dollars or 15 percent of one hundred thousand dollars which would you choose? The smart person would choose the 5 percent as it is equal to $50,000. The 15 percent is only equal to $15,000. Over time the 15 percent will pass the 5 percent but it will take a long time not a short time. While the gap between the United States and China is not as large as the illustration, it is large enough to make the point that Gerard Baker makes above, China still has a very long way to go even if the annual percentage of GDP growth is double the size of the United States'. As the Chinese economy matures its growth will level out to a more stable and steady rate. China may catch up but it will not likely be soon. This economic argument does not even touch the incredible asymmetrical difference between American military power and Chinese military power (the next section will talk about this in more detail).

Furthermore, unlike the major powers of the European Union, it would seem that this economic and military ascendancy is widely recognized within Asia capitals. Japan in particular seems to recognize this in its choice to continue its alliance with the United States. Japan is betting everything on American ascendancy. They are seeking no new allies. Every Japanese leader has followed this path since World War II. This is a staggering vote of confidence in the United States. India is also moving forward with closer security relations with the United States. George W. Bush's February 2006 visit to India clearly was aimed at China on the part of New Delhi and Washington. It would seem that Washington, like China, has renewed the old Cold War policy of encirclement. American policy seems to be to keep China worried about ALL its borders so that it is not tempted to EXPAND its borders.

The other nations of the region are also concerned about the lack of transparency in Chinese defense strategy and are hedging their bets by avoiding conflicts with both Washington (war on terror and Iraq) and China (economic and military). They know that in case of a threat or conflict that the United States will willingly accept allies and that they can always run to the United States in face of (potential) Chinese aggression as it is in American interest to contain China rather than to let it run unhindered. The next section will look at why United States policy toward China is so confident in its ability to contain possible Chinese aggression in East, Southeast, and South Asia.

Preparing to fight the last war?

In spite of China's recent spending spree, China is poised to fall further behind as the next Revolution in Military Affairs (RMA) takes place over the next three to five years. American military power is about to leap forward once again. In the study of military history there is the old adage the generals always prepare to fight and win the last war, only to learn too late that they are fighting with outdated equipment and tactics. The American military has made a conscious effort to avoid this potential pitfall. However, the same may not be said of China.

China, it would appear is preparing to fight the United States in a 1991 Persian Gulf War scenario or at the very best a 2003 Iraq War scenario. The problem for China is that they may be preparing to fight a conflict with equipment and tactics that are one to two generations out of date. As the United States is deploying its missile defense and developing the first generation of airborne directed energy weapons.[32] Directed energy weapons have the potential to revolutionize the battlefield in ways that have not been seen since the invention of the bow and arrow. This is "Star Wars" or "Star Trek" for real without the Hollywood special effects. China's missile-based nuclear deterrent could be rendered obsolete in the face of possible United States directed energy weapons.

It is important to understand that the United States is investing heavily in technology not just for economic advantage but in an effort to obtain capabilities. Framed from a position of capability this technology is just a way to obtain capabilities. The directed energy weapons mentioned in the preceding paragraph give capability to intercept supersonic/hypersonic weapons that could be launched at American military assets, particularly American aircraft carriers. If America acquires the capability to deploy these new technologies China's weapons strategy is irrelevant. China is trying to level the playing field through investment in current weapons systems while the United States is determined to maintain superiority through technological advances. As mentioned earlier Japan has bet its future on the United States continuing to dominate a unipolar world. If the United States acquires these capabilities then the high stakes gamble placed by Japan will have paid off.

The potential for problems here are twofold if China's nuclear deterrent is rendered obsolete by the weapons still in development. The first problem is the more obvious problem which is the scenario where China initiates a conflict with the United States thinking that it will be able to contain or control the United States military response. When Chinese military capacity proves to be inadequate, China will be faced with a huge humiliation and loss of face that may cause it to prolong the conflict unnecessarily to its own detriment. The second problem is for the United States in that the United States will be in a position were it could become overconfident and less willing to work for a peaceful resolution to a potential conflict. This could put the United States in a position of making policy choices that actually precipitate conflict.

Another way to look at potential and ongoing Sino-American hegemonic competition is from a decision-making perspective. Based on most of the decision-making research, we know that people and leaders are risk averse and are motivated by potential regret. They ask themselves "what is the worst that could happen," and if the answer is unpalatable they do not choose to take the risky action. The modernization and acquisition of greater military assets has the potential to make China less aggressive since they will have more to lose in a conflict with the United States. For example, in a conflict with the American Navy, the more ships they have, the greater the potential losses if they engage the Pacific Fleet.

To put it another way, the value of China's new military assets is context dependent. In a regional conflict with smaller countries such as Malaysia, the Philippines, or Vietnam, the modernized Chinese navy measurably improves China's bargaining position. The modern Chinese "blue water navy" would have no trouble intimidating the smaller naval, coastal defense forces of the region. On the other hand, in a hegemonic showdown with the United States, China's modern blue water navy would have very little impact except to potentially cost the United States more ammunition given current American technological superiority. Therefore, the modernization of the PLA Navy means that China risks losing its newly acquired power vis-à-vis regional actors with very little to no potential for gain in a conflict with the global hegemonic power, the United States. Therefore, from an American perspective, China will likely become a little more willing to avoid naval confrontation or to put it simply, it will be less aggressive. Thus in this coming era of greater American supremacy it behooves the American government to continue to engage China in a Liberal-institutionalist way in order to avoid conflict. One problem however is that the American supremacy could be quickly nullified if China (and others) were to obtain the technology and the wherewithal to deploy whatever weapons are state of the art. American economic supremacy would remain, but its military lead could be gone.

Conclusion: American policy toward China's rise is taking the long view

When examining long-term American policy toward China's rise, the assumption must be made that conflict between America and China would be disastrous for China, America, the region, and the world in general and that American policymakers know of this potential for disaster and will work to avoid it. The problem is that the boundaries defining "peaceful coexistence" may be different for Beijing and Washington. Whether the two sides can negotiate the boundaries remains to be seen. Over the last several American presidential administrations and dating back to Nixon's Secretary of State, Henry Kissinger, the American policy regarding China has taken the long view, engaging China through trade and economics while containing China security-wise. This policy has worked well for both countries. China is growing economically and is thus becoming more dependent on the global economic system—which would theoretically make it more cooperative and less adversarial. However, China's new-found wealth is being channeled heavily into the modernization of the PLA.

What should be America's policy toward China given the overall unknowns about China's intentions? If China's quest for supremacy is a multigenerational quest, then there is a real chance that diplomatic and economic engagement will make the question moot. A new generation of Chinese and Americans may not desire to see each other as strategic rivals. However, if the Chinese leadership grows impatient, then we may see an aggressor China assert itself into a conflict with the United States, which it currently stands to lose.

Given the choice between containment and engagement, American policy seems to be to simultaneously pursue both with equal effort. The current asymmetrical nature of any potential conflict with China gives the United States greater ability to pursue liberal institutionalist options without sacrificing its advantage from a realist perspective. However, direct conflict with the United States aside China's ability to destabilize the region through its ongoing weapons modernization program gives the United States great concern as to its ability to manage a non-direct conflict with China and pushes it toward a more realist policy toward China. It is for this last reason that the United States has been so willing to talk publicly about the "China threat" and China's status as a rising challenger to American hegemony.

This "China threat" is very important for United States policy in that it gives a focus (or an enemy if you will) for the United States military to focus on. As previously mentioned, without an enemy the United States military would lose support and funding in Washington's budget battles. China provides a real world threat that seemingly "must" be contained. It also fuels American ascendancy by spurring American hegemony to greater heights. In the ancient world, the Roman Empire grew in power as long as there were external threats to it. Once it realized that it had no challenger it began to crumble from within. Only when it was in an irreversible decline could others swoop in and divide up the pieces of a once great empire. America, like ancient Rome (and other empires throughout history) needs an outside threat to keep it from crumbling from within. China is currently providing this threat, intentionally or not. Accordingly, as the data indicates and contrary to conventional wisdom, American power is still growing and will likely continue to do so. America has still not reached the zenith of its power.

America is dealing with China's rise by engaging China economically while attempting to contain China security-wise. Little has changed in this policy over the last two decades of Republican and Democratic Administrations. Barring a "clear and present danger" security threat or crisis from China, America is likely to continue to take the long view toward Chinese growth by continuing to bank on the idea that China desires to grow economically more than it desires hegemonic domination. This long view is based on a liberal institutionalist belief that working with China is better than opposing China. However, this belief is still in line with the realist belief in the need to contain potential adversaries. The United States can always fall back on its economic and military superiority if China proves to be too aggressive or pose a direct threat to American security.

As long as China does not try to neutralize the American strategic advantage and an overconfident America does not unintentionally initiate a crisis, conflict is likely to be avoided as each nation develops a mutually dependant economic relationship. However, if China does pursue efforts to neutralize the American strategic advantage, the American reaction will likely be containment of the "China threat" by both military and economic means, thus increasing the likelihood of conflict. The American cultural tradition to deal with threats, real or imagined, is a long one, and the pre-emptive nature of the Bush Doctrine is not new to American policy.

NOTES

1. Earlier versions of this chapter under different titles were originally presented at the International Studies Association 2006 Annual Convention in San Diego, California, USA March 22–25, 2006 and the ASPC 2007 Annual Convention at the East-West Center in Honolulu, Hawaii, USA June 15–17, 2007.
2. For more on this please see: Yochiro Sato and Satu Limaye, *Japan in a Dynamic Asia: Coping with the New Security Challenges,* (Lanhan Maryland: Lexington Books, 2006), Chapters 1 and 3.
3. With apologies to U2 and their song "Bullet the Blue Sky" which is where this line comes from.
4. Department of Defense, *Annual Report to Congress: Military Power of the People's Republic of China 2006.* Accessed at: www.defenselink.mil/pubs/pdfs/China%20Report%20 2006.pdf
5. Ibid.
6. Steve Lohr; Andrew Ross Sorkin, and Jad Mouawad, "Unocal Bid Denounced At Hearing," *New York Times,* Section C, Page 1, Column 5 www.nytimes.com and *The China Daily,* July 14, 2005. www.chinadaily.com.cn/english/doc/2005–07/14/content_460173.htm.
7. Cragg Hines, "Why Hu needs the ranch instead of the South Lawn," *Houston Chronicle,* September 7, 2005. www.chron.com/cs/CDA/ssistory.mpl/editorial/outlook/3342368.

8. James C. Mulvenon, Murray Scot Tanner, Michael S. Chase, David Frelinger, David C. Gompert, Martin C. Libicki, and Kevin L. Pollpeter, *Chinese Responses to US Military Transformation and Implications for the Department of Defense*, (The RAND Corp., 2006).

9. Compiled and paraphrased by this author from NAPSnet daily report July 13, 2005. www.chinadaily.com.cn/english/doc/2005–07/13/content_459875.htm.

10. Israel has currently stopped publicly selling weapons to China under US diplomatic pressure, but is thought to be still selling some weapons and technology to China quietly.

11. The European Union currently does not sell advanced weapons to China because of its human rights record. It was contemplating dropping the arms sales ban in the spring of 2005 when China passed the anti-succession law against Taiwan. The passage of this law made it politically unpalatable to resume arms sales.

12. Supersonic cruise missile technology escaped the Soviets' technological abilities and to this day no nation has been able to overcome the technological hurdles. If the hurdles are overcome and China obtains the technology and the weapons, there will be a dramatic shift in the balance of power in East Asia unless the United States develops effective countermeasures to defend its aircraft carriers.

13. Summary from Naval-Technology.com. www.naval-technology.com/projects/sovremenny/.

14. Examples of this can be found from multiple sources: www.time.com/time/magazine/article/0,9171,1098961-1,00.html. www.theregister.co.uk/2006/10/09/chinese_crackers_attack_us/.

15. Computer World, www.computerworld.com/securitytopics/security/story/0,10801,105585,00.html.

16. Jing-dong Yuan, "Shenzhou and China's Space Odyssey," *The Jamestown Foundation*, Volume 5, Issue 24 (November 22, 2005) Accessed at: www.jamestown.org/images/pdf/cb_005_024.pdf.

17. "US, allies protest China's anti-satellite test," www.CNN.com, January 19, 2007.

18. Voice of America, July 9, 2005 as reported by *NAPSnet Daily Report*, July 9, 2005.

19. China's "city buster" deterrent is not based on Mutual Assured Destruction (MAD) like the US and the Soviet Union during the Cold War. China deterrent is based on being able to inflict the loss of 20 or more major cities on America as too high a price for aggression against China. The US nuclear arsenal would be able to destroy China several times over, but at the price of the US losing its largest cities.

20. Financial Times, July 14, 2005. http://news.ft.com/cms/s/28cfe55a-f4a7-11d99dd1-00000e2511c8.html.

21. Ibid.

22. As quoted by *ViewPoints* July 14, 2005 US Forces Japan www.usfj.mil. From: http://ebird.afis.mil/ Emphasis added.

23. Joseph Kahn, "China Courts Africa, Angling for Strategic Gains," *New York Times*, November 3, 2006. www.nytimes.com.

24. It is interesting to note that when Prime Minister Koizumi made his promised post election visit to Yasukuni Shrine in October 2005, China reverted back to making only official protests rather than permitting street demonstrations. The leadership in China had perhaps recognized that their policy was having undesired consequences.

25. 2004 Defense of Japan White Paper. www.jda.go.jp/e/pab/wp2004/.

26. 2005 Defense White Paper summary. www.fpcj.jp/e/mres/japanbrief/jb_560.html.

27. As quoted by *NAPSnet Daily Report*, July 19, 2005.

28. Jim Yardley, "A Deadly Fever, Once Defeated, Lurks in a Chinese Lake," *New York Times*, February 22, 2005, A1.

29. Edward Cody, "China's Rising Tide of Protest Sweeping Up Party Officials as Village Chiefs Share Anger Over Pollution," *Washington Post Foreign Service*, September 12, 2005, A01.

30. Gerard Baker, "America's Economic Hegemony is safe," *The Times*, April 25, 2006. http://business.Timesonline.co.uk.

31. David Brooks, *New York Times*, November 27, 2009. www.nytimes.com/2007/11/27/opinion/27brooks.html.

32. Doug Beason, *The E-Bomb* (Cambridge, MA: Da Capo Press, 2005).

A Just and Lasting Peace
Nobel Lecture, Oslo: December 10, 2009

BARACK H. OBAMA

Your Majesties, Your Royal Highnesses, distinguished members of the Norwegian Nobel Committee, citizens of America, and citizens of the world:

I receive this honor with deep gratitude and great humility. It is an award that speaks to our highest aspirations—that for all the cruelty and hardship of our world, we are not mere prisoners of fate. Our actions matter, and can bend history in the direction of justice.

And yet I would be remiss if I did not acknowledge the considerable controversy that your generous decision has generated. (Laughter.) In part, this is because I am at the beginning, and not the end, of my labors on the world stage. Compared to some of the giants of history who've received this prize—Schweitzer and King; Marshall and Mandela—my accomplishments are slight. And then there are the men and women around the world who have been jailed and beaten in the pursuit of justice; those who toil in humanitarian organizations to relieve suffering; the unrecognized millions whose quiet acts of courage and compassion inspire even the most hardened cynics. I cannot argue with those who find these men and women—some known, some obscure to all but those they help—to be far more deserving of this honor than I.

But perhaps the most profound issue surrounding my receipt of this prize is the fact that I am the Commander-in-Chief of the military of a nation in the midst of two wars. One of these wars is winding down. The other is a conflict that America did not seek; one in which we are joined by 42 other countries—including Norway—in an effort to defend ourselves and all nations from further attacks.

Still, we are at war, and I'm responsible for the deployment of thousands of young Americans to battle in a distant land. Some will kill, and some will be killed. And so I come here with an acute sense of the costs of armed conflict—filled with difficult questions about the relationship between war and peace, and our effort to replace one with the other.

Now these questions are not new. War, in one form or another, appeared with the first man. At the dawn of history, its morality was not questioned; it was simply a fact, like drought or disease—the manner in which tribes and then civilizations sought power and settled their differences.

And over time, as codes of law sought to control violence within groups, so did philosophers and clerics and statesmen seek to regulate the destructive power of war. The concept of a "just war" emerged, suggesting that war is justified only when certain conditions were met: if it is waged as a last resort or in self-defense; if the force used is proportional; and if, whenever possible, civilians are spared from violence.

Of course, we know that for most of history, this concept of "just war" was rarely observed. The capacity of human beings to think up new ways to kill one another proved inexhaustible, as did our capacity to exempt from mercy those who look different or pray to a different God. Wars between armies gave way to wars between nations—total wars in which the distinction between combatant and civilian became blurred. In the span of 30 years, such carnage would twice engulf this continent. And while it's hard to conceive of a cause more just than the defeat of the Third Reich and the Axis powers, World War II was a conflict in which the total number of civilians who died exceeded the number of soldiers who perished.

In the wake of such destruction, and with the advent of the nuclear age, it became clear to victor and vanquished alike that the world needed institutions to prevent another world war. And so, a quarter century after the United States Senate rejected the League of Nations—an idea for which Woodrow Wilson received this prize—America led the world in constructing an architecture to keep the peace: a Marshall Plan and a United Nations, mechanisms to govern the waging of war, treaties to protect human rights, prevent genocide, restrict the most dangerous weapons.

In many ways, these efforts succeeded. Yes, terrible wars have been fought, and atrocities committed. But there has been no Third World War. The Cold War ended with jubilant crowds dismantling a wall. Commerce has stitched much of the world together. Billions have been lifted from poverty. The ideals of liberty and self-determination, equality and the rule of law have haltingly advanced. We are the heirs of the fortitude and foresight of generations past, and it is a legacy for which my own country is rightfully proud.

And yet, a decade into a new century, this old architecture is buckling under the weight of new threats. The world may no longer shudder at the prospect of war between two nuclear superpowers, but proliferation may increase the risk of catastrophe. Terrorism has long been a tactic, but modern technology allows a few small men with outsized rage to murder innocents on a horrific scale.

Moreover, wars between nations have increasingly given way to wars within nations. The resurgence of ethnic or sectarian conflicts; the growth of secessionist movements, insurgencies, and failed states—all these things have increasingly trapped civilians in unending chaos. In today's wars, many more civilians are killed than soldiers; the seeds of future conflict are sown, economies are wrecked, civil societies torn asunder, refugees amassed, children scarred.

I do not bring with me today a definitive solution to the problems of war. What I do know is that meeting these challenges will require the same vision, hard work, and persistence of those men and women who acted so boldly decades ago. And it will require us to think in new ways about the notions of just war and the imperatives of a just peace.

We must begin by acknowledging the hard truth: We will not eradicate violent conflict in our lifetimes. There will be times when nations—acting individually or in concert—will find the use of force not only necessary but morally justified.

I make this statement mindful of what Martin Luther King Jr. said in this same ceremony years ago: "Violence never brings permanent peace. It solves no social problem: it merely creates new and more complicated ones." As someone who stands here as a direct consequence of Dr. King's life work, I am living testimony to the moral force of non-violence. I know there's nothing weak—nothing passive—nothing naïve—in the creed and lives of Gandhi and King.

But as a head of state sworn to protect and defend my nation, I cannot be guided by their examples alone. I face the world as it is, and cannot stand idle in the face of threats to the American people. For make no mistake: Evil does exist in the world. A non-violent movement could not have halted Hitler's armies. Negotiations cannot convince al Qaeda's leaders to lay down their arms. To say that force may sometimes be necessary is not a call to cynicism—it is a recognition of history; the imperfections of man and the limits of reason.

I raise this point, I begin with this point because in many countries there is a deep ambivalence about military action today, no matter what the cause. And at times, this is joined by a reflexive suspicion of America, the world's sole military superpower.

But the world must remember that it was not simply international institutions—not just treaties and declarations—that brought stability to a post-World War II world. Whatever mistakes we have made, the plain fact is this: The United States of America has helped underwrite global security for more than six decades with the blood of our citizens and the strength of our arms. The service and sacrifice of our men and women in uniform has promoted peace and prosperity from Germany to Korea, and enabled democracy to take hold in places like the Balkans. We have borne this burden not because we seek to impose our will. We have done so out of enlightened self-interest—because we seek a better future for our children and grandchildren, and we believe that their lives will be better if others' children and grandchildren can live in freedom and prosperity.

So yes, the instruments of war do have a role to play in preserving the peace. And yet this truth must coexist with another—that no matter how justified, war promises human tragedy.

The soldier's courage and sacrifice is full of glory, expressing devotion to country, to cause, to comrades in arms. But war itself is never glorious, and we must never trumpet it as such.

So part of our challenge is reconciling these two seemingly irreconcilable truths—that war is sometimes necessary, and war at some level is an expression of human folly. Concretely, we must direct our effort to the task that President Kennedy called for long ago. "Let us focus," he said, "on a more practical, more attainable peace, based not on a sudden revolution in human nature but on a gradual evolution in human institutions." A gradual evolution of human institutions.

What might this evolution look like? What might these practical steps be?

To begin with, I believe that all nations—strong and weak alike—must adhere to standards that govern the use of force. I—like any head of state—reserve the right to act unilaterally if necessary to defend my nation. Nevertheless, I am convinced that adhering to standards, international standards, strengthens those who do, and isolates and weakens those who don't.

The world rallied around America after the 9/11 attacks, and continues to support our efforts in Afghanistan, because of the horror of those senseless attacks and the recognized principle of self-defense. Likewise, the world recognized the need to confront Saddam Hussein when he invaded Kuwait—a consensus that sent a clear message to all about the cost of aggression.

Furthermore, America—in fact, no nation—can insist that others follow the rules of the road if we refuse to follow them ourselves. For when we don't, our actions appear arbitrary and undercut the legitimacy of future interventions, no matter how justified.

And this becomes particularly important when the purpose of military action extends beyond self-defense or the defense of one nation against an aggressor. More and more, we all confront difficult questions about how to prevent the slaughter of civilians by their own government, or to stop a civil war whose violence and suffering can engulf an entire region.

I believe that force can be justified on humanitarian grounds, as it was in the Balkans, or in other places that have been scarred by war. Inaction tears at our conscience and can lead to more costly intervention later. That's why all responsible nations must embrace the role that militaries with a clear mandate can play to keep the peace.

America's commitment to global security will never waver. But in a world in which threats are more diffuse, and missions more complex, America cannot act alone. America alone cannot secure the peace. This is true in Afghanistan. This is true in failed states like Somalia, where terrorism and piracy is joined by famine and human suffering. And sadly, it will continue to be true in unstable regions for years to come.

The leaders and soldiers of NATO countries, and other friends and allies, demonstrate this truth through the capacity and courage they've shown in Afghanistan. But in many countries, there is a disconnect between the efforts of those who serve and the ambivalence of the broader public. I understand why war is not popular, but I also know this: The belief that peace is desirable is rarely enough to achieve it. Peace requires responsibility. Peace entails sacrifice. That's why NATO continues to be indispensable. That's why we must strengthen U.N. and regional peacekeeping, and not leave the task to a few countries. That's why we honor those who return home from peacekeeping and training abroad to Oslo and Rome; to Ottawa and Sydney; to Dhaka and Kigali—we honor them not as makers of war, but of wagers—but as wagers of peace.

Let me make one final point about the use of force. Even as we make difficult decisions about going to war, we must also think clearly about how we fight it. The Nobel Committee recognized this truth in awarding its first prize for peace to <u>Henry Dunant</u>—the founder of the Red Cross, and a driving force behind the Geneva Conventions.

Where force is necessary, we have a moral and strategic interest in binding ourselves to certain rules of conduct. And even as we confront a vicious adversary that abides by no rules, I believe the United States of America must remain a standard bearer in the conduct of war. That is what makes us different from those whom we fight. That is a source of our strength. That is why I prohibited torture. That is why I ordered the prison at Guantanamo Bay closed. And that is why I have reaffirmed America's commitment to abide by the Geneva Conventions. We lose ourselves when we compromise the very ideals that we fight to defend. And we honor—we honor those ideals by upholding them not when it's easy, but when it is hard.

I have spoken at some length to the question that must weigh on our minds and our hearts as we choose to wage war. But let me now turn to our effort to avoid such tragic choices, and speak of three ways that we can build a just and lasting peace.

First, in dealing with those nations that break rules and laws, I believe that we must develop alternatives to violence that are tough enough to actually change behavior—for if we want a lasting peace, then the words of the international community must mean something. Those regimes that break the rules must be held accountable. Sanctions must exact a real price. Intransigence must be met with increased pressure—and such pressure exists only when the world stands together as one.

One urgent example is the effort to prevent the spread of nuclear weapons, and to seek a world without them. In the middle of the last century, nations agreed to be bound by a treaty whose bargain is clear: All will have access to peaceful nuclear power; those without nuclear weapons will forsake them; and those with nuclear weapons will work towards disarmament. I am committed to upholding this treaty. It is a centerpiece of my foreign policy. And I'm working with President Medvedev to reduce America and Russia's nuclear stockpiles.

But it is also incumbent upon all of us to insist that nations like Iran and North Korea do not game the system. Those who claim to respect international law cannot avert their eyes when those laws are flouted. Those who care for their own security cannot ignore the danger of an arms race in the Middle East or East Asia. Those who seek peace cannot stand idly by as nations arm themselves for nuclear war.

The same principle applies to those who violate international laws by brutalizing their own people. When there is genocide in Darfur, systematic rape in Congo, repression in

Burma—there must be consequences. Yes, there will be engagement; yes, there will be diplomacy—but there must be consequences when those things fail. And the closer we stand together, the less likely we will be faced with the choice between armed intervention and complicity in oppression.

This brings me to a second point—the nature of the peace that we seek. For peace is not merely the absence of visible conflict. Only a just peace based on the inherent rights and dignity of every individual can truly be lasting.

It was this insight that drove drafters of the Universal Declaration of Human Rights after the Second World War. In the wake of devastation, they recognized that if human rights are not protected, peace is a hollow promise.

And yet too often, these words are ignored. For some countries, the failure to uphold human rights is excused by the false suggestion that these are somehow Western principles, foreign to local cultures or stages of a nation's development. And within America, there has long been a tension between those who describe themselves as realists or idealists—a tension that suggests a stark choice between the narrow pursuit of interests or an endless campaign to impose our values around the world.

I reject these choices. I believe that peace is unstable where citizens are denied the right to speak freely or worship as they please; choose their own leaders or assemble without fear. Pent-up grievances fester, and the suppression of tribal and religious identity can lead to violence. We also know that the opposite is true. Only when Europe became free did it finally find peace. America has never fought a war against a democracy, and our closest friends are governments that protect the rights of their citizens. No matter how callously defined, neither America's interests—nor the world's—are served by the denial of human aspirations.

So even as we respect the unique culture and traditions of different countries, America will always be a voice for those aspirations that are universal. We will bear witness to the quiet dignity of reformers like Aung Sang Suu Kyi; to the bravery of Zimbabweans who cast their ballots in the face of beatings; to the hundreds of thousands who have marched silently through the streets of Iran. It is telling that the leaders of these governments fear the aspirations of their own people more than the power of any other nation. And it is the responsibility of all free people and free nations to make clear that these movements—these movements of hope and history—they have us on their side.

Let me also say this: The promotion of human rights cannot be about exhortation alone. At times, it must be coupled with painstaking diplomacy. I know that engagement with repressive regimes lacks the satisfying purity of indignation. But I also know that sanctions without outreach—condemnation without discussion—can carry forward only a crippling status quo. No repressive regime can move down a new path unless it has the choice of an open door.

In light of the Cultural Revolution's horrors, Nixon's meeting with Mao appeared inexcusable—and yet it surely helped set China on a path where millions of its citizens have been lifted from poverty and connected to open societies. Pope John Paul's engagement with Poland created space not just for the Catholic Church, but for labor leaders like Lech Walesa. Ronald Reagan's efforts on arms control and embrace of perestroika not only improved relations with the Soviet Union, but empowered dissidents throughout Eastern Europe. There's no simple formula here. But we must try as best we can to balance isolation and engagement, pressure and incentives, so that human rights and dignity are advanced over time.

Third, a just peace includes not only civil and political rights—it must encompass economic security and opportunity. For true peace is not just freedom from fear, but freedom from want.

It is undoubtedly true that development rarely takes root without security; it is also true that security does not exist where human beings do not have access to enough food, or clean water, or the medicine and shelter they need to survive. It does not exist where children can't aspire to a decent education or a job that supports a family. The absence of hope can rot a society from within.

And that's why helping farmers feed their own people—or nations educate their children and care for the sick—is not mere charity. It's also why the world must come together to confront climate change. There is little scientific dispute that if we do nothing, we will face more drought, more famine, more mass displacement—all of which will fuel more conflict for decades. For this reason, it is not merely scientists and environmental activists who call for swift and forceful action—it's military leaders in my own country and others who understand our common security hangs in the balance.

Agreements among nations. Strong institutions. Support for human rights. Investments in development. All these are vital ingredients in bringing about the evolution that President Kennedy spoke about. And yet, I do not believe that we will have the will, the determination, the staying power, to complete this work without something more—and that's the continued expansion of our moral imagination; an insistence that there's something irreducible that we all share.

As the world grows smaller, you might think it would be easier for human beings to recognize how similar we are; to understand that we're all basically seeking the same things; that we all hope for the chance to live out our lives with some measure of happiness and fulfillment for ourselves and our families.

And yet somehow, given the dizzying pace of globalization, the cultural leveling of modernity, it perhaps comes as no surprise that people fear the loss of what they cherish in their particular identities—their race, their tribe, and perhaps most powerfully their religion. In some places, this fear has led to conflict. At times, it even feels like we're moving backwards. We see it in the Middle East, as the conflict between Arabs and Jews seems to harden. We see it in nations that are torn asunder by tribal lines.

And most dangerously, we see it in the way that religion is used to justify the murder of innocents by those who have distorted and defiled the great religion of Islam, and who attacked my country from Afghanistan. These extremists are not the first to kill in the name of God; the cruelties of the Crusades are amply recorded. But they remind us that no Holy War can ever be a just war. For if you truly believe that you are carrying out divine will, then there is no need for restraint—no need to spare the pregnant mother, or the medic, or the Red Cross worker, or even a person of one's own faith. Such a warped view of religion is not just incompatible with the concept of peace, but I believe it's incompatible with the very purpose of faith—for the one rule that lies at the heart of every major religion is that we do unto others as we would have them do unto us.

Adhering to this law of love has always been the core struggle of human nature. For we are fallible. We make mistakes, and fall victim to the temptations of pride, and power, and sometimes evil. Even those of us with the best of intentions will at times fail to right the wrongs before us.

But we do not have to think that human nature is perfect for us to still believe that the human condition can be perfected. We do not have to live in an idealized world to still reach for those ideals that will make it a better place. The non-violence practiced by men like Gandhi and King may not have been practical or possible in every circumstance, but the love that they preached—their fundamental faith in human progress—that must always be the North Star that guides us on our journey.

For if we lose that faith—if we dismiss it as silly or naïve; if we divorce it from the decisions that we make on issues of war and peace—then we lose what's best about humanity. We lose our sense of possibility. We lose our moral compass.

Like generations have before us, we must reject that future. As Dr. King said at this occasion so many years ago, "I refuse to accept despair as the final response to the ambiguities of history. I refuse to accept the idea that the 'isness' of man's present condition makes him morally incapable of reaching up for the eternal 'oughtness' that forever confronts him."

Let us reach for the world that ought to be—that spark of the divine that still stirs within each of our souls.

Somewhere today, in the here and now, in the world as it is, a soldier sees he's outgunned, but stands firm to keep the peace. Somewhere today, in this world, a young protestor awaits the brutality of her government, but has the courage to march on. Somewhere today, a mother facing punishing poverty still takes the time to teach her child, scrapes together what few coins she has to send that child to school—because she believes that a cruel world still has a place for that child's dreams.

Let us live by their example. We can acknowledge that oppression will always be with us, and still strive for justice. We can admit the intractability of depravation, and still strive for dignity. Clear-eyed, we can understand that there will be war, and still strive for peace. We can do that—for that is the story of human progress; that's the hope of all the world; and at this moment of challenge, that must be our work here on Earth.

Thank you very much.

UNIT 3

✠

SECURITY

War Not A Biological Necessity

s war a biological necessity, a sociological inevitability, or just a bad invention? Those who argue for the first view endow man with such pugnacious instincts that some outlet in aggressive behaviour is necessary if man is to reach full human stature. It was this point of view which lay behind William James's famous essay, 'The Moral Equivalent of War', in which he tried to retain the warlike virtues and channel them in new directions. A similar point of view has lain behind the Soviet Union's attempt to make competition between groups rather than between individuals. A basic, competitive, aggressive, warring human nature is assumed, and those who wish to outlaw war or outlaw competitiveness merely try to find new and less socially destructive ways in which these biologically given aspects of man's nature can find expression. Then there are those who take the second view: warfare is the inevitable concomitant of the development of the state, the struggle for land and natural resources, of class societies springing not from the nature of man, but, from the nature of history. War is nevertheless inevitable unless we change our social system and outlaw classes, the struggle for power, and possessions; and in the event of our success warfare would disappear, as a symptom vanishes when the disease is cured.

One may hold a sort of compromise position between these two extremes; one may claim that all aggression springs from the frustration of man's biologically determined drives and that, since all forms of culture are frustrating, it is certain each new generation will be aggressive and the aggression will find its natural and inevitable expression in race war, class war, nationalistic war, and so on. All three of these positions are very popular

Margaret Mead, "Warfare is only an invention—not a biological necessity," from *Asia: Journal of the American Asiatic Association*, Vol. 40, No. 8, pp. 402–405. Published by Asia Publishing Company, 1940. Copyright by Indiawise. Permission to reprint granted by the rights holder.

War Not A Biological Necessity | 165

today among those who think seriously about the problems of war and its possible prevention, but I wish to urge another point of view, less defeatist, perhaps, than the first and third and more accurate than the second: that is, that warfare, by which I mean recognised conflict between two groups as groups, in which each group puts an army (even if the army is only fifteen pygmies) into the field to fight and kill, if possible, some of the members of the army of the other group—that warfare of this sort is an invention like any other of the inventions in terms of which we order our lives, such as writing, marriage, cooking our food instead of eating it raw, trial by jury, or burial of the dead, and so on. Some of this list anyone will grant are inventions: trial by jury is confined to very limited portions of the globe; we know that there are tribes that do not bury their dead but instead expose or cremate them; and we know that only part of the human race has had the knowledge of writing as its cultural inheritance. But, whenever a way of doing things is found universally, such as the use of fire or the practice of some form of marriage, we tend to think at once that it is not an invention at all but an attribute of humanity itself. And yet even such universals as marriage and the use of fire are inventions like the rest, very basic ones, inventions which were, perhaps, necessary if human history was to take the turn that it has taken, but nevertheless inventions. At some point in his social development man was undoubtedly without the institution of marriage or the knowledge of the use of fire.

THE CASE FOR warfare is much clearer because there are peoples even today who have no warfare. Of these the Eskimos are perhaps the most conspicuous examples, but the Lepchas of Sikkim described by Geoffrey Gorer in Himalayan Village are as good. Neither of these peoples understands war, not even defensive warfare. The idea of warfare is lacking, and this idea is as essential to really carrying on war as an alphabet or a syllabary is to writing. But, whereas the Lepchas are a gentle, unquarrelsome people, and the advocates of other points of view might argue that they are not full human beings or that they had never been frustrated and so had no aggression to expand in warfare, the Eskimo case gives no such possibility of interpretation. The Eskimos are not a mild and meek people; many of them are turbulent and troublesome. Fights, theft of wives, murder, cannibalism, occur among them—all outbursts of passionate men goaded by desire or intolerable circumstance. Here are men faced with hunger, men faced with loss of their wives, men faced with the threat of extermination by other men, and here are orphan children, growing up miserably with no one to care for them, mocked and neglected by those about them. The personality necessary for war, the circumstances necessary to goad men to desperation are present, but there is no war. When a travelling Eskimo entered a settlement, he might have to fight the strongest man in the settlement to establish his position among them, but this was a test of strength and bravery, not war. The idea of warfare, of one group organising against another group to maim and wound and kill them was absent. And, without that idea, passions might rage but there was no war.

But, it may be argued, is not this because the Eskimos have such a low and undeveloped form of social organisation? They own no land, they move from place to place, camping, it is true, season after season on the same site, but this is not something to fight for as the modern nations of the world fight for land and raw materials. They have no permanent possessions that can be looted, no towns that can be burned. They have no social classes to produce stress and strains within the society which might force it to go to war outside. Does not the absence of war among the Eskimos, while disproving the biological necessity of war, just go to confirm the point that it is the state of development of the society which accounts for war and nothing else?

We find the answer among the pygmy peoples of the Andaman Islands in the Bay of Bengal. The Andamans also represent an exceedingly low level of society; they are a hunting and food-gathering people; they live in tiny hordes without any class stratification; their houses are simpler than the snow houses of the Eskimo. But they knew about warfare. The army might contain only fifteen determined pygmies marching in a straight line, but it was the real thing none the less. Tiny army met tiny army in open battle, blows were exchanged, casualties suffered, and the state of warfare could only be concluded by a peacemaking ceremony.

Similarly, among the Australian aborigines, who built no permanent dwellings but wandered from water hole to water hole over their almost desert country, warfare—and rules of 'international law'—were highly developed. The student of social evolution will seek in vain for his obvious causes of war, struggle for lands, struggle for power of one group over another, expansion of population, need to divert the minds of a populace restive under tyranny, or even the ambition of a successful leader to enhance his own prestige. All are absent, but warfare as a practice remained, and men engaged in it and killed one another in the course of a war because killing is what is done in wars.

From instances like these it becomes apparent that an inquiry into the causes of war misses the fundamental point as completely as does an insistence upon the biological necessity of war. If a people have an idea of going to war and the idea that war is the way in which certain situations, defined within their society, are to be handled, they will sometimes go to war. If they are a mild and unaggressive people, like the Pueblo Indians, they may limit themselves to defensive warfare, but they will be forced to think in terms of war because there are peoples near them who have warfare as a pattern, and offensive, raiding, pillaging warfare at that. When the pattern of warfare is known, people like the Pueblo Indians will defend themselves, taking advantage of their natural defences, the mesa village site, and people like the Lepchas, having no natural defences and no idea of warfare, will merely submit to the invader. But the essential point remains the same. There is a way of behaving which is known to a given people and labelled as an appropriate form of behaviour; a bold and warlike people like the Sioux or the Maori may label warfare as desirable as well as possible, a mild people like the Pueblo Indians may label warfare as undesirable, but to the minds of both peoples the possibility of warfare is present. Their thoughts, their hopes, their plans are oriented about this idea—that warfare may be selected as the way to meet some situation.

SO SIMPLE peoples and civilised peoples, mild peoples and violent, assertive peoples, will all go to war if they have the invention, just as those peoples who have the custom of duelling will have duels and peoples who have the pattern of vendetta will indulge in vendetta. And, conversely, peoples who do not know of duelling will not fight duels, even though their wives are seduced and their daughters ravished; they may on occasion commit murder but they will not fight duels. Cultures which lack the idea of the vendetta will not meet every quarrel in this way. A people can use only the forms it has. So the Balinese have their special way of dealing with a quarrel between two individuals: if the two feel that the causes of quarrel are heavy, they may go and register their quarrel in the temple before the gods, and, making offerings, they may swear never to have anything to do with each other again. ... But in other societies, although individuals might feel as full of animosity and as unwilling to have any further contact as do the Balinese, they cannot register their quarrel with the gods and go on quietly about their business because registering quarrels with the gods is not an invention of which they know.

Yet, if it be granted that warfare is, after all, an invention, it may nevertheless be an invention that lends itself to certain types of personality, to the exigent needs of autocrats, to the expansionist desires of crowded peoples, to the desire for plunder and rape and loot which is engendered by a dull and frustrating life. What, then, can we say of this congruence between warfare and its uses? If it is a form which fits so well, is not this congruence the essential point? But even here the primitive material causes us to wonder, because there are tribes who go to war merely for glory, having no quarrel with the enemy, suffering from no tyrant within their boundaries, anxious neither for land nor loot nor women, but merely anxious to win prestige which within that tribe has been declared obtainable only by war and without which no young man can hope to win his sweetheart's smile of approval. But if, as was the case with the Bush Negroes of Dutch Guiana, it is artistic ability which is necessary to win a girl's approval, the same young man would have to be carving rather than going out on a war party.

In many parts of the world, war is a game in which the individual can win counters—counters which bring him prestige in the eyes of his own sex or of the opposite sex; he plays for these counters as he might, in our society, strive for a tennis championship. Warfare is a frame for such prestige-seeking merely because it calls for the display of certain skills and certain virtues; all of these skills—riding straight, shooting straight, dodging the missiles of the enemy and sending one's own straight to the mark—can be equally well exercised in some other framework and, equally, the virtues endurance, bravery, loyalty, steadfastness—can be displayed in other contexts. The tie-up between proving oneself a man and proving this by a success in organised killing is due to a definition which many societies have made of manliness. And often, even in those societies which counted success in warfare a proof of human worth, strange turns were given to the idea, as when the plains Indians gave their highest awards to the man who touched a live enemy rather than to the man who brought in a scalp—from a dead enemy—because the latter was less risky.

Warfare is just an invention known to the majority of human societies by which they permit their young men either to accumulate prestige or avenge their honour or acquire loot or wives or slaves or sago lands or cattle or appease the blood lust of their gods or the restless souls of the recently dead. It is just an invention, older and more widespread than the jury system, but none the less an invention.

But, once we have said this, have we said anything at all? Despite a few stances, dear to the instances of controversialist, of the loss of the useful arts, once an invention is made which proves congruent with human needs or social forms, it tends to persist. Grant that war is an invention, that it is not a biological necessity nor the outcome of certain special types of social forms, still once the invention is made, what are we to do about it? The Indian who had been subsisting on the buffalo for generations because with his primitive weapons he could slaughter only a limited number of buffalo did not return to his primitive weapons when he saw that the white man's more efficient weapons were exterminating the buffalo. A desire for the white man's cloth may mortgage the South Sea Islander to the white man's plantation, but he does not return to making bark cloth, which would have left him free. Once an invention is known and accepted, men do not easily relinquish it. The skilled workers may smash the first steam looms which they feel are to be their undoing, but they accept them in the end, and no movement which has insisted upon the mere abandonment of usable inventions has ever had much success. Warfare is here, as part of our thought; the deeds of warriors are immortalised in the words of our poets, the toys of our children are modelled upon the weapons of the soldier, the frame of reference within which our statesmen and our diplomats work always contains war. If we know that it is not inevitable, that it is due to historical accident that warfare is one of the ways in which we think of behaving, are we given any hope by that? What hope is there of persuading nations to abandon war, nations so thoroughly imbued with the idea that resort to war is, if not actually desirable and noble, at least inevitable whenever certain defined circumstances arise?

In answer to this question I think we might turn to the history of other social inventions, and inventions which must once have seemed as finally entrenched as warfare. Take the methods of trial which preceded the jury system: ordeal and trial by combat. Unfair, capricious, alien as they are to our feeling today, they were once the only methods open to individuals accused of some offense. The invention of trial by jury gradually replaced these methods until only witches, and finally not even witches, had to resort to the ordeal. And for a long time the jury system seemed the best and finest method of settling legal disputes, but today new inventions, trial before judges only or before commissions, are replacing the jury system. In each case the old method was replaced by a new social invention. The ordeal did not go out because people thought it unjust or wrong; it went out because a method more congruent with the institutions and feelings of the period was invented. And, if we despair over the way in which war seems such an ingrained habit of most of the human race, we can take comfort from the fact that a poor invention will usually give place to a better invention.

For this, two conditions, at least, are necessary. The people must recognise the defects of the old invention, and someone must make a new one. Propaganda against warfare, documentation of its terrible cost in human suffering and social waste, these prepare the ground by teaching people to feel that warfare is a defective social institution. There is further needed a belief that social invention is possible and the invention of new methods which will render warfare as out of date as the tractor is making the plough, or the motor car the horse and buggy. A form of behaviour becomes out of date only when something else takes its place, and, in order to invent forms of behaviour which will make war obsolete, it is a first requirement to believe that an invention is possible.

Reprinted from Margaret Mead, 'Warfare is only an invention—not a biological necessity' ASIA, XL (1940).

Excerpt from
All Quiet on the Western Front

We travel for several days. The first aeroplanes appear in the sky. We roll on past transport lines. Guns, guns. The light railway picks us up. I search for my regiment. No one knows exactly where it lies. Somewhere or other I put up for the night, somewhere or other I receive provisions and a few vague instructions. And so with my pack and my rifle I set out again on the way.

By the time I come up they are no longer in that devastated place. I hear we have become one of the flying divisions that are pushed in wherever it is hottest. That does not sound cheerful to me. They tell me of heavy losses that we have been having. I inquire after Kat and Albert. No one knows anything of them.

I search farther and wander about here and there; it is a wonderful feeling. One night and then another I camp out like a Red Indian. Then at last I get some definite information, and by the afternoon I am able to report to the Orderly Room.

The sergeant-major detains me there. The company comes back in two days' time. There is no object in sending me up now.

"What was it like on leave?" he asks, "pretty good, eh?"

"In parts," I say.

"Yes," he sighs, "yes, if a man didn't have to come away again. The second half is always rather messed up by that."

I loaf around until the company comes back in the early morning, grey, dirty, soured, and gloomy. Then I jump up, push in amongst them, my eyes searching. There is Tjaden, there is Müller blowing his nose, and there are Kat and Kropp. We arrange our sacks of

Erich Maria Remarque, *All Quiet on the Western Front*, pp. 122–128. Published by Fawcett Publications, 1967. Copyright by Ballantine Books. Permission to reprint granted by the rights holder.

All Quiet on the Western Front | 171

straw side by side. I have an uneasy conscience when I look at them, and yet without any good reason. Before we turn in I bring out the rest of the potato-cakes and jam so that they can have some too.

The two outer cakes are mouldy, still it is possible to eat them. I keep those for myself and give the fresh ones to Kat and Kropp.

Kat chews and says: "These are from your mother?"

I nod.

"Good," says he, "I can tell by the taste."

I could almost weep. I can hardly control myself any longer. But it will soon be all right again back here with Kat and Albert. This is where I belong.

"You've been lucky," whispers Kropp to me before we drop off to sleep, "they say we are going to Russia."

To Russia, it's not much of a war over there.

In the distance the front thunders. The walls of the hut rattle.

There's a great deal of polishing being done. We are inspected at every turn. Everything that is torn is exchanged for new. I score a spotless new tunic out of it and Kat, of course, an entire outfit. A rumour is going round that there may be peace, but the other story is more likely—that we are bound for Russia. Still, what do we need new things for in Russia? At last it leaks out—the Kaiser is coming to review us. Hence all the inspections.

For eight whole days one would suppose we were in a base-camp, there is so much drill and fuss. Everyone is peevish and touchy, we do not take kindly to all this polishing, much less to parades. Such things exasperate a soldier more than the front-line.

At last the moment arrives. We stand up stiff and the Kaiser appears. We are curious to see what he looks like. He stalks along the line, and I am really rather disappointed; judging from his pictures I imagine him to be bigger and more powerfully built, and above all to have a thundering voice.

He distributes Iron Crosses and speaks to this man and to that. Then we march off.

Afterwards we discuss it. Tjaden says with astonishment:

"So that is the All-Highest! And everyone, bar nobody, has to stand up stiff in front of him!" He meditates: "Hindenburg too, he has to stand up stiff to him, eh?"

"Sure," says Kat.

Tjaden hasn't finished yet. He thinks for a while and then asks: "And would a king have to stand up stiff to an emperor?"

None of us is quite sure about it, but we don't suppose so. They are both so exalted that standing strictly to attention is probably not insisted on.

"What rot you do hatch out," says Kat. "The main point is that you have to stand stiff yourself."

But Tjaden is quite fascinated. His otherwise prosy fancy is blowing bubbles. "But look," he announces, "I simply can't believe that an emperor has to go to the latrine the same as I have."

"You can bet your boots on it."

"Four and a half-wit make seven," says Kat. "You've got a maggot in your brain, Tjaden, just you run along to the latrine quick, and get your head clear, so that you don't talk like a two-year-old."

Tjaden disappears.

"But what I would like to know," says Albert, "is whether there would not have been a war if the Kaiser had said No."

"I'm sure of this much," I interject, "he was against it."

"Well, if not him alone, then perhaps if twenty or thirty people in the world had said No."

"That's probable," I agree, "but they damned well said Yes."

"It's queer, when one thinks about it," goes on Kropp, "we are here to protect our fatherland. And the French are over there to protect their fatherland. Now, who's in the right?"

"Perhaps both," say I, without believing it.

"Yes, well now," pursues Albert, and I see that he means to drive me into a corner, "but our professors and parsons and newspapers say that we are the only ones that are right, and let's hope so;—but the French professors and parsons and newspapers say that the right is on their side, what about that?"

"That I don't know," I say, "but whichever way it is there's war all the same and every month more countries coming in."

Tjaden reappears. He is still quite excited and again joins the conversation, wondering just how a war gets started.

"Mostly by one country badly offending another," answers Albert with a slight air of superiority.

Then Tjaden pretends to be obtuse. "A country? I don't follow. A mountain in Germany cannot offend a mountain in France. Or a river, or a wood, or a field of wheat."

"Are you really as stupid as that, or are you just pulling my leg?" growls Kropp. "I don't mean that at all. One people offends the other—"

"Then I haven't any business here at all," replies Tjaden, "I don't feel myself offended."

"Well, let me tell you," says Albert sourly, "it doesn't apply to tramps like you."

"Then I can be going home right away," retorts Tjaden, and we all laugh.

"Ach, man! he means the people as a whole, the State—" exclaims Müller.

"State, State"—Tjaden snaps his fingers contemptuously. "Gendarmes, police, taxes, that's your State;—if that's what you are talking about, no thank you."

"That's right," says Kat, "you've said something for once, Tjaden. State and home-country, there's a big difference."

"But they go together," insists Kropp, "without the State there wouldn't be any home-country."

"True, but just you consider, almost all of us are simple folk. And in France, too, the majority of men are labourers, workmen or poor clerks. Now just why would a French blacksmith or a French shoemaker want to attack us? No, it is merely the rulers. I had never seen a Frenchman before I came here, and it will be just the same with the majority of Frenchman as regards us. They weren't asked about it any more than we were."

"Then what exactly is the war for?" asks Tjaden.

Kat shrugs his shoulders. "There must be some people to whom the war is useful."

"Well, I'm not one of them," grins Tjaden.

"Not you, nor anybody else here."

"Who are they then?" persists Tjaden. "It isn't any use to the Kaiser either. He has everything he can want already."

"I'm not so sure about that," contradicts Kat, "he has not had a war up till now. And every full-grown emperor requires at least one war, otherwise he wouldn't become famous. You look in your school books."

"And generals too," adds Detering, "they become famous through war."

"Even more famous than emperors," adds Kat.

"There are other people back behind there who profit by the war, that's certain," growls Detering.

"I think it is more a kind of fever," say Albert. "No one in particular wants it, and then all at once there it is. We didn't want the war, the others say the same thing—and yet half the world is in it all the same."

"But there are more lies told by the other side than by us," say I; "just think of those pamphlets the prisoners have on them, where it says that we eat Belgian children. The fellows who write that ought to go and hang themselves. They are the real culprits."

Müller gets up. "Anyway, it is better that the war is here instead of in Germany. Just you take a look at the shell-holes."

"True," assents Tjaden, "but no war at all would be better still."

He is quite proud of himself because he has for once scored over us volunteers. And his opinion is quite typical here, one meets it time and again, and there is nothing with which one can properly counter it, because that is the limit of their comprehension of the factors involved. The national feeling of the soldier resolves itself into this—here he is. But that is the end of it; everything else from joining up onwards he criticizes from a practical point of view.

Albert lies down on the grass and growls angrily: "The best thing is not to talk about the rotten business."

"It won't make any difference, that's sure," agrees Kat.

As for the windfall, we have to return almost all the new things and take back our old rags again. The good ones were merely for the inspection.

Instead of going to Russia, we go up the line again. On the way we pass through a devastated wood with the tree trunks shattered and ground ploughed up.

At several places there are tremendous craters. "Great guns, something's hit that," I say to Kat.

"Trench mortars," he replies, and then points up at one of the trees.

In the branches dead men are hanging. A naked soldier is squatting in the fork of a tree, he still has his helmet on, otherwise he is entirely unclad. There is only half of him sitting up there, the top half, the legs are missing.

"What can that mean?" I ask.

"He's been blown out of his clothes," mutters Tjaden.

"It's funny," says Kat, "we have seen that a couple of times now. If a mortar gets you it blows you almost clean out of your clothes. It's the concussion that does it."

I search around. And so it is. Here hang bits of uniform, and somewhere else is plastered a bloody mess that was once a human limb. Over there lies a body with nothing but a piece of the underpants on one leg and the collar of the tunic around its neck. Otherwise it is naked and the clothes are hanging up in the tree. Both arms are missing as though they had been pulled out. I discover one of them twenty yards off in a shrub.

The dead man lies on his face. There, where the arm wounds are, the earth is black with blood. Underfoot the leaves are scratched up as though the man had been kicking.

"That's no joke, Kat," say I.

"No more is a shell splinter in the belly," he replies shrugging his shoulders.

"But don't get tender-hearted," says Tjaden.

All this can only have happened a little while ago, the blood is still fresh. As everybody we see there is dead we do not waste any more time, but report the affair at the next stretcher-bearers' post. After all it is not our business to take these stretcher-bearers' jobs away from them.

Terrorism and Weapons of Mass Destruction

MICHAEL D. INTRILIGATOR AND ABDULLAH TOUKAN

INTRODUCTION: MOTIVATION, DEFINITIONS AND A HISTORICAL EXAMPLE

The threat of terrorist use of nuclear weapons and other weapons of mass destruction (WMD), whether biological, chemical or radiological, is a real one that represents a most serious threat to the US and other nations that are potential targets of subnational terrorist groups or networks. Transnational terrorism and the potential acquisition by terrorists of weapons of mass destruction are part of the "asymmetric" dynamics of the various unexpected and new threats that have thrust the international community into a new and uncertain conflict. These dynamics have been witnessed in the 9/11 (September 11, 2001) al Qaeda terrorist attacks on New York and Washington, the 3/11 (2004) terrorist attacks against Madrid, and the 7/11 (2005) terrorist attacks against London. Terrorist acquisition and use of nuclear weapons is an extremely serious problem that must not be dismissed as the subject of works of fiction. Indeed, the US casualties and losses on 9/11 would be seen as relatively minor in comparison to a possible terrorist strike using nuclear weapons. One of the only things that both candidates in the US 2004 presidential elections agreed on was that this is the most serious threat the country faces.

Graham Allison[1] discusses this issue in his 2004 book *Nuclear Terrorism*, emphasizing that, as he puts it in the subtitle of this book, nuclear terrorism is the "*ultimate preventable catastrophe.*" Unfortunately, this conclusion may be overly optimistic in that his proposals for strict control over fissile material and the prevention of the acquisition of nuclear weapons by additional nations, while excellent policies, may not work perfectly. It is also

Michael D. Intriligator and Abdullah Toukan, "Terrorism and Weapons of Mass Destruction," from *Countering Terrorism and WMD: Creating a Global Counter-Terrorism Network*, pp. 69–84. Copyright © 2006 by Taylor & Francis Group. Permission to reprint granted by the publisher.

possible that terrorist groups have already obtained enough of this material to produce a nuclear weapon or even already possess such a weapon.

It is possible to identify various "nightmare scenarios." Most devastating would be a repeat of 9/11 but this time with a nuclear weapon. If a subnational terrorist group gained access to a nuclear weapon, it could use it or at least threaten to do so. If Osama bin Laden had even a crude nuclear weapon he could have used it on 9/11 or in other al Qaeda attacks. Some information exists about terrorists' intentions to obtain nuclear weapons. Osama bin Laden has specifically referred to the acquisition of nuclear weapons by the al Qaeda terrorist network as a "religious duty," and documents were found in the al Qaeda caves in Afghanistan regarding their intent to use WMD that even included a schematic diagram of a nuclear weapon. After the 9/11 attacks, al Qaeda spokesman Abu Gheith wrote:

> We have not reached parity with them. We have the right to kill 4 million Americans—2 million of them children—and to exile twice as many and wound and cripple hundreds of thousands. Furthermore, it is our right to fight them with chemical and biological weapons, so as to afflict them with the fatal maladies that have afflicted the Muslims because of the [Americans'] chemical and biological weapons.[2]

If this stated goal of retribution were true, the only way that al Qaeda could attain this objective would be to use nuclear weapons or a highly destructive and sophisticated biological agent.

Other nightmare scenarios involving terrorists using WMD include a strike with conventional weapons against a nuclear power plant near a major city such as Indian Point near New York City or a terrorist group placing a nuclear weapon in a container on a freighter entering a major port, such as the Los Angeles/Long Beach port complex, the largest in the US. It would not be difficult to place such a bomb in one of the many containers entering US ports, as almost none of them are inspected. Furthermore, the Los Angeles/Long Beach port represents an important potential target for terrorists, as it accounts for over 40 percent of all US foreign trade, so knocking it out of commission would have an enormous impact on the economies of the US and all its trading partners, potentially disrupting much of world trade.[3]

Garwin[4] most fears what he calls "megaterrorism," involving thousands of casualties, by means of biological warfare agents or nuclear weapons. He postulates that terrorists could use a nuclear weapon stolen from Russia or an improvised nuclear device based on highly enriched uranium built in the US. Some acts of megaterrorism, including 9/11, were foreseen by the US Commission on National Security in the 21st Century (the Hart-Rudman Commission) in its 1999 report, which stated that:

Terrorism will appeal to many weak states as an attractive option to blunt the influence of major powers … [but] there will be a greater incidence of ad hoc cells and individuals, often moved by religious zeal, seemingly irrational cultist beliefs, or seething resentment … The growing resentment against Western culture and values … is breeding a backlash … Therefore, the United States should assume that it will be a target of terrorist attacks against its homeland using weapons of mass destruction. The United States will be vulnerable to such strikes.[5]

It is customary to classify nuclear, biological, chemical and radiological weapons as WMD, but there are important differences among these weapons. In fact, it is misleading or even mistaken to lump together all of these weapons as one category of "weapons of mass destruction," since nuclear weapons are in a class all to themselves in view of their tremendous destructive potential, as shown in Table 4.1. While nuclear weapons are not now, as far as we know, in the hands of terrorists, they could be sometime in the future, given that this is an old technology that is well understood world-wide and given that there has recently been a proliferation of WMD-related technologies and material. Furthermore, recent trends in terrorist incidents indicate a tendency toward mass-casualty attacks for which WMD are well suited. There is even a type of rivalry between various terrorist groups to have the largest impact and the greatest publicity, topping the actions of other such groups.

The terrorist attacks on the World Trade Center (1993), the Tokyo subway (1995) and the Murrah Federal Building in Oklahoma (1995) clearly signaled the emergence of this new trend in terrorism mass-casualty attacks. Terrorists who seek to maximize both damage and political impact by using larger devices and who try to cause more casualties have characterized this new pattern of terrorism. There have also been the revelations that A.Q. Khan, the "father" of the Pakistan nuclear weapon, provided nuclear weapons technology to several nations, suggesting the emergence of a type of nuclear weapons "bazaar" that will sell components, technology, fissile material, etc. to the highest bidder, including another nation such as Libya, North Korea or Iran or possibly a well-financed terrorist group. If terrorists had access to the needed funding they could probably easily find another such expert or middleman to provide them the detailed plans and even the components for a nuclear weapon. Even without a full-fledged nuclear weapon they could assemble a radiological dispersal device that could cause massive disruption and also have massive psychological effects on the population.

There are many different types of terrorist groups or networks worldwide; they are not all fundamentalist Muslim or based in the Middle East or South and Southeast Asia. Table 4.2 shows the various terrorist groups that might resort to the use of WMD against the US. Their motivation is probably not merely poverty and ignorance, as is often alleged, but rather revenge for past humiliations and retribution as stated in the above quote from

Abu Gheith. As Friedman[6] states, "The single most underappreciated force in international relations is humiliation." Of course, different terrorist groups have different motivations and ideologies so there is no such thing as a "stereo-typical terrorist." Furthermore, a terrorist network would not be able to operate in the capacity that it does in the absence of the other components that engage in fundraising, recruitment and social support. In contrast to previous forms of transnational terrorism, the support base of transnational terrorist groups has spread throughout the globe rather than in any distinct geographical cluster.

Table 4.1A The comparative effects of biological, chemical and nuclear weapons delivered against the United States

	Area covered (sq. km)	Deaths assuming 3,000–10,000 people per sq. km
Using missile warheads		
Chemical: 300 kg of sarin nerve gas with a density of 70 milligrams per cubic meter	0.22	60–200
Biological: 30 kg of anthrax spores with a density of 0.1 milligrams per cubic meter	10	30,000–100,000
Nuclear: One 12.5 kiloton nuclear device achieving 5 lbs per cubic inch of over-pressure	7.8	23,000–80,000
1.0 megaton hydrogen bomb Using one aircraft dispensing 1,000 kg of sarin nerve gas or 100 kg of anthrax spores	190	570,000–1,900,000
Clear sunny day, light breeze:		
sarin nerve gas	0.74	300–700
anthrax spores	46	130,000–460,000
Overcast day or night, moderate wind:		
sarin nerve gas	0.8	400–800
anthrax spores	140	420,000–1,400,000
Clear calm night:		
sarin nerve gas	7.8	3,000–8,000
anthrax spores	300	1–3 million

One important consequence of the US invasion of Afghanistan was to eliminate the main base of al Qaeda, destroying its central command structure. In the absence of this central command structure, individual networks appear to have gained greater freedom and independence in tactical decisions than the traditional terrorist cells of the past. This particular trend in terrorism represents a different and potentially far more lethal one than that posed by the more familiar, traditional, terrorist adversaries. The 9/11 attacks have demonstrated that transnational terrorism is now more lethal and that it can have a fundamental political and strategic impact. Further, the threat of terrorist use of WMD is still possible and perhaps inevitable given the goals of al Qaeda, which is probably now rebuilding its central command structure.

Table 4.1B Biological weapons' estimated casualties using aerosol delivery mechanism

	Amount released	*Estimated damage/ lethality*
Anthrax	100 kg spores released over a city the size of Washington, DC	130,000–3 million deaths
Plague	50 kg Y. pestis released over city of 5 million people	150,000 infected 36,000 deaths
Tularemia	50 kg F. tularensis released over city of 5 million people	250,000 incapacitated 19,000 deaths

Sources:
World Health Organization, *Health Aspects of Chemical and Biological Weapons: Report of a WHO Group of Consultants*, 2nd edn. (Geneva: WHO, 1970).
Centers for Disease Control and Prevention (CDC), Fact Sheets on Biological and Chemical Agents, Atlanta, GA.
Anthony H. Cordesman material in the Office of Technology Assessment, *Proliferation of Weapons of Mass Destruction: Assessing the Risks*, US Congress, OTA–ISC–559, Washington, DC, Aug. 1993, pp. 53–4.

There has been to date only one example of a terrorist group using WMD. This historical example is the Japanese terrorist group Aum Shinrikyo's release of sarin nerve gas on the Tokyo subway on March 20, 1995. This attack represented the crossing of a threshold and demonstrated that certain types of WMD are within the reach of some terrorist groups. The attack came at the peak of the Monday morning rush hour, right under police headquarters, in one of the busiest commuter systems in the world, and resulted in 12 deaths and over 5,000 injuries. While the number of deaths was relatively small, this was the largest number of casualties of any terrorist attacks up to that time. This number of casualties is exceeded only by the 9/11 attacks on the World Trade Center in New York and the Pentagon in Virginia as well as in Pennsylvania that resulted in about

3,000 deaths and almost 9,000 nonfatal casualties.[7] Even before their attack on the Tokyo subway, Aum Shinrikyo had conducted attacks using sarin and anthrax.[8] Following this 1995 attack in Japan, President Clinton issued Presidential Decision Directive 39 stating that the prevention of WMD from becoming available to terrorists is the highest priority of the US government.

What is the threat of terrorists' use of WMD?

Owing to a number of global developments over the past decade, the threat that terrorists might resort to weapons of mass destruction has received increased attention from political leaders and the news media. These developments include: the proliferation of WMD-related technologies, materials and know-how; trends in transnational terrorist incidents, suggesting a growing tendency toward mass-casualty attacks for which WMD are well suited; and the interest in WMD that has been expressed by Osama bin Laden and al Qaeda.

Table 4.2. *Possible terrorist groups that might resort to the use of WMD against the US*

Group	Description	Possible reason
Non-state-sponsored terrorists	These are groups that operate autonomously, receiving no significant support from any government. These groups may be transnational, they don't see themselves as citizens of any one country, and groups that operate without regard for national boundaries carry out thereby transnational terrorism. Typical: al Qaeda terrorist organization	Terrorist organization backed in a corner, losing ground and support internationally. Terrorist organization trying to recapture public attention by resorting to higher levels of terrorism, resulting in mass casualties.
State-sponsored terrorists	International terrorist group that generally operates independently but is supported and controlled by one or more nation-states as part of waging asymmetric surrogate war against their enemies. The US has labeled Cuba, Iran, Libya, North Korea, Sudan and Syria as states sponsoring terrorism.	To undermine US policy and influence, and for the US to change its policy.

The events of September 11 and the wave of anthrax-laced envelopes mailed in the US during 2001—a case that still has not been solved—together constituted a watershed in the perception of the non-conventional terror threat in general and of bioterrorism in particular. These events heightened the potential link between transnational terrorism and WMD, with biological weapons in particular looming as a new and dangerous threat.

Overall, while there has been remarkably little historical use of WMD by terrorists and very few fatalities resulting from their use, one cannot rule out terrorist groups gaining such weapons and using them in the future. Sooner or later they could be available to terrorists. As former Secretary of Defense William Cohen stated concerning WMD terrorism: "The question is no longer if this will happen, but when." In addition, other groups have sought to gain access and use nuclear weapons and other WMD, which compounds the problem as new nations and subnational groups seek these weapons. Some terrorist groups may feel that, in order to attract worldwide attention, they should escalate from conventional to biological or nuclear weapons. The likely users of these and other WMD are probably fundamentalist terrorist groups, given both their motivation and their access to funding and expertise.[9]

It should be noted that nuclear weapons are "self-protecting"—they are difficult to acquire, to use and to take care of properly. This has the effect of keeping such weapons out of the reach of most national and subnational groups, including terrorists, and Table 4.3 summarizes some of the technical hurdles for nuclear, biological and chemical weapons programs. Nevertheless, a well-financed terrorist group could have the resources needed to hire the experts who could build and take care of such weapons, as was the case with Aum Shinrikyo. The CIA had predicted copycat phenomena in that case, but they did not in fact materialize, probably due to the difficulties of building and maintaining such a weapon. Also, each weapon is different and, while there are some weapons that can be developed easily, such as ricin, others are extremely difficult to build, including nuclear weapons. Nevertheless, with demand rising and marginal cost falling, as is also the case with other WMD technologies, it is only a matter of time before such weapons, including nuclear weapons, become available to terrorist groups.

Table 4.3 shows that, when addressing the supply and demand sides for WMD, the technical hurdles to produce such weapons should be taken into consideration. Owing to the complexity and expense of the processes needed to develop nuclear weapons, the *supply* side has to be addressed for such weapons. While few states are known to have nuclear weapons capability, those that have nuclear reactors should be addressed. With tight security measures at these plants and export controls, as well as all material under IAEA safeguards, no nuclear material would fall into the hands of terrorist organizations.

By contrast, owing to the relative ease with which biological, chemical and radiological weapons can be produced in a vast number of open laboratories and facilities that are designated as purely civilian, the *demand* side should be addressed for such weapons. This implies the need to identify and to destroy terrorist organizations that are pursuing the production or possession of these weapons.

Table 4.3. *Technical hurdles for nuclear, biological and chemical weapon programs*

	Nuclear	*Biological*	*Chemical*
Feed materials	Uranium ore, oxide widely available; plutonium and partly enriched uranium dispersed through nuclear programs, mostly under international safeguards.	Potential biological warfare agents are readily available locally or internationally from natural sources or commercial suppliers.	Many basic chemicals available for commercial purposes; only some nerve gas precursors available for purchase, but ability to manufacture them is spreading.
Scientific and technical personnel	Requires wide variety of expertise and skillful systems integration.	Sophisticated research and development unnecessary to produce commonly known agents. Industrial microbiological personnel widely available.	Organic chemists and chemical engineers widely available.
Plant construction and operation	Costly and challenging. Research reactors or electric power reactors might be converted to plutonium production.	With advent of biotechnology, small-scale facilities now capable of large-scale production.	Dedicated plant not difficult. Conversion of existing commercial chemical plants feasible but not trivial.
Comments	Black-market purchase of ready-to-use fissile materials or of complete weapons very possible.	Biological organisms are less expensive and easier to produce than nuclear material or many of the chemical warfare agents.	Legitimate commercial chemical plants and facilities can produce the required warfare agents.

Overall, the likelihood of terrorist groups acquiring WMDs is probably low in the short run but high in the long run. There is no way to demonstrate that terrorists will acquire and use such weapons, but, conversely, there is no way to demonstrate that they will not do so. Given the chance that this might happen and given the magnitude of potential losses involved, it is important to prevent this as well as to be prepared for such an eventuality, even at the cost of many billions of dollars. Using the concept of expected loss, the very low probability of a remote possibility, such as a terrorist group gaining access to and using nuclear weapons, is more than offset in terms of expected loss by the extraordinarily high losses such strikes would entail. It is also a serious mistake to underestimate the ability of terrorists to innovate new techniques of terror, such as using hijacked airplanes as suicide attacks, as occurred on 9/11. Both hijackings and suicide attacks were well known before but never combined effectively in this particular way.

There could be comparable innovations using nuclear weapons in the future, possibly combined with an unexpected delivery system, such as a rental van in a parking garage, a barge in a harbor or a cruise ship with thousands of people aboard. In fact, there are many possible targets. In addition to the typical open-air targets such as urban areas, the center of a city during rush hour, and port areas, smaller-scale attacks confined to enclosed areas would also be potential targets for terrorists. Some of these targets could be shopping malls, convention centers, domed sports stadiums, sealed buildings with central air-conditioning, subways, trains, airport terminals and passenger aircraft. In addition, terrorists could attack by the dispersal of chemical or biological weapons through building ventilation systems and by disabling the cooling systems of nuclear reactors, among a myriad of other possibilities.

It is important to study in detail how truly effective WMDs would be in furthering a terrorist group's ultimate agenda in both the short term and the long term. Of course, terrorist groups must choose among alternatives under constraints, but a well-financed group could choose to develop WMDs, following the model of Aum Shinrikyo, but possibly on an even larger scale, as an ultimate demonstration of its capabilities. It would be a mistake to underestimate the potential of terrorists to attack in new ways.

While certain types of WMD have been available for a long time, including nuclear weapons, these weapons have only been used by one country against another: the US against Japan at the end of World War II. That does not mean, however, that subnational terrorist groups would not use them in the future. The best policy choices for governments in the area of combating WMDs as opposed to combating conventional weapons would be to identify those policies that would best undermine resource availability for terror groups and force them into choice patterns that can be countered at least cost to these governments.[10]

What are the legal, political and other approaches that could be used to prevent terrorist use of WMD?

It is difficult even to consider the challenges presented by potential terrorist use of WMD since we are in a stage of denial, where the nightmare scenarios make even thinking about the problem and its remedies extraordinarily difficult. People find it hard to consider this threat seriously and instead consign it to fictional scenarios, such as in novels and films. It is necessary to overcome this denial mechanism and to take active steps to prevent potential terrorist threats to national and global security using WMD.

This problem is a global one that must be dealt with on that scale; international organizations must be involved and close international cooperation is necessary. Terrorism cannot be addressed by unilateral action when there is little or no support from other states. Each nation should realize that its major responsibility lies in protecting its citizens, but that it cannot do so without international cooperation and reliance on international organizations that may require it to give up some of its sovereignty.

The world's nuclear weapons stockpiles and the world's stockpiles of weapons-grade materials (both military and civilian) are overwhelmingly concentrated in the five nuclear weapon states (United States, United Kingdom, France, China and Russia). Additional nuclear weapons or components exist in Israel, India, Pakistan and, possibly, North Korea. In addition, civilian plutonium for many nuclear weapons also exists in Belgium, Germany, Japan, Switzerland and elsewhere, sometimes in quantities large enough to make a weapon.

Access to WMDs can be treated as a supply and demand problem: supplies must be limited, with the current huge supplies of WMDs safeguarded or destroyed. Russian stockpiles of tactical nuclear weapons should be safeguarded, while Russian stockpiles of chemical weapons and biological weapons, the largest in the world, should be destroyed through an expansion of the Nunn–Lugar Cooperative Threat Reduction program. As discussed by Allison, stockpiles of fissile material, both highly enriched uranium and plutonium, must be safeguarded under the same type of protection that the US gives to its stockpile of gold at Fort Knox, a new type of "gold standard."[11] Furthermore, Allison emphasizes the importance of preventing the acquisition of nuclear weapons by additional states, including Iran and North Korea. He notes that terrorists can obtain nuclear weapons only through theft of such a weapon or acquisition of the necessary fissile material, as they do not have the technical and financial capabilities to produce this material. Thus, preventing them from acquiring such capabilities can help make the problem of terrorist use of nuclear weapons a *preventable* one, although we believe he is too sanguine in this regard.

Allison stresses the supply side, noting, correctly, that the problem of nuclear terrorism would disappear if terrorists were to be denied access to nuclear weapons and to the fissile material necessary to produce them. It may be the case, however, that such access cannot be completely denied and it may also be the case that some of this materiel is already in the hands of terrorist groups, so it is important to treat the demand side as well as the supply side. To reduce the terrorist demand for nuclear weapons, a new form of deterrence must be developed, with a global deterrence system that would be used against any terrorist group using WMD. Such a system should be embodied in a formal agreement with a multi-pronged approach based on international cooperation with a credible enforcement mechanism.[12] An important step in this regard was the unanimous passage by the UN

General Assembly of the Nuclear Terrorism Convention of April 13, 2005, which makes criminal the possession or use of nuclear weapons or devices by non-state actors. It calls for an appropriate legal framework to criminalize nuclear terrorism-related offenses, allowing for arrest, prosecution and extradition of offenders, and it will enter into force after it is signed and ratified by at least 22 states.

There are several convincing reasons to acknowledge and address the possibility of loose nuclear materiel or even loose nuclear weapons floating in the international system. Intelligence agents are constantly discovering previously unknown networks through which the materials and information necessary to create a nuclear weapon may have passed unde-tected. On November 28, 2004, authorities thwarted a near-complete plan to smuggle the necessary elements of a uranium enrichment plant from South Africa to Libya. Another concern is that highly enriched uranium or plutonium may be missing from Russia's ill-protected supply, and that it could already be circulating among subnational networks. All of these concerns point to the need for a viable strategy on the demand side to reinforce treatment of the supply side. Put another way, traditional military analysis considers both *capabilities* and *intentions*. While Allison focuses on capabilities in terms of preventing ter-rorists from acquiring nuclear weapons, it is also necessary to look at intentions in terms of the demand for these weapons and how terrorists could be deterred from acquiring them or using them. The Cold War deterrence model is probably insufficient to protect national security, so the issue is that of developing a new model that can replace it.[13]

There are clearly serious challenges to adapting existing deterrence models, designed for state-to-state interaction, to non-state actors such as terrorist groups and networks. Thus, traditional concepts of deterrence will have to be reshaped to deal with the issue of how terrorist groups could possibly be deterred. It would be a mistake, however, to dismiss deterrence in this regard. For example, it is sometimes argued that suicide bombers cannot be deterred because they are already sacrificing their lives for their cause. This argument is flawed, however, as it is not the suicide bombers that must be deterred but rather their controllers, who make the decisions. There is the problem of knowing where to find the terrorist group in order to strike back.[14] Terrorists do have something to lose and could thus potentially be deterred. In particular, terrorists have a stake in overall group survival. In general, the possibility of deterring terrorism must be systematically analyzed to determine how that might be accomplished. This situation is somewhat analogous to the beginning of the Cold War before the doctrine of mutual assured destruction (MAD) was developed. The challenge to strategic analysts now is to develop a concept of deterrence that would be effective against terrorists.

Konishi[15] argues that preemptive/preventive military action has the potential to be a highly effective form of deterrence policy that has gone unrecognized because the US had "never [before] attempted to deter terrorists through military force." He states, "The United States has adopted a deterrence strategy that involves overwhelming military force aimed both at terrorists and states that harbor terrorists." He notes that "classic deterrence relies on the ability to convince potential adversaries that acts of aggression will result in greater costs than benefits. It is uncertain whether classic deterrence can succeed against asymmetrical threats such as terrorism. However, such a strategy is worth trying if over time it proves to limit a rapid escalation of terrorist activities." He notes that terrorists face an unprecedented threat from US forces, that such action would teach them to respect US military superiority, and that terrorists cannot sustain armed action in the long term. It is, however, unlikely that American military force would be able to deter al Qaeda in this way, given that the Vietcong were not dissuaded by the US preponderance of force during the Vietnam War and the Mujahedin, who were the base of the Taliban in Afghanistan, were not deterred by the Soviets during their invasion of that country.[16]

There are serious dangers in the current doctrine of preemption/preventive war as enunciated in the Bush administration Office of the National Security Advisor's September 2002 document "The National Security Strategy of the United States of America." The Bush administration introduced the doctrine of preemption, including striking suspect sites before obtaining "absolute proof." This "Bush doctrine" not only sets a precedent for other nations to follow but it also gives strong incentives for further nuclear weapons proliferation as states threatened by the US seek such weapons for their own protection, cases in point being North Korea and Iran. In 1997, then Secretary of Defense William Cohen stated that US military superiority was so great that potential adversaries, unable to compete in conventional arms, "may feel compelled to use apocalyptic weapons in a struggle against the United States." Along similar lines, after the 1991 Gulf War a Pakistani brigadier was asked what lesson he drew from the war and he responded that it was "don't fight the US with conventional weapons." Terrorist groups could reason the same way and seek nuclear weapons or other unconventional weapons. It should be noted that the European Union adopted a security strategy in December 2003 focusing on "preventive measures" as opposed to the Bush preemptive force doctrine.

Another non-solution would be the elimination of all nuclear weapons or making WMDs illegal. This is wishful thinking in the absence of an enforcement mechanism. Even if there were a treaty along these lines, for example the Non-Proliferation Treaty (NPT), Article VI of which calls for the eventual elimination of all nuclear weapons, a nation could opt out of it, as North Korea did.

How should the US respond after a nuclear terror attack?

An important question that has not been addressed in the open literature and has hardly been discussed at all is how the US ought to respond *after* a nuclear terror attack on a US city. We hope that there is some classified contingency planning for such an event.

In April 2005 the US Department of Homeland Security established the Domestic Nuclear Detection Office (DNDO) to provide a single accountable organization with the responsibility to develop and deploy a system to detect and report attempts to import or transport a nuclear device or fissile or radiological material intended for terrorist use. DNDO has been charged to work in close cooperation and coordination with federal, state and local governments and also with the private sector as part of a multi-layered defense strategy to protect the US from a nuclear or radiological terrorist attack. While it is important to establish such an office to detect these weapons, it is equally important to have contingency plans if this office does in fact detect a terrorist nuclear weapon and plans for what the appropriate response should be to the actual detonation of such a weapon of mass destruction on US soil.

One member of the House of Representatives, Congressman Tom Tancredo of Colorado, said that we should "take out" the Muslim holy sites like Mecca and Medina (or Jerusalem). This, however, is precisely the wrong way to respond, as it would only lead to much more terrorism and unify the Muslim world in a holy war against the US. Probably the best answer to what the US should do is to follow precedent. After 9/11, the US invaded Afghanistan, the host of al Qaeda, and cleared out their bases there. This retaliatory strike against those harboring the terrorists responsible for the attack was useful as a warning to other terrorist groups, and it has provided a brief period of respite from such attacks until al Qaeda rebuilds its command and control structure. Of course, the US may not know the location of the bases of the terrorists who were responsible, nor the particular terrorist group behind the attack. In that case we have to do everything we can to avoid a spasm response, such as the one suggested by Representative Tancredo. Rather we should work with our allies and the UN to identify the source and take out those responsible, including their hosts, their funding sources, etc.

It is important that the US show evidence to the world community before launching a military attack. This will not undermine or weaken the US; on the contrary, presenting the evidence to the world community and going through the United Nations will mobilize an international coalition that will stand with and support any US military actions. If the US immediately assumes that the terrorist group is state-sponsored and launches military strikes against Syria or Iran, these actions will inspire new hatreds against the US and its interests.

An immediate retaliation by the US to a WMD terrorist attack using nuclear weapons will be catastrophic for the US and many of its allies. Without any doubt, the US has the strongest military forces in the world, as well as the biggest nuclear arsenal. For this very reason, the US can wait for a while until it exhausts all avenues before it launches any military strikes. Indeed, US policy makers must address some basic questions before taking actions that could be of high risk, including:

- Is it of strategic interest to immediately strike an Islamic country using WMD?
- Does the US have adequate intelligence information to justify such an attack?
- Have all the other options been considered?
- What objectives will these actions achieve?

In short, the US must develop a comprehensive set of national strategies addressing terrorism, weapons of mass destruction, and homeland security. In close collaboration and cooperation with its close allies and the international community at large, the US just might succeed in deterring and eliminating the threat posed by terrorists and weapons of mass destruction.

CONCLUSIONS

First, we are probably not any safer overall now than we were before the implementation of the post-9/11 strategies. In some ways we are safer, possibly in terms of airplane hijackings, but in other ways not, or the situation is even worse, given the avowed goal of some terrorist groups to obtain nuclear weapons. Overall, we tend to be reactive rather than acting proactively.

Second, the major question is how can we prevent a terrorist attack using WMDs, such as a nuclear 9/11? We should recognize and avoid the denial syndrome and begin thinking about "worst-case scenarios" and working on ways to prevent them from happening. We certainly should not ignore the possibility that these events could ever happen, as we did before 9/11, where the weapons the terrorists used were merely box cutters, a far cry from WMD.

Third, there is need for more research on these matters. It is important to study how terrorists think and the nature of their motivation. Terrorists will likely be using the path of least resistance, so tightening up airport security, for example, will mean that they will substitute other vulnerable targets, such as ports, nuclear power plants, bridges, high-rise office buildings and other critical infrastructure. Clearly any protection should have a net benefit after taking into account its direct and indirect consequences. It is important to encourage analysts to engage in thinking as terrorists would, as in the "Red Team" exercises of the Cold War, and to act upon the conclusions of these studies. It is also important to recognize the importance of psychology in deterrence.[17]

Fourth, we must establish clear priorities for US counter-terrorism policies. Part of establishing clear priorities should be serious improvements in intelligence systems that have failed us repeatedly, including better organization, upgrading of capacities, better use of the private sector (including universities), holding intelligence services and individuals that lead them responsible for their failures, and so on. Some of the initiatives that have been undertaken at the local level, such as the Terrorism Early Warning (TEW) group that was initially established in Los Angeles County, should be expanded to the regional, state, national and international levels. Another initiative should be providing more resources for diplomatic efforts that have been starved for funds and personnel. Yet another point that somehow is not emphasized is destroying Russian stockpiles of chemical and biological weapons, which are larger than those of the rest of the world combined. Russia wants to destroy them and has committed itself to the Chemical Weapons Convention, but it cannot afford to build the necessary incinerators, which the US or a consortium of nations could provide. This could be the most cost-effective use of any US defense spending. Similarly, the Russian stockpiles of tactical nuclear weapons and biological weapons should be adequately protected or destroyed, as they could possibly be stolen by or sold to a terrorist group.

Fifth, and finally, new initiatives must be undertaken to deal with the issue of terrorist use of nuclear weapons and other WMD at the global level, including through international institutions. The recent proposals on reform of the UN system, in the Report of the High-Level UN Panel on Threats, Challenges and Change, are valuable in this regard.[18] They must, however, be supplemented by initiatives and reforms that deal directly with this threat, including the sharing of information and the creation of a task force that could take direct action against terrorist groups that could be planning to use WMD.

ACKNOWLEDGEMENTS

We would like to acknowledge the valuable research assistance of three UCLA graduate students who assisted in the preparation of this paper: Tracey DeFrancesco, Sarah Paulson and Josh Rosenfeld. We have also received useful comments on this paper from Gilbert Kim, another UCLA graduate student. All are students in the Master of Public Policy program in the UCLA School of Public Affairs. We have also received valuable suggestions from Jamus Jerome Lim, a graduate student in the Department of Economics at the University of California, Santa Cruz.

NOTES

1. Graham Allison, *Nuclear Terrorism: The Ultimate Preventable Catastrophe* (London: Times Books, 2004).

2. Abu Gheith, "'Why We Fight America': Al-Qaida Spokesman Explains September 11 and Declares Intentions to Kill 4 Million Americans with Weapons of Mass Destruction," MEMRI, No. 388, June 12, 2002, http://www.memri.org/bin/articles. cgi?Area=jihad&ID=SP38802. Al-Jazirah TV Broadcasts: Usama Bin Ladin's 1998 Interview with Jamal Ismail in Arabic, 20 Sept. 2001.

3. For other scenarios, see Anthony Lake, *Six Nightmares: Real Threats in a Dangerous World and How America Can Meet Them* (Boston, MA: Little, Brown, 2000), and Richard L. Garwin, "Nuclear and Biological Megaterrorism," 27th Session of the International Seminars on Planetary Emergencies, Aug. 21, 2002, http://www.fas.org/rlg/020821-terrorism.htm, part of which appears as "The Technology of Megaterror," *Technology Review*, Sept. 1, 2002.

4. See Garwin, "Nuclear and Biological Megaterrorism."

5. See US Commission on National Security in the 21st Century (chaired by former US Senators Gary Hart and Warren Rudman), *New World Coming: American Security in the 21st Century*, Sept. 1999.

6. See Thomas L. Friedman, "The Humiliation Factor," *New York Times*, Nov. 9, 2003. See also Jessica Stern, *The Ultimate Terrorists* (Cambridge, MA: Harvard University Press, 2000), and Jessica Stern, *Terror in the Name of God: Why Religious Militants Kill* (New York: Ecco, 2003).

7. It should be noted that most of the injuries in the Tokyo subway attack were not serious; most casualties were released from the hospital within one day. For the numbers of deaths and injuries from this and other terrorist strikes, see Johnston's archive, http://www.johnstonsarchive.net/terrorism/

8. See Bruce Hoffman, *Inside Terrorism* (New York: Columbia University Press, 1998).

9. See various articles in the journal *Terrorism and Political Violence*.

10. See Todd Sandler, "Fighting Terrorism: What Economics Can Tell Us," *Challenge*, 45, 2002, who argues that the way to prevent terrorism is to remove support for the terrorists in terms of funding, recruits, information, etc.

11. See Allison, *Nuclear Terrorism*.

12. See Graham Allison and Andrei Kokoshin (2002) "The New Containment: An Alliance against Nuclear Terrorism," *National Interest*, Fall 2002, and "US-Russian Alliance against Megaterrorism," *Boston Globe*, Nov. 16, 2001.

13. For a discussion of deterrence of terrorism, noting that deterrence still matters, see Jonathan Stevenson, *Counter-terrorism: Containment and Beyond*, Adelphi Papers (London: International Institute for Strategic Studies, 2004).

14. See Charles D. Ferguson, William C. Potter, Amy Sands, Leonard S. Spector and Fred L. Wehling, *The Four Faces of Nuclear Terrorism* (Monterey, CA: Center for Nonproliferation Studies, Monterey Institute, 2004).

15. See Weston Konishi, "The Case for Deterrence in the Anti-Terror Campaign," June 2002, http://www.weltpolitik.net/Sachgebiete/Internationale%20Sicherheitspolitik/Probilembereiche%20und%20L%F6sungsans%E4tze/Terrorismus/Analysen/The%20Case%20for%20Deterrence%20in%20the%20Anti-terror%20Campaign.html

16. See also Michael A. Levi, "Deterring Nuclear Terrorism," *Issues in Science and Technology*, Spring 2004.

17. See Michael D. Intriligator and Dagobert L. Brito, "The Potential Contribution of Psychology to Nuclear War Issues," *American Psychologist*, 43, Apr. 1988, pp. 318–21.

18. See United Nations, "A More Secure World: Our Shared Responsibility, Report of the High-Level UN Panel on Threats, Challenges and Change," Dec. 2, 2004, http://www.un.org/secureworld/

Walzer's Formulation of Just Cause

KIMBERLY HUDSON

W alzer elaborates his formulation of non-intervention and just cause across four broad categories: national self-defense, collective self-defense, pre-emption, and exceptions to the non-intervention rule. I'll summarize his views on each of those four categories here, highlighting the underlying reasons he gives for his positions.

National self-defense

Walzer's conception of just cause is among those threads of the tradition sometimes re-ferred to as the aggressor/defender paradigm. In Walzer's formulation, offensive war (war for any purpose other than defense) is always wrong. Defensive wars are assumed to be justified, except the defensive wars of societies engaged in massive human rights violations (genocide, enslavement, and widespread massacre). One element of Walzer's view is the idea that "no war, as medieval theologians explained, can be just on both sides."In Walzer's understanding, all offensive war, or any armed attack on the political independence or territorial integrity of a sovereign state is a crime of aggression. "Nothing but aggression can justify war," Walzer writes. "Nothing else warrants the use of force in international society."

> Aggression is the name we give to the crime of war. We know the crime because of our knowledge of the peace it interrupts—not the mere absence of fighting, but peace-with-rights, a condition of liberty and security that can only exist in

the absence of aggression itself. The wrong the aggressor commits is to force men and women to risk their lives for the sake of their rights. It is to confront them with the choice: your rights or (some of) your lives! ... Aggression is remarkable because it is the only crime that states can commit against other states.... Aggression is a singular and undifferentiated crime because, in all its forms, it challenges rights that are worth dying for.

The "rights worth dying for," according to Walzer, are the rights of individuals to a community: "the rights of contemporary men and women" to live as members of a historic community and to express their inherited culture through political forms worked out among themselves."Walzer does not require that these historic communities exhibit any particular characteristics except that they are not subject to foreign coercion, and in that way they are "self-determining."

He extends the right of self-defense (and the right to non-intervention) to severely repressive regimes: "Domestic heresy and injustice are never actionable in the world of states. Hence, again, the principle of non-intervention." Walzer does make an exception to this rule; it's not absolutely true for him that domestic injustice is *never* actionable in the world of states. Walzer holds that states are normally, but by no means always, the institutional arrangements by which people work out their community lives. He recognizes:

> If no common life exists, or if the state doesn't defend the common life that does exist, its own defense may have no moral justification. But most states do stand guard over the community of their citizens, at least to some degree: that is why we assume the justice of their defensive wars.

In other words, any first use of force (except justified pre-emptive self-defense) is aggression, and therefore, unjust. The party who retaliates is acting in self-defense, and this is almost always unconditionally justified for Walzer (except in the case of a slave society defending slavery or a genocidal government aiming to continue its genocide). The other *jus ad bellum* categories are assumed to be met if the situation is grave enough to say there is a just cause for war. I will say more about this in due course in Chapter 5, where I distinguish Walzer's views from my own views on last resort, proportionality, reasonable hope of success, legitimate authority, and right intention. In this chapter, I am focusing on Walzer's view of just cause.

There are wars where there is justice on neither side, "because justice doesn't pertain to them or because the antagonists are both aggressors, fighting for territory or power where they have no right."As a case in point, Walzer cites Lenin's hypothetical example of such a conflict, between "a slave-owner who owned 100 slaves warring against a slave owner who owned 200 slaves for a more 'just' distribution of slaves."Walzer thinks there is no right of self-defense on the part of a genocidal or slave state. However, all other states possess a right of self-defense against aggression. In Walzer's formulation, aggression includes wars of humanitarian intervention against tyrannical regimes if the regime's crimes do not rise to the level of genocide, widespread massacre, enslavement, or ethnic cleansing.

Collective self-defense: wars of law enforcement

Walzer writes, "Aggression justifies two kinds of violent response: a war of self-defense by the victim and a war of law enforcement by the victim and any other member of international society." If one state is a victim of aggression, other states are entitled to join in its defense. There is a "presumption in favor of military resistance once aggression has begun" according to Walzer, because future would-be aggressors ought to be deterred, and the rights of states to political independence and territorial integrity ought to be maintained. Walzer's view is that the victim of aggression fights back not only in his own defense, but in defense of the international order and the rights of all members of international society (states) to political independence and territorial integrity. An attack on one member of international society is an attack on the rights of all states and upon the international legal order. Any member of the international society, therefore, is entitled to defend that order, and thereby the stability of the international states-system. Although third-party states are entitled to join in the defense of the victim of aggression, they are not bound to do so; all states have a right to remain neutral.

One important quality to note about Walzer's view of collective self-defense is that it is not motivated by charity, compassion, or the duty to assist a neighbor as such. It is the norm of non-intervention that is being defended as much as the state under attack. The entitlement of the third-party state to intervene is generated by the attack on the norm against aggression. It is the attack on the system, and its generation of insecurity for the third-party state and all other states that unanswered aggression poses, that generates this right of response by the third-party state.

Pre-emption

Pre-emption, in *Just and Unjust Wars*, is a form of self-defense in which the victim of aggression defends itself with a first strike. For Walzer, pre-emption is justified "under sufficient threat," which is "conceptually between 'preventive war' and 'pre-emptive strike in response to imminent threat.'" Under sufficient threat means, according to Walzer, that three criteria are met:

> First, there is a manifest intent to injure, made clear by some evidence; second, there is a degree of active preparation that makes that intent a positive danger, and third, a general situation in which waiting, or doing anything other than fighting, greatly magnifies the risk.

Walzer's concrete example of such a situation is the three weeks immediately prior to the Israeli pre-emptive strike in the Six-Day War of 1967. In this case, Egypt responded to a false report of Israeli troops massing on the Syrian border by placing Egyptian troops on "maximum alert," massing their troops in the Sinai, expelling the United Nations from the Sinai and the Gaza Strip, and closing the Straits of Tiran to Israeli shipping on May 22, 1967—this closure itself a *casus belli*. By the end of May, the Egyptian President Gamal Abdel Nasser had announced that "if war came, the goal would be nothing less than the destruction of Israel"; Jordan, Syria, and Iraq announced their alliance with Egypt against Israel during the next two weeks. Diplomacy seemed to be useless. Israel pre-emptively launched attacks in what Walzer calls "a clear case of legitimate anticipation." Israel, against most expectations, won that war in six days.

In response to more recent events, noting that the "old arguments did not take into account weapons of mass destruction," Walzer has taken a slightly different view, but he has not fully elaborated a new doctrine. "Perhaps the gulf between preemption and prevention has now narrowed so that there is little strategic (and therefore little moral) difference between them." Walzer's discussion of pre-emption in *Just and Unjust Wars* does not include any mention of pre-emptive collective self-defense or pre-emptive humanitarian intervention.

Interventions

Generally speaking, for Walzer, the right to non-intervention and national self-defense is possessed by all sovereign states. Under normal circumstances, "Any use of force or imminent threat of force by one state against the political sovereignty or territorial integrity of another constitutes aggression and is a criminal act."[16] Walzer does, however, make three exceptions to this general rule. The three exceptions are in the cases of secession, counter-intervention in a civil war, and humanitarian intervention. I will discuss each of these rules of disregard in detail below, along with a fourth exception Walzer has added more recently, the case of failed states.

Walzer argues that the non-intervention norm may be disregarded in the following circumstances (the first three rules of disregard are elaborated in *Just and Unjust Wars*, the fourth in more recent work):

1. when the particular set of boundaries clearly contains two or more political communities, one of which is already engaged in a large scale military struggle for independence; that is, when what is at issue is secession or "national liberation";
2. when the boundaries have already been crossed by the armies of a foreign power, even if the crossing has been called for by one of the parties in a civil war, that is, when what is at issue is counter-intervention; and

3. when the violation of human rights within a set of boundaries is so terrible that it makes talk of community or self-determination or 'arduous struggle' seem cynical and irrelevant, that is, in cases of enslavement or massacre.
4. Intervention in the case of a less than fully capable state; this is acceptable either to aid the individuals inside the state or in self-defense. Intervention is permissible in a failed state to stop widespread suffering and death due to state collapse and the ensuing chaos. Intervention is also within the borders of a state that is incapable of controlling the population within its borders (for example, Walzer made this argument about Hezbollah in Lebanon and Hamas in Gaza).

Exception 1: Secessions

In his discussion of secessionist movements in *Just and Unjust Wars*, Walzer distinguishes between legitimate and illegitimate secessionist movements by what he calls the "test of self-help." The test of self-help applies to governments, revolutionary movements, and secessionist groups: if the government, movement, or group can fight its own internal war successfully, it has met the test of self-help.

Intervention is permitted to aid the government against the rebels until such time as the secessionist movement can garner sufficient support to meet the test of self-help. After that, intervention on the part of either side is prohibited. Foreign powers must stay out and let the local balance work out on its own; such a fight is part of the process of self-determination. If foreign powers do not stay out, a counter-intervention is permitted on behalf of the other side, to restore the balance of forces to what it would have been, had the first, unjust intervention not occurred. Counter-intervention (not an initial intervention) is only permitted to aid a secessionist movement if the movement would have had sufficient support among the people to win a war against its government, and it is not permitted if it does not.

First, if the movement could win its freedom without external interference because a sufficient portion of the people is willing and able to fight, the movement meets the "test of self-help." In such a case, foreign governments are no longer allowed to provide military assistance to the government; a strict rule of neutrality is now in force. Where a secessionist movement could win a revolt on its own without external assistance, Walzer's theory is permissive in allowing foreign support, even military assistance, for the revolt. When the movement is strong enough to win on its own, Walzer's theory endorses the movement's claim to a self-determining political community. Its ability to fight its own war, successfully, is evidence that the movement represents the historic community's self-determination.

For secessionist movements that cannot win a war of secession without foreign assistance, the rule of disregard does not apply. There is not a right to intervention (on the part of foreigners) to assist a secessionist movement, unless such assistance would not be necessary for the group to win in the absence of external force being brought to bear.

There is not a right of intervention to assist the secessionist movement, even if it has met the self-help test, unless another foreign power has already intervened on behalf of the government. Walzer holds that if the movement is truly a legitimate movement, with standing among the people, it will succeed on its own. If it cannot succeed, it is because the people do not want it or perhaps because they think it is imprudent to rebel. Walzer makes no moral distinction between these two reasons. Whatever the people's reasons, foreigners must respect their decision, as it is evidenced in practice by the strength or weakness of their movement. Walzer argues that freedom, to be meaningful, must be arrived at by a people in their own way, if they can achieve it. If they cannot achieve it, they are not fit for it, or they do not want it. There is no right to be rescued (or to rescue) from a bloody repression. To be freed by foreigners is not to be freed, but to be conquered. Walzer interprets John Stuart Mill's essay, "A Few Words on Non-intervention," to say that because of what freedom is, it necessarily must be earned by the people; freedom cannot be won for them by outsiders. A people get the government for which they are fit. Mill, according to Walzer, says a people must fight for their own freedom, just as an individual must cultivate his own virtue.

Walzer applies the self-help test to regimes as well as to secessionist movements: If the regime cannot compel its citizens to obedience, it is an illegitimate regime; if the regime is capable of repressing internal secessionist or revolutionary movements, the government passes the self-help test, and it is legitimate. "A legitimate government is one that can fight its own internal wars." Such a regime possesses rights to non-intervention and to national self-defense.

If a secessionist movement garners sufficient local support that the movement becomes capable of overthrowing the regime, the secessionist movement is legitimate, and an external force would be justified in assisting it. Although no external force would be necessary for the secessionists' victory, external intervention is permissible (*because* it is unnecessary). Walzer writes, however, that sometimes even a legitimate secessionist movement will not be justified in actually seceding if doing so "would remove not only land but also vitally needed fuel and mineral resources from some larger political community."

That was Walzer's position in *Just and Unjust Wars*. However, we have an indication that he may recently have reversed his position on this question. He has at least indicated a different position in one interview. In a 2004 interview in the *Harvard International Review*, Walzer gives three conditions under which foreign support for a secessionist movement is permissible. First, as in the *Just and Unjust Wars* formulation, there must be a secessionist movement that commands material support among the people it is claiming to liberate. Second, he adds the very different qualification that "the movement cannot be helped by any form of assistance short of war, and it will certainly be defeated without some external use of force." Third, the intervention must be likely to succeed at a less than "terrible" cost.

Exception 2: Counter-intervention

In the case where a revolutionary or secessionist movement challenges an established government, Walzer permits intervention to aid the government against the rebels. "After all, [the government] is the official representative of communal autonomy in international society." Intervention is permitted to aid the government, but not a nascent rebel group. If the rebels have a measure of success, and gain control over territory and population, they become "equal in status" with the established government, and neutrality is required. Once the parties are "equal in status," foreigners are neither permitted to continue (or start) aiding the government, nor are foreigners permitted to aid the rebels.

If neutrality is not respected and either side is aided by a foreign force, Walzer permits a counter-intervention.

> Self-determination is the right of a people 'to become free by their own efforts' if they can, and nonintervention is the principle guaranteeing that their success will not be impeded or their failure prevented by the intrusions of an alien power.

If an alien power is assisting a secessionist movement, foreign counter-intervention is permissible to aid the government. "Counter-intervention is morally possible only on behalf of a government (or a movement, party, or whatever) that has already passed the self-help test."

After the rebel movement has met the test of self-help by gaining control over substantial territory and population, if a foreign army is aiding the government, a counter-intervention would be permissible to aid the rebels. Walzer does not permit a counter-intervention to be decisive, but to restore the balance to what it would have been without the initial, unjust, intervention. The counter-intervention should restore the balance, to prevent the initial, unjust intervention from "establishing a sovereign, or a form of government, which the nation, if left to itself, would not have chosen." Imagine a fistfight broke out between two brothers, and a friend of one of the men came to his aid or came to restrain the other brother. In Walzer's formulation, the first intervention would have been impermissible, but it would be permissible for a fourth party to intervene to restore the balance between the first two belligerents—to remove the first intervener and let the brothers "duke it out." There is no judgment made about which of the brothers is in the right, or about who started the fight. The only justifiable aim for the intervener is to restore the balance of forces to what it would have been had the first unjust intervention not taken place: "The goal of a counter-intervention is not to win the war." The counter-intervention must only aim to restore the balance of forces between the government and the rebels, not to turn the tide. Such intervention ("to turn the tide" rather than to restore the balance) would constitute a denial of self-determination.

Exception 3: Humanitarian intervention

Walzer's third rule of disregard grants that unilateral humanitarian intervention is permissible in the case of massive human rights violations—in *Just and Unjust Wars*, this meant widespread massacre, official enslavement, or genocide. In a 1980 follow-up article to *Just and Unjust Wars*, Walzer added what we might now call ethnic cleansing:

> I think that I would now add to massacre and enslavement the expulsion of very large numbers of people (not simply the retreat of political opponents after a revolution or the transfer of populations that sometimes follows upon national liberation struggles—though these can be brutal enough).

In 1994, Walzer added the category of humanitarian intervention to rescue people in a failed state.[33] Although he is a passionate advocate of humanitarian military intervention under these circumstances, he is strongly opposed to intervention under any other circumstances.

In the case of massive human rights violations (genocide, widespread massacres, enslavement, or ethnic cleansing), Walzer says that the test of self-help does not apply. It is the victims' inability to help themselves and the horror of their situation that allows foreign armies to cross the outlaw state's border. Walzer says "the standard in the old law books was that [outsiders] had a right to intervene when there was a crime that 'outraged the conscience of mankind.'" In the preface to the third edition of *Just and Unjust Wars*, Walzer approvingly cites the Tanzanian intervention to remove Idi Amin in Uganda, the Vietnamese intervention in Pol Pot's Kampuchea, the Indian intervention in East Pakistan, and the NATO bombardment over Kosovo: "there were horrifying acts that should have been stopped," by foreign intervention if necessary.

In an article written just after the Rwandan Genocide in 1994, "The Politics of Rescue," Walzer writes a moving defense of humanitarian intervention in the case of widespread massacre, genocide, enslavement, or ethnic cleansing. In this article, Walzer expands the cases in which intervention is permissible to include failed states that cannot provide for the security of their people, and he defends the idea of protectorates and trusteeships as possibly the best way to secure decent conditions of life for people who have been the victims of genocide, massacre, ethnic cleansing, and the chaos of failed states (in particular, reference to Somalia and Rwanda):

> I don't mean to abandon the principle of non-intervention—only to honor its exceptions. It is true that right now there are a lot of exceptions. One reads the newspaper these days shaking. The vast numbers of murdered people; the men, women, and children dying of disease and famine willfully caused or easily preventable; the masses of desperate refugees—none of these are served by reciting high minded principles. Yes, the norm is not to interfere in other people's

countries; the norm is self-determination. But not for these people, the victims of tyranny, ideological zeal, ethnic hatred, who are not determining anything for themselves, who urgently need help from outside. And it is not enough to wait until the tyrants, the zealots, and the bigots have done their filthy work and then rush food and medicine to the ragged survivors. Whenever the filthy work can be stopped, it should be stopped. And if not by us, the supposedly decent people of the world, then by whom?

Humanitarian intervention, where it is permissible (that is, in the cases of genocide, widespread massacre, enslavement, or ethnic cleansing) is allowed (unilaterally) to any state that has the capability to stop the violence. In the absence of an international institution capable of acting swiftly enough to stop the bloodshed, "a plausible maxim for humanitarian intervention is 'who can, should.'"

Walzer has recently begun to argue that when "oppression carried out by the rulers reaches massacre and forced resettlement, then intervention is not merely right, it is morally required." Someone should intervene, but the duty does not fall on any one country or institution in particular; nor does Walzer specify how the agent should intervene. This argument seems inconsistent with his affirmation that even when genocide is occurring, all states individually retain their rights to neutrality, "even if its assertion seems ignoble." The assertion of the right of neutrality is more ignoble in the case of genocide, widespread massacre, or ethnic cleansing, for Walzer, than it is in the case of other types of wars. The reason Walzer gives is that we can predict, in advance, the result of standing by while genocide occurs, but the consequences of staying neutral in the case of other types of wars is often less clear.

Exception 4: Intervention in a failed or less than fully capable state

In his recent work, Walzer has also approved of interventions to stop widespread loss of life in cases of state failure. He has also approved of limited intervention in cases where the state has not collapsed completely but where sub-national actors such as terrorist groups cannot be controlled by the state and pose a hazard to neighboring states.

First, Walzer allows unilateral intervention to stop bloodshed in circumstances of state failure, although he "won't have much to say about it." He approves of "what the Nigerians did in Sierra Leone: they reduced the number of killings, the scope of the barbarism." In the absence of global institutions to care for people's needs, people need a decent and effective state.

Second, Walzer's doctrine permits cross-border anti-terrorist raids and targeted killings in a state that cannot control all of the population on its territory. Imagine a case where a state cannot control its territory and where a terrorist group is taking refuge or launching attacks from within its borders. The victim of the attacks has the right to cross the border of the state hosting the terrorist group, to conduct limited operations to kill the terrorists, and then leave. These targeted killings are legitimate when states do not have control over all their territory, such as in Lebanon or Pakistan. One example of justified targeted killing that Walzer gives is the American hellfire missile attack on several suspected Al-Qaeda operatives in the Yemeni desert in late 2001:

> It isn't a war zone, but it also isn't a zone of peace—and this description will fit many, not all, of the 'battlefields' of the 'war' against terrorism. In large sections of Yemen, the government's writ doesn't run; there are no police who could make the arrests (14 soldiers had already been killed in attempts to capture the Al Qaeda militants) and no courts in which prisoners could expect a fair trial. The Yemeni desert is a lawless land, and lawlessness provides a refuge for the political criminals called terrorists. The best way to deal with the refuge would be to help the Yemini government extend its authority over the whole of its territory. But that is a long process, and the urgencies of the 'war' against terrorism may require more immediate action. When that is true, if it is true, it doesn't seem morally wrong to target Al Qaeda militants directly—for capture, if that's possible, but also for death.

The limits of the rules of disregard

For Walzer, the "presumption against intervention is strong; we (on the left especially) have reasons for it, which derive from our opposition to imperial politics and our commitment to self-determination." The occasions for intervention are limited to genocide, official enslavement, widespread massacre, ethnic cleansing, and failed states. Short of this limit, Walzer insists that the justice or injustice of a state's domestic institutions has no bearing on its right to non-intervention. Alongside his support for humanitarian intervention in extreme cases, Walzer insists upon a "wide chasm" between genocide, systematic massacre, forced resettlement, and the failed state on the one side, and what he calls "common nastiness" or the "ordinary brutality of authoritarian regimes" on the other. "Ordinary brutality" includes routine, widespread political imprisonment, or murder, repression, and denial of political rights like free association, movement, and speech—anything except for genocide, widespread massacre, and forced resettlement. "Domestic tyrants are safe." Walzer believes that foreign intervention is wrong in the case of "ordinary brutality" because such intervention denies the people living inside the state to work out their own way of living together.

Walzer also cites prudential reasons not to intervene:

> The common brutalities of authoritarian politics, the daily oppressiveness of traditional social practices—these are not occasions for intervention; they have

to be dealt with locally, by the people who know the politics, who enact or resist the practices. The fact that these people can't easily or quickly reduce the incidence of brutality and oppression isn't a sufficient reason for foreigners to invade their country. Foreign politicians and soldiers are too likely to misread the situation, or to underestimate the force required to change it, or to stimulate a "patriotic" reaction in defense of the brutal politics and the oppressive practices. Social change is best achieved from within.

The state must not commit massive human rights abuses, and it must maintain enough control over its territory that chaos does not result in harms similar to genocide, massacre, and forced resettlement. It must also maintain enough control over its territory that terrorists cannot hide out there or launch attacks from its territory into neighboring states. Beyond those limitations, Walzer argues that outsiders must regard the regime as if it is legitimate, and they must respect the state's political independence and territorial integrity. The reason Walzer gives is not that the state is in fact legitimate with its own people. The state may have no standing with its own people, and it may perpetrate systematic abuses of human rights. But for Walzer, this domestic illegitimacy does not translate into international illegitimacy. Foreigners are bound to stay out.

Just The Good, No Bad and Ugly?
The Regional Impact of Externally Imposed Democracy

ANDREW J. ENTERLINE AND J. MICHAEL GREIG

T he chapters in this volume focus principally on the peacemaking process following a conflict, principally those conflicts that occur within states. Often, central to this peacemaking process is a change in the political system governing a post-conflict society. Historically, these changes in the political institutions in states afflicted with conflict are instigated or shepherded by third party actors, such as the United Nations, the major power states, or states neighboring the state experiencing the internal conflict. During, but principally following, the Cold War, the democratization of former autocratic states was argued to be an important component of a general strategy to prevent the recurrence of intrastate conflicts, as well as cultivating political systems that would have beneficial regional effects.

Recently, the claim that externally cultivated democratic institutions translate into positive regional benefits has been elaborated to suggest that this democratization promises rewards for the geographic regions into which democratic polities are introduced, such as greater peace, prosperity, and democracy. Furthermore, these regional outcomes are argued to be causally entwined and reinforcing, such that democracy increases peace, and peace and democracy provide the basis for stable and prosperous economic markets central to prosperity, and prosperity reinforces the desirability and effectiveness of democratic forms of governance, and so on. In light of developments in contemporary international relations, specifically the international occupations and democratization of Afghanistan and Iraq in 2002 and 2003, respectively, the regional implications of democratic institutions cultivated by third party states and international organizations is an important, yet rarely

Andrew J. Enterline and J. Michael Greig, "Just the Good, No Bad and Ugly? The Regional Impact of Externally Imposed Democracy," from *Conflict Prevention and Peacebuilding*, pp. 149–159. Copyright © 2006 by Taylor & Francis Group. Permission to reprint granted by the publisher.

Just The Good, No Bad and Ugly? | 205

studied, aspect of models of conflict resolution and peacemaking. We discuss our scientific inquiry into the veracity of this claim regarding the link between externally imposed democracy and the regional outcomes of peace, democracy, and prosperity in the remainder of this chapter.

Imposed democracy and regional peace, democracy and prosperity

In February 2003, American policymakers sought to place a possible war against Iraq in a broader, and more importantly, regional policy context.

This important shift in policy was generally interpreted in the media as a strategy by American policymakers to garner greater support from European and Middle Eastern allies for the use of military force against Iraq (Bumiller 2003). In formulating a broader policy, one that we refer to hereafter as the *regional-level* argument, American, and later British, policymakers sought to link war with Iraq, and implicity, military victory, and the eventual democratization of Iraq with a broad recipe for conflict resolution in the Middle East region, including greater interstate and intrastate peace, democracy, and economic prosperity.[1]

As stated publicly, policymakers sought first and foremost to reduce the interstate security threat posed by Hussein's Iraq and the destabilizing effect that policymakers argued this authoritarian regime had on other conflicts in the Middle East. Policymakers reasoned that the cultivation of a democratic regime in Iraq would address this problem, in part, because democratic polities, policymakers assumed, are more likely to exhibit peaceful foreign polities. Moreover, democratic polities are more likely to resolve disputes with other states through negotiation and compromise rather than resort to military force. This positive relationship between democracy and pacific foreign policy is fortified by several auxiliary assumptions implicit in contemporary policy statements and we discuss each in turn.

First, democratic polities are assumed to be less likely to support terrorist organizations, or pursue destabilizing policies in neighboring states, thereby providing a foundation for stable regional relations. Second, democratic polities reflect more inclusive political arenas in which ethnic, religious, and political differences between groups are moderated by inclusive, representative political institutions that preclude the need for groups to ground political mobilization in cultural identity. As a result, democratic states are less likely to experience domestic political instability, instability that is linked to interstate friction and militarized conflict. Finally, the very process of imposing democracy has important implications for regional politics. Specifically, democratizing authoritarian regimes through military force signals to non-democratic states, as well as to non-state actors supported by non-democratic states, that further pursuit of destabilizing regional policies might result in forceful responses by the international community, including further democratization of states through war.

Current scholarly research tends to substantiate the plausibility of the first assumption as it pertains to the regional-level argument. For example, Gleditsch and Hegre (1997) report evidence of a global system threshold at which point system democracy eventually begins to exert a negative effect on militarized conflict at the level of the interstate system. Crescenzi and Enterline (1999) confirm this finding, but conclude that there is considerable regional heterogeneity in the parabolic relationship between system democracy and war. Similarly, McLaughlin, Gates and Hegre (1999) conclude that while an increase in system democracy eventually corresponds to a decrease in system war, a fully parabolic relationship fails to materialize. Ray (2000) argues that the level of conflict in the global system is, in part, a function of how the shrinking population of non-democratic states responds to an increasingly democratic system, one that very well might be construed by non-democratic polities as threatening, thereby increasing the likelihood of militarized conflict.

The second dimension of the regional-level argument links the presence of an imposed democracy with further regional democratization. This relationship is grounded in the demonstrative properties of imposed democratic polities that flow out of the assumption that the more proximate a democratic polity, the greater the likelihood that liberal democratic ideals will become an issue of intellectual and public debate in neighboring non-democratic states. In turn, this public debate is anticipated to increase the pressure on non-democratic regimes to liberalize. Additionally, the presence of a liberal democracy in a region demonstrates the viability of democratic institutions in regions that are not traditionally democratic, thereby overcoming historical impediments to democratization such as colonial legacies and non-democratic regimes installed during the Cold War.

Finally, the regional-level argument assumes that individuals in all societies possess aspirations, if latent, for the liberties and institutions associated with liberal democracy. As a result, all societies can liberalize, even if the end product of this liberalization process varies significantly in form from the democratic institutions in the West European and North American states. As a result, the presence of an imposed democracy can act as a catalyst for further democratization in regions resistant to liberalization during previous waves, or surges, of democratization in the modern state system.

Again, current research suggests tangential support for the demonstration properties of imposed democracies. For example, in his well-known study, Huntington (1991) concludes that "snowballing" of national political systems occurs regionally. Similarly, Starr (1991, 1995) finds evidence of positive spatial dependence between democratic transitions, such that democratization can diffuse across, or spill over, national borders. More recently, Starr and Lindborg (2003) find further evidence that democratic and autocratic changes increase the likelihood of similar changes in neighboring states (i.e., democratization leads to further democratization, and autocratization leads to further autocratization), a finding that squares with the analysis of the domestic and international causes of democratization reported in Colaresi and Thompson (2003).

Other research emphasizes that state-system characteristics influence the probability of further democratization. The argument that imposed democracy promotes regional democracy is consistent with the conception of diffusion as emulation described by Siverson and Starr (1991). Thompson (1996) suggests that the emergence of "zones of peace" regionally can spur democratization. Pevehouse (2002) finds that state membership in democratic international organizations increases the odds that member states will democratize. Gleditsch (2002) finds strong evidence of spatial clustering among democracies within the international system. Kadera, Crescenzi and Shannon (2003) conclude that the greater the democratic community's power in a state-system, the more likely democratic polities are to persist, findings that square with the earlier work of Modelski and Perry (1991). Finally, Cederman and Gleditsch (2004), drawing upon the innovations in Gleditsch (2002), conclude that as the frequency of democracies within a geographic region increases, the more likely nondemocratic states in the region are to democratize.

In general, current research provides indirect, if consistent, support for the contemporary regional-level policy claim that imposed democratic polities provide a demonstration of liberal political ideals and institutions, a process that encourages further regional democratization. Indeed, this body of research, coupled with the oft-cited cases of West Germany and Japan following World War II, provides relatively strong evidence that the forceful democratization of authoritarian regimes can stimulate further regional political liberalization. However, aside from this tangential evidence reflected in the scholarly literature, as well as the anecdotal cases of post-WWII Germany and Japan, no direct test of relationship exists in the current literature.

Closely related to the theory linking imposed democracy with further regional democratization is the causal logic underlying the relationship between imposed democracy and regional prosperity. This causal linkage is achieved because the process of demonstration is one of liberal ideas and behavior in general, rather than solely the demonstration of democratic political institutions. Indeed, the political and economic dimensions of liberal thought, particularly the emphasis on individual agency, are mutually reinforcing. Therefore, in several ways, the regional impact of an imposed democratic, market-oriented state is a function of a causal logic that is similar to the logic identified in the discussion of regional democratization, wherein an imposed democracy demonstrates liberal ideas and debate as well as the general viability of liberal political institutions to citizens in non-democratic states.

In addition to the causal processes flowing from demonstration by imposed democracies, the economic dimension of the regional impact of imposed democracy is also anchored to the diffusion processes associated with economic interactions. The presence of a liberal, market economy in a region will, much like its impact on political thinking, demonstrate the viability and benefits of this economy to countries with non-market economies. Additionally, the presence of a market-oriented economy in a region functions as a foil for the economic stagnation that is often associated with centralized, nondemocratic economies. Much as the citizens of East European countries were subject during the Cold War to media reflecting the superior economic performance in the Western European democracies, the presence of a prosperous market economy in a region demonstrates the potential for greater economic prosperity to citizens in states with poor, centrally controlled economies. In turn, this positive economic foil encourages citizens of states in non-market economies to pressure their governments for greater economic liberalization. Finally, market economies are closely associated with foreign trade, and trade is also central to this diffusion argument. The presence of a liberal trading state encourages non-liberal states to engage in trade, a process that should increase the likelihood of further political and economic liberalization in non-democratic states.

Of the three causal claims advanced in the regional-level argument, the link between imposed democracy and regional prosperity is perhaps the least studied in the scholarly literature. Some scholarly research does examine the regional economic impact of post-WWII Japan and Germany, and these cases appear to provide support for this aspect of the regional-level argument. For example, during the post-war period, Japan steadily increased its regional economic influence such that by the 1980s in "almost every country in the region [Asia], Japan was simultaneously the largest investor; the largest exporter; the largest source of tourism; the largest foreign-aid donor; and the largest buyer of raw commodities" (Fallows 1995: 247). This expansion of Japanese economic influence in the region stimulated and coincided with increasingly market-oriented Asian economies and rapid economic growth in many countries. Similarly, West Germany played an important role in promoting economic and social change within Eastern Europe following World War II. For example, Lane (1995) argues that the West German policy of *Ostpolitik* increased the openness of the societies of Eastern Europe to new ideas and influences by stimulating contacts between Western Germany and Eastern Europe. The view from West Germany was that these linkages would open the societies of Eastern Europe to new ideas and influences.

Studies of the relationship between imposed political regimes and regional prosperity default to the familiar examples identified by American policymakers, i.e., the post-WWII democratic and capitalist success stories of West Germany and Japan.[2] In turn, the cases of West Germany and Japan appear to suggest firm evidence of the regional benefits that imposed democratic states can have on regional prosperity. However, beyond these two notable cases, little research exploring the relationship between imposed democratic regimes and regional prosperity exists.

Testing the regional-level argument

To verify empirically the regional-level argument, we identified a set of 27 externally imposed democratic polities (i.e., political institutions) during the twentieth century.[3] Externally imposed democratic polities are those political institutions that are installed in a state by one or more third party actors, including states or international organizations (e.g., democratic institutions installed by the United States in Japan following World War II). The 27 externally imposed polities that we analyze are reported in Table 7.1. In addition to exploring the general relationship between imposed democracies and regional outcomes, we wish to investigate whether this relationship is moderated by the strength or presence of democratic institutions in imposed democratic polities. To this end, we refer to imposed democracies with strong democratic institutions as "bright democratic beacons," and we refer to imposed democracies with weak democratic institutions as "dim democratic beacons." In testing the regional-level argument, we consider each regional outcome—i.e., peace, democracy, and prosperity—in turn, and with respect to the impact of bright and dim democratic beacons.

Table 7.1. *Externally imposed democratic polities in the twentieth century*

State	Start	End
Austria	1920	1934
Austria	1946	1994
Botswana	1966	1994
Canada	1867	1994
Cuba	1901	1955
Cyprus	1960	1994
West Germany/Germany	1949	1994
Guyana	1966	1978
Haiti	1918	1935
Honduras	1908	1936
Ireland	1922	1994
Jamaica	1959	1994
Japan	1952	1994
Kenya	1963	1969
Lebanon	1941	1990
Lesotho	1966	1970
Malaysia	1957	1994
Mauritius	1968	1994
New Zealand	1857	1994
Nigeria	1960	1966
Philippines	1935	1972
Singapore	1959	1965
Sri Lanka	1948	1994
Sudan	1954	1958
Syria	1944	1950
Uganda	1962	1967
Zimbabwe	1923	1987

Source: McLaughlin *et al.* (1998).

With respect to the relationship between externally imposed democratic polities and regional interstate war, our empirical analysis indicates that a state's war propensity declines by approximately 32 percent when it is geographically contiguous to a bright democratic beacon. By contrast, this relationship attenuates when we consider states beyond those directly contiguous to an externally imposed democracy. As encouraging as these results are regarding the relationship between imposed democracy and regional interstate war, further analysis suggests the need for caution. First, although the analysis for the twentieth century suggests a significant pacifying effect by bright democratic beacons on neighboring states, this effect is considerably weaker in a sample corresponding to the post-WWII period. Indeed, we find that bright democratic beacons have their weakest impact on regional peace during precisely that historical interval, the post-WWII period.

Most striking, however, are the findings corresponding to the performance of dim democratic beacons during the post-WWII interval. Specifically, it appears that rather than enhancing regional peace, these beacons actually undermine regional peace. Indeed, a state neighboring a dim democratic beacon is 87 percent more likely to engage in war in any given year relative to a state that is not. In general, our analysis suggests that the degree to which an imposed democratic polity is democratic has significant implications for regional war. The brighter the imposed democratic beacon, the greater the negative impact on regional war; conversely, the dimmer the democratic beacon, the greater the regional tendency toward war.

In sum, our analysis of regional peace suggests that externally imposed democratic polities can stimulate regional peace, but only under conditions in which imposed democratic beacons burn brightly. If an imposed democracy reflects strong democratic institutions, then this bright democratic beacon does reduce conflict among its closest neighbors, stimulating greater regional peace and conflict resolution. Yet, our analysis suggests that dim democratic beacons do not merely exert a benign impact on the regions in which they reside. Rather, our analysis suggests that these dim democratic beacons increase their own conflict propensity, as well as the war-proneness of neighboring states, a dynamic that undermines regional peace, ongoing peacemaking processes, and general political stability.

Next, we now consider the impact of such polities on regional democratization. In general, our empirical analysis suggests little empirical support for the claim that the presence of imposed democratic polities stimulates further democratization in the regions that they occupy. Indeed, there appears to be no significant effect of these polities upon the likelihood of democratization of states in their region. While bright democratic beacons do not seem to influence regional democratization, dim democratic beacons negatively influence the democratization of their neighbors.

Interestingly, dim democratic beacons do not appear to have the same effect upon the states directly contiguous to them as they do to other non-contiguous neighbors. Indeed, our analysis suggests that states geographically contiguous to dim democratic beacon are neither more nor less likely to experience democratization. At first glance, this result seems surprising since it makes sense to expect that imposed regimes are likely to have the most direct effect upon the bordering states. Yet, these results may reflect the presence of two opposed effects that dim democratic beacons potentially exert upon their immediate neighbors. On one hand, the weak form of democracy associated with dim democratic beacons, as well as the instability that these polities seem to interject into the regions they occupy, would likely decrease the likelihood of further regional democratization. Conversely, the military presence of the imposing state or states (e.g., the United States in Iraq) in the state receiving the imposed polity, a presence that would encourage democratization both within the imposed polity and the region at large, would be felt most directly by states directly contiguous to the dim democratic beacon. Such an explanation might explain the two effects that would account for the null findings for states directly contiguous to dim democratic beacons.

Our third and final theoretical expectation links the presence of imposed democratic polities with increased regional prosperity, a concept that we operationalize with per capita Gross National Product (GNP). Our analysis of prosperity suggests that the variable describing the minimum distance of a state to the nearest bright democratic beacon is negative and statistically significant. This finding indicates that per capita GNP growth becomes more likely the *nearer* a state is to a bright imposed democratic beacon. Indeed, we find that states that are proximate, but not contiguous, to a bright democratic beacon are approximately 13 percent more likely to experience GNP growth than other states. Interestingly, states contiguous to a bright democratic beacon were neither significantly more or less likely to experience GNP growth. Similar to our analysis of regional democracy, dim democratic beacons have a negative effect on prosperity in the regions they occupy, such that the presence of a dim beacon within a 1–950 kilometer band of a state reduces the likelihood of growth in per capital GNP in given year by approximately 16 percent.

In sum, our analysis lends additional support to the conjecture that factors associated with dim democratic beacons exert two separate effects upon their immediate neighbors. On one hand, the influence of the imposing power may have a spill-over effect upon the states contiguous to the imposed state, promoting greater stability and, in turn, increasing the likelihood of economic growth. At the same time, based on our analysis of peace, above, the presence of dim democratic beacons seems to promote instability in neighboring states. As a result, the null findings obtained for states contiguous to dim democratic beacons may reflect the impact of these two cross-cutting influences.

CONCLUSION

In crafting the policy argument for the invasion of Iraq, policymakers repeatedly referenced the post-World War II experiences of Germany and Japan as epicenters of subsequent peace, democracy, and prosperity in their respective geographic regions. Our study of this regional-level policy claim with data for the twentieth century leads us to conclude that, under conditions in which bright democratic beacons persist in a region, regional peace and prosperity are promoted, but democratization is not. Furthermore, we find that imposed democratic polities that are weakly democratic generally reduce the odds that a region will achieve greater peace, prosperity, and democracy.

Based on these general findings, our analysis provides some insight into the likely regional impact of a post-Hussein democracy in Iraq. On the positive side, if Iraq emerges as a bright democratic beacon, there exists a chance for greater regional peace and prosperity. Such an achievement in a region racked by recurring, high-intensity conflict would without a doubt be a favorable development. However, the road to a fully functioning democracy on the order of Germany or Japan, i.e., quintessential bright democratic beacons, is likely to be difficult, given Iraq's ethnic and religious cleavages, near absence of a democratic tradition, the impact of the American occupation, and the potential hostility of Iraq's neighbors. Under conditions of a dimly lit democratic beacon in Iraq, our analysis suggests that regional peace, prosperity, and democracy are unlikely to follow in the Middle East.

The implications of our analysis of externally imposed democratic polities for thinking about peace in post-conflict societies are significant. As we know, nation-states do not exist in isolation. Rather, virtually every nation-state in the modern state system has some geographic, economic, social, or political links to other nation-states in this system. Therefore, attempts by the international community to resolve disputes between and within states do have important implications beyond the state where democratic political institutions are imposed. Indeed, our study indicates that the translation of imposed democracy into positive regional outcomes turns on the strength of the democratic institutions in an imposed democracy. If the beacon of democracy is strong, then most, but not all, of the promised benefits have, on average, accrued regionally. Conversely, if the beacon of democracy is weak, then the regional byproducts of imposed democracy are alarming and likely to be counter-productive. Ultimately, despite the positive regional benefits derived from the presence of bright democratic beacons, we conclude that relying on externally imposed democracy as a vehicle for regional conflict resolution is a risky strategy for achieving regional conflict resolution, democracy, and prosperity.

NOTES

1. The most explicit outline of this policy shift is reflected in two speeches by American President George W. Bush in 2003 (Bush 2003a, 2003b).
2. See President George W. Bush's speech to the American Enterprise Institute (Bush 2003a).
3. Detailed coding rules for identifying these polities, as well as more extensive reporting of our empirical tests of the regional-level argument, are reported in Enterline and Greig

(forthcoming). Due to data limitations, we define the twentieth century to include the period 1909–1994.

REFERENCES

Bumiller, E. (2003) "Bush Says Ousting Hussein Could Aid Peace in the Middle East," *New York Times* February 27.

Bush, G.W. (2003a) "In the President's Words: 'Free People Will Keep the Peace of the World,'" *New York Times* February 27.

Bush, G.W. (2003b) "Iraqi Democracy Will Succeed," *New York Times* November 6.

Cederman, L. and Gleditsch, K.S. (2004) "Conquest and Regime Change: An Evolutionary Model of the Spread of Democracy and Peace," *International Studies Quarterly* 48: 603–629.

Colaresi, M. and Thompson, W.R. (2003) "The Economic Development-Democratization Relationship: Does the Outside World Matter?," *Comparative Political Studies* 36 (4): 381–403.

Crescenzi, M.J.C. and Enterline, A.J. (1999) "Ripples from the Waves? A Systemic, Time-Series Analysis of Democracy, Democratization, and Interstate War," *Journal of Peace Research* 36: 75–94.

Enterline, A.J. and Greig, J.M. (2005) "Beacons of Hope? The Impact of Imposed Democracy on Regional Peace, Democracy and Prosperity," *Journal of Politics* 67(4): 1075–1098.

Fallows, J. (1995) *Looking at the Sun: The Rise of the New East Asian Economic and Political System.* New York: Vintage.

Gleditsch, K.S. (2002) *All International Politics Is Local: The Diffusion of Conflict, Integration, and Democratization.* Ann Arbor, MI: University of Michigan.

Gleditsch, N.P. and Hegre, H. (1997) "Peace and Democracy: Three Levels of Analysis," *Journal of Conflict Resolution* 41: 283–310.

Huntington, S.P. (1991) *The Third Wave: Democratization in the Late Twentieth-Century.* Norman, OK: University of Oklahoma.

Kadera, K.M., Crescenzi, M.J.C., and Shannon, M.L. (2003) "Democratic Survival, Peace, and War in the International System," *American Journal of Political Science* 47: 234–247.

Lane, C. (1995) "Germany's New Ostpolitik," *Foreign Affairs* 74: 77–89.

McLaughlin, S., Gates, S., and Hegre, H. (1999) "Evolution in Democracy-War Dynamics," *Journal of Conflict Resolution* 43: 771–792.

McLaughlin, S., Gates, S., Hegre, H., Gissinger, R., and Gleditsch, N.P. (1998) "Timing the Changes in Political Structures: A New Polity Database," *Journal of Conflict Resolution* 42: 231–242.

Modelski, G. and Perry, G. (1991) "Democratization in Long Perspective," *Technological Forecasting and Social Change* 39: 23–34.

Pevehouse, J.C. (2002) "Democracy from the Outside-In? International Organizations and Democratization," *International Organizations* 56: 515–49.

Ray, J.L. (2000) "On the Level(s): Does Democracy Correlate with Peace?" in John A. Vasquez (ed.) *What Do We Know About War?* Lanham, MD: Rowman and Littlefield.

Siverson, R.M. and Starr, H. (1991) *The Diffusion of War: A Study of Opportunity and Willingness.* Ann Arbor, MI: University of Michigan.

Starr, H. (1991) "Democratic Dominoes: Diffusion Approaches the Spread of Democracy in the International System," *Technological Forecasting and Social Change* 35: 356–381.

Starr, H. (1995) "D2: The Diffusion of Democracy Revisited," paper presented at the International Studies Association Meeting, Chicago, Illinois, February 20–26.

Starr, H. and Lindborg, C. (2003) "Democratic Dominoes Revisited: The Hazards of Governmental Transitions, 1974–1996," *Journal of Conflict Resolution* 47: 490–519.

Thompson, W.R. (1996) "Democracy and Peace: Putting the Cart Before the Horse?" *International Organization* 50: 141–174.

Just War – or a Just War?
March 9, 2003 Op-Ed Contributor

JIMMY CARTER

ATLANTA—Profound changes have been taking place in American foreign policy, reversing consistent bipartisan commitments that for more than two centuries have earned our nation greatness. These commitments have been predicated on basic religious principles, respect for international law, and alliances that resulted in wise decisions and mutual restraint. Our apparent determination to launch a war against Iraq, without international support, is a violation of these premises.

As a Christian and as a president who was severely provoked by international crises, I became thoroughly familiar with the principles of a just war, and it is clear that a substantially unilateral attack on Iraq does not meet these standards. This is an almost universal conviction of religious leaders, with the most notable exception of a few spokesmen of the Southern Baptist Convention who are greatly influenced by their commitment to Israel based on eschatological, or final days, theology.

For a war to be just, it must meet several clearly defined criteria.

The war can be waged only as a last resort, with all nonviolent options exhausted. In the case of Iraq, it is obvious that clear alternatives to war exist. These options—previously proposed by our own leaders and approved by the United Nations—were outlined again by the Security Council on Friday. But now, with our own national security not directly threatened and despite the overwhelming opposition of most people and governments in the world, the United States seems determined to carry out military and diplomatic action that is almost unprecedented in the history of civilized nations. The first stage of our widely publicized war plan is to launch 3,000 bombs and missiles on a relatively defenseless Iraqi population within the first few hours of an invasion, with the purpose of so damaging and demoralizing the people that they will change their obnoxious leader, who will most likely be hidden and safe during the bombardment.

The war's weapons must discriminate between combatants and noncombatants. Extensive aerial bombardment, even with precise accuracy, inevitably results in "collateral damage." Gen. Tommy R. Franks, commander of American forces in the Persian Gulf, has expressed concern about many of the military targets being near hospitals, schools, mosques and private homes.

Its violence must be proportional to the injury we have suffered. Despite Saddam Hussein's other serious crimes, American efforts to tie Iraq to the 9/11 terrorist attacks have been unconvincing.

The attackers must have legitimate authority sanctioned by the society they profess to represent. The unanimous vote of approval in the Security Council to eliminate Iraq's weapons of mass destruction can still be honored, but our announced goals are now to achieve regime change and to establish a Pax Americana in the region, perhaps occupying the ethnically divided country for as long as a decade. For these objectives, we do not have international authority. Other members of the Security Council have so far resisted the enormous economic and political influence that is being exerted from Washington, and we are faced with the possibility of either a failure to get the necessary votes or else a veto from Russia, France and China. Although Turkey may still be enticed into helping us by enormous financial rewards and partial future control of the Kurds and oil in northern Iraq, its democratic Parliament has at least added its voice to the worldwide expressions of concern.

The peace it establishes must be a clear improvement over what exists. Although there are visions of peace and democracy in Iraq, it is quite possible that the aftermath of a military invasion will destabilize the region and prompt terrorists to further jeopardize our security at home. Also, by defying overwhelming world opposition, the United States will undermine the United Nations as a viable institution for world peace.

What about America's world standing if we don't go to war after such a great deployment of military forces in the region? The heartfelt sympathy and friendship offered to America after the 9/11 attacks, even from formerly antagonistic regimes, has been largely dissipated; increasingly unilateral and domineering policies have brought international trust in our country to its lowest level in memory. American stature will surely decline further if we launch a war in clear defiance of the United Nations. But to use the presence and threat of our military power to force Iraq's compliance with all United Nations resolutions—with war as a final option—will enhance our status as a champion of peace and justice.

Jimmy Carter, the 39th president of the United States, is chairman of the Carter Center in Atlanta and winner of the 2002 Nobel Peace Prize.

Iraq and the Democratic Peace

JOHN M. OWEN IV

John M. Owen IV is Associate Professor of Politics at the University of Virginia and the author of "Liberal Peace, Liberal War: American Politics and International Security."

WHO SAYS DEMOCRACIES DON'T FIGHT?

Seldom if ever has the hostility between academics and the U.S. president been so pronounced. Of course, political scientists always seem to complain about the occupant of the White House, and Republicans fare worse than Democrats: Herbert Hoover was called callous, Dwight Eisenhower a dunce, Richard Nixon evil, Ronald Reagan dangerous, and George H.W. Bush out of touch. But professors have consigned George W. Bush to a special circle of their presidential hell. And the White House seems to return the sentiment.

According to the academics, Bush's chief transgressions have had to do with foreign policy, especially the Iraq war—a mess that could have been avoided if only the president and his advisers had paid more attention to those who devote their lives to studying international relations.

The irony of this argument is that few other presidents—certainly none since Woodrow Wilson, a former president of the American Political Science Association, scribbled away in the Oval Office—have tied their foreign policies more explicitly to the work of social science. The defining act of Bush's presidency was grounded in a theory that the political

John M. Owen IV, "Iraq and the Democratic Peace," from *Foreign Affairs*, November/December 2005. Copyright © 2005 by Council on Foreign Relations. Permission to reprint granted by the publisher.

Iraq and the Democratic Peace | 219

scientist Jack Levy once declared was "as close as anything we have to an empirical law in international relations," namely, that democracies do not fight one another.

The theory, which originated in the work of the eighteenth-century philosopher Immanuel Kant and was refined in the 1970s and 1980s by several researchers working independently, has, since the 1990s, been one of the hottest research areas in international relations. Although some skeptics remain and no one agrees about why exactly it works, most academics now share the belief that democracies have indeed made a separate peace. What is more, much research suggests that they are also unusually likely to sign and honor international agreements and to become economically interdependent.

The administrations of Presidents George H.W. Bush and Bill Clinton made frequent appeals to the theory in public, and it seems to have informed their support for democratization in former communist lands and in Haiti. The current Bush administration, however, has gone much further in its faith in the idea, betting the farm that the theory holds and will help Washington achieve a peaceful, stable, and prosperous Muslim world as, over time, Iraq's neighbors, following Iraq's example, democratize. The United States' real motives for attacking Iraq may have been complex, but "regime change"—the replacement of Saddam Hussein's gruesome tyranny with a democracy—was central to Washington's rhetoric by the time it began bombing Baghdad in March 2003.

Why has a president who set his defining policy around one of political science's crown jewels come in for so much venom from the same academics who endorse the idea? After all, a host of peer-reviewed journal articles have implicitly supported the president's claim that a democratic Iraq would not threaten the United States or Israel, develop weapons of mass destruction, or sponsor terrorism. Are professors simply perpetual critics who refuse to take responsibility for the consequences of their ideas? Or does Bush hatred trump social science?

The Bush administration's desire to break with its predecessors and alter the authoritarian status quo in the Middle East was admirable. But the White House got its science wrong, or at least not completely right: the democratic peace theory does not dictate that the United States can or should remake Iraq into a democracy. In *Electing to Fight: Why Emerging Democracies Go to War*, the veteran political scientists Edward Mansfield and Jack Snyder make two critical points. Not only is turning authoritarian countries into democracies extremely difficult, much more so than the administration seems to have anticipated. The Middle East could also become a much more dangerous place if Washington and the rest of the world settle for a merely semidemocratic regime in Baghdad. Such an Iraq, Mansfield and Snyder imply, would be uncommonly likely to start wars—a bull in the Middle Eastern china shop. Unfortunately, such an Iraq may also be just what we are likely to end up with.

ILLIBERAL DEMOCRACIES

At first glance, the realists' critique of the Iraq war is easier to understand than that of the democratic peace theorists. Indeed, realism—which holds that a country's type of government has no systematic effects on its foreign policy—is enjoying a revival in Washington these days, precisely because of the war. According to the realists, the best way to have dealt with Saddam would have been not to overthrow him but to use coercive bargaining: to have threatened him with annihilation, for example, if he ever used nuclear weapons.

Even the democratic peace theory, however, does not necessarily prescribe the use of force to transform despotisms such as Iraq into democracies. Indeed, by itself, the argument that democracies do not fight one another does not have any practical implications for the foreign policymaker. It needs an additional or minor premise, such as "the United States can make Iraq into a democracy at an acceptable cost." And it is precisely this minor premise about which the academy has been skeptical. No scholarly consensus exists on how countries become democratic, and the literature is equally murky on the costs to the United States of trying to force them to be free.

This last part of the puzzle is even more complicated than it first appears. Enter Mansfield and Snyder, who have been contributing to the democratic peace debate for a decade. Their thesis, first published in 1995, is that although mature democracies do not fight one another, democratizing states—those in transition from authoritarianism to democracy—do, and are even more prone to war than authoritarian regimes. Now, in *Electing to Fight*, the authors have refined their argument. As they outline in the book, not only are "incomplete democratizing" states—those that develop democratic institutions in the wrong order—unlikely ever to complete the transition to democracy; they are also especially bellicose.

According to Mansfield and Snyder, in countries that have recently started to hold free elections but that lack the proper mechanisms for accountability (institutions such as an independent judiciary, civilian control of the military, and protections for opposition parties and the press), politicians have incentives to pursue policies that make it more likely that their countries will start wars. In such places, politicians know they can mobilize support by demanding territory or other spoils from foreign countries and by nurturing grievances against outsiders. As a result, they push for extraordinarily belligerent policies. Even states that develop democratic institutions in the right order—adopting the rule of law before holding elections—are very aggressive in the early years of their transitions, although they are less so than the first group and more likely to eventually turn into full democracies.

Of course, politicians in mature democracies are also often tempted to use nationalism and xenophobic rhetoric to buttress their domestic power. In such cases, however, they are usually restrained by institutionalized mechanisms of accountability. Knowing that if they lead the country into a military defeat or quagmire they may be punished at the next election, politicians in such states are less likely to advocate a risky war. In democratizing states, by contrast, politicians know that they are insulated from the impact of bad policies: if a war goes badly, for example, they can declare a state of emergency, suspend elections, censor the press, and so on. Politicians in such states also tend to fear their militaries, which often crave foreign enemies and will overthrow civilian governments that do not share their goals. Combined, these factors can make the temptation to attack another state irresistible.

Mansfield and Snyder present both quantitative and case-study support for their theory. Using rigorous statistical methods, the authors show that since 1815, democratizing states have indeed been more prone to start wars than either democracies or authoritarian regimes. Categorizing transitions according to whether they ended in full democracies (as in the U.S. case) or in partial ones (as in Germany in 1871–1918 or Pakistan throughout its history), the authors find that in the early years of democratic transitions, partial democracies—especially those that get their institutions in the wrong order—are indeed significantly more likely to initiate wars. Mansfield and Snyder then provide several succinct stories of democratizing states that did in fact go to war, such as the France of Napoleon III (1852–70), Serbia between 1877 and 1914, Ethiopia and Eritrea between 1998 and 2000, and Pakistan from 1947 to the present. In most of these cases, the authors find what they expect: in these democratizing states, domestic political competition was intense. Politicians, vying for power, appeased domestic hard-liners by resorting to nationalistic appeals that vilified foreigners, and these policies often led to wars that were not in the countries' strategic interests.

Although their argument would have been strengthened by a few comparative studies of democratizing states avoiding war and of full democracies and authoritarian states starting wars, Mansfield and Snyder are persuasive. In part this is because they carefully circumscribe their claims. They acknowledge that some cases are "false positives," that is, wars started by states that have wrongly been classified as democratizing, such as the Iran-Iraq War, started by Iraq in 1980. They also answer the most likely objections to their argument. Some skeptics, for example, might counter that Mansfield and Snyder get the causality reversed: it is war or the threat of it that prevents states from becoming mature democracies. Others might argue that democratizing states become involved in more wars simply because their internal instability tempts foreign states to attack them—in other words, that democratizers are more sinned against than sinning. Analyzing data from 1816 through 1992, Mansfield and Snyder put paid to these alternative explanations. Bad domestic institutions usually precede wars, rather than vice versa, and democratizing states usually do the attacking.

Where does Electing to Fight leave realism, the dominant theory of international conflict? The quantitative data support the realist claims that major powers are more likely to go to war than minor ones and that the more equal are the great powers, the more likely are wars among them. But democratization makes war more likely even after one takes these factors into account. Furthermore, the case studies suggest that democratizing states very often lose more than they gain from the wars they begin, which implies that they do not respond to international incentives as rationally as realism would expect. That said, notwithstanding its preference for viewing states from the inside, the Mansfield-Snyder theory is still "realist" in the general sense that it assumes that politicians and other actors are rationally self-interested. Their self-interest simply involves building and maintaining domestic power as well as external security—and sometimes trading some of the latter in order to gain the former.

The authors' conclusions for foreign policy are straightforward. The United States and other international actors should continue to promote democracy, but they must strive to help democratizing states implement reforms in the correct order. In particular, popular elections ought not to precede the building of institutions that will check the baleful incentives for politicians to call for war. Mansfield and Snyder are unsparing toward well-intentioned organizations that have pressured authoritarian governments to rush to elections in the past—often with disastrous consequences. As the authors show, for example, it was organizations such as the World Bank and the National Democratic Institute that pushed Burundi and Rwanda to increase popular sovereignty in the early 1990s—pressure that, as Mansfield and Snyder argue, helped set off a chain of events that led to genocide. Acknowledging their intellectual debt to writers such as Samuel Huntington (particularly his 1968 book *Political Order in Changing Societies*) and Fareed Zakaria, Mansfield and Snyder have written a deeply conservative book. Sounding like Edmund Burke on the French Revolution but substituting statistics and measured prose for rhetorical power, the authors counsel against abruptly empowering people, since premature elections may well usher in domestic upheavals that thrust the state outward against its neighbors.

BACK IN BAGHDAD

This brings the conversation back to Iraq, and in particular the notion that the United States can turn it into a democracy at an acceptable cost. In effect, Mansfield and Snyder have raised the estimate of these costs by pointing out one other reason this effort may fail—a reason that few seem to have thought of. Forget for a moment the harrowing possibility of a Sunni-Shiite-Kurdish civil war in Iraq. Set aside the prospect of a Shiite-dominated state aligning itself with Iran, Syria, and Lebanon's Hezbollah. What if, following the departure of U.S. troops, Iraq holds together but as an incomplete democratizer, with broad suffrage but anemic state institutions? Such an Iraq might well treat its own citizens better than the Baathist regime did. Its treatment of its neighbors, however, might be just as bad.

Although Saddam was an unusually bellicose and reckless tyrant, attacking Iran in 1980 and Kuwait in 1990 and engaging in foolish brinkmanship with the United States, as Mansfield and Snyder imply, a democratic Iraq may be no less bellicose and reckless. In the near future, intensely competitive elites there—secularists, leftists, moderates, and both Shiite and Sunni Islamists—could compete for popularity by stirring up nationalism against one or more of Iraq's neighbors. And Iraq lives in a dangerous neighborhood.

Already, Iraqi Shiite parties have been critical of Sunni-dominated Jordan; Iraqi Sunni parties, of Shiite-dominated Iran; and Iraqi Kurdish parties, of Turkey.

One hopes that the White House contemplated this scenario prior to March 2003. Whether it did or not, the possibility must be considered now, by U.S. civilian and military leaders, academics, and U.S. allies who agree with those academics. If Mansfield and Snyder are correct about the bellicose tendencies of young, incompletely democratized states, the stakes of Iraq's transition are higher than most have supposed. They are high enough, in fact, that those who called so loudly in the 1990s for an end to UN sanctions because Iraqis were dying but who are silent about the Iraqis who are dying now ought to reconsider their proud aloofness from the war. An aggressive Iraq, prone to attack Kuwait, Iran, Saudi Arabia, Syria, or Israel, is in no one's interest. The odds may be long that Iraq will ever turn into a mature democracy of the sort envisaged by the Bush administration. But those odds are lengthened by the refusal of those states in Europe and the Middle East that could make a difference actually to do so.

UNIT 4

✛

HUMAN RIGHTS

International Law
Amid Power, Order and Justice

RICHARD FALK

INTRODUCTORY CONSIDERATIONS

The history of international law has been decidedly mixed. It has functioned for several centuries both as a sword for the strong and a shield for the weak. It has developed over the course of the Westphalian Era, stretching back to the Peace of Westphalia in 1648, as a regulatory and cooperative framework for the interplay of sovereign states. Throughout this history the juridical logic of equality that is embodied in international law has been consistently subordinated to the geopolitical framework of world politics based on the logic of relative power. The same ratio of law to power pertains today. This means that the quality of world order is very dependent on the prudence, wisdom and legitimacy of the global leadership provided at a given time and in various settings by the main geopolitical actors.

During the early stages of the Cold War this leadership was provided mainly by the United States, with the Soviet Union in a defensive and reactive pattern. Under this leadership the United Nations was established, the Nuremberg/Tokyo war crimes trials were held, and the Universal Declaration of Human Rights (UDHR) was adopted. Each was a major *geopolitical* acknowledgement of the importance of strengthening the relative role of the normative side (that is, law plus morality) of international relations. This strengthening related to three major world order deficiencies that had been disclosed by the great devastation of the two world wars, and the human suffering associated with oppressive regimes: ending the discretionary status of war by UN Charter prohibition on recourse to force except in self-defence (Articles 2(4) and 51), holding political leaders accountable for crimes of state (Nürnberg and Tokyo Judgements, as supplemented by the Genocide Convention), and challenging a central tenet of the Westphalian ethos, which holds that whatever takes places *within* the territory of a state is a matter of sovereign right and not subject to external review. Such initiatives were tentative and provisional steps, but opening wide horizons of possibility, which unfortunately have not been successfully implemented. These initiatives were from the outset subject to major qualifications and regressive moves in geopolitics that occurred throughout the Cold War. At the same time such steps gave grounds for hope that future world order could be an improvement on the past, and that the essence of this improvement would be a greater effort to reconcile international law with global justice. This hope, while often crushed by persisting geopolitical Machiavellianism, has remained important as an inspiration and source of legitimation for normatively inclined governments and visionary elements of civil society. Even when states have cynically cast aside or defied these normative promises of the Charter, Nuremberg and UDHR, civil society actors have done their best, especially in war/peace and human rights situations, to fulfil these higher expectations. The sad truth remains, that international law operates as an essentially *voluntary* system of constraints for major states, and is selectively, and often unfairly, enforced in relation to weaker states. The non-proliferation regime governing development and possession of nuclear weapons illustrates both sides of this dynamic: exemptions for the powerful; enforcement for the weak.

The United Nations Charter and practice is a major arena within which these tensions were expressed. For instance, the Charter affirms sovereign rights in rather unconditional terms, famously declaring that the UN shall refrain from intervening in matters 'essentially within the domestic jurisdiction of any state' (Article 2(7)), which effectively nullifies any prospect that international human rights will be implemented in relation to abusive governments. Going further, it seems clear that the only reason that the UDHR could be agreed upon in the first place was the tacit understanding among participating governments that it would *not* be enforced. But civil society took more seriously the norms contained in the UDHR, and found ways to convert this instrument from the statist intention to compile a list of pieties into a viable political project. This political project took hold as a result of pressures exerted by an array of trans-national human rights organizations founded and funded by civil society, and given historical relevance in the course of a variety of struggles against oppressive rule, including in East Europe, in the form of the promotion of the right of self-determination in the movement against colonialism, and at the core of the global anti-apartheid movement. In this sense, states, including geopolitical actors, *rediscovered* human rights as a useful instrument of world order *after* these norms of political behaviour had been first taken seriously at the level of civil society.

In a sense, the same dynamic is manifest with respect to the legacy of the Nuremberg/Tokyo tradition. This tradition always suffered from the taint of victors' justice, exempting from legal scrutiny such wartime atrocities of the winning side as the indiscriminate bombing of German and Japanese cities, and the initiation of the Nuclear Age with the atomic bombs dropped on Hiroshima and Nagasaki. At Nuremberg it was declared that the standards used to judge the defeated Germans would only be vindicated if in the future those who sat in judgement accepted accountability by reference to the same legal constraints on the behaviour of sovereign states. This 'Nuremberg Promise' was repeatedly broken by the subsequent official crimes of the Second World War victors. But the promise was not forgotten by representatives of civil society. In the course of the Vietnam War, in the United States many acts were committed by anti-war Americans based on their reading of Nuremberg that were seeking to implement over the heads of the geopoliticians norms of limitations associated with the prohibition of aggressive war and the obligations of international humanitarian law with respect to the conduct of war. The impact of these acts of civil resistance is hard to assess, but it would seem at the very least that they contributed to the delegitimation of the Vietnam War, and when coupled with battlefield failures, led to its eventual repudiation even by policy-making elites. With a similar effect was the Bertrand Russell War Crimes Tribunal set up in 1967 on the basis of civil society concerns about the criminality of the Vietnam War, engaging the participation of the leading European intellectuals of the day (Jean-Paul Sartre, Simone de Beauvoir) and later inspiring the formation of the Permanent People's Tribunal in Rome that has for 20 years relied upon the progressive elements in international law to assess the injustices, wrongdoing and crimes of leading geopolitical actors that are met with silence by the state system and even by the United Nations.

The Charter itself embodied the contradictory impulses of international law and geopolitics. On the one side, principles of non-interntvention, self-determination and equality of states are affirmed, as well as the prohibition of all non-defensive uses of force to resolve international disputes. On the other side, there is imposed no legal obligation to disarm or to submit disputes to the International Court of Justice, and the five permanent members of the Security Council (picked from the winners of the Second World War plus China) are given a veto power, which in effect exempts them from the Charter. Such deference to political realism is an explicit acknowledgement that international legal authority cannot be imposed upon leading political actors. In practice this exemption, combined with the geopolitical stalemate in the Cold War and the refusal of either superpower to go forward with the Chapter VII (Articles 39–49) efforts to establish procedures and capabilities to provide collective security in the face of aggression, doomed the effort to end recourse to discretionary war by geopolitical actors and their friends. Again to the extent that this normative expectation has been kept alive, it has been a result of the action of world citizens and peace movements that base their demonstrations and other initiatives on an unconditional acceptance of the outlawry of aggressive war for all states, big and small alike.

What is evident, then, over the course of the last century is a long struggle to curtail the primacy of geopolitics and territorial sovereignty as the pillars of world order. This struggle has had ebbs and flows. Its positive results often depend on some sort of convergence between the demands of civil society and either the moderation or weakness of geopolitical forces. Its negative experiences usually reflect the impact of extremist geopolitical orientations and militarist orientations toward the fulfilment of geopolitical world order goals. This pattern has been given great prominence in the period since the end of the Cold War. The next section examines the optimistic mood of the 1990s associated with the first normative 'revolution' in world politics that raised hopes as the millennium approached despite some discouraging aspects. The third section focuses on the return to regressive geopolitics as a consequence of the American approach to the pursuit of grand strategy goals in the aftermath of the 9/11 attacks. A final section discusses prospects as of the early twenty-first century for reviving the normative revolution, taking some account of three impinging trends: the growing dysfunction of war and militarism as geopolitical instruments; the tightening energy/ecological squeeze that will require transition to a post-petroleum world economy by stages during the decades ahead, requiring painful adjustments; and the growing need for a more institutionalized form of global governance to cope effectively and fairly with the growing complexity and fragility of the world.

Notes on the normative revolution of the 1990s

The period immediately following the Cold War seemed to present strong opportunities for global reform, giving the West lots of political space to take initiatives to make the world safer and more equitable. It was a moment of liberal capitalist global ascendancy in the aftermath of the Soviet collapse, with a virtually worldwide acceptance of only those forms of political governance based on a combination of a strong market economy and constitutional democracy. Additionally, there was a virtual completion of the decolonization process, with only South Africa and Palestine remaining important remnants of the colonial era at the start of the 1990s. The United States emerged as the undisputed global leader, claiming for itself a special role as 'indispensable nation' given the geopolitical background of unipolarity. In such a favourable context there were several promising world order initiatives that might have been encouraged by the US either on its own or in concert with other leading governments: serious nuclear disarmament and negotiated demilitarization (e.g. a worldwide 1 per cent of GNP ceiling on military expenditures for national security); a UN peace force and independent revenue base; limitations on the use of the veto and mandatory reference of contested policy issues to ICJ for resolution; serious and balanced diplomatic efforts to promote a fair settlement of the Israel-Palestine conflict. But instead, the geopolitical preoccupation of major states was devoted to global economic growth along neo-liberal lines, producing both a prevailing sense that 'globalization' was the true new world order and an anti-globalization backlash by those social forces around the world being victimized by this latest phase of predatory world capitalism. The intergovernmental basis for reformist action lacked any forward energy. The supposed 'new world order' proclaimed by the first George Bush was an opportunistic packaging of recourse to war to legitimize a coalition formed under a UN mandate in 1990 to push Iraq out of Kuwait. It was never meant to be anything more than a temporary effort to mobilize support within the US and the world for a dubious war that was intended to be controlled from Washington but backed by the United Nations. In this sense, rather than the *new* world order, it was a dramatic reminder of the resilience of the *old* world order, with the geopolitical ventriloquist making use of its UN puppet.

Despite this disappointing failure to take advantage of the global setting to introduce needed changes, the 1990s did produce some notable developments that were based on the potentially constructive contributions of international law to global justice and humane global governance. In all instances, and this is a dramatic expression of the rise of non-state, civil society actors, these developments depended on the rise of global civil society as a political force, acting either autonomously or in collaboration with those statist forces that wanted to restrict sovereign rights and geopolitical discretion, which historically were the two main sources of human wrongs and warmaking within the Westphalian frame-work. International law played a central role in giving substance to these undertakings and confidence to activists. Several of these initiatives can be mentioned to show a continuity with the global reformist surge evident after 1945: to restrict warmaking, to hold leaders criminally accountable for violations of fundamental rules about the use of force and with respect to the treatment of persons under sovereign control, and to move toward the *international* protection of the fundamental human rights of vulnerable peoples subject to severe abuse from territorial governments. Despite the forward movement in each domain, there were also major setbacks, and contradictory tendencies, but overall there was a widespread appreciation that these efforts to globalize liberal legality were improving the quality of world order.

Several significant legal developments involved moves to restrict certain tactics in relation to warfare over the opposition of geopolitical actors. Two illustrations can be given. 'A new internationalism' involving a coalition of civil society actors and moderate govern-ments managed to produce a treaty that was rapidly negotiated and widely supported by most governments to ban the use of anti-personnel landmines. Such a move was impressive symbolically as it suggested a certain space for global reforms without geopolitical backing in the face of American opposition to this move. At the same time, the success was of only marginal relevance to modern warfare as the dependence on anti-personnel landmines was mainly a matter of cost efficiency, and military substitutes existed to achieve similar battlefield results.

More challenging was an initiative of the General Assembly, responsive to well-orchestrated civil society pressures, to refer to the World Court the question of the legality of nuclear weapons. Once again, with greater resolve than in relation to landmines, the US government energetically used its political leverage to oppose this reference, and again failed. This failure was reinforced when the World Court in 1996 issued its legal opinion, which cast grave doubt on the legality of almost every contemplated use of nuclear weapons, casting legal doubt on strategic thinking in the nuclear weapons states, and unanimously reminded nuclear weapons states of their solemn obligation under Article VI of the Non-Proliferation Treaty to pursue in good faith nuclear disarmament. This set of World Court directives, while completely ignored by the nuclear weapons states, did contribute to the general climate of illegitimacy, even criminality, associated with any future threat or use of nuclear weapons. In this respect the gap between an objective reading of international law requirements and the attitude of nuclear weapons states suggests two lines of interpretation: the inability of international law to overcome the priorities of geopolitical actors with respect to the most urgent of war/peace issues; and the importance of future collaborations between non-nuclear weapons states and antinuclear civil society forces in seeking the implementation of international legal standards with respect to these weapons of mass destruction if the Preamble of the UN Charter 'to save succeeding generations from the scourge of war' is ever going to take on entrenched militarism that continues to dominate the grand strategy of geopolitical actors.

Perhaps of more immediate substantive impact was the effort to revive the Nuremberg tradition of accountability of leaders. The victims of the Pinochet regime in Chile were particularly active around the world in seeking some kind of justice in response to years of abuse. In 1998, Pinochet was detained in Britain because of a request for extradition that came from Spain where a prosecutor was prepared to indict the former Chilean dictator for torture and other international crimes. The litigation in British courts that followed focused world attention on this issue of criminal accountability of heads of sovereign states. Although Pinochet was eventually allowed to escape prosecution in Spain and returned to Chile because he was deemed unfit to stand trial, there was great enthusiasm generated in civil society for moving toward the establishment of an international criminal court, as well as to extend the authority of domestic courts throughout the world to enforce international criminal law, what is called by international lawyers 'universal jurisdiction'. Again, a global coalition of civil society actors and moderate, reform-minded governments was effective in generating a process that has led to an international treaty that brought the International Criminal Court into being in 2002. Whether such an institution and accountability can operate effectively in the face of intense American opposition remains to be seen. This opposition has taken various forms. One of the most obstructive of these is for the US government to negotiate a large number of bilateral agreements with governments to exempt its citizens from ever being turned over for prosecution. It requires only a touch of irony to appreciate that it is American policy-makers and commanders that would stand in the greatest jeopardy of indictment and prosecution if an international criminal procedure of the sort foreshadowed at Nuremberg were allowed to go forward in the early twenty-first century and have the capacity to extend its reach to those who acted on behalf of *all* states, and not just, as at present, the leadership of weak or defeated states. As the criminal trials of Slobodan Milosevic and Saddam Hussein show, the US government is not opposed to the Nuremberg legacy if narrowly confined, but only to its extension to the activities of dominant geopolitical actors.

A third kind of initiative during the 1990s was associated with 'humanitarian intervention' in circumstances where a vulnerable population faced catastrophe. The first major attempt to move in this direction involved the break-up of former Yugoslavia, with some earlier halfhearted and pathetic efforts under UN auspices to avoid ethnic cleansing in Bosnia in the early 1990s. A second early humanitarian effort involved Somalia, where the UN was tasked with the job of alleviating a massive human crisis brought about by governmental collapse. Its role was to provide emergency food and medical assistance, and the mission enjoyed initial success. However, when followed by a more ambitious UN peacekeeping undertaking, led by the US, to restructure the country politically, armed resistance ensued, the operation was rather abruptly ended and international forces were withdrawn to avoid any deeper involvement in factional struggles that were ripping Somalia apart, and making the goal of restoring stable governance seem unattainable. The difficulties encountered in Somalia that led to failure contributed to an American-led unwillingness to allow protective action by the UN to prevent, or minimize, a set of genocidal developments in Rwanda in 1994, and this show of global apathy was followed by the ignominy of UN peacekeepers standing by while Muslim males were slaughtered in the thousands in the supposed UN safe haven of Srebrenica in 1995.

Humanitarian concerns converged with some geopolitical priorities a few years later, generating political backing for humanitarian intervention in Kosovo under NATO command in 1999. The undertaking, although criticized for bypassing the UNSC and thus contrary to international law, was politically supported by most European governments, seemed welcomed at the time by the overwhelming majority of the Kosovar population, and did successfully avert what appeared to be a new cycle of ethnic cleansing in the region. The effectiveness of this response, as compared to Somalia and Rwanda failures, is certainly associated with the geopolitical commitment to the use of sufficient force that was based on giving NATO a new set of security roles after the Cold War, showcasing the continuing seriousness of American involvement in European affairs, and reinforcing the message that military force under American leadership can achieve desired political results at acceptable costs. In other words, the geopolitical stakes associated with the post-Cold War credibility of NATO combined with the display of a continuing American commitment to European issues ensured that the humanitarian concern would not be shortchanged if difficulties emerged.

There were also some serious criticisms of the NATO approach: it undermined the proper UN role with respect to global peace and security; the aerial bombardment from high altitudes shifted the burden of risk to the civilian population of Serbia and Kosovo; inadequate steps were taken in the immediate post-conflict setting to protect Serbs from Albanian acts of revenge; and insufficient resources were devoted to enable a successful reconstruction effort. The Kosovo War remains a normatively ambiguous experience in which the role of global civil society was marginal, partly because civic attitudes were not unified, and the geopolitical stakes overshadowed the humanitarian challenge.

The Kosovo precedent is also ambiguous with respect to international law. It definitely seemed to authorize an evasion of the supposedly total authority of the UNSC over non-defensive uses of force, setting an unfortunate precedent that looks worse in retrospect. At the same time, the effect of the NATO undertaking was to rescue a vulnerable population from probable imminent catastrophe, and to induce the return from refugee camps of hundreds of thousand of Kosovars who had fled in fear across borders. It also illustrated the degree to which the convergence of normative and geopolitical priorities has the capacity to produce effective action.

The 1990s gave rise to additional efforts to improve the quality of world order. There were an unprecedented number of efforts to redress historic wrongs either by apologies, commissions of truth and reconciliation, and reparations and compensation. Long suppressed issues involving the victims of Japanese and German abuses during the Second World War (slave labour comfort women, confiscated assets) or the dispossession of indigenous peoples in various settings around the world suddenly received meaningful official attention. There seemed to be a definite set of moves designed to bring international law into closer conformity with the requirements of global justice, as well as to set limits on the sovereign rights of states. At the same time, these moves toward normative revolution were preliminary, and as subsequent developments have made clear, quite reversible due to adverse geopolitical developments in almost all respects. The 1990s did nothing to displace the central observation that world order continues to be shaped by geopolitical actors. This role is inconsistent with aspirations to achieve a bottom-up, more democratic world order, but it is not necessarily malevolent. It depends on the orientation and behaviour of the dominant geopolitical actors. Compare the relatively constructive role of the US in the period immediately following the Second World War and its role after the 9/11 attacks. One dimension of this comparison can be made by emphasizing the degree of congruence between global reform and the strengthening of international law and institutions in 1945, and the hostility toward such goals since 2001. This latter pattern is the focus of the next section.

American lawnessness in the twenty-first century

The US government has long adopted double standards when it comes to respecting international law, especially in the setting of national security issues. It promotes a generalized respect for the rule of law in world politics, is outraged by violations of international law by its enemies, and chooses selectively when to comply and when to violate. This pattern can be traced far back in American history, but it is convenient to take note of American violations of international law in the setting of the Vietnam War, as well as periodic interventions in Central and South America. I would argue that this pattern has diminished

America's global reputation and capacity for leadership, as well as worked against its own national interests.

It seems clear that the US, and the American people, would have benefited over the years from a foreign policy carried out subject to the discipline of international law. If the US government had abided by international law, the dreadful experience of the Vietnam War would never have occurred. More recently, an observation that will be discussed further below, upholding international law would have avoided the fiasco of the Iraq War. Contrary to popular belief, respecting the restraints of international law better serves the national interest of a powerful country at this stage of history far better than does an attitude, so prevalent in neoconservative circles and since 9/11, that international law poses inconvenient, unnecessary, unwise and removable obstacles on the path toward national and global security.

It is important to understand that the restraints embodied in international law have been voluntarily developed on the basis of international experience and changing attitudes toward war by representatives of sovereign states acting to uphold the realist interests and professed values of their governments. The intent of international law, even with respect to warmaking, is practical rather than aspirational or idealistic. The core principles of international law encode the wisdom of diplomacy accumulated over the course of the last several centuries. International law is of particular importance in relation to uses of force as an instrument of foreign policy, and more generally, as it bears upon issues relating to security, especially war and peace. The US Constitution declares in Article VI(2) that, 'duly ratified treaties are the supreme law of the land'. This puts the key rules and principles of international law on a par with Congressional acts within the American legal system. The Supreme Court has ruled that in the event of an unavoidable clash between these two sources of legal authority, the last in time should prevail, but that to the extent possible both forms of legal authority should be validated by interpretative flexibility.

The basic argument in support of a foreign policy that is respectful of the constraints of international law deserves to be expressed vigorously: in a globalizing world of great complexity it is overwhelmingly in the interest of all states, large and small, that their relations be reliably and peacefully regulated by international law. This observation is uncontroversially applicable to the daily operations of the world economy and many other types of international behaviour, including maritime safety, environmental protection, tourism, immigration, disease control and criminal law enforcement. The stability of international life depends on a closely woven fabric of law as providing a needed foundation of reliability for almost all activity that partly or wholly takes place outside the borders of a sovereign state.

What is a cause for deepest current worry is that the US government has seemed to abandon this elementary understanding of the relevance of law to the establishment of world order. As suggested, this tendency is not entirely new. It runs like a great river throughout the entire course of American history, but it has taken a serious turn for the worse during the Bush presidency, especially in the aftermath of the 9/11 attacks. Even prior to the attacks, the foreign policy of the Bush administration made it a point of pride to disclose its disdain for widely respected international treaties. The Bush White House contended that existing and pending treaties limited its military and political options in undesirable ways. In the early months of the Bush presidency, the White House announced its opposition to the Comprehensive Test Ban Treaty prohibiting nuclear weapons testing, its withdrawal from ABM Treaty design to avoid an arms race in space, its unwillingness to submit for Senate ratification the Kyoto Protocol regulating greenhouse gas emissions, and its defiant and gratuitous withdrawal of its signature from the Rome Treaty establishing the International Criminal Court. Such a pattern of unilateralist and undisguised hostility to international treaties and multilateral cooperation was unprecedented in American history. It led to a strong negative reaction at home and abroad. Normally friendly governments were clearly disturbed by this strident display of unilateralism and international nihilism by the new American president. This American repudiation of widely endorsed multilateral treaty arrangements upset large segments of world public opinion. These treaty arrangements dealing with important matters of global policy were generally viewed as important contributions to a peaceful world, making their repudiation seem contrary to common sense, as well as dangerous for the overall well-being of the peoples of the world. These expressions of unilateralism by the US to global policy issues did not involve violating existing international law. What was exhibited was a diplomacy based on an outmoded and ultra neo-conservative opposition to almost any form of multilateral undertaking in the security area other than by way of alliance relationships such as NATO or the aggressive partnership with Israel. This unilateralism dysfunctionally limits the capacity of America to make constructive use of its status as the sole remaining superpower in the aftermath of the Cold War, as well as privileges excessive reliance on military approaches to problem-solving and wasteful expenditures on over-investment in unusable military hardware.

The US Congress, and American public, are also not exempt from blame on these counts. It was in Congress even before George W. Bush came to Washington in 2001 that militarist pressures were brought to bear in such a way as to oppose beneficial multilateral treaty constraints on US policy. The Senate refused to ratify the Comprehensive Test Ban in the Clinton years, in addition to being so strongly opposed to the International Criminal Court and Kyoto Protocol that there was no prospect for such treaties to be approved by the required 2/3s vote if submitted to the Senate for ratification. What mainly distinguished the Bush approach to international law were two developments: its alignment of the Executive Branch with an anti-internationalist set of policies; and its avowedly ideological and emphatic repudiation of treaty instruments in order to signal a unilateralist approach to foreign policy premised upon military dominance and interventionary diplomacy. It was this geopolitical posture by the Bush leadership that frightened world public opinion. Before 9/11 a rising crescendo of domestic and international opposition to the Bush policies led to mounting criticism of this approach to world affairs, which hardened the perception that Bush's credentials as president were already unusually weak given his contested electoral mandate. Many observers who scrutinized the results in 2000 believed that a fair count of the votes in Florida would have resulted in Bush's defeat, and victory for Al Gore.

This concern and opposition has dramatically intensified outside the US since 9/11 because the Bush White House has moved from this earlier hostility to multilateralism to a posture of pronounced unwillingness to abide by fundamental international legal rules and standards that this country, along with other constitutional democracies, had previously accepted and applied as a matter of course. These rules include humane treatment of prisoners taken during armed combat, unconditional prohibitions on torture and assassination of political opponents, and the duty to protect civilians in any foreign territory under occupation. The most important of all these legal restrictions on foreign policy is the rule of international law prohibiting non-defensive uses of force without a mandate from the UN Security Council. In his 2004 State of the Union Address, President Bush told Congress that the US would never seek 'a permission slip' in matters bearing on its security. But it is precisely a permission slip that international law, and the UN Charter, requires if force is used outside the scope of self-defence *against a prior armed attack*. This strict limitation on recourse to war was written into the Charter largely at the behest of the US government after the Second World War. The basic idea was to bind the states of the world to a legal framework that unconditionally prohibited wars of aggression, what has more brashly been recently called 'wars of choice'. German and Japanese leaders were sentenced to death at war crimes tribunals in 1945 because they had initiated and conducted aggressive wars, a precedent not entirely lost on the peoples of the world.

The Iraq War is a notorious example of an aggressive war (or war of choice) that violates this fundamental rule of international law set forth authoritatively in Article 2(4) of the United Nations Charter. As such, according to the Nuremberg Principles embodied in general international law after the conviction of German leaders for their criminal conduct, the invasion of Iraq in 2003 constitutes a Crime Against Peace. The American prosecutor at Nuremberg, Justice Robert Jackson, famously said to the tribunal, '… let me make clear that while this law is first applied against German aggressors, the law includes, and if it is to serve a useful purpose it must condemn, aggression by other nations, including those which sit here now in judgement.' It is this Nuremberg Promise that is being repeatedly and defiantly broken by the US and Israel, thereby undermining any prospect for peace and normalcy in the world.

The pattern of illegality associated with the Iraq War, and subsequent occupation, continues to shock the conscience of humanity. American officials have strained to redefine 'torture' so as to permit what the rest of the world, and common sense, understand to be 'torture'. The abuse of prisoners detained in Guantanamo, Abu Ghraib and elsewhere has severely damaged America's reputation in the world, as well as discredited a genuine and necessary struggle against extremist enemies engaged in terrorism. Government lawyers and their neoconservative supporters in society have argued in favour of assassinating terrorist suspects in foreign countries, and have justified under the terminology of 'extraordinary rendition' deliberately handing over suspects to foreign governments notorious for their reliance on torture as their normal mode of prisoner interrogation. The detrimental impact of American lawlessness on the protection of human rights worldwide and within the US has been set forth in great detail by such respected organizations as the American Civil Liberties Union, Amnesty International and Human Rights Watch. This record of American abuse has badly undercut the capacity of the US government to exert pressure on other governments to protect human rights, rendering such pressure suspect and hypocritical.

It is notable to observe that the events of 9/11 produced a patriotic surge within the US that has given the Bush administration the political space needed to embark on a foreign policy aimed at 'geopolitical preeminence', and only incidentally concerned with the defeat of Al Qaeda and the containment of transnational terrorism. Such an ambitious priority was stated clearly before 9/11 in the report of the Project for a New American Century published in September 2000 under the title of 'Repairing America's Defenses', and endorsed by many individuals who later became leading advisors to the Bush presidency. This wider grand strategy was explicitly embraced, and set forth in detail, subsequent to 9/11, in the important White House document entitled, 'The National Security Strategy of the United States of America' (2002), which has been itself updated by a new document released by the White House in 2006 with the same title. In other words, violating international law, especially embarking on wars of aggression, has been integral to the realization of pre-existing American global ambitions that were politically non-viable before 9/11. To sustain a climate of acquiescence within the US it has been necessary to rely upon a manipulative politics of fear and anger associated with the 9/11 experience that has largely led to a suspension of mainstream criticism by the media, an absence of debate reinforced by the passivity of the opposition Democratic Party, and by the US Congress. In this crucial respect, Congress is failing in its constitutional duties by its unwillingness to exert principled pressure on the Executive to uphold the rule of law by demanding compliance with international law. The public outrage associated with the derelictions of governmental duty in the setting of Hurricane Katrina in 2005 seemed temporarily to have finally opened a space for challenging the legitimacy of the present government, but then the critical mood vanished, despite the fact that the Bush presidency has been steadily losing popular support. There is still no indication that Congress or the public is willing to cancel the blank cheque issued to the Bush presidency in the setting of foreign policy in the feverish atmosphere following 9/11. And despite all that has happened, it appears to remain politically viable for the US government in collaboration with Israel to move toward a new aggressive warfare in the Middle East.

This focus on American behaviour obscures the larger framework of argument. It has become a requirement of a constitutional democracy in the twenty-first century for a government's foreign policy, as well as its domestic behaviour, to be conducted in a manner consistent with the discipline of international law. In a globalizing world the extension of law to international activity almost always serves the national interest of even powerful states. The constraints of international law keep the leaders of democratic states from embarking on dangerous geopolitical ventures that would not be supported by an informed citizenry. The refusal of one state, particularly if it is seen to be a leading state, to abide by international law creates a precedent that gives other states a reciprocal right, as well as political encouragement, to violate their legal obligations.

Finally, adherence to international law in matters of war and peace is in the interest of the peoples of the world. There may be humanitarian emergencies or dangerous threats of attack that might justify recourse to war as the UN Secretary General's report 'In Larger Freedom' and as the UN High-level Panel on Threats, Challenges and Change recommends, but such recourse to war is only legally valid if it is authorized by the Security Council. America and the world will be better off when non-defensive warfare requires in every instance the issuance of 'a permission slip'. The bad American example should not confuse political leaders around the world. It will be beneficial for the peoples of the world to strengthen the global rule of law, and to encourage a pedagogy of peace and security that emphasizes the relevance of international law to a peaceful and equitable world order. Perhaps the disadvantages of American lawlessness in this period can stimulate a global swing by other political actors back toward lawfulness, thereby emulating the broad tendencies toward law-oriented global policies associated with the European Union. It would be helpful if leaders in global civil society would give attention to the importance of effective legal regimes to regulate many sectors of international life, and move to reinforce efforts to hold criminally accountable those who are responsible for aggressive warfare and abusive conduct. The world is now morally sensitive and politically integrated to ignore or tolerate the commission of Crimes Against Peace or Crimes Against Humanity.

Concluding comments

International law remains subordinate to geopolitics, and is shaped to a considerable extent by the priorities and prudence of the leading political actor at a given historical interval. But such an overview is not the entire story. International law, especially as embodied in Nuremberg, the UN Charter and the UDHR, as well as the many recent rulings by the World Court, also offers and encourages resistance to geopolitically driven projects destructive of human values and to particular abuses of sovereign rights. The emergence of global civil society actors represents a further geopolitical challenge in a number of domains of international life. The World Tribunal on Iraq, organized as a civil society undertaking in 2005, held in Istanbul, confirmed the unlawfulness of the American and British invasion of Iraq and its subsequent occupation, as well as implored global institutions to hold those responsible for these policies criminally accountable in the Nuremberg sense. Such a decision by a civil society tribunal, now spread to all parts of the planet by virtue of the Internet, definitely contributes to a climate of illegitimacy surrounding the persisting war policies of the US and Israel, despite being unable to implement its 'legal' findings in a manner that would alter behaviour.

There are several developments that suggest an important potential role for law in shaping the future of humanity on a global scale:

- Accepting the practical need for agreed patterns of order amid the complexity and fragility of many aspects of trans-national activity.
- Acknowledging the growing evidence that warfare and military expenditures are dysfunctional means by which to pursue political ends, and that adherence to legal standards and procedures offer promising alternatives.
- Meeting the challenge of globally delimited problems such as global warming, polar melting, mass migration, energy and water shortages.
- Recognizing the success of the European Project in providing a model of post-Westphalian political order on a regional scale that relies on regional law, procedures and institutions to address conflict, and has managed to instill a culture of peace among the participants.

At the same time, this potential role can only become actual if the US as rogue hegemon changes its approach toward these issues, becoming less unilateralist, abandoning the pursuit of global empire, and growing to appreciate the benefits of a law-oriented foreign policy in which self-discipline accomplishes much of what law enforcement requires. The prospect of an American defeat in Iraq, and the frustration of the main plan to bring 'democracy' to the Middle East by freely elected secular leaders who rush off to Washington to pledge allegiance once in control, may open enough space for alternative visions of world order to become relevant. Before such an adjustment occurs, we are likely to experience a downward spiral that will diminish still further respect for the core norms of international law. In the summer 2006 regional crisis, Israel, with the backing of the US, used large-scale border-crossing military action to punish the whole of Lebanon for allowing Hezbollah, claiming falsely that this is 'self-defence' as understood in international law. Of course, it was nothing of the sort. The media went along with the confusion caused by affirming that a state subject to attack enjoys a right of response, but unless the attack is of a scale to qualify as 'an armed attack' across a border it does not give rise to a right of self-defence by the attacked government, but only a legal option of retaliation in kind, limited and focused. What is discouraging, although not surprising, is that Turkey took advantage of what its foreign minister called 'Israel's precedent in international law' to frame an argument about a comparable Turkish right to intervene militarily in northern Iraq to deal with an allegedly mounting Kurdish threat.

But civil society actors need not be merely reactive with respect to international law. It would seem quite appropriate to frame a future world order by two different, although complementary, legal directives: (1) the affirmations in Articles 25 and 28 of the UDHR that everyone enjoys 'the right to a standard of living' adequate to meet basic human needs' and that 'everyone is entitled to a social and international order' that realizes all of the specific enumerated human rights. Such normative affirmations are almost too good to be true, but provide civil society actors with official criteria by which to legitimate their struggles to achieve global justice and humane global governance; and (2) to articulate and act upon a new globalist ethos of human solidarity that informs a concept of responsible global citizenship, mindful of specific national and regional identities, but dedicated to the *whole* rather than to its *parts*, whereby 'global law' comes to anchor world order rather than Westphalian 'international law.'

International Humanitarian Law

INTERNATIONAL HUMANITARIAN LAW (IHL)

Background

Whatever the practicalities of armed conflict, the rules that govern war are not chaotic. There are laws that govern under what circumstances war may be declared, and how a war may be fought. In 1945, war was declared an unacceptable way to settle political differences, and was made illegal, except in the case of self-defense. States retain the right to defend themselves, individually or collectively, against attacks on their independence or their territory, in response to a (legal or illegal) use of force. The United Nations Charter allows member States the use of force in collective action to maintain or restore international peace and security, as a form of self-defense.

Wars do, however, occur for reasons other than self-defense, and may be the result of retaliation to numerous localized situations. Whatever the provocation or justification for war, there is a need for objective international rules to limit the effects of war on people and property. The International Humanitarian Law (IHL) has been set up and developed to protect certain particularly vulnerable groups of persons.

International Humanitarian Law (IHL) consists of a series of about 30 treaties, or laws, which aim both to control the effect of a war on civilians, and to control military acts during war: The treaties have been accepted, or 'ratified', by the international community, and have become truly universal law. For example, one of the most famous treaties is the Geneva Convention, which has been ratified by over 150 states.

Many of these treaties were made in response to new methods of warfare that were used in preceding wars. The World Wars, for example, witnessed the use of methods of warfare that by far superceded previous conflicts in terms of both military and civilian casualties.

- The First World War (1914–1918) witnessed the first large-scale use of poison gas, the first-ever aerial bombardments and the capture of hundreds of thousands of prisoners of war. The Geneva Conventions of 1925 and 1929 were a response to those developments.
- The Second World War (1939–1945) saw civilians and military personnel killed in equal numbers, as against a ratio of 1:9 in the First World War. In 1949 the international community responded to those tragic figures, and more particularly to the terrible effects the war had on civilians, by revising the Conventions then in force and adopting a new instrument: the Fourth Geneva Convention for the protection of civilians.
- According to Norway's International Peace Research Institute, civilians are targeted more than ever. At the beginning of the century nine soldiers were casualties of war for every single civilian who suffered the same fate. Today the ratio has reversed, approaching 1 soldier for every 8 civilians. [www.time.com/time/magazine]

It is important to mention that the IHL is not only designed to protect victims of international armed conflict—it also protects victims of fighting carried out within a country between recognizable armed groups. It also protects the victims of other internal disturbances not carried out between armed groups, but due to internal disruption and disorder resulting from acts of violence (such as riots, struggles between factions or against the authorities).

Summary of IHL:

The law governing conduct during war has three fundamental concerns.

First, the IHL aims to protect people who are not, or who are no longer fighting in the armed conflict. These people may be civilians who live and work in a country at war, wounded soldiers who are no longer able to fight, or members of the military who have surrendered. This is known as the law of Geneva. The essential rules of IHL seek to protect those people who are not directly involved in the war, and to treat them with humanity, without any unfavorable distinction. Not all civilian deaths in wartime are unlawful. In military terms, 'collateral damage', including civilian casualties, is to be expected in war. But there are clear rules that set limits on the conduct of hostilities. For example, the IHL makes it illegal to harm or capture medical teams bearing the flag of the Red Cross (or Red Crescent) on a white background, because they collect and care for the wounded. IHL also makes it illegal for prisoners of war to be treated without dignity or respect for their lives.

Prisoners must legally be entitled to their personal rights and their political and religious convictions, to exchange news with their families, and to receive medical help.

Second, the IHL restricts the methods of warfare that the military are legally allowed to use. This is known as the law of The Hague. Neither side of the armed conflict may use weapons that are likely to cause unnecessary losses or excessive suffering. For example, it is illegal for armies to use land mines, asphyxiating, poisonous gases or bacteriological (often called biological) warfare, because these methods of combat will cause continuing harm to civilians, and to military personnel, after the war has ended. One of the cornerstones of the IHL is the principle that all possible measures must be taken to distinguish between civilian persons and objects, and military objectives. Part of the Geneva Convention sets out the 'basic rule' regarding the protection of civilians (often referred to as the principle of distinction').

> 'In order to ensure respect for and protection of the civilian population and civilian objects, the Parties to the conflict shall at all times distinguish between the civilian population and combatants and between civilian objects and military objects and accordingly shall direct their operations only against military objectives.'

Third, the IHL is specially intended to resolve matters of humanitarian concern arising directly from war. It provides the laws under which people who break humanitarian law during armed conflict, war criminals, can be brought to justice. If any of the conventions (laws) of the IHL are violated (broken) by specific individuals, the individuals can be taken to court and tried. A good example of this is the Nuremberg tribunal, which occurred after WW2. The tribunal aimed to bring Adolf Hitler and the principal members of his administration to justice, and to punish them for the murder of millions of Jewish civilians in the concentration camps of World War II. Presently, the International Tribunal for the Former Yugoslavia is trying suspected criminals of war from the conflicts in the Balkan Peninsula. The most publicized case involves that of the former President of the Republic of Serbia, Slobodan Milosevic, who is accused of Crimes Against Humanity and Violations of the Customs or Laws of War by the planning, instigating and ordering of a campaign of terror and violence directed against the Kosovo Albanian citizens.

Respect for IHL

Humanitarian law is not always respected and violations of them are not always prosecuted. Opinions vary as to why IHL is often breached without prosecution. Some opinions include:

* ignorance of the law

- the very nature of war so wills it
- humanitarian law is not matched by an effective centralized system for implementing sanctions

Yet simply giving up in the face of breaches and halting all action that seeks to gain greater respect for humanitarian law would be far more discreditable. This is why, pending a more effective system of sanctions, acts that breach IHL should be relentlessly condemned and steps taken to prevent and punish them.

Lastly, the international community's efforts to create a permanent international criminal court should also be noted. As the project stands at present (1997), the court would be competent to try war crimes and crimes against humanity, including genocide.

> *"War is in no way a relationship of man with man but a relationship between States, in which individuals are enemies only by accident; not as men, nor even as citizens, but as soldiers … since the object of war is to destroy the enemy State, it is legitimate to kill the latter's defenders as long as they are carry arms; but as soon as they lay them down and surrender, they cease to be enemies or agents of the enemy, and they again become mere men and it is no longer legitimate to take their lives."*
> *- Jean Jacques Rousseau*

SOURCES

www.icrc.org/icrceng.nsf
www.amnesty.org
From: *September 11: Crisis Response Guide*
Copyright: Human Rights Education Program, Amnesty International USA, 2001.

The Universal Declaration of Human Rights

On December 10, 1948 the General Assembly of the United Nations adopted and proclaimed the Universal Declaration of Human Rights the full text of which appears in the following pages. Following this historic act the Assembly called upon all Member countries to publicize the text of the Declaration and "to cause it to be disseminated, displayed, read and expounded principally in schools and other educational institutions, without distinction based on the political status of countries or territories."

PREAMBLE

Whereas recognition of the inherent dignity and of the equal and inalienable rights of all members of the human family is the foundation of freedom, justice and peace in the world,

Whereas disregard and contempt for human rights have resulted in barbarous acts which have outraged the conscience of mankind, and the advent of a world in which human beings shall enjoy freedom of speech and belief and freedom from fear and want has been proclaimed as the highest aspiration of the common people,

Whereas it is essential, if man is not to be compelled to have recourse, as a last resort, to rebellion against tyranny and oppression, that human rights should be protected by the rule of law,

Whereas it is essential to promote the development of friendly relations between nations,

Whereas the peoples of the United Nations have in the Charter reaffirmed their faith in fundamental human rights, in the dignity and worth of the human person and in the equal rights of men and women and have determined to promote social progress and better standards of life in larger freedom,

Whereas Member States have pledged themselves to achieve, in co-operation with the United Nations, the promotion of universal respect for and observance of human rights and fundamental freedoms,

Whereas a common understanding of these rights and freedoms is of the greatest importance for the full realization of this pledge,

Now, Therefore THE GENERAL ASSEMBLY proclaims THIS UNIVERSAL DECLARATION OF HUMAN RIGHTS as a common standard of achievement for all peoples and all nations, to the end that every individual and every organ of society, keeping this Declaration constantly in mind, shall strive by teaching and education to promote respect for these rights and freedoms and by progressive measures, national and international, to secure their universal and effective recognition and observance, both among the peoples of Member States themselves and among the peoples of territories under their jurisdiction.

Article 1.

- All human beings are born free and equal in dignity and rights. They are endowed with reason and conscience and should act towards one another in a spirit of brotherhood.

Article 2.

- Everyone is entitled to all the rights and freedoms set forth in this Declaration, without distinction of any kind, such as race, colour, sex, language, religion, political or other opinion, national or social origin, property, birth or other status. Furthermore, no distinction shall be made on the basis of the political, jurisdictional or international status of the country or territory to which a person belongs, whether it be independent, trust, non-self-governing or under any other limitation of sovereignty.

Article 3.

- Everyone has the right to life, liberty and security of person.

Article 4.

- No one shall be held in slavery or servitude; slavery and the slave trade shall be prohibited in all their forms.

Article 5.

- No one shall be subjected to torture or to cruel, inhuman or degrading treatment or punishment.

Article 6.

- Everyone has the right to recognition everywhere as a person before the law.

Article 7.

- All are equal before the law and are entitled without any discrimination to equal protection of the law. All are entitled to equal protection against any discrimination in violation of this Declaration and against any incitement to such discrimination.

Article 8.

- Everyone has the right to an effective remedy by the competent national tribunals for acts violating the fundamental rights granted him by the constitution or by law.

Article 9.

- No one shall be subjected to arbitrary arrest, detention or exile.

Article 10.

- Everyone is entitled in full equality to a fair and public hearing by an independent and impartial tribunal, in the determination of his rights and obligations and of any criminal charge against him.

Article 11.

- (1) Everyone charged with a penal offence has the right to be presumed innocent until proved guilty according to law in a public trial at which he has had all the guarantees necessary for his defence.

- (2) No one shall be held guilty of any penal offence on account of any act or omission which did not constitute a penal offence, under national or international law, at the time when it was committed. Nor shall a heavier penalty be imposed than the one that was applicable at the time the penal offence was committed.

Article 12.

- No one shall be subjected to arbitrary interference with his privacy, family, home or correspondence, nor to attacks upon his honour and reputation. Everyone has the right to the protection of the law against such interference or attacks.

Article 13.

- (1) Everyone has the right to freedom of movement and residence within the borders of each state.
- (2) Everyone has the right to leave any country, including his own, and to return to his country.

Article 14.

- (1) Everyone has the right to seek and to enjoy in other countries asylum from persecution.
- (2) This right may not be invoked in the case of prosecutions genuinely arising from non-political crimes or from acts contrary to the purposes and principles of the United Nations.

Article 15.

- (1) Everyone has the right to a nationality.
- (2) No one shall be arbitrarily deprived of his nationality nor denied the right to change his nationality.

Article 16.

- (1) Men and women of full age, without any limitation due to race, nationality or religion, have the right to marry and to found a family. They are entitled to equal rights as to marriage, during marriage and at its dissolution.
- (2) Marriage shall be entered into only with the free and full consent of the intending spouses.

- (3) The family is the natural and fundamental group unit of society and is entitled to protection by society and the State.

Article 17.

- (1) Everyone has the right to own property alone as well as in association with others.
- (2) No one shall be arbitrarily deprived of his property.

Article 18.

- Everyone has the right to freedom of thought, conscience and religion; this right includes freedom to change his religion or belief, and freedom, either alone or in community with others and in public or private, to manifest his religion or belief in teaching, practice, worship and observance.

Article 19.

- Everyone has the right to freedom of opinion and expression; this right includes freedom to hold opinions without interference and to seek, receive and impart information and ideas through any media and regardless of frontiers.

Article 20.

- (1) Everyone has the right to freedom of peaceful assembly and association.
- (2) No one may be compelled to belong to an association.

Article 21.

- (1) Everyone has the right to take part in the government of his country, directly or through freely chosen representatives.
- (2) Everyone has the right of equal access to public service in his country.
- (3) The will of the people shall be the basis of the authority of government; this will shall be expressed in periodic and genuine elections which shall be by universal and equal suffrage and shall be held by secret vote or by equivalent free voting procedures.

Article 22.

- Everyone, as a member of society, has the right to social security and is entitled to realization, through national effort and international co-operation and in accordance with the organization and resources of each State, of the economic, social and cultural rights indispensable for his dignity and the free development of his personality.

Article 23.

- (1) Everyone has the right to work, to free choice of employment, to just and favourable conditions of work and to protection against unemployment.
- (2) Everyone, without any discrimination, has the right to equal pay for equal work.
- (3) Everyone who works has the right to just and favourable remuneration ensuring for himself and his family an existence worthy of human dignity, and supplemented, if necessary, by other means of social protection.
- (4) Everyone has the right to form and to join trade unions for the protection of his interests.

Article 24.

- Everyone has the right to rest and leisure, including reasonable limitation of working hours and periodic holidays with pay.

Article 25.

- (1) Everyone has the right to a standard of living adequate for the health and well-being of himself and of his family, including food, clothing, housing and medical care and necessary social services, and the right to security in the event of unemployment, sickness, disability, widowhood, old age or other lack of livelihood in circumstances beyond his control.
- (2) Motherhood and childhood are entitled to special care and assistance. All children, whether born in or out of wedlock, shall enjoy the same social protection.

Article 26.

- (1) Everyone has the right to education. Education shall be free, at least in the elementary and fundamental stages. Elementary education shall be compulsory. Technical and professional education shall be made generally available and higher education shall be equally accessible to all on the basis of merit.
- (2) Education shall be directed to the full development of the human personality and to the strengthening of respect for human rights and fundamental freedoms. It shall promote understanding, tolerance and friendship among all nations, racial or religious groups, and shall further the activities of the United Nations for the maintenance of peace.

- (3) Parents have a prior right to choose the kind of education that shall be given to their children.

Article 27.

- (1) Everyone has the right freely to participate in the cultural life of the community, to enjoy the arts and to share in scientific advancement and its benefits.
- (2) Everyone has the right to the protection of the moral and material interests resulting from any scientific, literary or artistic production of which he is the author.

Article 28.

- Everyone is entitled to a social and international order in which the rights and freedoms set forth in this Declaration can be fully realized.

Article 29.

- (1) Everyone has duties to the community in which alone the free and full development of his personality is possible.
- (2) In the exercise of his rights and freedoms, everyone shall be subject only to such limitations as are determined by law solely for the purpose of securing due recognition and respect for the rights and freedoms of others and of meeting the just requirements of morality, public order and the general welfare in a democratic society.
- (3) These rights and freedoms may in no case be exercised contrary to the purposes and principles of the United Nations.

Article 30.

- Nothing in this Declaration may be interpreted as implying for any State, group or person any right to engage in any activity or to perform any act aimed at the destruction of any of the rights and freedoms set forth herein.

Current Trends in UN Peacekeeping
A Perspective from Asia

Dipankar Banerjee

The opening paragraph of the Brahimi Report presented to the UN General Assembly in September 2000 clearly highlighted the dilemma the world faces over peacekeeping today:

> The United Nations was founded … in order to save succeeding generations from the scourge of war. Meeting this challenge is the most important function of the Organization, and to a very significant degree it is the yardstick with which the Organization is judged by the peoples it exists to serve. Over the last decade, the United Nations has repeatedly failed to meet the challenge, and it can do no better today.[1]

This is indeed a stringent critique but perhaps a bit harsh. Actually the achievements of UN peacekeeping measured over its entire history have been remarkable and successful. In numerous cases it has prevented further blood-letting by intervening in situations that could have degenerated into all-out war, maintained peace in very complex situations of impending conflict, monitored the truce between armies after an often shaky ceasefire, helped disengage forces arrayed in battle and provided security to permit humanitarian assistance in conflict zones. Yet, the challenges it faced in the last decade are also significant, casting doubts in many minds regarding the efficacy of UN peace operations.

More people have died in violent armed conflicts in the twentieth century than perhaps in all earlier centuries combined. This is as much due to global population increase and developments in the means of inflicting death and destruction than to any increase in human proclivity for violence. Civilization has not evolved sufficiently to prevent conflicts or prevent them early enough to minimize casualties and reduce suffering. The evolution of warfare in the twentieth century has demonstrated how complex is the source of conflict today and varied are the means of waging war. Additional complexities of trans-border attack with an unknown face yet devastating consequences were revealed in September 2001. US responses in Afghanistan and Iraq have raised further concerns, and events since 9 September 2001 have emphasized as never before the need to direct all international actions, particularly in areas of war and peace, through the UN.

Stages in the Evolution of UN Peacekeeping Operations

Even after the extraordinary violence of 1939–45 there was neither a strong commitment nor a clear policy for maintaining peace. The concept of 'peacekeeping operations' evolved slowly and in an ad hoc manner, for there is no mention of this in the United Nations Charter. As a former Under Secretary-General for the Department of Peacekeeping Operations has remarked: 'There is still no definition on what it entails, no criteria when operations are to be established and no guidelines on how to plan and deploy the forces'.[2] There is no specific provision for 'peacekeeping' in the Charter. It evolved over the Cold War years as an extra-ordinary art, calling for the use of military personnel not to wage war but to prevent fighting between belligerents. However, UN peacekeeping operations have passed through four phases, each with its somewhat distinct characteristics.

The first phase, often called traditional peacekeeping, refers to the 'non-interventionist buffer zone deployments' of the Cold War era. It relied on a situation where there was a peace to keep, and peacekeeping operations usually followed a ceasefire, the terms of which were generally accepted by the belligerents. The UN Security Council and all parties connected with the conflict agreed to the deployment of a force, which was international in composition and enjoyed complete freedom of movement in the host territories. It was meant to act impartially, and armed force was to be used only in self-defence.[3] There was also one Chapter VII intervention where a force was used by major powers under Security Council approval in Korea. This force was provided by major powers under their operational command and was not a blue-helmet operation. There is a distinct difference between the two. Where the former is essentially political, impartial and non-coercive, the latter is a punitive process, conducted as a military operation and is not necessarily impartial, even though there is likely to be a degree of discrimination.

The next stage may be described as second-generation peacekeeping and came about after the end of the Cold War. These operations eventually became more complex.

The unique challenges of the era appeared to signal to the world an opportunity for the UN, and there were high expectations from its peacekeeping activities. Conflicts tended to be more intra-state than inter-state, even though neighbouring countries may have been involved in providing support. The cause of conflict was more often ethnic unrest, a consequence perhaps of the sudden realization of new identities. There was seldom a peace to keep and instead there was an expectation that by the very presence of the UN force somehow peace might prevail. The permanent members of the Security Council sometimes had different views and interests on a particular conflict and often played a contrary role. There was greater reluctance in western developed countries to participate in operations. It usually took a long time for the force to be assembled, and the mandates assigned to it were not matched in the composition of the force, its resources, or its equipment and weaponry. Finally, there was usually a humanitarian dimension that had to be attended to simultaneously while dealing with the conflict.[4]

By the mid-1990s the euphoria of UN peacekeeping efforts tended to peter out. The experiences of Somalia, Rwanda, Bosnia and Herzegovina, and Angola all had a sobering effect. First, they demonstrated that each conflict was unique and a 'one size fits all' approach would not work. It was one thing to maintain peace when both sides were exhausted and seriously wishing for an end to conflict and another when it was but an interval in the fighting, with the protagonists keen to have another go. Second, non-state armed actors had no regard for international norms and in such a situation traditional peacekeeping was not effective. Third, when major powers had different interests, their commitment also differed widely. Finally, with developed countries increasingly reluctant to participate, the burden fell on the developing world, countries that were sometimes unable to provide forces with the weapons, resources and training essential for the conduct of these operations.[5]

With the Srebrenica tragedy in 1995, the prospect of UN peacekeeping looked bleak. It then entered what may be called the third phase, a period when serious attempts were made to regionalize peacekeeping. The expectation was that with their local expertise perhaps regional organizations were better suited to maintaining peace in their respective areas. NATO in Europe, the Commonwealth of Independent States in the Caucasus and African regional organizations in their respective regions in Africa were considered to be better suited for such tasks and were expected to take a larger responsibility. The world's commitment also declined during this period, and UN peacekeeping forces and expenditures were reduced to about one-third of those that had prevailed in the early 1990s.[6] But regional and sub-regional organizations were no panacea, and when they did not have the infrastructure or the resources such as could be provided by NATO, they were less well placed than the UN for these tasks. Second, countries within a region were often a party to the conflict or their interests were affected and hence they were not appropriate to the task. Third, regional organizations particularly when less developed lacked the moral legitimacy of the UN, a severe disadvantage in any role in conflict prevention.[7]

The exponential resurgence of peacekeeping from 1999 was a phenomenon that arose to intervene in failing and failed states, many drawn out of humanitarian considerations, and this may be considered as a fourth, overlapping, phase. Major operations were launched in Kosovo, East Timor, Sierra Leone, Democratic Republic of Congo, and in Eritrea/Ethiopia. Perhaps more importantly, these developments led to a serious soul searching to understand the limitations of earlier approaches and a determination to set in place corrective measures to strengthen and improve UN peacekeeping efforts.

Corrective Measures

This return to the UN and confidence in its role and importance in peacekeeping is what determined subsequent developments. The Secretary-General initiated a fundamental reorientation of UN responsibilities to identify areas of weakness as well as areas of concern and actions required to rectify them. Three major reports that emerged are examined briefly in this connection. First, Kofi Annan's own report on *Prevention of Armed Conflicts* submitted to the fifty-sixth session of the General Assembly on 7 June 2001 attempted to fulfil his pledge 'to move the United Nations from a culture of reaction to a culture of prevention'.[8] The other two were reports of two commissions. *The Report of the Panel on United Nations Peace Operations*, under the chairmanship of Lakhdar Brahimi, was submitted to the Millennium Assembly in August 2000. It examined the state of peace operations under the UN and made many important recommendations.[9] *The Report of the International Commission on Intervention and State Sovereignty* instituted by the Canadian Government and co-chaired by Gareth Evans and Mohamed Sahnoun was the third, published on 30 September 2001. The Commission examined the dilemma facing the international community in intervening in acute humanitarian catastrophes that might infringe on state sovereignty. Its highly nuanced and sensitive report, appropriately titled *The Responsibility to Protect*, has been widely acclaimed and has been debated around the world.[10]

These documents provide the basis for new approaches to peacekeeping and raise serious questions, particularly from the perspective of nations in Asia. What are the commitments and responsibilities of states and are these being met equitably? If the Security Council is the principal body entrusted with peace-keeping is it fully representative? How is conflict to be prevented and who is responsible for implementing corrective measures? What should be done to improve the operational dimension of peacekeeping? Where does one draw the line between intervention and state sovereignty? This essay will briefly highlight the findings of the above reports and provide the Asian perspectives on issues that need our attention.

Preventing Armed Conflict

Conflict prevention, according to Secretary-General Kofi Annan, lies at the heart of the UN's responsibility. Accordingly, he set two principal objectives: first, to review the progress made in conflict prevention under the UN; second, to make specific recommendations to enhance the UN's capability. Only the key conclusions and specific recommendations are mentioned here. First, primary responsibility for conflict prevention rests with national governments. The role of the UN and the international community is principally to support and help develop capacity. Second, preventive actions should ideally be initiated at the earliest possible opportunity. More important, these have to address the deep-rooted socio-economic, cultural, environmental, institutional and other structural causes that often underlie conflict in a region. Third, an effective preventive strategy requires a comprehensive approach which has to take both a short-term view to end the conflict and a long-term perspective encompassing political, diplomatic, humanitarian, human rights, developmental, institutional and other measures that should enlist the support of the international community and national and regional actors. Fourth, conflict prevention and sustainable and equitable development are mutually reinforcing activities and can best take place in an environment of sustainable peace. Finally, a successful preventive strategy depends on the cooperation of many international bodies including the Bretton Woods institutions. In his report, the Secretary-General particularly emphasized the role of regional and sub-regional organizations, the private sector, non-governmental organizations and other civil society actors.[11]

The issue of sustainable development assumes great importance in any conflict. Major inequities within a state are an important condition that could lead to conflict. When exacerbated by ethnic, linguistic, cultural and religious differences they deepen into a complex situation which leads to intractability. The underlying causes are still economic imbalance and lack of opportunities. In a globalized world many of the principal causes and their remedies do not often lie within the purview and the control of a sovereign nation. When international actions are not equitable their adverse impact on weaker states is likely to be severe. The Secretary-General has highlighted these connections, but as he has mentioned, the solutions to these issues are not mainly within the UN organization but in the hands of international financial and economic institutions.

The adverse impact of globalization on some countries poses a serious challenge today. Their continued economic travails have not merited the kind of response from the International Monetary Fund and the World Bank that will contribute towards preventing conflicts. Instead the approach is often to put undue pressure on these countries and to emphasize human rights, insist on opening up national economies and similar economic liberalization policies, without adequately taking into account the conditions in a particular state or how individual countries are affected by them. The case of Malaysia after 1997 is particularly notable in this regard. When the country was affected by an exodus of capital, Prime Minister Mahathir of Malaysia adopted a fixed exchange rate for the Ringgit (instead of devaluing the currency), closed part of the economy from foreign competition and restructured it against prevailing international opinion. The Malaysian economy soon stabilized and there were no adverse social impacts from the short period of economic downturn that may otherwise have led to internal conflict. By contrast, Indonesia's response led to deep social unrest.

The Brahimi Report

The Brahimi Report concluded that the UN had for too long been used by member states as a means to be seen as 'doing something', rather than focusing on the right things to do.[12] The report offers general recommendations for the conduct of successful UN peacekeeping operations, especially:

- the need for a clear and specific mandate;
- consent to the operations by parties involved in the conflict;
- ensuring adequate resources for the task at hand.[13]

The report also contained some 57 explicit and more than 100 implicit recommendations. Some of the specific recommendations were under the following heads:

- institution of fact-finding missions in an attempt to prevent future crises;
- the need for more robust peacekeeping in situations where peace has broken down due to the intransigence of one or more parties;
- the proposal for a UN Information and Strategic Analysis Secretariat (EISAS) to support the Executive Committee on Peace and Security;
- call for a rapid deployment capability and greater on-call expertise;
- enhance the capacity of the DPKO and provide it with more funds;
- establishment of integrated mission task forces.[14]

These recommendations are all very positive and have been well received by the international community. The report is already being acted on at the Secretariat and a number of steps have already been taken. The staff at the DPKO has been increased by 50 per cent to 600 persons. Administrative aspects are being streamlined and areas falling within the purview of the Secretary-General have been expedited, especially in the management and planning areas. The UN Stand-by Arrangement System (UNSAS) has been streamlined. The On-Call List concept has been improved and 154 positions have been identified. The Rapid deployment level of UNSAS went into effect from mid-2002, which is expected to substantially reduce the deployment time for future operations. The General Assembly has approved over US$140 million to create strategic deployment stocks. A modern inventory management system began functioning in mid-2003. A Stand by High-Readiness Brigade (SHIRBRIG) has helped to provide a rapid deployment capability for emergent situations.[15]

Commendable improvements have been affected in peace operations in the last two years based on the Brahimi Report, which may set a trend for future effectiveness. Operations in Timor-Leste were successfully concluded. An Interim Authority in Afghanistan has been established. Peace and security was restored to Sierra Leone where UN-supported demobilization has been a success. Assistance in training police and border forces in Bosnia and Herzegovina were concluded after seven years.[16]

At the end of 2003 the UN had deployed 14 peacekeeping operations of which five were in Africa, four in the Middle East (including UNIKOM, the mission in Iraq-Kuwait that closed in October), two in Asia and the Pacific and three in Europe. It also had 15 political and peacebuilding missions—eight in Africa (including one in Angola that closed in February), four in Asia and the Pacific, two in the Middle East and one in Central America. Deployment of peacekeepers in these operations reached its high point for the year in December, as did the number of contributors. At that time almost 46,000 military and civilian police personnel from 94 countries were serving in the field. Civilian personnel included approximately 3,700 international and 7,600 local staff.[17]

Other trends in peacekeeping also merit our attention. First, peacekeeping forces are now provided from the developing rather than the developed world. All ten top force-contributing nations at the end of 2003 were from developing countries, in descending order: Pakistan, Bangladesh, Nigeria, India, Ghana, Nepal, Jordan, Uruguay, Kenya and South Africa.[18] Three South Asian countries are among the first four troop-contributing countries and in the last decade have collectively contributed about 30 per cent of the entire peacekeeping strength. India has borne the highest casualties in peacekeeping since its inception.[19] We need to ask, are their voices sufficiently represented in shaping the decisions affecting peace operations, particularly at the planning stage and mandate formulation?[20] The answer unfortunately is no.

The overall responsibility for peace operations rests with the Security Council. Its members decide on all aspects of a particular operation and formulate the rules governing their mandate. Its permanent members in effect decide which operations will actually be deployed. Yet, in times of crisis they are unwilling to take the responsibility or support early corrective measures with necessary resources. The lack of timely intervention in the case of Rwanda is perhaps the strongest indictment of this state of affairs. The structure of the Security Council reflected the international order of 1945, not of the twenty-first century. Is this an equitable division of responsibility and will it lead to effective participation by all nations? Today's war on terror is somewhat mischievously defined as between Islam and the rest. But, if it is truly a war by all against the fanatical few, are Islamic countries sufficiently represented in the higher echelons of international decision-making on war and peace?

The Responsibility to Protect

In his Millennium speech, Kofi Annan asked the world body to consider, 'armed intervention' as an 'option of last resort, but in the face of mass murder it is an option that cannot be relinquished'. He made compelling cases at the UN General Assembly both in 1999 and in 2000 and asked the international community to develop a new consensus on how to approach these issues: 'If humanitarian intervention is, indeed, an unacceptable assault on sovereignty, how should we respond to a Rwanda, to a Srebrenica—to gross and systematic violations of human rights that offend every precept of our common humanity?'[21]

The Report goes on to lay down the basic principles of intervention. First, it identifies the responsibility to protect, which it presumes will be the state itself. Next, in the condition for international intervention, it defines both the extent of state failure and the condition, only when the state is 'unable to halt or avert it'. The report then suggests the guiding principles for the international community.

A right to intervention embraces three specific responsibilities: the responsibility to *prevent*, the responsibility to *react* and the responsibility to *rebuild*. It also emphasizes that this right should be guided by four precautionary principles: *right intention*, which is to avert human suffering; *last resort*, that is after every non-military option has been explored; *proportional means*, based on minimum force; and finally, *reasonable prospects*, both of success and that the consequences should not outweigh the results of inaction. Overall the principles and recommendations are very well thought through and they ensure adequate safeguards against misuse. Yet, as the debate over this issue is joined globally, the concerns in Asia should also be put firmly on the agenda.

In addition to practical issues a larger disquiet arises from the challenge posed to the very basis of the international state system—national sovereignty. We too often forget that many liberal democratic states of today were founded on vicious intra- and inter-state violence of the sixteenth to nineteenth centuries, a stage that many developing countries are now experiencing in their efforts at state formation.

A strong sense of state sovereignty pervades much of Asia. The region remains firmly beholden to sovereignty, taking that as the fundamental basis of stability and identity.[22] Having emerged from colonial domination and the ravages of the Second World War only half a century ago, there is a strong sense that more time is needed for state formation and consolidation, particularly where post-colonial conflicts were long-drawn-out. While national sovereignty must not be used as a shield to mask the atrocities perpetrated against its citizens by a state, any international action that violates this principle of state sovereignty must be founded on extremely solid ground.

Both India and China have strongly endorsed this concept of state sovereignty in all their dealings with the international community. In numerous statements made by the Indian head of the Permanent Mission at the UN, particularly during the Kosovo crisis, the question of state sovereignty and principle of upholding it by the international community was stressed many times by its representative. China too has held strongly to these views. According to a key study by Bates Gill of the Brookings Institution: 'The crucial principle is that the national authorities which rule over the people within a specific area are the ultimate authority for dealing with all domestic and foreign affairs faced by the nation state. These authorities alone enjoy these rights and responsibilities, to the exclusion of any other actor'.[23] Given these views, the international community should carefully consider before undertaking any interventionary peacekeeping operations affecting Asia.

If humanitarian interventions have to occur, decisions to intervene must be taken with great deliberation and through a transparent, impartial and legitimate mechanism, which does not favour the national interest of intervening powers. A number of other issues will have to be taken into account:

- Is the objective attainable militarily? Has a clear strategic assessment been done? Are the resources available? Is support to the operation strong within the region and internationally?
- Essential requirements include: early warning, preliminary planning, well-trained and equipped forces ready at short notice, good logistics and sound planning and support back-up.
- Should time and conditions permit, all measures other than force must first be considered.
- Participation in such humanitarian intervention, if necessary, should be by trained forces but from countries without any strategic interests in the region. Let us not underestimate the fact that training for such tasks needs to be of an even higher order. Use of force is easy. Restraint in the use of force in situations of grave provocation is much more difficult.
- Only the United Nations under exceptional conditions can permit such an intervention. However, the Security Council as presently constituted and empowered is not an acceptable body to many nations in the world.
- There must be a clear exit policy.

Review of Peacekeeping Operations

A Comprehensive Review of Peacekeeping Operations in all their aspects was conducted at the General Assembly in March 2002. A few conclusions are of particular interest. The Under Secretary-General for Peacekeeping noted that since the Brahimi Report, the DPKO had been strengthened and its resource base enlarged. The General Assembly was committed to ensure that adequate resources were made available to it to fulfil all its responsibilities. In particular military capacity within the Secretariat would be enhanced. The integrated mission task force concept was accepted and the standby arrangement system which had come into effect was to be strengthened. There was concern regarding suitable geographic representation in missions and the principle of transparency in selecting contingents. Weaknesses in the DPKO were also noted and areas for improvement acknowledged.[24]

The Brahimi Report and subsequent actions at the UN headquarters have done much in recent years to improve the quality of peacekeeping. The challenge is to harness this and develop the political support for more effective operations around the world.

UN peace operations in Asia remained generally satisfactory at the end of 2003 and at a lower key than in most preceding years. The UN Transitional Administration in East Timor (UNTAET) successfully conducted the presidential elections, and administrative power was handed over to the new administration on 20 May 2002. Subsequently, a revised and a much smaller UN support team, the UN Mission of Support in East Timor

(UNMISET), was established with responsibility for policing and some administrative and advisory functions. The second oldest UN Mission in India-Pakistan, UNMOGIP, remains deployed in the disputed region of Jammu and Kashmir, but its ability to monitor the ceasefire is severely restricted. India no longer recognizes its jurisdiction and does not allow it to function, but tolerates its presence. In Tajikistan the situation has improved dramatically in recent years and the UN Tajikistan Office of Peacebuilding continues to help the country build institutions and promote the rule of law. The UN Political Office in Bougainville (UNPOB) remains deployed to oversee the Peace Agreement, and a mission was sent in May 2002 to enhance disarmament efforts.[25]

The most significant UN activity is focused on Afghanistan. After the Bonn Agreement an Interim Authority and a Transitional Administration were established at the end of 2001. A donor meeting took place in Tokyo in January 2002. A Loya Jirga was convened for seven weeks (April–June 2002) of some 1500 tribal representatives, including 200 women, which legitimized Karzai's leadership of the Transitional Administration. Sixteen UN agencies are currently working in Afghanistan. Enormous efforts at nation building are going on there under extremely difficult circumstances. But international commitment to Afghanistan seemed to diminish in 2003 and the situation overall remained somewhat critical. Afghanistan may yet remain the one issue on which the success of UN peacebuilding efforts will be judged in the post-September 11 era.

The Lessons from Iraq

Even more than Afghanistan, lessons from Iraq will determine UN peacekeeping in the years ahead. The situation is presently poised at a delicate stage. The unilateral intervention by the United States and the UK once again bypassed the UN Security Council as it had done earlier in Kosovo. Neither principles of self-defence nor the possibility of an attack by weapons of mass destruction (WMDs), which subsequently were proved to be without foundation, justified pre-emptive attack on another nation in the absence of a clear Security Council resolution. The other objective emphasized subsequently, of ending the dictatorial rule of a despot, was even less convincing and has set a dangerous precedent. The issues related to Iraq will need serious discussion before clear guidelines are accepted by the international community. Indeed initial steps to learn from these processes have been initiated by the Secretary-General by appointing a High Level Panel to study global security threats and make recommendations for developing the elements of a collective response.[26]

The lessons that can already be drawn from Iraq begin with the point that interventionary actions, whatever the condition, are best achieved only under the legitimate authority of the UN. Second, the purpose and intent of such operations has also to be clearly determined by independent authorities, which alone will have any chance of international legitimacy. Suspicions of illegal possession of WMDs, which were neither effectively proved nor later verified by ground inspections, has further undermined the credibility of the initial steps. When an attempt was made to modify that justification through the 'democracy option' route, it found no credibility. Finally, the nature of military operation, which quickly transformed from a pretext of liberation to one of aggression and conquest further undermined the legitimacy of the intervening force and will surely hamper its successor.

Challenges of Peacekeeping Operations in Asia

Given the above evolving situation in peacekeeping operations under the UN, what are the challenges particularly as perceived from Asia? There are seven principal issues that should be foremost in our considerations.[27]

- *A new concept of human security.* Accepting that a concept of security has never been static, there is indeed a fundamental difference in perception over the last decade, particularly in Asia. Since the publication of the Human Rights Development Report by the UNDP in 1994, alternative concepts of security, particularly 'human security', have gained much acceptance around the world. This cut across cultures and bridged the gap between the rich and poor, bringing all under the umbrella of a similar human condition. Here, the focus of security is on the people and not the state. Development, empowerment, meeting legitimate aspirations and meeting basic human needs are the central issues.

- *Regional organizations and the UN.* As future conflicts become even more intra-state and complex, involving ethnic groups and leading to state failures, peace operations will become more complex. In these conditions, situations will need to be dealt with within the region, preferably under regional security organizations. There are two principal reasons for this: first, such local issues are better understood locally and solutions too are best evolved at local levels; and second, the UN cannot be everywhere—it should seriously consider doing less, but what it does undertake to do must be done well. In Asia there exists today only the Asian Regional Forum (ARF), which is not chartered to deal with peace operations and in any case does not cover the more disturbance-prone regions of Asia. Serious thought will have to be given to this in future.

- *Doctrinal challenges to peace operations and the use of force.* Complex peacekeeping operations need to be embedded in doctrinal clarity. The Brahimi Report did not seriously address issues of doctrine. A vexing question that has emerged again and again in complex peacekeeping operations is the nature and amount of force that may be used. The mandate for a particular operation is likely to provide guidelines in that respect, but more clarity is desirable. In situations in Asia, there may be conditions of ethnic strife where counter violence at an early stage by well-trained peacekeepers may well avoid considerable bloodshed later. Also, there may be situations where effective threat of use of force rather than actual force itself is likely to be sufficient.

- *Preventive action.* Much debate has taken place in recent years focusing on preventive action by the UN and other organizations, rather than responding to a situation after violence has broken out. Many early warnings related to conflict can be detected in advance of the outbreak of violence. Absence or lack of governance is a principal condition in many situations in Asia and may be observed at an earlier stage. Tackling root causes may require establishing foundations for developing improved governance.

- *Using police forces.* Many recent peace operations around the world have used civil police forces to maintain the peace, as these were often primarily a law and order issue. That may well be a distinguishing feature in the future. This should be welcomed, particularly in Asia, where sensitivities regarding use of regional military forces remain high. Yet, in deciding the type of forces, a critical question will continue to be the effectiveness of the force concerned. In complex peacekeeping operations the civil police are not expected to perform satisfactorily.

- *Disarmament, demobilization and reintegration.* Around the world a major question in halting the fighting and establishing peace is disarming the combatants, permanently putting out of commission the weapons involved, demobilizing the combatants and integrating them within societies through gainful employment. This is relevant to Asian situations as well. In Cambodia in particular, demobilization and reintegration have been important issues. Reintegration is a complex operation, involving social, political and psychological integration of combatants, which is not easily achieved without careful planning and expert guidance. This becomes a part of peace-building and needs to be funded adequately from the beginning.

- *Safety and security of UN personnel.* Sanctity and associated security connected with the UN emblem has been undermined in many instances in recent years. In some parts of the world this even symbolizes a target. While good training can address some concerns, other aspects will need to be seriously considered at an appropriate stage. In addition to combat security, other issues concern disease, health and hygiene and adequate treatment to counter them.

CONCLUSION

The period from 1999 has again seen an increase in international peacekeeping. This has become necessary because of the continuing conflict in Africa and new issues emerging in different areas as a consequence of the 11 September 2001 terrorist attacks. The challenge to the international community has also grown as a result. The UN and other regional organizations have to find ways to make these operations more effective and responsive to today's needs. Most importantly, these responses have to be based on international law, uphold human rights and respect the rights of states. In an article in *Foreign Affairs*, 'The New Interventionism', Michael Glennon ended with the sentence: 'If power is used to do justice, law will follow'.[28] The view from Asia would suggest that it is law, fairly and equitably developed, that must define justice and the use of interventionary force. For too long and in its recent history Asia has been the victim of interventionist force. While developing greater commitment to internationalism it would like to see greater not less caution against unilateral intervention. Intervention should be sanctioned by the majesty of international law but with sufficient guarantees against misuse. Above all, international peacekeeping must continue to be the responsibility of the UN, the world's only truly international organization.

NOTES

1. See UN doc. A/55/305-S/2000/809 on *Report of the Panel on United Nations Peace Operations*, accessed at: www.un.org/peace/reports/peace_operations.
2. Jean-Marie Guehenno, 'On the Challenges and Achievements of Reforming the UN Peace Operations', in Edward Newman and Albrecht Schnabel (eds), *International Peacekeeping (Special Issue: Recovering from Civil Conflict)*, Vol.9, No.2, Summer 2002, p.69.
3. Sandra Cummer, 'The Challenges Faced by the Military in Adapting to Peacekeeping Missions', in *Peacekeeping and International Relations*, Vol.27, No.1, Jan/Feb 1998, p.13.
4. Ibid.
5. Guehenno (n.2 above), p.70.
6. Ibid., p.71.
7. Ibid.
8. See, *Prevention of Armed Conflicts*, UN doc. A/55/985-S/2001/574, A/55/985/Corr.1-S/2001/574/Corr., 7 June 2001.
9. See *Report of the Panel on the United Nations Peace Operations* (n.1 above).
10. See Report of the International Commission on Intervention and State Sovereignty: *The Responsibility to Protect*, Ottawa: International Development Research Centre, Dec. 2001.
11. *Prevention of Armed Conflicts* (see n.8 above).
12. *Report of the Panel on the United Nations Peace Operations* (n.1 above), p.73.
13. See UN doc. A/55/305-S/2000/809, accessed at www.un.org/Depts/dpko/dpko/faq/q3.
14. Ibid.
15. 'Issues related to UN Peace Operations—2003', accessed at: www.un.org/Depts/dpko/dpko/pub/year_review03.
16. 'Overview in 2002', in *Year in Review*, accessed at: www.un.org/Depts/dpko/dpko/pub/year_review03/Overview.htm.
17. Ibid.
18. See www.un.org/Depts/dpko/pub/year_review03.
19. See www.un.org/Depts/dpko/fatalities/totals.htm.

20. In recent years their representation in executive functions has increased. Maj.-Gen. Chitra Bahadur Gurung from Nepal is the Acting Military Adviser in the DPKO and Col. Virinder Dadhwal from India is the Chief of the Force Generation Service.

21. Quoted in the Foreword, *The Responsibility to Protect* (n.10 above), viii.

22. Amitav Acharya, 'Sovereignty', *International Herald Tribune*, 23 Jan. 2003.

23. Bates Gill and James Reilly, 'Sovereignty, Intervention and Peacekeeping: The View from Beijing', *Survival*, Vol.42, No.3, autumn 2000, pp.41–59.

24. See 'Report of the Special Committee on Peacekeeping Operations', UN Doc. A/56/863, 11 March 2002.

25. *The Year in Review 2003*, accessed at: www.un.org/Depts/dpko/dpko/pub/year_review03/Asia-Pacific_peace_operations.htm.

26. See www.un.org./News/Press/docs/2003/sga857.doc.htm.

27. *Challenges of Peace Operations in the 21st Century, 2002*, report prepared by the Government of Sweden, accessed at: www.peacechallenges.net/pdf/Concluding1.pdf.

28. Michael Glennon, The New Interventionism: The Search for a Just International Law, Vol.78, No.3, *Foreign Affairs*, May/June 1999, p.7.

The 1994 Rwanda Genocide

RENÉ LEMARCHAND

Since April 1994 Rwanda has become a synonym for one of the worst genocides of the 20th century. An estimated half a million people, mostly Tutsi, were killed in the course of a carnage that claimed twice as many victims in one month as the Bosnian civil war in two years. To this must be added almost as many deaths caused by military engagements, cholera, dysentery, famine, and sheer human exhaustion.

As much as the appalling scale of the bloodletting, it is the element of planned annihilation that gives the Rwanda killings their genocidal quality. The parallel with the 1972 genocide in Burundi immediately comes to mind (see Chapter 10, "The Burundi Genocide"). Although the threats to the ruling ethnocracies—the Hutu in Rwanda, the Tutsi in Burundi—came from identifiable groups of armed opponents, in the end entire civilian communities became the targets of ethnic cleansing (i.e., large-scale ethnic massacres)—the Hutu in Burundi, the Tutsi in Rwanda. In both states, the enemy was demonized, made the incarnation of evil, and dealt with accordingly; in both instances, the killings were planned and orchestrated from above, and owed little or nothing to a supposedly spontaneous outburst of anger from below.

Where Rwanda differs from Burundi is not just that the "rebels" happen to be Tutsi, but Tutsi refugees, or sons of refugees, who were driven out of the country in the wake of the 1959–1962 Hutu-led revolution. Few would have imagined that 30 years later the sons of the refugee diaspora in Uganda would form the nucleus of a Tutsi-dominated politico-military organization—the *Front Patriotique Rwandais* (FPR)—that would successfully fight its way back into the country and defeat an army three times its size. Fewer still would have anticipated the price of their victory. Between the FPR invasion on October 1, 1990, and the fall of the capital (Kigali) on July 4, 1994, the killings wiped out one tenth of Rwanda's population of 7 million.

Seen in the broader context of 20th century genocides, the Rwanda tragedy underscores the universality—one might say the "normality"—of African phenomena. The logic that set in motion the infernal machine of the Rwanda killings is indeed no less "rational" than that which presided over the extermination of millions of human beings in Hitler's Germany or Pol Pot's Cambodia. The implication, lucidly stated by Helen Fein (1994), is worth bearing in mind: "Genocide is preventable because it is usually a rational act; that is, the perpetrators calculate the likelihood of success, given their values and objectives" (p. 5).

Mythologies

It is imperative to explode the myths surrounding the Rwanda genocide. Contrary to the image conveyed by the media, there is nothing in the historical record to suggest a kind of tribal meltdown rooted in "deep-seated antagonisms," or "long-standing atavistic hatreds." Nor is there any evidence in support of the "spontaneous action from below" thesis. From this perspective, the killings are largely reducible to a collective outburst of blind fury set off by the shooting down of President Juvenal Habyarimana's plane on April 6, 1994. However widespread, both views are travesties of reality. What they mask is the political manipulation that lies behind the systematic massacre of innocent civilians.

It is not my intention to dispose of one myth by promulgating another—the fantasy of a precolonial society where Hutu and Tutsi lived in an eternally blissful harmony. Precolonial Rwanda was unquestionably one of the most centralized and rigidly stratified societies in the Great Lakes Region. Representing approximately 85 percent of a total population estimated at 2 million at the turn of the century, the Hutu peasants were clearly at the bottom of the heap, socially, economically and politically; but if power, status, and wealth were generally in Tutsi hands, not every Tutsi was powerful and wealthy.

Inequality was inscribed in the differential treatment accorded to each group, and within each group. Nonetheless, Hutu and Tutsi shared the same language and culture; the same clan names, the same customs, and the symbols of kingship served as a powerful unifying bond between them. Nor was conflict necessarily more intense or frequent between Hutu and Tutsi than between Tutsi and Tutsi. Much of the historical evidence suggests precisely the opposite (Vidal, 1991).

Although the potential for conflict existed long before the advent of European rule, it was the Belgian colonial state that provided the crucible within which ethnic identities were reshaped and mythologized. The result was to drastically alter the norms and texture of traditional Rwanda society. It was the colonial state that destroyed the countervailing mechanisms built around the different categories of chiefs and subchiefs, thus adding significantly to the oppressiveness of Tutsi rule. It was the colonial state that insisted on individuals carrying an identity card specifying their ethnic background, a practice perpetuated until 1994, when "tribal cards" often spelled the difference between life and death. It was with the blessings of the colonial state that Christian missionaries began to speculate about the "Hamitic" origins of the kingdom, drawing attention to the distinctively Ethiopian features, and hence the foreign origins, of the Tutsi "caste" (Linden, 1977). Indirect rule, synonymous with Tutsi rule, found added legitimacy in the Hamitic lucubrations of Christian clerics; and, they eventually provided the ideological ballast of the Hutu revolution, before reappearing in 1994 in the form of a violently anti-Tutsi propaganda.

The Legacy of Revolution

After decades of unrelenting support of Tutsi rule, Belgian policies underwent a radical shift in the mid-1950s (Lemarchand, 1970). Partly in response to pressure from the UN Trusteeship Council, and partly as a result of the arrival in Rwanda of a new generation of Catholic missionaries, imbued with the ideals of Christian Democracy, a sustained effort was made to extend educational opportunities to an increasing number of Hutu elements. This radical policy shift provoked immediate resistance from the custodians of Tutsi supremacy—i.e., chiefs, subchiefs, and Tutsi intellectuals generally—while prompting educated Hutu elements to press their claims for social reform upon the trusteeship authorities.

Ethnic violence suddenly erupted in November 1959, in the form of a Hutu *jacquerie* directed against Tutsi chiefs. Hundreds of people were killed on both sides of the ethnic fault line. Though quickly brought under control by the intervention of Belgian troops, the rural uprising marked the first phase of a revolutionary process culminating in January 1961 with a Hutu-led, Belgian-assisted coup that formally abolished the monarchy and led to the proclamation of a de facto republican regime under Hutu rule. By the time Rwanda acceded to independence on July 1, 1962, some 200,000 Tutsi had been forced into exile, the majority seeking asylum in Uganda, Burundi, and Zaire. Not until 32 years and a million deaths later would the destiny of Rwanda be once again entrusted to Tutsi hands.

The Hutu revolution constitutes a critical element in the background of the genocide: by forcibly displacing tens of thousands of Tutsi from their homeland—now in a homeless limbo and determined to go back to their country, by force if necessary—the revolution planted the seeds of the refugee-warrior militancy that led to the creation of the FPR in 1990 (Reyntjens, 1993). By the same token, to the extent that the Hutu revolution came to be identified with a "democratic," "anti-feudal" mass movement, its enemies could only be described in opposite terms, as feudal counter-revolutionaries bent upon restoring minority rule. It is not by accident that, during the killings, the Tutsi were collectively identified by Hutu ideologues with the "Feudo-Hamitic" enemy.

The Ideology of Genocide

The root cause of the Rwanda genocide lies in the extent to which collective identities have been mythologized and manipulated for political advantage. Today Hutu and Tutsi are not just ethnic labels; rather, they are social categories that carry an enormous emotional charge. Tutsi are seen by many Hutu as culturally alien to Rwanda, their presence traceable to "Hamitic invaders from the north" who used ruse and cunning—gifts of cattle and beautiful women—to enslave the unsuspecting Hutu agriculturalists. Only the Hutu—that is, the Bantu people, as distinct from the Hamites—qualify as authentic Rwandans. That such portrayals are at odds with every shred of evidence available is immaterial. The point is that they are critical elements in the cognitive map of Hutu ideologues. The Hamitic frame of reference is central to an understanding of the ideology of genocide. This is where the legacy of missionary historiography—evolving from speculation about cultural affinities between Hamites and Coptic Christianity to politicized dogma about the Ethiopian origins of the Tutsi—contributed a distinctly racist edge to the discourse of Hutu politicians.

Already the ideological stock-in-trade of Hutu revolutionaries in the 1950s, official references to the Hamitic peril gained renewed salience in the wake of the FPR invasion. The attack on Kagitumba on October 1, 1990, suddenly gave ominous credibility to the image of the Tutsi as an alien invader: Did they not invade the country from the north, like their forefathers, this time with arms and ammunition provided by Uganda? Is it not the case that many of the soldiers enlisted in the ranks of the FPR were born in Uganda, and that its leaders had close ties with President Museveni of Uganda, whose Hima origins are sufficient proof of his Hamitic sympathies? And, with characteristic cunning, did they not try to dupe President Habyarimana into accepting the Arusha Accords, which, if implemented, would have posed a mortal threat to the democratic heritage of the Hutu revolution?

What emerges from the incitements to violence distilled by Radio Mille Collines and other vectors of Hutu propaganda is an image of the Tutsi as both alien and clever—not unlike the image of the Jew in Nazi propaganda. His alienness disqualifies him as a member of the national community; his cleverness turns him into a permanent threat to the unsuspecting Hutu. Accordingly, nothing short of physical liquidation can deal with such danger.

The Road to Apocalypse

With the birth of several opposition parties in 1991, a whole new set of actors entered the political arena, adding an entirely new dimension to the security threats posed by the FPR invasion. For the first time since the Hutu revolution of 1959, the circumstances were ripe for a strategic alliance between the enemies from within and those from without.

Predictably, this convergence of external and internal threats generated intense fears within the ruling party, the *Mouvement Revolutionnaire National pour le Developpement*

(MRND). At stake was not just the monopoly of power exercised by the party leadership, or even the structure of Hutu domination, but the political survival of a regime entirely controlled by northern Hutu elements. It is worth remembering in this connection that during much of the First Republic (1962–1973), power lay in the hands of Hutu politicians from the south-central regions; not until the coup of July 1973, instigated by Major-General Juvenal Habyarimana, and the proclamation of the Second Republic (1973–1994), did the northerners emerge as the dominant force in the government, the administration, the Party, and the army.

Given the nature of their ethno-regional underpinnings, and shared resentment of northern Hutu rule, it is hardly surprising that the three major opposition parties—the ethnically mixed *Parti Liberal* (PL), the *Parti Social Democrate* (PSD), and the *Mouvement Democratique Republicain* (MDR)—should have been perceived by MRND hard-liners as potential allies of the FPR, and therefore as presumptive traitors: the PL because of its mixed Hutu-Tutsi membership, the PSD and MDR because they drew much of their support from the Hutu masses of the south-central regions.

In this three-cornered politico-military struggle, the Tutsi civilian populations became political pawns. Courted by the PL, solicited for cash and food (and sometimes threatened) by the FPR, thoroughly distrusted by the MRND, a good many Tutsi ended up joining hands with the FPR because they felt they had no other option. Official suspicions that every Tutsi, by ethnic definition, harbored pro-FPR sympathies created the conditions of a self-fulfilling prophecy. The wholesale slaughter of hundreds of Bagogwe (a Tutsi subgroup) in northern Rwanda in January 1991, followed by the coldblooded murder of thousands of Tutsi civilians in the Bugesera region in March 1992, set off a pattern of localized ethnic cleansing that went on almost uninterruptedly in the months preceding the genocide.

Anti-Tutsi violence increased in proportion to the magnitude of the threats posed by the FPR, but also as a result of the organizational steps taken to counter such threats. Reference must be made here to the massive recruitment and training of Hutu militias. Known in Kinyarwanda as *interahamwe* ("those who stand together"), they were ostensibly organized to protect civilians against FPR attacks; their real function, however, was to serve as a paramilitary force trained to provide auxiliary slaughterhouse support to the police, the *gendarmerie,* and the regular army. While the interahamwe came to be identified with the MRND, another group, the *impunza mugambi* ("the single-minded ones"), linked up with an even more fanatically anti-Tutsi party, the *Coalition pour la Defense de la Republique* (CDR). On the eve of the genocide the militias claimed a total membership of 50,000.

Most of the militias were recruited from among the vast pool of Hutu internally displaced persons (IDPs) driven from their homes by the advance of the FPR in the north. On the eve of the genocide about 1 million of the IDPs were registered in the whole of Rwanda, living in 40 IDP camps, for the most part in extremely harsh conditions. The

IDPs, according to James Gasana (2000), who once served as minister of defense in the Habyarimana government, "were explicitly targeted by the FPR rebellion, expelled from their homes and continuously shot at in the camps to force them to move farther into the government-controlled zone. Families were separated and scattered—health centers were overwhelmed, mortality increased; suspension of schooling and lack of occupation for the young led to increased delinquency and crime" (p. 12). It is hardly a matter of coincidence that among the scores of young thugs manning the checkpoints in the capital, the vast majority were recruited among the IDPs of the Nyacinga camp, near Kigali. Seething hatred of every Tutsi in sight is what lay behind the scenes of mayhem in Kigali, Butare, and Gikongoro.

By 1992 the institutional apparatus of genocide was already in place. It involved four distinctive levels of activity or sets of actors:

1. The so-called *akazu* ("little house" in Kinyarwanda), consisting of Habyarimana's wife (Agathe), his three brothers-in-law (Protais Zigiranyirazo, Seraphim Rwakumba, and Elie Sagatwa), and a sprinkling of trusted advisers. This core group was directly responsible for planning and orchestrating the genocide.

2. The rural organizers: recruited among communal and prefectoral personnel—i.e., *prefets, sous-prefets, bourgmestres, conseillers communaux,* etc.—and numbering anywhere from 300 to 500. They supplied the middle-level cadres in charge of engineering and supervising the killings in the communes.

3. The militias *(interahamwe),* often operating in tandem with the police and the *gendarmerie,* formed the ground-level operatives in charge of doing the actual killing. Many also played a key role in "persuading" (at gunpoint) Hutu civilians to kill their Tutsi neighbors. Although the term came to designate a variety of self-appointed killers, the core group has been described as "forming up to 1 or 2 percent of the population; they killed out of conviction; they were trained to kill, they often smoked hashish and are thought to have killed between 200–300 people each" (Physicians for Human Rights, 1994, p. 11).

4. The presidential guard, numbering approximately 6,000 and recruited exclusively among northerners, were trained specifically to assist civilian death squads. The systematic killing of opposition figures, Hutu and Tutsi, in the days immediately following the crash of the presidential plane, on April 6, 1994, was essentially the work of the presidential guard.

The sociological profile of the killers reflects the diversity of their social and institutional ties. Especially noteworthy, however, is the number of intellectuals and professional people who participated in the slaughter. Despite many exceptions to the rule, one cannot fail to notice the number of journalists, medical doctors, agronomists, teachers, university lecturers, and even priests who were identified by survivors as accomplices in the massacre of innocent civilians. At the other end of the social spectrum were the hundreds and thousands of landless Hutu peasants and unemployed city youth whose prime motivation for killing was to steal their victims' property, their land, their furniture, their radio, or what little cash they happened to carry.

What set in motion the wheels of this infernal machine was complex, a sequence of events that began with the Arusha Accords conference in Tanzania (June 1992–August 1993) and ended with the shooting down of President Habyarimana's plane in April 1994.

Although compromise was the very essence of the power-sharing formula hammered out at Arusha—whereby the FPR would have as many seats in the transitional government and legislature as the MRND, and would contribute 40 percent of the troops and 50 percent of the officer corps to the new Rwandan army—for the hard-liners within the party and the *akazu,* this was tantamount to betrayal. By instigating ethnic violence on a substantial scale in several localities, MRND/CDR extremists had every intention to derail the peace process. The wanton killing of innocent civilians thus became the quickest way of eliminating all basis for compromise with the FPR.

The decisive event that played directly into the hands of the extremists and sounded the death knell of the Arusha Accords, however, was the assassination of Burundi President Melchior Ndadaye on October 21, 1993. As the first popularly elected Hutu president in the history of Burundi, his election brought to a close 28 years of Tutsi hegemony, and this after a transition widely described by outside observers as "exemplary" (Lemarchand, 1994). His death at the hands of an all-Tutsi army had an immediate and powerful effect on the Hutu of Rwanda. The message came through loud and clear: "You simply cannot trust the Tutsi!" With Ndadaye's death vanished what few glimmers of hope remained that Arusha might pave the way for a lasting compromise with the FPR.

The shooting down of Habyarimana's plane, on April 6, 1994, on a return flight from a regional summit in Dar-es-Salaam, must be seen as the critical turning point in the sequence of events leading to the bloodbath. On board were not one but two Hutu presidents, Habyarimana and Cyprien Ntaramyira of Burundi, thus bringing to three the number of Hutu presidents killed in six months. Among other passengers killed in the crash were Burundi ministers Bernard Ciza and Cyriaque Simbizi, Major General Déogratias Nsabimana, Rwanda's Chief of Staff, Juvénal Renzaho, presidential advisor and former ambassador to Germany, Colonel Elie Sagatwa, the president's brother-in-law and special counselor, Major Thaddée Bagaragaza, head of the presidential guard, and Dr. Emmanuel Akingeneye, Habyarimana's personal physician.

Despite continuing speculation by some analysts of an *akazu*-sponsored plot intended to eliminate the "moderates," there is growing evidence to suggest that Kagame was indeed the central actor behind the crash. (Editor's note: There, in fact, continues to be speculation that various actors might have planned and carried out the downing of the plane. Among those under suspicion are: the akazv, the French government and the Rwandan Patrivtie Force. In regard to the alleged involvement of France see Linda Melvern's 2008 article, "The Perfect Crime?", in prospect.) Debate and disagreements persist between those who stubbornly adhere to the view that *akazu*-linked extremists committed the deed to rid the country of a president turned too liberal (such as Linda Malvern and Gérard Prunier, among others) and those who point to Kagame as the chief villain. Those holding the anti-Kagame brief note that he has steadfastly refused to allow an international commission to investigate the matter, and that among the victims of the crash were some of the key supporters of the *akazu,* such as Sagatwa, Renzaho and Nsabimana. None could be described as moderates. Even more revealing are the detailed testimonies offered by former FPR officers and defectors, most notably Abdul Ruzibiza's account of how he and other members of the crack unit known as the Network Commando went about the task of preparing the ground for the shooting down of the presidential plane (Ruzibiza 2005). Ruzibiza's disclosures fully corroborate the findings of the French investigating magistrate Jean-Louis Bruguière in his brief on behalf of the three French crew members who died in the crash.

It is important to add that there were compelling political reasons for Kagame to render null and void the road map established at the Arusha conference. Seen from the perspective of the electoral calendar drawn at Arusha, it is easy to see why Kagame might have found it imperative to chart an alternative course, even if it meant planning Habyarimana's murder: with general elections scheduled to take place 22 months after the inauguration of the Broadly Based Transition Government (BBTG) there could be little doubt that the FPR would end up the loser; meanwhile with only 5 cabinet seats out of 21 in the BBTG the FPR was in no position to introduce an amendment to the Arusha provisions. The only way to prevent the nightmare scenario of a defeat at the polls was to either scrap the Arusha accords or seize power. Shooting down Habyarimana's plane would have allowed Kagame to score on both counts.

Descent into Hell

The news of Habyarimana's death spread instantly throughout the land, ushering a climate of intense fear and uncertainty. For Hutu extremists the exigencies of security, indeed survival, called for an immediate response. The decision to apply the full force of genocidal violence against all Tutsi as well as every Hutu suspected of Tutsi sympathies stemmed from a straightforward rational choice, dictated by the logic of survival: Either we kill them first, or else we'll be killed. Thus framed, the logic of the "security dilemma" left no alternative but to annihilate the enemies of the nation, the Tutsi.

In practice, setting in motion the wheels of the killing machine turned out to be a far more complex and difficult task than has been assumed by most commentators. Recent research into the dynamics of violence at the local level shows just how central to the whole genocidal process were the intra-Hutu struggles for power between moderates and extremists (Straus, 2006). In a number of communes, efforts to tip the scales on the side of the hard-liners met with considerable local resistance. As Scott Straus (2006) conclusively demonstrates, the genocide was by no means the sudden, irresistible, uniformly orchestrated butchery that some might imagine; it came about as "a cascade of tipping points, and each tipping point was the outcome of local, intra-ethnic contests for dominance (among Hutu)" (p. 93). Furthermore, as Straus (2006) shrewdly observes, the protracted struggles for supremacy that went on in many communes makes it all the more probable that a more determined stance on the part of the international community would have prevented the worst from happening.

In Kigali, the killing of opposition figures, Hutu and Tutsi, began a few hours after the crash, on the basis of pre-established lists. The first to be targeted were moderate Hutu politicians affiliated with the MDR and PSD, and the Tutsi leadership and rank-and-file of the PL, including its president, Lando Ndasingwa. At this stage, little attention was paid to ethnic criteria. Anyone suspected of FPR sympathies was seen as traitor. Included in this category were Prime Minister Agathe Uwilingiyimana, the president of the Constitutional Court, the minister of labor and social affairs, and countless other lower ranking officials.

Opposition figures were disposed of in a matter of hours. Doing away with hundreds of thousands of Tutsi civilians—and thousands of Hutu in the Gitarama and Butare prefectures—proved a more difficult undertaking. Where local authorities refused to yield to the murderous injunctions coming from Kigali (as in Butare, where the *prefet* managed to keep things relatively peaceful for ten days after the slaughter began in Kigali), they were the first to be killed when the *interahamwe* showed up.

Forty-eight hours after the crash, the carnage began to spread through the countryside, causing thousands of panic-stricken Tutsi to flee their homes. Some were sheltered by Hutu neighbors, others tried to flee to FPR-controlled areas, and still others sought refuge in churches or went into hiding in neighboring swamps. The worst massacres occurred in churches and mission compounds, as in Nyamata, Musha, Karubamba. In Musha, 40 kilometers north of the capital, where some 1200 Tutsi had sought refuge, the militias went to work at 8:00 A.M. on April 8; not until the evening was the "job" *(akazi)* done.

Throughout the carnage, "the militias were exhorted by the privately owned Radio Mille Collines, which continued to broadcast messages such as 'The enemy is out there—go get him!' and 'The graves are only half full!'" (Richburg, 1994, p. 4) In a number of localities, Hutu were ordered by the militias to kill their Tutsi neighbors; failure to comply meant a death warrant for themselves and their families.

The methods used by the militias are described with clinical precision in a report by Physicians for Human Rights (1994): "The *interahamwe* used the following methods of killing: machetes, *massues* (clubs studded with nails), small axes, knives, grenades, guns, fragmentation grenades, beatings to death, amputations with exsanguination, live burials, drowning, or rape. Many victims had both their Achilles tendons cut with machetes as they ran away, to immobilize them so that they could be finished off later" (p. 11).

When death has been dispensed so massively and cruelly, one wonders whether the wounds will ever heal. The legacy of horror casts a long shadow on the capacity of Rwandan society to rise from its own ashes. And it raises problematic questions about the chances of national reconciliation: Can justice and accountability erase the haunting memories of the past? Can the RPF soldiers be prevented from dispensing a more brutal form of justice in dealing with returning refugees suspected of participating in the genocide? How can Tutsi hegemony meet both the exigencies of security and the demands of the Hutu majority for a meaningful participation in the economic and political life of the country?

Postgenocide Rwanda: The Quest for National Reconciliation

In seeking answers to these questions it is important to recall how the new Rwanda authorities interpret the root cause of the genocide, how they estimate the rate of participation in the killings, and how best to mete out punishment. While all three are closely related to the goal of national reconciliation, in practice they raise major obstacles in the way of a viable *modus Vivendi* between Hutu and Tutsi.

Despite considerable evidence to the contrary, official interpretations of the genocide are reducible to one single overriding variable: inter-ethnic hatreds. Hence the need to drastically alter Rwanda's social map. In practice, this means that at the stroke of a pen ethnic identities have been legislated out of existence. In today's Rwanda, there are no longer Hutu, Tutsi and Twa, but only Banyarwanda—the "people of Rwanda"—and anyone suspected of encouraging "divisionism" by making loaded references to ethnic labels is liable to legal sanctions. Article 13 of the constitution deals explicitly with "revisionism, denial and trivialization *(banalisation)*" of the genocide: all are punishable by law; Article 33 further stipulates that "the propagation of ethnic, regional and racial discrimination or any other form of division is punishable by law." The rationale behind this legislation is straightforward: since ethnic enmities lie at the root of the carnage, the path to peace lies in the elimination of ethnicity from political discourse.

Given that these legal restrictions are ostensibly designed to exclude Hutu parties from participating in the political life of the country, it should come as no surprise that President Paul Kagame ran virtually unopposed in the 2003 presidential and parliamentary elections, winning 95 per cent of the vote. The next largest vote getter, MDR leader Faustin Twagiramungu, a Hutu, managed 3.7 per cent of the vote. While the Hutu have been given cosmetic representation in the government (with 13 out of 18 ministerial portfolios) this does not detract from the fact that they are being denied all legitimate avenues for making their voices heard. The banning of the main opposition party, MDR, on the eve of the elections, along with the dissolution of the principal human rights group, the League for the Promotion and Defense of Human Rights (Liprodhor) and four other civil society organizations on the grounds that they allegedly supported genocide ideas, bears testimony to the extensiveness of human rights abuses committed under the pretense of attempting to prevent "divisionism."

Another key assumption relates to the presumed massive participation of Hutu in the killings, officially estimated at three million, meaning in effect that "the entire adult Hutu population at the time of the genocide participated in it" (Straus, 2006, pp. 115, 116). Although the figure of 175,000 to 210,000 is closer to the mark (see Straus, 2006, p. 117), official estimates of Hutu participation help explain why so many were arrested on the flimsiest grounds in the days following the genocide, as well as the extreme suspicion surrounding the Hutu population in general, and the sustained efforts made to ensure the full control of the ruling RPF at every level of government.

Although decentralization lies at the heart of Rwanda's reconciliation strategy, the dominant position of the RPF at the communal and district levels makes a mockery of the notion that "decentralization (will) enhance the reconciliation of the people of Rwanda via the empowerment of the local populations." Local elections were held in March 1999 and March 2001, respectively, at the sector and district levels. The 154 communes were transformed into 91 districts, each consisting of a district council of 20 people indirectly elected by an electoral college made up of representatives of the sectors included in the district. Both were accompanied by widespread irregularities and political manipulation. Widely criticized in the sector elections was the queuing system which denied the voters the secrecy of their ballots. With the sector representatives largely under RPF control, there was little mystery about the political complexion of the electoral colleges in charge of electing district representatives.

What is known in Rwanda as "grassroots consensual democracy" rules out electoral party competition. Local elections are expected to reflect "the consensus of the people." But if the latest sector and district polls are any index, the government spares no effort to ensure that the candidates are pro-RPF sympathizers. Both in 1999 and 2001, as reported by local observers, the electors were in no doubt as to which candidates they were expected to elect. Decentralization became—for all intents and purposes—an exercise in facilitating the penetration of the RPF in the rural sectors.

Much the same purpose has been served by "villagization" policies, involving the massive relocation of rural populations. What is officially labeled the "national habitat policy" is ostensibly designed to "resolve the problem of land scarcity by redistributing the land." At the core of this initiative is a major effort to reorganize rural life by moving people away from their hillside compounds into villages. Over the last few years, hundreds of thousands of peasant families have been forcefully expelled from their homes and moved into villages *(imidugudu)*. While doubts have been raised about the economic benefits of villagization, most observers would agree that the immediate result has been to greatly facilitate the political control of Hutu peasant families.

Decentralization has also been a key feature of the reform of the judicial system through the introduction of grass-roots tribunals known as *gacaca,* after the traditional councils that once handled local disputes the immediate objective of the reform is to shift the jurisdiction of the courts to *gacaca* tribunals so as to deal more effectively with the huge backlog of cases involving accusations of genocide. Ultimately, the aim is to bring impunity to an end and thus promote reconciliation among local communities.

The process began with twelve "pilot" tribunals in June 2002; by 2005, the system was implemented on a nation-wide basis, reaching out from districts to sectors and cells. Sitting as judges were some 260,000 *inyangamugayo* ("persons of integrity") elected by their local communities. Integrity, however, is no substitute for legal training. Despite the lack of systematic assessments, the consensus of opinion among knowledgeable observers is that the experiment has fallen short of its stated objectives. In the words of Eugenia Zorbas (2007), "the lack of provisions for the defense of alleged perpetrators, the poor training of judges, the failure to respect the principle of 'double jeopardy' and the fact that only crimes of genocide (i.e. Hutu crimes) are allowed to be discussed are among the main sources of concern for *gacaca* observers" (p. 26).

For the most part, the hearings unfold in a climate of fear—fear of taking a stand in defense of the accused, fear of giving testimony that might be held against them, fear of retribution by the families of the accused, fear of violating the pact of silence *(ceceka)* by which Hutu sometimes agree not to give testimony against another Hutu. The flight to Burundi of some 4,000 Hutu involved in *gacaca* proceedings in 2006 speaks volumes for the perception that many Hutu have of the tribunals as yet another trap set by Tutsi authorities. Their suspicions are not unfounded. According to Human Rights Watch, the *gacaca* courts have issued a very large number of sentences, frequently involving the maximum of 30 years in jail, with the result that by 2007 the prisoner population was at its highest level since the genocide, roughly 90,000 leaving out the population held in the *cachots* (lock-ups) (cited in Zorbas, 2007, p. 27). In short, if the aim of the experiment was to reduce the number of detainees and promote reconciliation, the net result has been exactly the opposite.

Scarcely more impressive is the record of the Arusha-based International Criminal Tribunal for Rwanda (ICTR). Although the Rwanda authorities voted against it, the ICTR came into existence by a resolution of the UN Security Council in 1998 for the purpose of promoting national reconciliation, peace-keeping and the fight against impunity. Rwandan national courts were given concurrent jurisdiction with the ICTR, but the latter has priority to select and bring to trial Hutu suspects; since 2007 Rwandan domestic courts are no longer free to mete out capital punishment, and thus life imprisonment is the maximum sentence given at the ICTR and Rwandan National Courts.

Among the shortcomings of the ICTR that were identified by the International Crisis Group (ICG) in 2001 were the lack of professionalism of some judges, and the extreme slowness and the high cost of the proceedings. With more than 800 employees, three trial chambers presided over by nine judges, and an annual budget of around $100 million, the performance of the ICTR has been the target of scathing criticism from journalists, scholars and advocacy groups. Its record speaks for itself: by mid-2002 only nine verdicts had been issued; as of October 2007, 27 defendants out of a total of 33 accused of genocide crimes have been tried, five of whom were acquitted, 27 cases are on appeal, while nine detainees are still awaiting trial. A number of key suspects have been extradited to Arusha, notably Théoneste Bagosora, Ferdinand Nahimana and Joseph Nzizorera, but only one (Nahimana) has been tried and found guilty. Meanwhile, the ICTR has yet to offer a coherent explanation for what happened in 1994. In the words of the ICG: "The ICTR has still not been able to shed light on the design, mechanism, chronology, organization, and financing of the genocide, nor has it answered the key question: Who committed the genocide?" (ICG, 2001, p. 1).

Nor did the ICTR succeed in its attempt to bring to trial current Rwandan army officers guilty of committing war crimes. As is by now clear, tens of thousands of innocent Hutu civilians were murdered by Kagame's army before, during and after the genocide. According to the Gersony report, long held confidential by the UN High Commission for Refugees (UNHCR), anywhere from 20,000 to 40,000 Hutu civilians were killed by FPR soldiers in 1993 and 1994 (Des Forges, 1999, p. 726). But this is a fraction of the total number of Hutu killed by FPT units in Rwanda and eastern Congo. Since the ICTR mandate is restricted to crimes committed in 1994 it has no authority to initiate legal proceedings against human rights violations committed by the FPR from 1995 to 1997.

The efforts of former ICTR Prosecutor Carla Del Ponte to include such crimes in the ICTR's agenda were effectively thwarted by the decision of the UN Security Council to remove her from her post. As Del Ponte's former spokesperson Florence Hartman makes clear, this would not have happened without the strongest pressures brought to bear on the UN Secretary General by the Bush administration, ever anxious to take the defense of its Rwandan ally (Hartmann, 2007). Kagame's plea won the day. His troops, Kagame said, were "under no obligation to render accounts to the justice system of an international community which allowed the massacre of Tutsi" (Hartmann, 2007, p. 26). In sum, the justice of the ICTR, like that of the *gacaca*, is the victor's justice, hardly the kind conducive to reconciliation.

National reconciliation seems even less promising when one considers the repressive character of the regime. The Kagame government is a thinly veiled military ethnocracy, which rules through fear, assassination and intimidation. All dissenting voices have been silenced through the ever-present threat of being accused of "divisionism." Wealth and power are the privileges of the Tutsi oligarchs within the army and the government. The "premise of inequality"—the phrase once used to describe the texture of the Rwanda monarchy—has returned with a vengeance.

The ICG summed up the political climate at the close of 2002 in terms that have lost none of their pertinence:

The political parties have either been dismantled or forced to accept the consensus imposed by the RPF [Rwandan Patriotic Front], the independent press has been silenced, and civil society forced to exist between repression and coercion. The RPF wields almost exclusive military, political and economic control and tolerates no criticism or challenge to its authority. The opposition has been forced into exile, and anti-establishment speeches relegated to secrecy. In the name of unity and national reconciliation, the various segments of Rwanda society are subjected to a paternalistic and authoritarian doctrine and cannot express themselves freely (International Crisis Group, 2002, p. 1).

The absence of a significant political overture is a source of immense frustration not just for Hutu; among Tutsi, the survivors of the genocide, numbering some 150,000, are not the least resentful of their growing marginalization. Meanwhile, the selective homage paid to the victims of the genocide through the annual ritual of commemorative ceremonies makes it abundantly clear to the Hutu that they are collectively seen as perpetrators. Symbolic memory thus reflects the pattern of exclusion inscribed in the new political dispensation. How to restore the impulses of truthfulness, civility and democratic governance will remain the central issue faced by the new Rwanda in the years to come; only then will the prospects for national reconciliation—as distinct from grudging mutual tolerance—enter the realm of the possible.

EYEWITNESS ACCOUNTS

Unlike the events surrounding the 1972 genocide in Burundi, a number of eyewitness accounts of the horrors surrounding the Rwanda genocide are available from a variety of sources. Journalists, human rights activists, and members of the clergy have collected a rich harvest of firsthand testimonies. Nowhere, however, are the human dimensions of the cataclysm conveyed in more chilling detail than in the London-based African Rights publication, *Rwanda: Death, Despair and Defiance* (Omaar, 1994). Except for Account 3, excerpted from a report by Physicians for Human Rights (1994), all of the testimonies below are drawn from the African Rights report.

Account 1

The following account addresses the critical role played by local government authorities—*bourgmestres,* communal counselors, *prefets,* and *sous-prefets*—in organizing the killings in the countryside. It draws from the testimonies of Antoine Mugambira, from the Kivu commune (Gikongoro prefecture), and Francois Nzeyimana, from the Muganza commune, also in Gikongoro.

We were attacked by *interhamwe,* CDR [the *Coalition pour la Defense de la Republique*], *MDR-Power* [Hutu hard-liners in the MDR], and MRND [the *Mouvement Revolutionnaire National pour le Developpement*]. Among those who led the attack were a certain Mukama, a soldier, together with the *bourgmestre* of the commune Kivu. They set fire to houses, destroyed our property and ate our cows. We fled to Muganza parish. When we arrived there we met many other people from Muganza. … We were with white nuns who said, "Fight those people because they are killers." The second day they came back with four soldiers, reservists from Ngara and two from Nyabimata. They shot at us and left us with fourteen wounded and six dead. That was on Saturday. On Sunday, we fled again, to Cyahinda. Soldiers shot at us. *Interahamwe* too. We fought them one day, the day we arrived there.

Two of my children were killed, Nkusi and Muhire. I know the killer. He was a soldier, Mukama. He had a gun; he is the one who shot many people. They would shoot at a hundred or two hundred people. … It is all former soldiers who killed us. Those who fell over were beaten up with clubs or hacked to death.

In the night we decided to flee to Burundi. On the Mubuga side we saw many dead bodies, for example children on top of their dead mothers. … When we arrived in a place called Kukibuga, in a market place called Kugisenyi, we saw more than 300 people who had been killed with their children. They were piled up.

With other peasants we fled together at Muganza and we put up some fight against the killers by throwing stones at them but later they brought guns and shot indiscriminately. So many people were killed. Some fled to Cyahinda but there was burning and killing, so some are dead.

The killers included the *bourgmestre* called Juvenal Muhitira, helped by some local police. One of the policemen was called Mukama, another one was called Ngenzi and [there were] others who were armed. Others who killed my parents were *gendarmes* who were supposed to be protecting them. They were led by Damien Biniga who was the *sous-prefet*. I saw more than 15 dead bodies in all when I took my brother to the parish. We tried to take the worst off for treatment but the white doctors and nurses had fled themselves. When we went to the Nahihi commune, the local people threw spears and stones at us. The *gendarmes* drove us into the forest and many people were killed. We were about 400 people when we entered the forest but only 45 got out (Omaar, 1994, pp. 366–8).

Account 2

Nothing is more revealing of the extent of the moral breakdown engendered by the geno-cide than the wholesale desecration of churches. More people were killed in churches and church compounds than in any other site. Among many others, the churches of Ntamara, Nyarabuye, and the Centre Christus in Kigali became the scene of incredible cruelties. The first testimony, by Josianne Mukeshimana, a 15-year-old school girl, recounts what happened in Ntamara; the second, by a 13-year-old girl named Makuramanzi, describes the scene after she survived the massacre at Nyamata.

The day after the President died, houses started burning in our commune. Refugees began streaming in from other areas. We panicked as we saw *interahamwe* following people everywhere. The second day we left home and went to look for protection in the church of Ntamara. But we were not to find any protection in the church.

About five days after we had been there, there was an attack against the church. When we saw them coming, we closed the doors. They broke the doors down and tore down some of the bricks in the back wall. They threw a few grenades through the holes where the bricks had been. But most people who died were killed by machetes. When they came in, they were obviously furious that we had closed the doors. So they really macheted the refugees. The attackers were *interahamwe* but they were not from our sector. They were ordinary villagers from somewhere else. They surrounded the church to knock down anyone who escaped.

In a fury, those *[interahamwe]* inside really desecrated the church, destroying the statues. They told us: "We are destroying your church!" People could not leave. But it was also intolerable to remain in one's position as the macheting continued. So like the mad, people ran up and down inside the church. All around you, people were being killed and wounded.

Eventually I decided to drop down among the dead. I raised my head slightly; an *interahamwe* hurled a brick at me. It hit me just on top of my eye. My face became covered with blood which was useful in making them think I was even more dead. I tried to stop breathing so they would really believe that I was dead. The macheting continued all round me.

Once they thought most people were dead, they paid more attention to looting the dead. Most of them left. But one of them was not satisfied with his loot. He remained in the church. … He came to search my pockets and discovered that I was alive. He threatened to kill me unless I paid him. I said I had no money. He took my watch. In the meantime the other attackers were calling out to him, warning him that he might be killed if he delays any longer. He left.

I tried to get up but it was in vain. I was very weak from my injuries and there were so many bodies everywhere that you could hardly move. A few children, perhaps because they were unaware of the dangers, stood up. I called one of the children to help me. She was a girl of about nine. She replied that she could not help me because they had cut off her arms. I struggled and managed to sit up. But what I could not do was to stand up. I tried and tried but just could not do it. Finally I saw a young woman I knew, a neighbor. I called out to her. At first she did not answer. I insisted and finally she responded. When I looked closely I saw she too had had her arms cut off.

By now I don't know if what I am feeling and seeing is real life or a nightmare. I asked her if it was real life. She tried to get someone else to help me but could not find anyone. Eventually I forced myself to get up and out of the church. When I got out I got so scared that I returned to the church in spite of the dead bodies. I spent the night there with all the corpses around me (Omaar, 1994, pp. 3, 488–9).

Account 3

Next to churches, hospitals became a prime target for the massacre of civilians. The search for, and subsequent killing of, wounded survivors of previous massacres were frequent occurrences at the Centre Hospitalier in Kigali, at the Caraes Psychiatric Hospital at Ndera, and the Butare Hospital. On April 23, militias and soldiers from the Rwandan army killed 170 patients and medical personnel at the Butare Hospital. Dr. Claude-Emile Rowagoneza was present at the hospital when the massacre began on April 21. This is his testimony.

The massacres were delayed until April 20. That day everyone was asked to stay at home except those working in the hospital. Medical staff were transported to the hospital. Nurses had to walk and many were stopped at the checkpoint, asked to show their identify cards, and killed if they were Tutsi. There were 35 doctors at the hospital, of which 4 were Tutsi. Because of the danger, all four Tutsi stayed at the hospital as did some nurses. Drs. Jean-Bosco Rugira and Jean-Claude Kanangire are known to have been killed, and the fate of Dr. Isidore Kanangare, who was hiding in the hospital and may have been evacuated by the French, is unknown.

In mid-May, injured soldiers from the Kanombe barracks started being brought to Butare Hospital and no more civilians were being admitted. They also started deciding who were Tutsi on the basis of their features, looking at the nose, height, and fingers because the identity cards were no longer accurate. Some of the doctors at the hospital risked their lives by helping threatened staff by hiding and feeding them. ...

When the patients' wounds had healed, some of the doctors—the "bad" doctors—expelled the Tutsi even though everyone knew they would be killed outside. At night, the *interahamwe* and the soldiers came in but these doctors were colluding willingly. If people refused to go, they were taken out at night. They could be seen being killed by the *interahamwe* waiting at the gates. Later the prime minister came down to Butare—apparently the educated people in Butare asked him to come—and while here he had a meeting with medical staff. They all said peace had returned and told the patients that it was safe to return home. They wanted those who were remaining here to go. Those who did were then killed. ...

No one knew who my family were. We had good neighbors who said my family were Hutu. My wife was taken twice by *interahamwe* but neighbors insisted that she was Hutu. We have a 6-month-old daughter. My sister, mother, and father fled to Burundi but all my aunts and uncles and in-laws were killed except for my mother-in-law. In other words, more than 40 of my relatives were killed.

I spent my time hiding in a toilet at the hospital. Eventually I left the hospital and stayed with another friendly Hutu doctor who took me to another Hutu friend who hid me in his toilet. ... On July 2, there was general panic as the FPR arrived. That night I moved from his friend's house to my own home (Omaar, 1994, pp. 27–8).

Account 4

Attempts by the perpetrators of genocide to dehumanize their victims took many forms. Particularly horrible were the methods used to force members of the same family to kill their immediate relatives. The following account by a 24-year-old Tutsi, Venuste

Hakizamungu, tells how he was forced by a group of *interahamwe* to kill his own brother, Theoneste Ruykwirwa, suspected of FPR sympathies.

When the killings started, our family was not aware that Tutsi were the target. Therefore, we had had no time to plan our escape. Trouble began in another part of our sector, at Nyagasambu, but soon spread to our *cellule*. In both *cellules* people were chased by *interahamwe* who had been brought in from Bugesera. They assembled everyone in a group. When it came to our family, Hutu residents from both *cellules* tried to pass us off as Hutu by saying that "there was no tutsiship in our family." Those neighbors who we thought were trying to defend us told us to escape to a neighboring village. We left. We realized later that they were not trying to defend us. There was pressure on them to kill us and they did not want to kill us themselves. So they sent us to be killed to another village. …

My brother Theoneste went to the nearest village. But the people there refused to kill him. … The next day he came home and went straightway to a roadblock surrounded by *interahamwe*. He told them to kill him themselves and end the story there. These *interahamwe* ahim back to the house. They told us that he had to be killed in order to prove that the whole family were not agents of the FPR. They left him in the house, knowing that he would not try to escape. During this time messages were coming in every hour, urging our family to kill Theoneste. The whole family was threatened with death unless we killed Theoneste. He begged us to kill him, saying that the only alternative was death for the whole family and a very cruel death for him. …

After these four days, about 20 *interahamwe*, armed with machetes, hoes, spears, and bows and arrows, came to the house. They stood over me and said: "Kill him!" Theoneste got up and spoke to me. "I fear being killed by a machete; so please go ahead and kill me but use a small hoe." He himself brought the hoe and handed it to me. I hit him on the head. I kept hitting him on the head but he would not die. It was agonizing. Finally I took the machete he dreaded in order to finish him off quickly. The *interahamwe* were there during the whole time, supervising what they called "work." When Theoneste was dead they left. The next day I buried him. And I escaped immediately afterwards (Omaar, 1994, pp. 344–5).

Account 5

The rape of women and girls constitutes yet another form of dehumanization. Many of the victims were subsequently killed. One of the few survivors is a 17-year-old girl, named Louise. This is how she described her ordeal.

They came back for me. They were three delinquents. As they came towards me, they were discussing how they were going to kill me. But then one of the thugs recognized me, saying, "But she is the daughter of so and so. He is a rich man." They said I should give them money since my father is well off. I confessed I had no money. They continued to discuss ways of killing me.

Then one of them suggested that they should rape me instead. The three of them raped me in turns. Each having finished, he walked away. As the last one finished, a new group of *interahamwe* arrived. They ordered the man who raped me last to rape me again. He refused. Then they threatened to burn both of us alive unless he raped me again. So he raped me again.

When he was through, the new group of *interahamwe* beat me up. Then they said, "OK let's go. We want to show you where you are going to go." They threw me into the pit latrine. The man who pushed me pushed me so hard that instead of falling in I fell across. He dragged me back by the legs and I fell in upright, on top of my aunt. I could still hear the thugs talking. One of them said I might still be alive and suggested throwing a grenade in. Another commented, "Don't waste your grenade. A kid thrown that deep cannot be alive." They left.

I tried to climb out. But I had bled so much I was feeling dizzy. I felt I had no strength left in me. I kept falling down. Finally I collapsed. … When somebody came to take me out of the pit, I didn't know who it was. I realized I was out of the pit when I regained consciousness. I saw a soldier standing next to me … (Omaar, 1994, p. 425).

REFERENCES

Ball, Howard (1999). *Prosecuting War Crimes and Genocide: The Twentieth Century Experience.* Emporia, KS: University Press of Kansas.

Des Forges, Alison (1999). *Leave None to Tell the Story: Genocide in Rwanda.* New York: Human Rights Watch.

Fein, Helen (1994). "Patrons, Prevention and Punishment of Genocide: Observations on Bosnia and Rwanda," p. 5. In Helen Fein (Ed.) *The Prevention of Genocide: Rwanda and Yugoslavia Reconsidered: A Working Paper of the Institute for the Study of Genocide.* New York: The Institute for the Study of Genocide.

Hartmann, Florence (2007). *Paix et Chatiment.* Paris: Editions Flammarion.

International Crisis Group (2001). *International Criminal Tribunal for Rwanda: Justice Delayed, Africa Report No. 30.* June 7. Nairobi/Arusha/Brussels: Author.

International Crisis Group (2002). *Rwanda at the End of the Transition: A Necessary Political Liberalisation, Africa Report No. 53.* November 13. Nairobi/Brussels: Author.

Lemarchand, René (1970). *Rwanda and Burundi.* London: Pall Mall.

Lemarchand, René (1994). *Burundi: Ethnocide as Discourse and Practice.* Washington and Oxford: Woodrow Wilson Center Press and Oxford University Press.

Linden, Ian (1977). *Church and Revolution in Rwanda.* Manchester: Manchester University Press.

Omaar, Rakiya (1994). *Rwanda: Death, Despair and Defiance.* London: African Rights.

Physicians for Human Rights (1994). *Rwanda 1994: A Report of the Genocide.* London: Author, p. 11 (typescript).

Reyntjens, Filip (1993). *L'Afrique des Grands Lacs en Crise.* Paris: Karthala.

Richburg, Keith (May 9, 1994). "In Rwanda, 'Highly Organized' Slaughter." *International Herald Tribune,* p. 4.

Straus, Scott (2006). *The Order of Genocide: Race, Power and War in Rwanda.* Ithaca and London: Cornell University Press.

Vidal, Claudine (1991). *Sociologie des Passions.* Paris: Karthala.

Zorbas, Eugenia (2007). *Reconciliation in Post-Genocide Rwanda: Discourse and Practice.* Ph.D Dissertation in Development Studies, London School of Economics and Political Science, University of London.

The Problems of Doing Good
Somalia As a Case Study in Humanitarian Intervention

ALBERTO R. COLL

The concept of humanitarian intervention has an ancient and noble lineage in the history of international relations. It refers to the forceful intervention in the domestic affairs of a state by another state or group of states for the purpose of stopping outrageous human rights abuses and alleviating human suffering. Medieval legal theorists such as St. Thomas Aquinas, and later international law thinkers in the sixteenth and seventeenth centuries such as Vitoria and Grotius, agreed that a prince's right to rule undisturbed over his people could be superseded in cases where he committed egregious injustices or was incapable of maintaining basic justice, order, and human well-being as a result of natural calamities or his own moral or intellectual turpitude. In those cases, foreign princes had an obligation to intervene, by force if necessary, to uphold the basic rights of those being abused and to alleviate human suffering. This obligation was based on the idea of the common humanity of all peoples in which the entire world was a single human community ruled by basic standards of natural law and justice.

The notion of humanitarian intervention fell in disfavor in the eighteenth century as international law became progressively dominated by the notion of state sovereignty. In the conception of international law that first became prevalent in the eighteenth century and has continued down to our own time, states are seen as autonomous units with the right to exercise complete sovereignty over the people within their boundaries. Under this system, states were no longer obligated to intervene in another state to protect basic human rights. The only kind of humanitarian intervention recognized by this view of international law was in situations in which the state intervening was doing so to protect the lives and safety of its own citizens living in another state. Throughout the nineteenth century a number of European powers carried out a few of these interventions, invariably against less technologically advanced states outside European society, such as the Ottoman empire and China.

As late as the 1970s, while the governments of Uganda and Cambodia engaged in wholesale slaughter and genocide that cost several million lives, the international community refused to sanction a humanitarian intervention on behalf of the peoples of either country. The suggestions by critics such as the late Senator George McGovern that the United Nations mount an effort to stop the atrocities of the Pol Pot regime in Cambodia met with little enthusiasm either in the United States or anywhere else. Third World countries were particularly suspicious of the idea, which they saw as a Trojan horse for new forms of Western imperialism and paternalism in the developing world. Eventually, Tanzania invaded Uganda and Vietnam intervened in Cambodia, thereby ousting Idi Amin and Pol Pot, respectively, and putting an end to the mass killings. But in spite of each country's claims that it had staged a humanitarian intervention, and in spite of the worldwide relief that at last someone had done something, the international community refused to sanction the incidents, seeing them instead as self-interested actions by Tanzania and Vietnam rather than as humanitarian interventions benevolently aimed at protecting human rights and ending widespread suffering.

In early 1991, with the end of the Cold War, the growth of fresh hopes for a rebirth in the United Nations' fortunes, and the successful conclusion of the Persian Gulf War, the classical notion of humanitarian intervention underwent a dramatic revival. The first major case came in the aftermath of the Gulf War, when the United States, Great Britain, and France, with the authorization of the United Nations, carried out a humanitarian intervention in Northern Iraq on behalf of the Kurds. The large Kurdish minority in Iraq has long sought its own independent state, or at least a substantial degree of autonomy, neither of which the Iraqi government has ever accepted. When Saddam Hussein's armies were defeated by the allied coalition in the Persian Gulf War of 1991, the Kurds grasped at what seemed an ideal opportunity to rise up in arms and achieve their dream of statehood. They were to be bitterly disappointed. Saddam had salvaged enough of his military forces from the wreckage of Desert Storm to mount a savage counterattack against the Kurdish rebels. As the Iraqi offensive intensified in its ferocity, the Western powers, however belatedly, finally stepped in and established a protected zone from which all Iraqi military forces were barred, and within which the United Nations was able to carry out extensive emergency relief activities to assist the beleaguered Kurdish population. Since Hussein had used chemical weapons against the Kurds during a similar rebellion in the 1980s, killing tens of thousands, it is not difficult to estimate that the allied/UN intervention of 1991 saved tens of thousands of lives at very low cost to the participants.

The Kurdish intervention was hailed as a harbinger of future humanitarian interventions. Interestingly, a survey of the major international law and foreign policy journals throughout the 1970s and 1980s reveals little discussion on the subject of humanitarian intervention, and whenever the subject was addressed, it was usually treated by academics and policymakers with the greatest skepticism as to its morality or practical relevance in a system of sovereign states. Beginning in 1991, however, a massive sea change took place. Scholars and practitioners alike began to admit that the end of the Cold War had created opportunities for international action of a much wider scope and of greater intrusiveness across increasingly permeable national boundaries. National sovereignty was no longer considered as rigid an obstacle, or as great a moral value, as before.

Today the international consensus—which is not shared by a number of non-Western states such as China—seems to be that humanitarian intervention is legitimate as long as it meets several criteria. First, it must be sanctioned by the United Nations. Second, the purpose must be truly humanitarian: there must be a large number of lives at risk, or the human rights abuses in question need to be truly egregious. (Both of these are issues obviously subject to conflicting interpretations in specific cases.) Third, the intervention should be no more intrusive and last no longer than necessary for the international community to accomplish its humanitarian objectives.

SOMALIA AND THE BUSH ADMINISTRATION

On December 4, 1992, President George Bush, recently defeated in his reelection bid by Arkansas Governor Bill Clinton, announced his decision to send over 20,000 U.S. troops to Somalia. The purpose of this military force was to insure that the large amount of food being donated to the Somali people by the international community would reach its intended beneficiaries. There was widespread fear among international relief organizations and the United Nations that large numbers of Somalis were on the verge of starving to death. The country was wracked by civil war, and the various rival groups struggling for power were keeping much of the international aid from reaching its final destination points. Unless military force was used to reopen seaports, roads, and the main airport at Mogadishu, and to convoy the food supplies throughout the country, the famine would take a devastating toll. The American contingent, assisted by much smaller forces from other countries, would be under the command of a senior U.S. military officer and would operate in support of ongoing relief efforts by the United Nations and a number of nongovernmental international humanitarian organizations (NGOs). The president's decision to use American military force for such a seemingly worthwhile objective was widely applauded around the world and within the United States. Thus began Operation Restore Hope.

The president's decision to send American troops to Somalia was surprising to those who in the previous two years had urged the administration, in vain as it turned out, to intervene in places of greater national interest to the United States than Somalia. In the spring of 1991, for example, Saddam Hussein, then staggering from the destruction of most of his army in Operation Desert Storm, had begun to massacre thousands of rebellious Shi'is and Kurds. In spite of repeated pleas for help, the United States did not move against Saddam for several weeks. When it finally did so, it limited its intervention to the imposition of a ban on Iraqi military aircraft in southern Iraq and the establishment of a protected zone in the northwestern Kurdish region of Iraq.

A few months later, war in the former Yugoslavia broke out, and the United States refused to intervene. By late spring of 1992, with all of Europe concerned about the Serbian military onslaught against Croatia and the Muslim regions of Bosnia-Herzegovina, and despite such distinguished critics as Margaret Thatcher and former Secretary of State George Shultz urging vigorous American political and military efforts to end the conflict before it further damaged the fabric of European stability, the Bush administration took the position that this was a crisis beyond the capacity of American power to resolve at a reasonable cost, and that it was up to the Europeans to take the lead in resolving it. In the summer and fall of that year, Democratic presidential nominee Bill Clinton highlighted George Bush's inaction as illustrative of the president's alleged passivity and moral insensitivity.

Why, then, did President Bush decide to intervene in Somalia? In the days of the Cold War, Somalia had been of some importance to the United States because of its geographical position astride the Horn of Africa. As the Soviets consolidated their hold over Ethiopia in the late 1970s, their relationship with Somali dictator Siad Barre deteriorated. In 1977, much to the United States' elation, Barre expelled all Soviet advisers, and in 1980 he offered the U.S. Navy use of the port of Berbera in exchange for American arms and financial aid. Washington received another indirect benefit. Barre continued to support the Eritrean secessionist guerrillas in Ethiopia, which were creating serious difficulties for the Soviet-supported Ethiopian regime.

Barre was overthrown in January of 1991 at the same time the Cold War ended. For a short time, Somalia seemed to disappear from the map of America's strategic interests. The country became engulfed in a bloody civil war as different factions struggled to gain control. By late 1991, the civil war had begun to seriously disrupt the country's food production. Over a million Somalis became displaced from their homes and famine began to spread. By early 1992 conditions had become so serious that the United Nations, along with a host of international nongovernmental organizations, was carrying out a massive famine relief effort. In the United States, newspapers and the Cable News Network (CNN) were carrying daily stories showing dramatic photographs of starving children with bloated bellies and emaciated bodies. By the summer, the dead count had passed the 200,000 mark and was still rising.[1]

On August 15, shortly before the Republican National Convention, President Bush, then trailing Bill Clinton in the polls by a wide margin, decided to step up American support for the famine relief efforts of the United Nations and various other international charitable organizations. The United States would increase the amount of food it was donating and would provide different kinds of technical and logistical support to insure the food was widely distributed once it reached Somalia. The new American measures, however, turned out to be insufficient to stop the famine.

The key problem was Somalia's political and military chaos. Central governmental authority had ceased to exist. The country had broken up into a series of fiefdoms controlled by rival warlords. Getting food shipments to various parts of the country required massive bribes to secure the permission of the roving militias and armed groups in control of those territories through which the food had to pass. In many cases the warlords outright obstructed the food shipments, trying to seize the food for their army's use or for sale in the black market, or simply to deny it to their enemies. In addition, the civil war had taken a severe toll on the country's roads and bridges. The ports and the major airport in the capital of Mogadishu were often shut down as a result of military violence.

By late fall of 1992 it was obvious that the famine was continuing. Even though the volume of food entering the country had risen from 20,000 to 37,000 metric tons per month between September and November, the amount of donated food reaching those in need had declined from 60 to 20 percent.[2] The United Nations warned that unless more drastic measures were taken, many Somalis would die within the next six months. In Washington, a number of officials began to think an American military intervention might be the best step to take, given the scale of the problem.

At the same time, President Bush began to turn his full attention to Somalia after a disappointing defeat to Bill Clinton in the November election. He wanted to end his presidency on a high note. Foreign policy had always been George Bush's strength, and indeed the president intended before leaving office to complete a major arms control accord with Russia that would remind the world and future historians of his key contribution, as he saw it, to ending the Cold War between the superpowers. UN Secretary-General Boutros Boutros-Ghali had made it clear to the president that he wanted to see the United Nations mount a major effort, with substantial American military support, to break the logjam of food distribution in Somalia. During the second week of November, the president instructed his senior advisers to prepare a set of policy options for dealing with the Somalia crisis, indicating that he wanted to put an end to the famine. Certainly it should be possible to bring American power to bear to save innocent lives at a reasonable cost to the United States.

At the Pentagon, word arrived in mid-November that the president was serious about an American military intervention in Somalia, and the main question became what form it should take. On this issue there was a difference of opinion between the military and the civilian staff in the Defense Department. The military staffers were led by the chairman of the joint chiefs of staff, General Colin Powell. Born in Brooklyn of West Indies immigrant parents, Powell had risen by dint of hard work and unparalleled political skills to become the first African-American to occupy the highest post in the U.S. military. As with many other Vietnam veterans, his service in that disastrous war had been the key formative experience shaping his professional outlook. The chief lesson Powell had carried from Vietnam was the need to avoid entangling the American military in wars that lacked popular support, and the requirement that, if the military was sent to war, it should be sent with all the massive strength necessary to win decisively and quickly.

In the year following the 1991 war against Iraq, Powell had capitalized on the success of the American military to institutionalize his views through what became known in the Pentagon as the Powell Doctrine. A restatement of the earlier Weinberger Doctrine (1984), which Powell had helped to draft in his capacity as secretary of defense Weinberger's military assistant, the Powell Doctrine stated that the United States should employ combat troops only (1) if vital American interests were at stake, (2) it could achieve a clear-cut victory, and (3) military power was employed with overwhelming force. While the war against Iraq was an example of this use, a humanitarian intervention in the murky political complexities of Somalia was not. For months, Powell and his senior staff had been quietly lobbying against a U.S. military intervention in Somalia.

On the civilian side, the outlook was somewhat different. The principal policy adviser to Defense Secretary Cheney was Paul Wolfowitz, a thoughtful official who, after receiving his Ph.D. from Cornell in 1967, had taught at Yale and subsequently entered public service as a young intern, quickly gaining the attention of Paul Nitze, and rose through successive Democratic and Republican administrations to become the third-highest ranking civilian in the Pentagon. Out of intellectual conviction, Wolfowitz kept his focus on what he considered the key strategic problems facing the United States in late 1992: strengthening NATO at a difficult time of uncertainty over the alliance's future and the increasing disagreements over Bosnia, encouraging Russia and Ukraine to reduce their nuclear arsenals while maintaining tight control over them, and keeping a set of dangerous regional rogue states such as Iraq, Iran, and North Korea in check. In Under-Secretary Wolfowitz's set of priorities there was little room for Somalia.

When word arrived that the White House expected imminent serious action on Somalia, Wolfowitz passed the tasking to two offices in his staff: the deputy assistant secretary of defense for international security affairs, Africa (ISA-Africa) and the assistant secretary of defense for special operations and low-intensity conflict (SOLIC). In the large bureaucratic battles of late 1991 and early 1992 over future U.S. military strategy and force structure, these two offices had been largely on the sidelines. Now their hour had come.

While SOLIC had been repeatedly a strong advocate of using American special operations forces in various parts of the world in missions of broad military support to U.S. diplomacy, the position it took regarding Somalia was surprisingly conservative. Somalia was not important to U.S. interests. Thus, any commitment of U.S. resources should be limited. If American troops had to be used in a humanitarian intervention, they should be used in support of a broader UN operation in which the United Nations, not the United States, should bear the risks and pay any political costs that might accrue. A high-profile U.S. military intervention with the United States in the lead was inappropriate given Somalia's low ranking in America's strategic priorities.

Ironically, it was General Powell who did the most to sink SOLIC's proposed policy option and ensure that the American intervention in Somalia would be a *solo* effort, with the United States taking the lead and most of the potential risks. If the U.S. military was to be involved in Somalia and the politically sensitive general knew that George Bush had decided as much it would come as close as possible to the overwhelming force model favored by Powell. The notion of placing American combat forces under UN command was distasteful to Powell, who had little confidence in the United Nations' ability to perform military operations competently, much less to safeguard American lives in the same way a U.S.-led and U.S.-commanded force would. For Powell, unlike for the civilians at SOLIC, Somalia was an all-or-nothing affair. Either the United States should not intervene (the general's preferred alternative), or if it did it should do so on a large scale so as to accomplish its putative mission as bloodlessly and as quickly as possible and then get out. Powell's view was shared by the theater commander, General Joseph Hoar, commander in chief of the Central Command, who would have overall responsibility for directing the military intervention.

Within the Pentagon, Powell's standing was so high, and his political prestige and capital so immense, that his victory in the bureaucratic battle over the shape of the Somalia military intervention came as no surprise to anyone. Certainly, the general enjoyed the well-earned confidence of both the secretary of defense and the president, the latter having become particularly fond of his counsel. The die was cast.

As the massive force began to land in Somalia on December 9 under the incongruous glare of the lights of television cameramen who had gathered on the beaches to film the historic event, the Bush administration went out of its way to indicate that this was a limited humanitarian intervention. The American forces were there to make sure that the food reached the hungry. Once they accomplished this objective, the troops would be withdrawn and the mission would be turned over to the United Nations. In comments to journalists, National Security Adviser Brent Scowcroft hinted that he expected some of the U.S. troops involved would be returning home by January 21, the date of President-elect Clinton's inauguration, or shortly thereafter, and though Secretary Cheney and General Powell distanced themselves from any such optimistic assessments, they insisted that this would be a mission limited in both its scope and duration.

International and domestic support for Bush's decision was overwhelming and included the strong endorsement of President-elect Clinton and the Congressional Black Caucus. Yet, there were a few dissenting voices, though at the time no one paid much attention to them. On December 1, several days before the intervention began, Smith Hempstone, U.S. ambassador to Kenya and a seasoned observer of African affairs, sent to Washington a long cable opposing the intervention. Hempstone was pessimistic about the prospects for success of a humanitarian intervention in Somalia. He believed that the efforts to end the famine would be no better than a temporary palliative. The rival factions would return to all-out civil war as soon as the international forces withdrew from the country. As for the intervention being a catalyst for producing long-lasting economic and political reforms in Somalia, Hempstone had little hope of that happening. Somalia was simply too backward, and too dominated by semi-feudal social traditions in which the highest allegiances were to oneself, to one's family, and to one's clan, in that order of priority, with the nation-state occupying a rather distant place in the average Somali's affections and loyalties. Once the United States stepped into the morass of the Somali civil war, Hempstone warned, it would find it difficult to extricate itself. In somewhat injudicious language that had the unfortunate effect of lessening the power of his arguments, Hempstone wrote that Somalia would prove to be "a tar baby" that the United States would be unable to hand over to someone else.

Elsewhere, one of America's most celebrated diplomats and scholars of foreign affairs, George F. Kennan, had written in his diary on December 9 that the Somalia operation would turn out to be a dreadful error of American policy. With cool logic, he reasoned that

> The situation we are trying to correct has its roots in the fact that the people of Somalia are wholly unable to govern themselves and that the entire territory is simply without a government ... this dreadful situation cannot possibly be put to right other than by the establishment of a governing power for the entire territory, and a very ruthless, determined one at that. It could not be a democratic one, because the very prerequisites for a democratic political system do not exist.[3]

In his diary reflections, Kennan raised another important set of ethical issues: given the United States' massive budget deficits—which would have to be paid for by future generations of Americans—and its inability to address adequately its domestic human and social needs—particularly in America's decaying cities—was it morally appropriate to pour several billion dollars into faraway Somalia? These questions certainly had to be part of the moral calculus by which the United States needed to assess whether or not it should intervene in Somalia. Yet, as Kennan noted, no one was asking these questions, certainly not in the White House, Congress, or the news media, all of which seemed to be caught up in a fever of humanitarian enthusiasm. Had Kennan published his gloomy reflections instead of keeping them to himself, he would have seemed like a modern-day Scrooge to the American people and the first family, all of whom received much cheer that Christmas from the images of young American soldiers diligently alleviating the hunger pangs of millions of Somalis.

THE CLINTON ADMINISTRATION

When Bill Clinton took the oath of office on the steps of the Capitol on January 21, 1993, the humanitarian mission was not over, and the process of bringing the troops home had not yet begun. Indeed, American troop strength reached its peak of 25,000 that month. The process of clearing the political and physical obstacles to the relief effort and distributing the food supplies was taking longer than anticipated. Yet, success, as measured by the number of Somalis being fed and the quickly receding prospects for mass famine, was at hand. By late February it was clear that the mission, as narrowly defined initially, was about to end. It was at this point that policy discussions in Washington became complicated.

The Clinton administration was divided on what to do next. On the one hand, the senior military leadership, including General Powell, believed that the United States should withdraw as quickly as possible and hand over the reins to the United Nations force then being assembled for the purpose of restoring some political stability to Somalia, UNOSOM II. According to this viewpoint, any American troops remaining in Somalia after the hand-over to the United Nations should be few in number and should play a supporting rather than a leading role.

On the opposite side of the debate was a growing number of political appointees in the State and Defense Departments, supported by the career Africa region experts at the State Department and large segments of the press, who believed that now that the U.S. military was in Somalia, it should go beyond the narrow task of providing emergency relief and engage in a substantial degree of "nation-building"—the process of reconstructing Somalia's shattered political and economic infrastructure. It would be a great pity, they argued, if not an outright tragedy, if the United States, having already spent large amounts of money and political energy alleviating the famine, were to leave Somalia without addressing some of the root causes of the instability and violence that had brought about the famine in the first place. Only after Somalia was on a course toward political reconciliation and economic stability would the United Nations be capable of taking over the task of reconstruction from the United States.

It is important to point out that even though the advocates of immediate withdrawal seemed to carry the day—the United States handed over its mission to UNOSOM II on May 4—the underlying sentiment that favored a more thoroughgoing American involvement in Somalia's internal political and economic affairs than the Bush administration had considered remained an immensely powerful force in shaping subsequent American policy. Indeed, this sentiment was to guide efforts by the Clinton administration as it worked to support UNOSOM II from March 1993 on.

After taking over from the Americans, UNOSOM II began to run into problems for a number of reasons. First, its political objectives were both highly ambitious and ill-defined. In late March, the UN Security Council, with the full support of the Clinton administration, had passed Resolution 814 setting forth UNOSOM II's mandate. Its goals were no less than

> the economic rehabilitation of Somalia ... to help the people of Somalia to promote and advance political reconciliation, through broad participation by

all sectors of Somali society, and the re-establishment of national and regional institutions and civil administration in the entire country … the restoration and maintenance of peace, stability, and law and order … [and the creation] of conditions under which Somali civil society may have a role, at every level, in the process of political reconciliation and in the formulation and realization of rehabilitation and reconstruction programs.[4]

Given the giant scale of Somalia's political and economic troubles, and the almost feudal condition of its institutions, not even the most ardent advocates of "nation-building" would be able to agree on the precise point at which UNOSOM II could consider that it had achieved success. Promoting Somalia's transition toward political reconciliation was a case in point. Did this objective, hazily defined as it was, encompass merely the end of hostilities between warring factions in the country? Or did it also embrace reviving the old system of clan assemblies, in the hope that it would produce a national leadership acceptable to most Somalis? How far should UNOSOM II interfere in these processes? How should UNOSOM II relate to the warlords, most of whom saw themselves as representing large clans within the country and therefore as entitled to a large share of power if not the preeminent position of political power in the country? Should UNOSOM II simply prevent any renewed outbreaks of large-scale violence, or should it go further and disarm the warlords, by force if necessary? Although similar quandaries confronted UNOSOM II in the field of economic policy, it was in the political and military arena that UNOSOM II was most vulnerable to incoherence. Not only did the Clinton administration not attempt to clarify UNOSOM II's objectives, but in its own internal debates and in its policymakers' guidelines for supporting UNOSOM II, the administration, dominated by those who wanted to see Somalia reconstructed, showed an equal degree of conceptual confusion.

In addition to objectives that were at best unclear and at worst overly ambitious, UNOSOM II faced a classic "Lippmann gap" between its goals and the military and economic resources available to implement them. The sums of money pledged by United Nations' members to UNOSOM II's work, large as they were, were insufficient for the enormous task at hand. Militarily, the UNOSOM II force was far weaker than the American contingent had been, and was hobbled by the typical problems facing UN military operations: an awkward command structure, a multiplicity of national subcommands below the UNOSOM II command level, and sharp disagreements among UNOSOM II members about the operation's military objectives and strategy. To these were added substantial shortfalls in mobility and heavy firepower. All of these problems were particularly worrisome given UNOSOM II's ambitious agenda and the likelihood that in order to implement it, UNOSOM II might have to take on some of the warlords, a number of whom were heavily armed, had years of military experience, and knew the country's terrain well.

During the five months of their preliminary mission, the Americans had avoided conflict with the warlords by combining their superior and unquestionable military strength with a policy of talking and negotiating with the warlords whenever any difficulties arose. The American commander on the ground, Marine General Robert Johnston, was a veteran of the ill-fated 1983 Beirut "peacekeeping" mission. So was his political counterpart, Ambassador Robert Oakley, the U.S. special envoy to Somalia. They were determined not to get the United States entangled in Somalia's civil war, and to avoid any appearance that they were favoring one faction over another. Given that their objective was simply to feed the starving, the Americans' policy made sense and was a replay of the old Teddy Roosevelt adage, "speak softly and carry a big stick." Perhaps inadvertently, and certainly unavoidably, given its limited resources and broad agenda, UNOSOM II began to move in the opposite direction shortly after it began operations, uttering rather ambitious rhetoric but carrying an inadequate stick to back it up. By then, General Johnston and Robert Oakley had left Somalia, and their places had been taken by Jonathan Howe and Robert Gosende, neither of whom had the same degree of sensitivity to the pitfalls of intervening in civil war situations.

UNOSOM II's presence and its agenda soon were perceived as a threat by some of the warlords, especially those who were strong enough to hope that, were UNOSOM II out of the way, they would gain power. Notable among these was Mohamed Farah Aideed, a shrewd, charismatic Somali politician and clan leader. Married four times and the father of fourteen children, Aideed had grown rich from extortionist activities he had carried out in connection with the 1992–94 famine and the international relief effort. During Siad Barre's 21-year dictatorship, Aideed had been a political prisoner for several years. Barre later pardoned him and sent him to India as ambassador, hoping to co-opt him or at least him keep him at a safe distance. In 1990, as the dictatorship began to crumble, Aideed took up arms against Barre, and of all the warlords was the most effective militarily in helping to push the dictator out of the country and keep him from returning. Aideed considered himself entitled to lead the country, and he had amassed substantial military forces both inside and outside of Mogadishu.

Aideed calculated, with good reason, that the further UNOSOM II succeeded in implementing its "nation-building" agenda, the less likely he would be to gain control of the country and the greater the risk that one of his rivals would. In May of 1993, he launched a virulent nationalist political campaign designed to persuade Somalis that UNOSOM II was bent on returning Somalia to colonial status and that it was time for the UN forces, including its small contingent of Americans, to depart from the country. His suspicions toward the United Nations were inseparable from the deep ill will he harbored toward its secretary-general. Boutros Boutros-Ghali, who, as Egypt's foreign minister a few years earlier, had been, in Aideed's view, excessively supportive of the corrupt and tyrannical Siad Barre.

In response to the inflammatory rhetoric emanating from Aideed's radio station, Radio Mogadishu, UNOSOM II decided to shut it down. Before doing so, it notified Aideed that it was sending teams of peacekeepers to inspect several of his weapons storage sites. On June 5, 1993, a team of Pakistanis, after inspecting the storage site located at the radio station, was attacked by Aideed's militia, the SNA. The violence soon spread into a city-wide rampage that left 24 Pakistani soldiers dead and scores injured. There was now a direct military conflict underway between UNOSOM II and the country's most powerful warlord.

It was at this point that a prominent retired U.S. navy admiral, serving as special representative of the UN secretary-general to Somalia in his capacity as a private citizen, began to play a role that was to enmesh the United States further into UNOSOM II's growing difficulties. Admiral Jonathan Howe had served his country with distinction as a naval officer for three decades. Before joining UNOSOM II, Howe had served as deputy national security adviser to President Bush and had been closely involved in the Bush administration's decision to intervene in Somalia. Widely known as a "hard charger" who got things done when no one else could, Howe was extremely well connected in Washington throughout both the civilian and military bureaucracies. Shortly after taking the UNOSOM II job in the spring of 1993—with the full blessing of the Clinton administration—he began to use his extensive connections and his intricate knowledge of America's military capabilities to lobby for a more vigorous American involvement in Somalia in support of the troubled UNOSOM II operation. Senior officials at the highest levels in the National Security Council, the State Department, and the Pentagon received frequent calls from Howe at all hours of the day and night requesting more American resources for UNOSOM II.

By late June, with the Pakistani soldiers dead. Aideed in full open defiance, and his supporters roaming through the streets of Mogadishu, it was clear to Howe that UNOSOM II was in danger of collapsing unless the United States acted energetically to prop it up. Howe also worried that the contingent of American forces remaining in Somalia was becoming increasingly vulnerable to the spreading violence and might suffer an attack from Aideed similar to the one that ended in the loss of Pakistani lives. On June 17, after a bloody melee between Aideed's SNA and UNOSOM II forces, Howe forsook whatever possibilities might have remained for negotiations with Aideed by issuing a warrant for his arrest and offering a $25,000 bounty for his capture. He also began to ask persistently that the United States send the famed Delta Force to Somalia to help UNOSOM II capture Aideed. (Delta is a highly classified, superbly trained U.S. special counterterrorist unit.)

In the Pentagon, Howe's request met with considerable ambivalence. While the senior special forces commanders were eager to see the Delta Force sent into action. General Powell and much of the Joint Chiefs were leery of the considerable political and military risks involved. On the civilian side, the SOLIC office once again counseled restraint, reminding senior decision makers that Delta was a powerful and lethal military instrument inappropriate for this case, given the political uncertainties of Somalia and the limited nature of American interests at stake there.

The new under-secretary for policy (and successor to Paul Wolfowitz), Ambassador Frank Wisner, agreed for the time being with SOLIC's assessment that Delta should not be sent, even though he had been pushing for months for a more activist U.S. effort in Somalia. A brilliant foreign service officer who had served as ambassador to Egypt and later as under-secretary of state, Wisner had moved over to the Pentagon in late January of 1993 with an activist agenda. He was a strong believer in U.S. engagement in the Third World and the value of the United Nations to American interests in the post–Cold War world. As a young foreign service officer, Wisner served in Vietnam alongside Anthony Lake, who was now President Clinton's national security adviser. Unlike many of his contemporaries, he gained in Vietnam a good deal of respect for the American military, particularly the Special Forces.

Wisner was one of the senior Washington officials whom Howe contacted regularly from his Mogadishu post. While Wisner was reticent to back the use of the Delta Force to hunt down Aideed, he did agree with Howe on the need for more active American political and military support for UNOSOM II. As early as April, he had been mulling over the use of U.S. special operations forces to help disarm the warlords and destroy some of their large weapons stockpiles. By late June, he was warning the somewhat indecisive secretary of defense, Les Aspin, that the failure of the United Nations in Somalia would deal a severe blow to America's national interest. The UN's future potential as a useful peacekeeping organization was at stake. Failure in Somalia would spell an end to U.S. efforts to use the United Nations in crises which, though not significant enough to merit direct American involvement, were nevertheless sufficiently important to require active resolution.

The month of July saw unremitting escalation of the military conflict between UNOSOM II and Aideed, with the United States using its small but powerful remaining contingent in Somalia—the Quick Reaction Force—in increasingly heavier strikes against Aideed as part of the Clinton administration's strategy to bolster UNOSOM II. A major threshold was crossed on July 12 when the Quick Reaction Force, without any warning, carried out a devastating raid against Aideed's command post. The military operation had been approved all the way up the chain of command to the White House and UN headquarters in New York. The helicopter gunships fired sixteen missiles into the compound, killing a number of prominent Aideed supporters and SNA leaders. The International Committee of the Red Cross put the Somali casualty figures at 54 killed and 161 wounded.[5] In the wake of the raid, a top aide to Aideed warned that "there was no more United Nations, only Americans. If you could kill Americans, it would start problems in America directly."[6]

Following a number of SNA attacks in early August that killed several American soldiers, President Clinton on August 22 secretly ordered the Delta Force to Somalia, augmented by the equally legendary Army Rangers. Once more, another Rubicon was crossed: the United States had again decided to stake its international reputation and the credibility of its elite military forces in a direct challenge to a minor Third World warlord. There was high confidence in Washington that Aideed would be the loser in this gambit.

As in Vietnam, the United States was unable to translate its overwhelming technological superiority over ragtag forces into either a military or a political victory. With impressive skill and daring, the special forces searched for Aideed constantly, but he always managed to stay just a step ahead of them. His numerous sympathizers kept him well-informed of the special forces' whereabouts and movements. He avoided radio communication to prevent interception of his messages. They never captured him. An intelligent man who, unlike Saddam Hussein, knew the United States well as a result of having spent considerable time living there, Aideed figured that the United States might tire of the whole enterprise if he could raise the political costs to them just a bit. After all, precisely because Somalia was not important to the United States, a few well-placed blows might induce the Americans to give up.

By now, the U.S. Congress, including many Democrats, had become restless with the inconclusive and escalating Somalia operation. Besides, the president, still only eight months in office, seemed uninterested in foreign policy and uncomfortable with its details, thereby providing a tempting target for his Republican adversaries. As congressional opposition began to mount, a number of thoughtful critics in and outside Capitol Hill began to ask whether the administration had any exit strategy for Somalia, any notion of when and under what conditions it was prepared to bring to an end the U.S. intervention.

The administration's responses to these queries were less than reassuring. In various fora, the president and his secretary of defense argued that the situation was improving, that America could not be seen as retreating, and that the United States would be able to fulfill its mission and bring its forces home in the near future. Revealing how little he understood what the American forces were doing, or perhaps in a deliberate effort to tap into the American people's humanitarian impulse even at the cost of misleading the public, the president kept insisting that the central purpose of the U.S. forces was to feed the starving, even though by then the famine had been over for several months.

By late September, the U.S. special envoy to Somalia, Robert Gosende, had begun to reconsider the wisdom of the policy of waging war against Aideed, and submitted to the State Department a recommendation that the policy be changed to one of dialogue and negotiations. Unfortunately, however, the wheels of the State Department and National Security Council bureaucracies moved too slowly. On October 3, tragedy struck. A U.S. special forces team swooped down by helicopter on a Mogadishu building to arrest several prominent Aideed lieutenants who were in hiding. Within a few minutes, the special forces had rounded up the suspects and were ready to carry them away, the operation an apparent success. But by then, word of the raid had spread and hundreds of armed Aideed sympathizers, mixed with large numbers of women and children, began to gather around the building. They fired their weapons at the Americans, shooting down the helicopters that were hovering above the building preparing to take away the Americans and their prisoners, and trapped the U.S. force in a small area with the intention of killing them. In the ensuing battle that lasted several hours, the handful of American troops killed over 300 of Aideed's militia and wounded some 1,000, including a large number of women and children who were part of the crowd. The besieged American team was eventually rescued, but not before losing eighteen soldiers. Like the Tet offensive of 1968, the battle was a military victory for the United States but a political defeat.

Pandemonium broke out in Washington. A beleaguered and exhausted secretary of defense was called to testify immediately before a congressional committee and set off a firestorm of outrage when, in an uncharacteristic outburst of genuine humility, he asked the congressmen their opinion of what American policy toward Somalia should be. To make matters worse, some Pentagon sources leaked the story that several weeks earlier the U.S. field commander in Somalia, General Montgomery, had requested heavy armored vehicles to protect the American forces but Aspin had turned down the request because of concerns that sending the heavy equipment might alarm Congress unduly by feeding suspicions about further escalation. In fairness to Aspin, none of his military advisers at the Pentagon, including General Powell, had been particularly adamant about the need for the vehicles. The secretary's military advisers had not given him an accurate idea of the serious risk to which the American forces were exposed in Mogadishu, and thus it was understandable that he had decided the matter as he did. But now that a debacle was in the making, not one of Les Aspin's advisers—or for that matter not even his superior, the president—stepped in to his rescue. He was allowed to twist slowly under withering congressional and media fire, the clear scapegoat for a disaster to which many others had contributed. To his credit, Aspin took most of the blame on himself, unfair as that may have been. With his credibility and reputation in tatters, he was to resign a few months later from the job to which he had aspired all his life, and in which he had lasted less than eleven months. He would die a broken man less than two years later.

A few days after the October 3 debacle, President Clinton, eager to cut his mounting political losses, announced that the United States would withdraw its military forces from Somalia within a few months. There were no preconditions attached. Two weeks later, UNOSOM II opened negotiations with Aideed. By the spring of 1994, the United States had withdrawn most of its remaining forces from Somalia and the other states participating in UNOSOM II had begun to pull out their troops. Surrounded by cheering throngs of supporters, Aideed entered Mogadishu triumphantly on May 20. The last UN forces left the country under protection of the U.S. military in March of 1995. Aideed, however, proved unable to consolidate his power, and the civil war continued. In August of 1996, in the course of a military skirmish with one of his rivals, he was mortally wounded and died a few days later. While there was no famine in the country, peace seemed as elusive as ever.

THE MORAL DEBATE

From the United States' perspective, after spending $2 billion on military operations alone, exclusive of the nonmilitary aid donated to Somalia, and with a total of 30 Americans dead and another 175 wounded, was it worth it? The answer to this question runs across a wide spectrum of opinion. On one end are those best described as *interest-driven realists* who argue that, no matter how powerful the United States is, and no matter how broad and global its interests are, its economic and political resources are still limited, and therefore it needs to choose carefully where and to what extent it becomes involved in the numerous crises dotting today's world. For example, the significant sums of money that the Defense Department spent on Somalia came out of some other account in the Department's budget; some important program had to be downgraded or sacrificed altogether, some significant investment neglected or postponed, in order to pay for the Somali intervention.

Similarly, the political resources of the United States government are limited, as are the reservoirs of public support for foreign commitments. The enormous amounts of time, energy, intellectual focus, and political capital that the president and his top diplomatic and military advisers spent on Somalia came at the expense of other critical issues, some of them of possibly greater relevance to the well-being and security of the American people than Somalia. In a world of limited U.S. resources and multiple demands on these resources, the United States has to be selective and tough-minded as it chooses among competing priorities.

The interest-driven realists argue that, in the context of the size and multiplicity of major international problems confronting the United States in the last decade of the twentieth century, Somalia should have been ranked low in American priorities. It is true that in the age of instant communication and CNN the American people were shocked and disturbed by the spreading famine, but not so much as to demand that the government intervene to stop it. Even though the president received wide popular support when he decided to intervene, there is no evidence that a failure to intervene would have led to strong public disapproval outside the Beltway.

Furthermore, even if some form of intervention had been agreed upon, its scope, duration, and the size of the forces involved needed to be measured in the context of the limited U.S. interests at stake and the potential costs and risks involved. This was not an unopposed humanitarian intervention, as was the 1991 Operation Blue Angel in which the U.S. military, with the full support of the Bangladesh government, had extended humanitarian assistance to that country in the aftermath of a devastating cyclone. In Somalia there was a full-blown civil war among heavily armed factions, and the intervention ran the risk of becoming opposed by some of those factions, especially the more deeply it engaged in "nation-building" missions.

Among interest-driven realists, especially those outside the isolationist or neo-isolationist camp, there are many that have what we might call an interest-driven "domino theory" of international precedent and consequences. They appreciate that isolated events and actions can have strategic consequences far beyond their original narrow context. This is why, in foreign policy and defense, realists tend to favor the exercise of American strength and resolve, as long as the *interests* at stake are significant. A tough stance on behalf of American interests in one country will affect perceptions of U.S. credibility and strength in another. A show of weakness in one place will embolden U.S. adversaries elsewhere.

On the whole, interest-driven realists are skeptical of humanitarian interventions, especially those involving high costs and risks in places of marginal strategic importance to the United States. Lest we see these realists as bereft of a moral compass, they point out that selectivity in choosing whether to intervene, the weighing of costs and risks, and an appreciation of the nation's limited resources in a world of multiple dangers are all morally worthwhile concerns. Moreover, they warn, costly interventions in places of limited value to the United States wind up leaving the American public with a sour taste for international commitments, thereby imperiling future public support for action in places that really matter, be they Kuwait, Korea, or Europe.

As their final trump card, the realists like to point to the apparently inexhaustible reservoir of humanitarian crises around the world and the seemingly arbitrary choice of Somalia. Why not Sudan, where more people were dying from hunger? Why Haiti and not Cuba? Is it morally appropriate to allow CNN to dictate America's strategic priorities? These are legitimate questions in a world of seemingly limitless human suffering and limited resources.

At the other end of the spectrum in the debate over Somalia are those we might call *value-driven globalists*. Most of them consider themselves to be as aware of the realities of power politics and as concerned about promoting U.S. national interests as the interest-driven realists. The key differences are, first, their broader conception of the national interest in the light of contemporary global economic and political interdependence, and second, a value-driven "domino theory" of precedent and consequences. The globalists' viewpoint has been expressed forcefully by the veteran American diplomat Chester Crocker, himself no starry-eyed idealist:

> President Bush was right—politically, strategically, and ethically to launch Operation Restore Hope, and President Clinton was right to support his decision. The judgment that U.S. forces could and should stop humanitarian disaster in Somalia was a proper assertion of global leadership … As the end of the century nears, it is surely wise that we and others broaden our understanding of national interest to include consideration of interests related to global order (sanctity of borders, extension of the Nuclear Nonproliferation Treaty) and global standards (avoiding genocide, mass humanitarian catastrophe).[7]

Value-driven globalists focus on the degree to which the well-being and security of the United States is tied to a certain kind of benign international order. They would agree with the realists that this order needs American military power at its foundation, but it also depends for its health and vibrancy on global institutions of cooperation, including the United Nations, and the strengthening of shared international legal and moral norms that provide some restraints on state behavior. The spread of civil war and mass famine, even in a small country such as Somalia, could not be written off as a tragic but ultimately inconsequential event. To allow it to continue would have had repercussions beyond the purely humanitarian aspects. It would have contributed further to the overall deterioration of Africa. Moreover, once the United Nations intervened, a U.S. refusal to support the operation would have led to UN failure and thereby would have undermined that organization's credibility. In keeping with their value-driven domino theory of precedent and consequences, globalists argue that allowing extreme suffering and degradation in a place like Somalia has its costs, imperceptible as these might seem to the realists. International passivity in the face of gross human suffering and violations of human rights in one particular place contributes to a generalized loss of respect for life and human dignity in the world as a whole. International society, morality, and basic decency form one whole fabric. A tear somewhere affects the fabric's quality and strength everywhere else, and though obviously not all tears are of the same kind, one should fix them whenever feasible. It is interesting to note that the just war tradition has recognized these global communitarian links to which the globalists pay so much attention. In his sixteenth-century treatise *The Indies*, for example, Francisco de Vitoria argued that human rights violations in one country affected everyone else as a consequence of all persons being part of the same larger human society spanning the whole world.

Globalists argue that, given the United States' enormous resources, aid to Somalia and support for the UN intervention was a reasonable, feasible course of action. The fact that the intervention eventually became resented by many Somalis and perceived by most Americans as a fiasco does not erase several fundamental realities. First, thanks to American leadership, the famine ended and many Somali lives were saved, though a serious study has shown that by the time the Marines landed in December the famine had peaked and the total number of lives saved by the intervention may have been as low as 10,000[8]

Second, in spite of the affair's ambiguous denouement, Somalia did not revert to the same degree of chaos as before. Although the civil war has continued, its level of violence is lower and the country is out of the worst throes of internal strife that almost destroyed it. Economically, Somalia also has a long way to go, but its agricultural production is considerably above 1991–92 levels. On balance, a modicum of order and well-being was restored to a corner of Africa. All of these achievements justify the entire operation in the globalists' eyes, in spite of the tragic loss of American lives, the financial cost to the Defense Department, the mistakes made along the way by all parties, and the incomplete and anticlimactic ending. To the degree that Somalia and the corner it occupies in Africa is a slightly more orderly place today, and the international system has one fewer point of chaos, the benefits to the United States of the Somalia intervention were indirect but not insubstantial.

Finally, the globalists have an answer for the realists' question of why Somalia was chosen. There may have been even more serious crises elsewhere, but there were practical opportunities to act in Somalia, and so it was appropriate and useful to step in even if it meant giving less attention to other humanitarian emergencies. We face similar dilemmas in our personal lives and in domestic policy. The fact that we are unable to assist all the deserving poor to the fullest extent of their needs does not prevent us from engaging in some forms of charity. Our choice of those charities is shaped by circumstances that are largely accidental if not arbitrary, yet no one would argue that it would be best not to give to any charity at all rather than give to some on the basis of less than fully systematic reasons.

CONCLUSION

The substantive debate between the interest-driven realists and the value-driven globalists, and among the various points in the spectrum between these two poles of opinion, will not be settled soon. In the Somalia intervention, good intentions were mixed with miscalculations in roughly equal proportions to produce an outcome that was as full of ambiguities and failures as it was of undeniable achievements. The United States started out its mission with high confidence that it could do some good at low cost, and without becoming entangled in Somalia's conflict. As the humanitarian effort proceeded successfully, American officials and their UN counterparts fell to the temptation of expanding the mission in order to address Somalia's wider political and economic problems. This was the fateful step. For in expanding the mission to include the country's wholesale political and economic reconstruction, they put themselves on a collision course with powerful Somali forces that had a different vision of where the country should go. The error of expanding the mission was compounded when, after encountering resistance from such forces, notably Aideed, they proceeded to underestimate him and to forsake compromise in favor of all-out war. Although grossly outmatched technologically, Aideed fought this war skillfully, mindful that given Somalia's relative unimportance to the United States if he could evade capture and continue killing American soldiers it would not be long before the Americans gave up. In the end, the United States did do some good, but not without incurring significant economic, political, and human costs. What started out as an effort to demonstrate American global leadership wound up leaving the United States embarrassed and humiliated. Clausewitz's old-fashioned warning that "in war even the seemingly most simple things turn out not to be so simple" is as applicable to the use of military force in humanitarian interventions as it is to the larger conflicts with which we usually associate his somber words.

NOTES

1. Refugee Policy Group, *Lives Lost, Lives Saved: Excess Mortality and the Impact of Health Interventions in the Somalia Emergency* (Washington: Center for Policy Analysis and Research on Refugee Issues, 1994), 16–17, 21, 24.
2. Andrew Natsios, "Food Through Force: Humanitarian Intervention and U.S. Policy," *Washington Quarterly* (Winter 1994), 135.
3. George F. Kennan, "Somalia, Through a Glass Darkly." *The New York Times,* September 30, 1993, A25.
4. *The United Nations and Somalia, 1992–1996* (New York: United Nations Department of Public Information, 1996), 261–263.
5. John L. Hirsch and Robert B. Oakley, *Somalia and Operation Restore Hope: Reflections on Peacemaking and Peacekeeping* (Washington: United States Institute of Peace, 1995), 121–22.
6. Keith B. Richburg, "In War on Aideed, UN Battled Itself," *Washington Post,* December 6, 1993, cited by Hirsch and Oakley, *Somalia and Operation Restore Hope,* 121–22. Hirsch and Oakley add: "There is no doubt that the militia leaders had studied not only Operation Desert Storm but Vietnam and Lebanon to understand the domestic political impact of American casualties."
7. Chester Crocker, "The Lessons of Somalia", *Foreign Affairs* (May/June 1995), 7
8. *Lives Lost, Lives Saved,* 32.

UNIT 5

INTERNATIONAL POLITICAL ECONOMY AND ENVIRONMENT

Constructing an International Economic Worldview

AMY L. S. STAPLES

During July 1944, the forty-four Allied and Associated states arrayed against the Axis powers met at the Mount Washington Hotel in Bretton Woods, New Hampshire, where they drafted the Articles of Agreement for the World Bank and the International Monetary Fund (IMF)—the most powerful international financial institutions ever created. The Bretton Woods Conference thereby launched a new era in international economic cooperation. As a discipline, economics itself was barely a half-century old, and cooperation across national boundaries to this point had been largely informal, tentative, and voluntaristic. The conference changed this; cooperation was now systematized and centered in these new UN agencies, which were run by economic professionals. The perceived lessons of the previous fifty years, notably the conviction that nationalistic and autarchic economic and financial policies had contributed to the Great Depression and the Second World War, were the impetus for the change. Peace and prosperity in the future, the delegates believed, required multilateral trade and convertible currencies, but the delegates held that in addition to these automatic economic stabilizers, new international regulatory, coordinating, and stabilizing institutions were needed. Professionals, much like themselves, would run these organizations, analyzing economic problems scientifically and dispassionately applying their expertise in order to coordinate national policies, promote development, and regulate the global economy. These were the lessons and goals that shaped policymaking at Bretton Woods and that guided the World Bank in the years ahead.

Also guiding the World Bankers in this new endeavor was a shared sense of professionalism, developed in the discipline over the previous half-century and clearly evident throughout the conference. U.S. treasury undersecretary Harry Dexter White and John Maynard Keynes of the British Treasury were central in drafting the Bretton Woods accords. White, the son of Jewish immigrants, and Keynes, the son of British aristocrats, were different in many ways, but they saw the world in similar terms—terms defined much more by profession and experience than by nationality or class. As part of this common professional ideology, they shared a progressive faith in the ability of experts to act objectively on behalf of the common good, which meant acting on the basis of "the facts" regardless of political considerations or national interests. This shared professionalism allowed the two men to write into the Bretton Woods accords a sense of international purpose and ultimately to lay the foundation for an international identity that characterized the individuals who later worked for the World Bank and the IMF.

EARLY FORMATIVE EXPERIENCES

This ideology and worldview were a direct outgrowth of the professionalization of economics, which combined an emphasis on the new social science methodologies with a continuing commitment to social improvement. Anglo-American economics evolved into an independent academic discipline by using new statistical and "scientific" methods to command authority and to differentiate itself from the humanities, but it did not entirely abandon its ethical and religious roots. Indeed, the most influential economist of the time, Alfred Marshall, who chaired the Economics Department at Cambridge University, embodied both the scientific and ethical dimensions of the new profession; he influenced an entire generation of economists, including John Maynard Keynes. Marshall convinced Cambridge to create an economics curriculum separate from history and moral science, because he believed that economists could and should meet the objective, apolitical, and impartial standards of the physical sciences. But he also pioneered the concept of welfare economics—the notion, in other words, that economic analysis must supply policymakers with the tools and information needed to improve the lot of humankind.

The same sense of social purpose suffused the American economics profession, which also came into its own around the turn of the century, when such public issues as currency reform, the growth of trusts and railroads, and the rise of the labor movement encouraged a strong interest in the discipline and its ability to solve difficult economic and political problems. Influenced by this sense of purpose and confident of their own professional abilities, American academic economists rejected many of the ideas attached to laissez-faire and the neoclassical economic theory that supported it. In fact, the declaration of principles they drafted for the fledgling American Economic Association envisioned "the State as an agency whose positive assistance is one of the indispensable conditions of human progress." Although economists later abandoned this rhetoric as they strove to become more apolitical and dispassionate, the sense of social purpose it conveyed and the belief in government responsibility (which was emblematic of the Progressive Era) remained relatively constant in the American economics profession.

On both sides of the Atlantic, economists and their professional cousins in banking sought to act on this sense of social purpose by translating their professional worldview and growing authority into prominent roles in national economic policymaking and international relations. On the national level, progressive American bankers and economists urged the creation of the Federal Reserve System, in response to the financial instability and attendant social problems that plagued the United States between 1873 and 1907. This system and similar reforms sought to remove questions of currency, banking, and money from the partisan political arena and instead to entrust them to nonelected economic experts, thereby enhancing the role of these experts in governmental policymaking and their self-constructed identity as apolitical professionals.

American economists and bankers, together with their British counterparts, also tried to spread their newly acquired professionalism to other, usually less-developed, areas. Financial and governmental officials from both the United States and Great Britain energetically promoted the gold-exchange standard in the countries of eastern Europe and Latin America. They also urged these same countries to adopt a centralized banking system, tax and accounting reforms, and a formal system of revenue collection, all of which, they claimed, would lay the foundation for financial stability, increased trade, and more private investment. Montagu Norman, who headed the Bank of England, sent his employees across Europe, Latin America, and the British Dominions carrying this message. He also invited banking officials from these areas to visit London, where they could study the British system of centralized banking and learn firsthand how an institution like the Bank of England, which was supposedly run by disinterested professional experts, could contribute to financial stability and growth.

All of these activities demonstrate the sense of mission that infused American and British economists and bankers in the early years of the century as well as their faith in experts, their belief that financial management offered solutions to far-ranging economic, social, and political problems, their conviction that fiscal restraint and responsibility were key to economic progress, and their tendency to equate economic progress with advancement toward "civilization." These financial experts believed that their prescribed reforms would replace revolution and anarchy with order and stability as well as integrate these less-developed nations into a mutually advantageous system of world trade. Economic regulation ensured the proper functioning of the mechanisms of credit and markets, which these Anglo- American officials believed were capable of instilling the "manly" virtues of discipline, regularity, and responsibility. In other words, these financial missionaries also saw themselves as advocates of moral and social as well as economic uplift.

In the United States of the 1920s, these convictions seemed to be embodied in Herbert Hoover, who served first as secretary of commerce under Presidents Warren G. Harding and Calvin Coolidge and then as president himself. Although Hoover believed that American prosperity rested in part on an expanding world economy, he did not believe that the government should be primarily responsible for promoting economic growth and stability, in large part because government involvement would actually politicize economic affairs and lead to inefficiency, waste, and war. Instead Hoover wanted the government to rely heavily on private, nonpolitical experts, who would supposedly act on a rational, scientific basis—not on the basis of political considerations. With these ideas as a guide, he encouraged Benjamin Strong, governor of the New York Federal Reserve Board, to cooperate informally with British and European central bankers to stabilize currencies and foster trade. Hoover also backed the formation of the Dawes Commission, a committee of business and banking experts appointed to reorganize German finances and determine that country's ability to pay reparations. He hoped to construct similar machinery to deal with the inter-Allied debts, which were a drag on the international economy, and he asked private banks to consult voluntarily with the Treasury, Commerce, and State departments to ensure that their loans did not conflict with national policy, were made only for "reproductive purposes," and would therefore contribute to global growth and stability. Unfortunately, Hoover overestimated the ability of bankers, economists, and other professionals to solve the world's problems, just as he underestimated the negative effect that a high American tariff, war debt collections, and poor lending policies would have on the international economy.

The Great Depression convinced many that private bankers alone could not solve the world's economic problems, that more effective economic management was necessary, and that that management had to be more official and more international than Hoover had anticipated. Gradually, the locus of economic decision making began to shift from informal to formal mechanisms of cooperation and from the private banking community to national governments. To be sure, governments sometimes acted with little regard for the effects of their policies on other countries, as was the case with the London Economic Conference of July 1933, which collapsed when the conferees were unable to agree on a common approach to economic stabilization. But more typical was the realization that new international institutions and new forms of collaboration and government action were needed not only to deal with the Depression but also to guarantee growth and stability over the long term.

Indeed, the Depression eventually precipitated new efforts at international economic collaboration. In 1934, for example, the United States established an exchange stabilization fund to sustain the dollar and then expanded the fund to support a number of other currencies and provide for consultation on common economic problems. In 1936, the Treasury Department formalized this arrangement in the Tripartite Declaration between the United States, France, and Great Britain, under which the three countries pledged to consult on ways to expand trade, end exchange controls, and avoid new international monetary disturbances. As it turned out, however, the signatories were unable to make progress toward their economic goals in the face of autarchic German trade and currency policies, and most came to believe that international monetary stability was only possible within a more broadly based international system.

The Tripartite Declaration called for national treasuries to deal with each other directly rather than through central banks or private banking interests, a change that placed a new emphasis on government action. Reinforcing this new emphasis was the introduction of Keynesian economic theories, which stressed the paramount importance of government management of the economy, especially in spending and control of interest rates. These theories began to gain wide credence after 1936 among professional economists, who brought these ideas into government, where they began to shape public policy on a variety of issues, including those having to do with the international economy.

Keynesian economists and government officials also moved toward more formal governmental efforts to alleviate the Depression when they focused on economic development. Traditional wisdom held that economic growth occurred as the result of large-scale private investment, but the New Deal seemed to demonstrate that the government itself could mobilize the resources necessary to promote development, at least in some areas. The Tennessee Valley Authority (TVA), begun in 1933, was the marquee example of this kind of government-funded economic development. It became the model for similar river-development schemes throughout the United States and the world, as well as for the Rural Electrification Administration, which brought electricity to rural areas across the country in order to encourage their economic development and modernization.

By the beginning of World War II, therefore, the economics profession had become confident in its ability to improve both economies and societies. Not only had the profession distinguished itself within academia but governments had also begun to seek regularly the advice of economists. This had begun informally, as economists advised legislators on economic reforms and became more formalized as governments took increasing control of national economies. These governments also built upon the informal coordination of the international economy that had flourished in the Progressive and interwar periods. Now they were ready to build an international organization to formalize this economic work.

BRETTON WOODS: CONSTRUCTING A COOPERATIVE INTERNATIONAL ORDER

The movement toward formalized international economic cooperation seen in the Tripartite Declaration accelerated during the Second World War and culminated at the Bretton Woods Conference. Shortly after Pearl Harbor, U.S. treasury secretary Henry Morgenthau Jr. appointed Harry Dexter White to begin American postwar economic planning. White had fought in World War I, studied economics at Stanford and Harvard, and taught economics briefly before entering the Treasury in 1934, where he quickly became second in charge. Recognizing the close relationship between domestic and international economic issues, White was convinced that U.S. prosperity depended on the world's countries being wealthy enough to buy American goods and being willing to sell their raw materials. Because such an open trading system demanded a level of exchange-rate stability that could only be achieved through the cooperation of all countries, White considered establishing an international stabilization fund that would provide formal cooperative machinery as well as assets to support national currencies. At the heart of the plan was the New Deal concept of shifting responsibility for international economic policy from private and central bankers to national governments acting through international organizations.

To create such a system, however, required some sacrifice of national sovereignty. In order to maintain stable exchange rates, each country would have to abandon high tariffs, export subsidies, foreign-exchange restrictions and controls, bilateral clearing arrangements, and domestic policies that promoted inflation or deflation. White knew that such sacrifices would be difficult for governments, but he believed that the benefits of doing so would be enormous. Keynes was not so certain. He and other British leaders who believed that the premature return to the gold standard in the 1920s was at the root of Britain's financial woes wanted to avoid any postwar system that would allow automatic stabilizers or powerful international institutions to deny national governments the flexibility they needed to determine their own economic policies. Therefore, Keynes and his colleagues sought to limit the power of the proposed International Monetary Fund while simultaneously seeking a well-endowed World Bank that would float large loans, build investors' confidence, and restore international capital flows to underwrite Britain's postwar reconstruction. But whatever differences in emphasis existed between Keynes and White, they shared a professional ideology, a common view of the shortcomings of the interwar period, and similar visions of a postwar economic order based on formal international institutions staffed by experts. In the sometimes contentious three-year process of hammering out draft accords for these international institutions, the Allied economists came to think of themselves as "a group of friends working together for a common cause." This sense of common purpose and professionalism found its way into the *Joint Statement by Experts on the Establishment of an International Monetary Fund.*

Central to the *Joint Statement*'s broad outline of the World Bank's operations was the clear desire for a bank with the necessary independence to pursue an international agenda. To establish sufficient financial strength, World Bank vaults would hold member contributions totaling $200 million in scarce gold and dollars, but to build its own economic resources and to attain a greater degree of independence, the bank would also charge borrowing nations a "fairly substantial flat rate commission." The bank's internationalism and professionalism, however, were as important as economic independence. To these ends, Keynes and the other Europeans believed that it should charge all borrowers the same rate of interest, that its lending should be based only on expert analysis of the desirability of a loan and the ability of the nation to repay it, and that its loans should be completely untied so that the proceeds could be spent in any country offering the needed goods and services at a competitive price. In other words, to Keynes and the other drafters of the statement, the World Bank was to be an international organization that so far as possible promoted the best interests of the international economy as a whole—a revolutionary idea that later became key to the identity of the World Bank and its staff as international public servants operating independently of national governments.

A sense of optimistic possibility animated the Bretton Woods Conference, a spirit that grew out of a common sense of professionalism, the "lessons" of the interwar period, and the desire to construct a new global economy. Almost everyone at the Mount Washington Hotel seemed to view the world economy as a single organic unit that required international institutions to ensure its proper regulation. They also seemed to believe that the absence of effective international regulators, together with economically nationalistic policies, had been responsible for the Depression and world wars of the previous decades.

At Bretton Woods, construction of the new international order required balancing different national interests without allowing any concession that could unbalance the multilateral system. There were a great many national issues to be balanced: the Mexicans wanted to move toward the monetarization of silver; the Indian delegation demanded the return of its blocked sterling balances in London; the Europeans were more concerned with the bank's role in the reconstruction of their economies, while the Latin Americans fought to advance the development function of the World Bank; the Soviets were suspicious of the Western powers and protective of their socialist system; and a large segment of the American people and Congress were only slowly abandoning their suspicion of international institutions. The task of reconciling these differences fell largely to the American delegation (aided by the conference's technical experts), but out of the process of reconciliation came the renewed conviction that it was possible to reconcile national interests with a new spirit of internationalism, that new international institutions could succeed where strictly national policies had failed, and that a new class of professional experts and international civil servants could avoid the problems that had marred the interwar era.

In negotiating with Great Britain and the Soviet Union, for example, the American delegation went as far as possible toward meeting those nations' reservations without compromising the core of the institutions' missions. In the case of the United Kingdom, the framework for cooperation had been laid during three years of preparatory talks, and this habit of cooperation, according to a British delegate, was the key to the conference's success. The U.S. delegates appreciated the willingness of Great Britain to contribute $1.2 billion to the lending pool of the World Bank, and they sought at every turn to consult with the British delegation, to work together on controversial issues, and to maintain good relations. Toward the end of the conference, Keynes went so far as to describe relations between the American and British delegations as "perfect." More challenging was the task of cultivating the cooperation of the Soviet delegation and easing its suspicions, but Morgenthau was determined to secure full Soviet participation in the Bretton Woods institutions. Although Dean Acheson of the State Department thought that Morgenthau "coddled the Russians," and some of the Europeans also accused the U.S. delegation of caving in to Moscow, Morgenthau unabashedly emphasized his role in the Roosevelt administration's reestablishment of diplomatic relations with the USSR in 1933 and sought to portray himself as a friend, even a "grandfather," to the Soviet delegation. To garner the goodwill of the Soviet delegation, he and other Americans also acceded to the USSR's request for an IMF quota of slightly more than a billion dollars, an amount close to that of the British and one the Soviets thought emblematic of their standing as a major power. The Soviets appeared to be pleased with this concession, though they were less than happy when the U.S. delegation rejected their proposal that they and all war-devastated countries be allowed to reduce the amount of the capital they paid into the bank and the fund without a corresponding reduction in voting power. Fears that all nations would claim such an exemption and that the subsequent reduction in available capital would cripple the institutions had led the United States to issue this rare refusal.

In addition to assuaging British and Soviet concerns, the American delegation at Bretton Woods also tried to meet the concerns of other countries in constructing the new international economy. Although these countries could not contribute as much to the resources of the fund or the bank, their participation was necessary if the international system was to function correctly. China and France, for example, were still important to the continuing war effort as well as effort to the stability of the postwar world, and because of this the U.S. delegation was willing to allot each a sizeable quota in the fund and bank, which gave them automatic seats on the executive boards of both institutions. The Third World nations represented at the conference, primarily India and the Latin American countries, also sought effective representation on these boards, primarily to promote their own interests, which lay largely in tapping international resources for their economic development. In these cases, too, the American delegation made concessions: India received a permanent seat on the boards of both organizations, while the Latin Americans received enough votes collectively to elect two executive directors.

In spite of these national issues and the need to accommodate them, a spirit of internationalism continued to suffuse the conference, use and many delegates hoped that it would also permeate the Bretton Woods institutions. They hoped the World Bank would become a community of countries that came together cooperatively to solve international problems in a rational manner, just as the conference had managed to deal effectively with national concerns at Bretton Woods. To be sure, the bank and the fund were not to be supranational institutions with the power to dictate national policies, but the charter of both institutions pledged member states to common policies and obliged each to uphold those policies. In addition, both organizations had the power to make recommendations to member countries and to refuse to underwrite their loan projects. They also had the ability to mobilize more capital than any single nation or private investor and to make this capital available without regard to political considerations. In these and other ways, they were empowered to act as truly international institutions of global cooperation and to do so, at least in theory, on the basis of professional, businesslike principles, not political or national considerations.

Clearly, the Bretton Woods delegates hoped that their creations would bring a new day of international economic progress and cooperation. Hopes for the World Bank were particularly high, as the delegates believed that it would prevent a relapse into the horrible political and economic conditions that had characterized the interwar period and would usher in a new age of rising productivity, employment, and living standards through international cooperation. This hope for postwar cooperation and appreciation for the achievements of the conference was well expressed by Keynes, who had headed the commission responsible for drafting the bank's Articles of Agreement, when he moved to accept the final act at the closing plenary session of the conference:

> We have not been trying, each one to please himself, and to find the solution most acceptable in our own particular situation. That would have been easy. It has been our task to find a common measure, a common standard, a common rule applicable to each and not irksome to any …We have shown that a concourse of 44 nations are actually able to work together at a constructive task in amity and unbroken concord … We have been learning to work together. If we can so continue, this nightmare, in which most of us here present have spent too much of our lives, will be over. The brotherhood of man will have become more than a phrase.

The cooperative nature of the new world order being constructed at Bretton Woods was not limited to cooperation between countries; on the contrary, the conferees also sought to foster a partnership between the bank and private enterprise to rejuvenate the international economy and to provide some regulation of private lending. To do so the bank would guarantee the bonds of nations undertaking reconstruction or development projects, in order to make those bonds attractive to private investors, and it would finance loans from its own resources when private investors were not available. Its relatively low interest rates and high standards would hopefully prevent both usurious rates in the private market and a relapse into the poor lending policies of the 1920s. In addition, the bank's lending to Third World countries was supposed to foster an environment conducive to private foreign investment while at the same time underwriting the kind of infrastructural projects—roads, railroads, communications, port facilities, and public utilities—that attracted few private investors. "If you build a public road you get no returns at all," explained Alvin Hansen, Keynesian Harvard economist and Bretton Woods adviser, "and yet it is extremely productive and induces private investment. It is that kind of loans this Bank has to make."

The Bretton Woods delegates also realized that cooperation with private businessmen and bankers was a two-way street. If the World Bank was to be able to rely on Wall Street to buy its bonds and support its approach to international lending, the bank would have to win the New York financial community's confidence. For this reason the drafters of the bank's Articles of Agreement established a very conservative lending posture for the fledgling organization, under which it could not lend more than its $10 billion in subscriptions. Although most private banks could lend two or three times their reserve capital, the American delegation argued that Wall Street would not purchase the bank's bonds or recognize its guarantee of national bonds unless the World Bank adopted a very fastidious lending posture.

As they left the Mount Washington Hotel, the Bretton Woods delegates could be justifiably proud of what they had achieved. The Articles of Agreement seemed to lay a sound foundation for international economic cooperation, and they had been provisionally approved by all the Allies, including the Soviet Union. But it remained to be seen whether they would pass muster with the U.S. Congress, which had been the bane of the League of Nations, and whether they would work in practice.

PASSAGE OF THE BRETTON WOODS LEGISLATION

If Wall Street's support was essential to the World Bank's success, congressional support was first needed to give it and the IMF life. To assuage concerns on Capitol Hill, Morgenthau and his colleagues had included congressional leaders from both political parties in the Bretton Woods delegation, and they also made sure that the United States would exercise a degree of influence over the World Bank and the IMF commensurate with its financial contribution to both institutions. With the latter goal in mind, Congressman Brent Spence (D-KY), a Bretton Woods delegate and chair of the House Committee on Banking and Currency, was "unalterably opposed" to locating the headquarters of either the bank or the fund anywhere but in the United States. He believed that congressional ratification of the accords would be impossible under other circumstances and urged Morgenthau to express this to Keynes "as plainly as diplomacy will allow." Said Spence, "I don't know how plain that is, [but] profanity wouldn't hurt." For similar reasons, he and other members of the American delegation also demanded a system of weighted voting that tied voting power to the size of a member's financial contribution. This system gave the United States something like a veto in both the bank and the fund and went a long way toward assuaging the concerns of conservatives like Republican senator Robert A. Taft of Ohio, who had proclaimed that Congress would never approve a "plan which places American money in a fund to be dispensed by an international board in which we have only a minority voice."

Despite such conservative opposition, the U.S. delegation was confident that both Congress and the American people would ultimately approve the Bretton Woods accords, and not only because they secured the concessions that Spence and others had in mind.

According to Edward E. "Ned" Brown, chairman of the First National Bank of Chicago and a conference delegate, the bank and fund were "clearly to the direct interest of American investors and the American public." Because the United States was certain to emerge from the war as the world's dominant financial, industrial, and agricultural power, it needed markets for its surplus capital and production if it hoped to avoid a recession, perhaps even another depression. The fund and bank promised to loan Europe and the Third World the dollars they needed to buy American goods and at the same time spread the risk of such loans across the international community rather than leaving it on the shoulders of U.S. taxpayers. Also, because the entire international community was, in effect, making the loans, the members of the U.S. delegation believed that "no country would dare default to an international organization of this kind."

The hearings before the House and Senate Committees on Banking and Currency that followed the 1944 election vindicated the confidence and hard work of the Bretton Woods delegation and the Treasury Department. During the course of the hearings, the Treasury was able to reverse initially negative press coverage of the Bretton Woods accords and build something close to a consensus behind the notion that it was necessary to stabilize the entire international economy with fixed exchange rates and ample reconstruction loans. Over one hundred organizations adopted resolutions and statements recommending approval of the Bretton Woods legislation, and of these organizations none was more aggressive in its support than the Congress of Industrial Organizations (CIO). In a pamphlet titled *Bretton Woods Is No Mystery*, which closely followed the Treasury's line of argument, the labor union asserted that currency instability disrupted international trade and hurt employment in the United States, that the total U.S. capitalization of both institutions would cost less than the country spent in a single week during World War II, and that the bank would create "a decent relationship between nations," "more exports and imports," and "more jobs." Indeed, the CIO claimed that foreign trade could create five million jobs in the United States, which was "the difference between prosperity and depression," and it lashed out at the private bankers who constituted the most persistent opposition to the Bretton Woods legislation. It accused the American Bankers' Association (ABA) and its chairman, Winthrop Aldrich, of seeking to monopolize the international economy in order to advance their own interests. According to the CIO, people knew that a banker-run international economy would again lead to world depression, fascism, and war and that far better results could be expected from the Bretton Woods agreements, which had been formulated over three years by economic experts who had "studied the problem not for personal gain but for the good of their own nations and for the good of the world."

Nonetheless, opposition to the Bretton Woods accords came from a number of quarters. In addition to the ABA, organizations going on record as against the new institutions were the Association of Reserve City Bankers, the Bankers Association for Foreign Trade, the New York State Bankers Association, the Los Angeles Chamber of Commerce, the U.S. Chamber of Commerce, and the Guaranty Trust Company. Several individual economists also expressed reservations, particularly about the IMF. Together with the bankers, they supported international monetary stabilization but wanted it to begin with the British pound and other key currencies. They argued that the World Bank could provide the necessary currency stabilization loans, in addition to its reconstruction and development loans, without the extensive rules and regulations envisioned in the IMF accords. Congressmen Frederick C. Smith and Howard H. Buffett summed up this point of view in a minority report to the House Committee on Banking and Currency.

But the committee report, some business and bankers' organizations, many Republicans, and, eventually, Congress as a whole concluded that large changes to the Articles of Agreement formulated at Bretton Woods would make it difficult for the legislatures of other signatories to ratify the articles. Any delay in doling out reconstruction loans or encouraging currency stabilization, they feared, would result in a repeat of post–World War I economic chaos. To those few critics who had argued for a return to the gold standard or individual and bilateral national currency stabilization, the committee responded that international monetary and financial cooperation was essential to a rebirth of global trade and investment. Two months of congressional testimony resulted in no substantial change to the agreements. The most substantive alteration in the enabling legislation was a new provision creating the National Advisory Committee on International Monetary and Financial Matters (NAC), which merely formalized consultation between representatives from the Treasury and State departments and the American executive directors of the World Bank and IMF. Now the sole remaining question was how the Bretton Woods accords would work in practice.

SAVANNAH: THE FIRST MEETING OF THE WORLD BANK

Keynes's opening address at the inaugural meeting of the World Bank and IMF in Savannah, Georgia, in March 1946 suggested appropriate christening gifts for the newborn institutions. First on his list was "a many-coloured raiment to be worn by these children as a perpetual reminder that they belong to the whole world and that their sole allegiance is to the general good." He then suggested vitamins that would instill in the bank and fund "energy and a fearless spirit, which does not shelve and avoid difficult issues, but welcomes them and is determined to solve them." Finally, as a complement to this fearless spirit, he urged "wisdom, patience and grave discretion." For if the new institutions were to "win the full confidence of the suspicious world," he said, they would have to act with a Solomon-like wisdom and "without prejudice or favour" in all their actions. Keynes's words well reflected the optimism of the Bretton Woods Conference, but these high hopes were not to be realized, if the Savannah meeting was any indication. Compared to the relative consensus and international goodwill achieved at Bretton Woods, the proceedings in Savannah generated a surprising level of national bickering and hard feelings. The divisiveness stemmed from the ebbing of the spirit of international cooperation that the U.S.

delegation had tried to foster at Bretton Woods. The new president, Harry S. Truman, and his treasury secretary, Fred Vinson, seemed to pay little heed to the reservations and concerns of other countries and opted instead for what the *Manchester Guardian* termed "steam-roller tactics."

France, India, and Great Britain had assumed that the headquarters of the Bretton Woods institutions would be in New York City, close to the United Nations and the world's financial capital and away from the political influences of the U.S. capital. "These bodies could not be regarded as international institutions," warned Keynes, if they "were being treated as an appanage of the American Administration," which would be the case if they were headquartered in the nation's capital. The American delegation, however, believed that a Washington location was desirable, because the bank and the fund would be close to foreign legations (which would make consultation easier) and because it would symbolize the shift in responsibility for international economic stabilization from private banking interests to national governments. But rather than seeking the views of other national delegations or even enunciating his own justification for the decision, Vinson had gone directly to Truman, obtained authority to demand that Washington be the headquarters' site, and curtly informed Keynes and the other delegates that the decision was final.

A similar confrontation occurred over the role of the executive directors. The Americans saw full-time executive directors as key to making the World Bank an independent and professional authority. Keynes, on the other hand, wanted the directors to be "in close touch with their own central banks and Treasuries," which would be impossible if they were full-time, Washington-based employees. Similar differences led the British and Americans to disagree on bank officials' salaries. The Americans favored substantial salaries, seeing this as the way to attract talented individuals and thereby enhance the bank's stature and authority, whereas the British did not want to create a new class of international bureaucrats who had more prestige, authority, and money than national leaders. They eventually agreed on a compromise figure of thirty thousand dollars for the bank president and seventeen thousand for the executive directors, but the British, who were still disgusted that the head of the World Bank would be paid more than their prime minister, refused to go along and cast the only negative vote on the matter. Their thinking was accurately summed up in a *Manchester Guardian* editorial: "The American Treasury... seems to have made no secret of its belief that the United States, which pays the piper, has a right to call the tune. In fact, the worst fears of those who had always warned us that this was what the United States meant by international economic co-operation were borne out at Savannah."

Keynes might have believed that Vinson had cursed the christening of his "twins," but the animosity at Savannah largely proved to be an aberration. In the next twenty years, the bank lived up to many of the hopes of the Bretton Woods planners and, to a large extent, recaptured the cooperative, international spirit of that conference. This reflected the professional heritage of the World Bankers (which combined equal parts of social responsibility, scientific expertise, and belief in the efficacy of cooperation) as well as the hard lessons of the Depression about the organic unity of the global economy. With this background, they constructed an identity for themselves and their bank that emphasized internationalism, professionalism, objectivity, and an apolitical nature, the very things that Keynes and the fathers of economics had stressed. Now the World Bankers were ready to undertake the new work of economic development on a global scale, a task they believed would change the world. They did ultimately do so, but often not in the ways they had anticipated.

Introduction
New Confessions and Revelations from the World of Economic Hit Men

Economic hit men (EHMs) are highly paid professionals who cheat countries around the globe out of trillions of dollars. They funnel money from the World Bank, the U.S. Agency for International Development (USAID), and other foreign "aid" organizations into the coffers of huge corporations and the pockets of a few wealthy families who control the planet's natural resources. Their tools include fraudulent financial reports, rigged elections, payoffs, extortion, sex, and murder. They play a game as old as empire, but one that has taken on new and terrifying dimensions during this time of globalization. I should know; I was an EHM.

I wrote that opening paragraph to *Confessions of an Economic Hit Man* as a description of my own profession. Since the book's first publication in early November 2004, I have heard TV, radio, and event hosts read those words many times as they introduced me to their audiences. The reality of EHMs shocked people in the United States and other countries. Many have told me that it convinced them to commit themselves to taking actions that will make this a better world.

The public interest aroused by *Confessions* was not a foregone conclusion. I spent a great deal of time working up the courage to try to publish it. Once I made the decision to do so, my attempts got off to a rocky start.

By late 2003, the manuscript had been circulated to many publishers—and I had almost given up on ever seeing the book in print. Despite praising it as "riveting," "eloquently written," "an important exposé," and "a story that must be told," publisher after

John Perkins, "Introduction: New Confessions and Revelations from the World of Economic Hit Men," from *A Game as Old as Empire*, pp. 1–12, Copyright © 2007 by Berrett-Koehler Publishers, Permission to reprint granted by the publisher.

Introduction: New Confessions and Revelations from the World of Economic Hit Men | 325 publisher—twenty-five, in fact—rejected it. My literary agent and I concluded that it was just too anti-corporatocracy. (A word introduced to most readers in those pages, *corporatocracy* refers to the powerful group of people who run the world's biggest corporations, the most powerful governments, and history's first truly global empire.) The major publishing houses, we concluded, were too intimidated by, or perhaps too beholden to, the corporate elite.

Eventually a courageous independent publisher, Berrett-Koehler, took the book on. *Confessions'* success among the public astounded me. During its first week in bookstores it went to number 4 on Amazon.com. Then it spent many weeks on every major bestseller list. In less than fourteen months, it had been translated into and published in twenty languages. A major Hollywood company purchased the option to film it. Penguin/Plume bought the paperback rights.

Despite all these successes, an important element was still missing. The major U.S. media refused to discuss *Confessions* or the fact that, because of it, terms such as *EHM*, *corporatocracy*, and *jackal* were now appearing on college syllabuses. The *New York Times* and other newspapers had to include it on their bestseller lists—after all, numbers don't lie (unless an EHM produces them, as you will see in the following pages)—but during its first fifteen months in print most of them obstinately declined to review it. Why?

My agent, my publicist, the best minds at Berrett-Koehler and Penguin/ Plume, my family, my friends, and I may never know the real answer to that question. What we do know is that several nationally recognized journalists appeared poised on the verge of writing or speaking about the book. They conducted "pre-interviews" with me by phone and dispatched producers to wine and dine my wife and me. But, in the end, they declined. A major TV network convinced me to interrupt a West Coast speaking tour, fl y across the country to New York, and dress up in a television-blue sports coat. Then—as I waited at the door for the network's limo—an employee called to cancel. Whenever media apologists offered explanations for such actions, they took the form of questions: "Can you prove the existence of other EHMs?" "Has anyone else written about these things?" "Have others in high places made similar disclosures?"

The answer to these questions is, of course, yes. Every major incident described in the book has been discussed in detail by other authors—usually lots of other authors. The CIA's coup against Iran's Mossadegh; the atrocities committed by his replacement, Big Oil's puppet, the Shah; the Saudi Arabian money-laundering affair; the jackal-orchestrated assassinations of Ecuador's President Jaime Roldós and Panama's President Omar Torrijos; allegations of collusion between oil companies and missionary groups in the Amazon; the international activities of Bechtel, Halliburton, and other pillars of American capitalism; the unilateral and unprovoked U.S. invasion of Panama and capture of Manuel Noriega; the coup against Venezuelan President Hugo Chávez— these and the other events in the book are a matter of public record.

Several pundits criticized what some referred to as my "radical accusation"—that economic forecasts are manipulated and distorted in order to achieve political objectives (as opposed to economic objectivity) and that foreign "aid" is a tool for big business rather than an altruistic means to alleviate poverty. However, both of these transgressions against the true purposes of sound economics and altruism have been well documented by a multitude of people, including a former World Bank chief economist and winner of the Nobel Prize in economics, Joseph Stiglitz. In his book *Globalization and Its Discontents*, Stiglitz writes:

> To make its [the IMF's] programs *seem* to work, to make the numbers "add up," economic forecasts have to be adjusted. Many users of these numbers do not realize that they are not like ordinary forecasts; in these instances GDP forecasts are not based on a sophisticated statistical model, or even on the best estimates of those who know the economy well, but are merely the numbers that have been negotiated as part of an IMF program … [1]
>
> Globalization, as it has been advocated, often seems to replace the old dictatorships of national elites with new dictatorships of international finance … For millions of people globalization has not worked … They have seen their jobs destroyed and their lives become more insecure. [2]

I found it interesting that during my first book tour—for the hardcover edition, in late 2004 and early 2005—I sometimes heard questions from my audiences that reflected the mainstream press. However, they were significantly diminished during the paperback edition tour in early 2006. The level of sophistication among readers had risen over the course of that year. A growing suspicion that the mainstream press was collaborating with the corporatocracy—which, of course, owned much of it or at least supported it through advertising—had become manifest. While I would love to credit *Confessions* for this transformation in public attitude, my book has to share that honor with a number of others, such as Stiglitz's *Globalization and Its Discontents*, David Korten's *When Corporations Rule the World*, Noam Chomsky's *Hegemony or Survival*, Chalmers Johnson's *Sorrows of Empire*, Jeff Faux's *Global Class War*, and Antonia Juhasz's *Bush Agenda*, as well as films such as *The Constant Gardener*, *Syriana*, *Hotel Rwanda*, *Good Night, and Good Luck*, and *Munich*. The American public recently has been treated to a feast of exposés. Mine is definitely not a voice in the wilderness.

Despite the overwhelming evidence that the corporatocracy has created the world's first truly global empire, inflicted increased misery and poverty on millions of people around the planet, managed to sabotage the principles of self-determination, justice, and freedom that form the foundations upon which the United States stands, and turned a country that was lauded at the end of World War II as democracy's savior into one that is feared, resented, and hated, the mainstream press ignores the obvious. In pleasing the moneymen and the executives upstairs, many journalists have turned their backs on the truth. When approached by my publicists, they continue to ask: "Where are the trenches?" "Can you produce the trowels that dug them?" "Have any 'objective' researchers confirmed your story?"

Although the evidence was already available, Berrett-Koehler and I decided that the proper response was to answer such questions in terms that no one could ignore and that only those who insisted on remaining in denial could dispute. We would publish a book with many contributors, an anthology, further revealing the world of economic hit men and how it works.

In *Confessions*, I talked about a world rooted in the cold war, in the dynamics and proxy conflicts of the U.S.–Soviet conflict. My sojourn in that war ended in 1981, a quarter of a century ago. Since then, and especially since the collapse of the USSR, the dynamics of empire have changed. The world is now more multipolar and mercantile, with China and Europe emerging to compete with the U.S. Empire is heavily driven by multinational corporations, whose interests transcend those of any particular nation-state.[3] There are new multinational institutions and trade agreements, such as the World Trade Organization (WTO) and North American Free Trade Agreement (NAFTA), and newly articulated ideologies and programs, such as neoliberalism and the structural adjustments and conditionalities imposed by the IMF. But one thing remains unchanged: the peoples of the Third World continue to suffer; their future, if anything, looks even bleaker than it did in the early 1980s.

A quarter-century ago, I saw myself as a hit man for the interests of U.S. capitalism in the struggle for control of the developing world during the cold war. Today, the EHM game is more complex, its corruption more pervasive, and its operations more fundamental to the world economy and politics. There are many more types of economic hit men, and the roles they play are far more diverse. The veneer of respectability remains a key factor; subterfuges range from money laundering and tax evasion carried out in well-appointed office suites to activities that amount to economic war crimes and result in the deaths of millions of people. The chapters that follow reveal this dark side of globalization, show-ing a system that depends on deception, extortion, and often violence: an officer of an offshore bank hiding hundreds of millions in stolen money, IMF advisors slashing Ghana's education and health programs, a Chinese bureaucrat seeking oil concessions in Africa, a mercenary defending a European oil company in Nigeria, a consultant rewriting Iraqi oil law, and executives financing warlords to secure supplies of coltan ore in Congo.

The main obstacle to compiling such stories should be obvious. Most EHMs do not think it is in their best interests to talk about their jobs. Many are still actively employed in the business. Those who have stepped away often receive pensions, consultant fees, and other perks from their former employers. They understand that whistle-blowers usu-ally sacrifice such benefits—and sometimes much more. Most of us who have done that type of work pride ourselves on loyalty to old comrades. Once one of us decides to take the big leap—"into the cold," to use CIA vernacular—we know we will have to face the harsh reality of powerful forces arrayed to protect the institutional power of multinational corporations, global banks, government defense and security agencies, international agencies—and the small elite that runs them.

In recent years, the people charged with deceiving ordinary citizens have grown more cunning. *The Pentagon Papers* and the White House Watergate tapes taught them the dangers of writing and recording incriminating details. The Enron, Arthur Andersen, and WorldCom scandals, and recent allegations about CIA "extraordinary renditions," weapons of mass destruction deceits, and National Security Agency eavesdropping serve to reinforce policies that favor shredding. Government officials who expose a CIA agent to retaliate against her whistle-blowing spouse go unpunished. All these events lead to the ultimate deterrent to speaking the truth: those who expose the corporatocracy can expect to be assassinated—financially and by reputation, if not with a bullet.

Less obvious deterrents also keep people from telling the truth. Opening one's soul for public scrutiny, confessing, is not fun. I had written many books before *Confessions* (five of them published). Yet none prepared me for the angst I would encounter while exposing my transgressions as an EHM. Although most of us humans do not want to think of ourselves as corrupt, weak, or immoral, it is difficult—if not impossible—to ignore those aspects of ourselves when describing our lives as economic hit men. Personally, it was one of the most difficult tasks I have ever undertaken. In approaching prospective contributors to a book such as this I might tell them that confessing is, in the end, worth the anguish. However, for someone setting out on this path, that end seems very distant.

I discussed these obstacles and the potential benefits of overcoming them with Steve Piersanti, the intrepid founder and CEO of Berrett-Koehler, who made the decision to publish *Confessions*. It did not take us long to decide that the benefits were well worth the struggle. If my *Confessions* could send such a strong message to the public, it made sense that multiple confessions—or stories about people who need to confess—might reach even more people and motivate them to take actions that will turn this empire back into the democratic republic it was intended to be. Our goal was nothing less than convincing the American public that we can and must create a future that will make our children and grandchildren—and their brothers and sisters on every continent—proud of us.

Of course we had to start by showing journalists the trowels *and* the trenches. We decided that we should also include well-researched analyses by observers who came from a more objective perspective, rather than a personal one. A balance between firsthand and third-party accounts seemed like the prudent approach.

Steve took it upon himself to find someone who could be an editor and also serve as a sleuth: he'd have to ferret out prospective writers and convince them that loyalty to country, family, and future generations on every continent demanded that they participate in this book. After an extensive selection process, he, his staff, and I settled on Steven Hiatt. Steve is a professional editor—but he also has a long history as an activist, first against the

Vietnam War and then as a teachers' union organizer. In addition, he worked for a number of years at Stanford Research Institute, a think tank and consultancy organization serving multinationals and government agencies around the world and closely linked to Bechtel, Bank of America, and other players in the EHM world. There he worked on research reports that he describes as essentially "the corporatocracy talking to itself."

Once the process of assembling this anthology began, I started speaking about it. When people asked those questions—"Can you prove the existence of other EHMs?" "Has anyone else written about these things?" "Have others made similar disclosures?"—I told them about the upcoming book. The wisdom of making that decision to publish an anthology was supported on February 19, 2006, when the *New York Times* ran a major article that featured *Confessions* on the front page of its Sunday Business Section. The editors, I am sure, were comforted by the results of a background check confirming my account of my life and the episodes described in *Confessions*; however, the fact that other EHMs and researchers had committed to writing this book was, I suspect, the most important factor in their decision to publish that article.

The contributors to this book uncover events that have taken place across a wide range of countries, all EHM game plans under a variety of guises. Each sheds more light on the building of an empire that is contrary to American principles of democracy and equality. The chapters are presented in an order that follows the fl ow of money and power in the Global Empire. The chart on page 10 shows that progression: the selling of loans to Third World countries, the fl ow of dirty money back to First World control via secret offshore accounts, the failure of debt-led development models to reduce poverty, the accumulation of mountains of unpayable debt, the gutting of local economies by the IMF, and military intervention and domination to secure access to resources. Steve Hiatt, in "Global Empire," gives an overview of the web of control that First World companies and institutions use to rule the global economy; each subsequent chapter exposes another facet. In brief summary:

- S.C. Gwynne joined Cleveland Trust and quickly moved into the heady atmosphere of international banking, where he learned that ability to pay had little to do with placing loans. In "Selling Money—and Dependency: Setting the Debt Trap" he describes a culture of business corruption in which local elites and international banks build mutually supportive relationships based on debts that will have to be repaid by ordinary citizens.
- John Christensen worked for a trust company on the offshore banking haven of Jersey, one of Britain's Channel Islands. There he found himself at the center of the EHM world, part of a global offshore banking industry that facilitates tax evasion, money laundering, and capital fl ight. In "Dirty Money" he reveals the workings of a system that enables the theft of billions from Third World (and First World) citizens; the lures of an opulent lifestyle; and why he decided to get out.

- The Bank of Credit and Commerce International was for two decades a key player in offshore/underground banking. It provided off-the-books/ illegal transactions for a startling range of customers—from the CIA to the Medellín cartel to Osama bin Laden and al-Qaeda. In "BCCI's Double Game," Lucy Komisar recounts the bank's rapid rise and fall—and its $13 billion bankruptcy.

- Congo remains one of the world's poorest countries and is caught in a civil war that has cost at least 4 million lives over the last ten years, with western multinationals financing militias and warlords to ensure access to gold, diamonds, and coltan. In "The Human Cost of Cheap Cell Phones," Kathleen Kern provides an eyewitness account of the high price the Congolese have paid to bring cheap electronics to First World consumers.

- Some 30 percent of America's supply of oil is expected to come from Africa in the next ten years, but U.S. and UK oil companies will be competing with China for access to these reserves. Local communities have been campaigning to gain a share of this new wealth and to prevent environmental destruction of their region. In "Mercenaries on the Front Lines in the New Scramble for Africa," Andrew Rowell and James Marriott tell how a British expat security officer found himself in the middle of this struggle for oil and power.

- According to most estimates Iraq has the world's second largest oil reserves— and access to Iraq's oil has been one of the essential elements of U.S. foreign policy. The occupation regime is planning to sign oil production sharing agreements with U.S. and UK companies that will cost the Iraqi people $200 billion that they need to rebuild their country. In "Hijacking Iraq's Oil Reserves," Greg Muttitt reveals the EHM behind this high-level hit.

- "Have you brought the money?" a Liberian official asked World Bank staffer Steve Berkman, clearly expecting him to hand over a satchel full of cash. In "The World Bank and the $100 Billion Question," Berkman provides an insider's account of how and why the Bank looks the other way as corrupt elites steal funds intended for development aid.

- In the 1970s, the Philippines were a showcase for the World Bank's debt-based model of development and modernization. In "The Philippines, the World Bank, and the Race to the Bottom," Ellen Augustine tells how billions in loans were central to U.S. efforts to prop up the Marcos dictatorship, with the World Bank serving as a conduit.

- Export credit agencies have a single job: to enrich their countries' corporations by making it easier for poor countries to buy their products and services. In "Exporting Destruction," Bruce Rich turns a spotlight on the secretive world of ECAs and the damage they have caused in selling nuclear plants to countries that cannot manage them and pushing arms in war-torn regions.

- The G8 finance ministers announced before their Gleneagles meeting that they had agreed on $40 billion of debt relief for eighteen Third World countries. In "The Mirage of Debt Relief," James S. Henry, an investigative journalist, economist, and lawyer, shows how little debt relief has actually been granted—and why dozens of countries remain caught in the West's debt trap.

Feel free to read the chapters according to your interests. Skip around, focus on one geographic area at a time or on one particular discipline, if you wish. Then turn to Antonia Juhasz's "Global Uprising" to learn what you can do to resist global domination by the corporatocracy.

As you read, please allow yourself to think about and feel the implications of the actions described for the world and for our children and grandchildren. Permit your passions to rise to the surface. Feel compelled to take action. It is essential that we—you and I—do something. We must transform our country back into one that reflects the values of our Declaration of Independence and the other principles we were raised to honor and defend. We must begin today to re-create the world the corporatocracy has inflicted on us.

This book presents a series of snapshots of the tools used by EHMs to create the world's first truly global empire. They are, however, a mere introduction to the many nefarious deeds that have been committed by the corporate elite—often in the name of altruism and progress. During the post–World War II period, we EHMs managed to turn the "last, best hope for democracy," in Lincoln's words, into an empire that does not flinch at inflicting brutal and often totalitarian measures on people who have resources we covet.

After reading the chapters you will have a better understanding of why people around the world fear, resent, and even hate us. As a result of the corporatocracy's policies, an average of 24,000 people die every day from hunger; tens of thousands more—mostly children—die from curable diseases because they cannot afford available medicines. More than half the world's population lives on less than $2 a day, not nearly enough to cover basic necessities in most places. In essence our economic system depends on modern versions of human exploitation that conjure images of serfdom and slavery.

We must put an end to this. You and I must do the right thing. We must understand that our children will not inherit a stable, safe, and sustainable world unless we change the terrible conditions that have been created by EHMs. All of us must look deep into our hearts and souls and decide what it is we can best do. Where are our strengths? What are our passions?

As an author and lecturer, I know that I have certain skills and opportunities. Yours may be different from mine, but they are just as powerful. I urge you to set as a primary goal in your life making this a better world not only for you but also for all those who follow. Please commit to taking at least one action every single day to realize this goal. Think about those 24,000 who die each day from hunger, and dedicate yourself to changing this in your lifetime. Write letters and e-mails—to newspapers, magazines, your local and national representatives, your friends, businesses that are doing the right thing and those that are not; call in to radio shows; shop consciously; do not "buy cheap" if doing so contributes to modern forms of slavery; support nonprofit organizations that help spread

Global Empire North and South
FLOWS OF MONEY AND POWER

The Global North has for decades sold a model of development based on debt. Loans pushed by First World lenders and eagerly grabbed by corrupt Third World elites have left Global South countries in a debt trap $3.2 trillion deep—often with little real development to show for it. Much of the money simply round-trips back to First World suppliers or offshore banking havens. Meanwhile, a new era of imperial domination has begun with interventions to secure control of scarce resources like oil and coltan.

GLOBAL NORTH
G8 NATIONS · MULTINATIONALS · WORLD BANK · IMF

1. FOLLOW THE MONEY

S.C. GWYNNE
Selling Money—
and Dependency

JOHN CHRISTENSEN
Dirty Money: Offshore Banking

LUCY KOMISAR
BCCI: Banking on America,
Banking on Jihad

4. THE DEBT TRAP

JAMES S. HENRY
The Mirage of Debt Relief

3. INTERVENTION AND DOMINATION: ACCESS TO RESOURCES

KATHLEEN KERN
The Human Cost of Cheap Cell Phones

ANDREW ROWELL/ JAMES MARRIOTT
Oil, Mercenaries, and the New Scramble for Africa

GREG MUTTITT
Hijacking Iraq's Oil: EHMs at Work

2. DEBT-LED DEVELOPMENT

STEVE BERKMAN
The $100 Billion Question

ELLEN AUGUSTINE
The World Bank and the Philippines

BRUCE RICH
Exporting Destruction

GLOBAL SOUTH
THE UNDERDEVELOPED WORLD

the word, protect the environment, defend civil liberties, fight hunger and disease, and make this a sane world; volunteer; go to schools and teach our children; form discussion groups in your neighborhood—the list of possible actions is endless, limited only by imagination. We all have many talents and passions to contribute. The most important thing is to get out there and do it!

One thing we all can—and must—do is to educate ourselves and those who interact with us. Democracy is based on an informed electorate. If we in the United States are not aware that our business and political leaders are using EHMs to subvert the most sacred principles upon which our country is founded, then we cannot in truth claim to be a democracy.

There is no excuse for lack of awareness, now that you have this book, plus many others and a multitude of films, CDs, and DVDs to help educate everyone you connect with. Beyond that, it is essential that every time you read, hear, or see a news report about some international event, do so with a skeptical mind. Remember that most media are owned by—or dependent on the financial support of—the corporatocracy. Dig beneath the surface. The appendix, "Resources of Hope," provides a list of alternative media where you can access different viewpoints.

This may well be the most pivotal and exciting time in the history of a nation that is built on pivotal and exciting events. How you and I choose to react to this global empire in the coming years is likely to determine the future of our planet. Will we continue along a road marked by violence, exploitation of others, and ultimately the likelihood of our self-destruction as a species? Or will we create a world our children will be proud to inherit? The choice is ours—yours and mine.

NOTES

1. Joseph E. Stiglitz, *Globalization and Its Discontents* (New York: Norton, 2003), p. 232.
2. Ibid., pp. 247–48.
3. For more on the corporatocracy as an international, interlinked power elite, see Jeff Faux, "The Party of Davos," *Nation*, January 26, 2006.

High-Tech Trash
Will Your Discarded TV End Up in a Ditch in Ghana?

CHRIS CARROLL

June is the wet season in Ghana, but here in Accra, the capital, the morning rain has ceased. As the sun heats the humid air, pillars of black smoke begin to rise above the vast Agbogbloshie Market. I follow one plume toward its source, past lettuce and plantain vendors, past stalls of used tires, and through a clanging scrap market where hunched men bash on old alternators and engine blocks. Soon the muddy track is flanked by piles of old TVs, gutted computer cases, and smashed monitors heaped ten feet (three meters) high. Beyond lies a field of fine ash speckled with glints of amber and green—the sharp broken bits of circuit boards. I can see now that the smoke issues not from one fire, but from many small blazes. Dozens of indistinct figures move among the acrid haze, some stirring flames with sticks, others carrying armfuls of brightly colored computer wire. Most are children.

Choking, I pull my shirt over my nose and approach a boy of about 15, his thin frame wreathed in smoke. Karim says he has been tending such fires for two years. He pokes at one meditatively, and then his top half disappears as he bends into the billowing soot. He hoists a tangle of copper wire off the old tire he's using for fuel and douses the hissing mass in a puddle. With the flame retardant insulation burned away—a process that has released a bouquet of carcinogens and other toxics—the wire may fetch a dollar from a scrap-metal buyer.

Another day in the market, on a similar ash heap above an inlet that flushes to the Atlantic after a downpour, Israel Mensah, an incongruously stylish young man of about 20, adjusts his designer glasses and explains how he makes his living. Each day scrap sellers bring loads of old electronics—from where he doesn't know. Mensah and his partners—friends and family, including two shoeless boys raptly listening to us talk—buy a few computers or TVs. They break copper yokes off picture tubes, littering the ground with shards containing lead, a neurotoxin, and cadmium, a carcinogen that damages lungs and kidneys. They strip resalable parts such as drives and memory chips. Then they rip out wiring and burn the plastic. He sells copper stripped from one scrap load to buy another. The key to making money is speed, not safety. "The gas goes to your nose and you feel something in your head," Mensah says, knocking his fist against the back of his skull for effect. "Then you get sick in your head and your chest." Nearby, hulls of broken monitors float in the lagoon. Tomorrow the rain will wash them into the ocean.

People have always been proficient at making trash. Future archaeologists will note that at the tail end of the 20th century, a new, noxious kind of clutter exploded across the landscape: the digital detritus that has come to be called e-waste.

More than 40 years ago, Gordon Moore, co-founder of the computer-chip maker Intel, observed that computer processing power roughly doubles every two years. An unstated corollary to "Moore's law" is that at any given time, all the machines considered state-of-the-art are simultaneously on the verge of obsolescence. At this very moment, heavily caffeinated software engineers are designing programs that will overtax and befuddle your new turbo-powered PC when you try running them a few years from now. The memory and graphics requirements of Microsoft's recent Vista operating system, for instance, spell doom for aging machines that were still able to squeak by a year ago. According to the U.S. Environmental Protection Agency, an estimated 30 to 40 million PCs will be ready for "end-of-life management" in each of the next few years.

Computers are hardly the only electronic hardware hounded by obsolescence. A switchover to digital high-definition television broadcasts is scheduled to be complete by 2009, rendering inoperable TVs that function perfectly today but receive only an analog signal. As viewers prepare for the switch, about 25 million TVs are taken out of service yearly. In the fashion-conscious mobile market, 98 million U.S. cell phones took their last call in 2005. All told, the EPA estimates that in the U.S. that year, between 1.5 and 1.9 million tons of computers, TVs, VCRs, monitors, cell phones, and other equipment were discarded. If all sources of electronic waste are tallied, it could total 50 million tons a year worldwide, according to the UN Environment Programme.

So what happens to all this junk?

In the United States, it is estimated that more than 70 percent of discarded computers and monitors, and well over 80 percent of TVs, eventually end up in landfills, despite a growing number of state laws that prohibit dumping of e-waste, which may leak lead, mercury, arsenic, cadmium, beryllium, and other toxics into the ground. Meanwhile, a staggering volume of unused electronic gear sits in storage—about 180 million TVs, desktop PCs, and other components as of 2005, according to the EPA. Even if this obsolete equipment remains in attics and basements indefinitely, never reaching a landfill, this solution has its own, indirect impact on the environment. In addition to toxics, e-waste contains goodly amounts of silver, gold, and other valuable metals that are highly efficient conductors of electricity. In theory, recycling gold from old computer motherboards is far more efficient and less environmentally destructive than ripping it from the earth, often by surface-mining that imperils pristine rain forests.

Currently, less than 20 percent of e-waste entering the solid waste stream is channeled through companies that advertise themselves as recyclers, though the number is likely to rise as states like California crack down on landfill dumping. Yet recycling, under the current system, is less benign than it sounds. Dropping your old electronic gear off with a recycling company or at a municipal collection point does not guarantee that it will be safely disposed of. While some recyclers process the material with an eye toward minimizing pollution and health risks, many more sell it to brokers who ship it to the developing world, where environmental enforcement is weak. For people in countries on the front end of this arrangement, it's a handy out-of-sight, out-of-mind solution.

Many governments, conscious that electronic waste wrongly handled damages the environment and human health, have tried to weave an international regulatory net. The 1989 Basel Convention, a 170-nation accord, requires that developed nations notify developing nations of incoming hazardous waste shipments. Environmental groups and many undeveloped nations called the terms too weak, and in 1995 protests led to an amendment known as the Basel Ban, which forbids hazardous waste shipments to poor countries. Though the ban has yet to take effect, the European Union has written the requirements into its laws.

The EU also requires manufacturers to shoulder the burden of safe disposal. Recently a new EU directive encourages "green design" of electronics, setting limits for allowable levels of lead, mercury, fire retardants, and other substances. Another directive requires manufacturers to set up infrastructure to collect e-waste and ensure responsible recycling—a strategy called take-back. In spite of these safeguards, untold tons of e-waste still slip out of European ports, on their way to the developing world.

In the United States, electronic waste has been less of a legislative priority. One of only three countries to sign but not ratify the Basel Convention (the other two are Haiti and Afghanistan), it does not require green design or take-back programs of manufacturers, though a few states have stepped in with their own laws. The U.S. approach, says Matthew Hale, EPA solid waste program director, is instead to encourage responsible recycling by working with industry—for instance, with a ratings system that rewards environmentally sound products with a seal of approval. "We're definitely trying to channel market forces, and look for cooperative approaches and consensus standards," Hale says.

The result of the federal hands-off policy is that the greater part of e-waste sent to domestic recyclers is shunted overseas.

"'We in the developed world get the benefit from these devices," says Jim Puckett, head of Basel Action Network, or BAN, a group that opposes hazardous waste shipments to developing nations. "But when our equipment becomes unusable, we externalize the real environmental costs and liabilities to the developing world."

Asia is the center of much of the world's high-tech manufacturing, and it is here the devices often return when they die. China in particular has long been the world's electronics graveyard. With explosive growth in its manufacturing sector fueling demand, China's ports have become conduits for recyclable scrap of every sort: steel, aluminum, plastic, even paper. By the mid-1980s, electronic waste began freely pouring into China as well, carrying the lucrative promise of the precious metals embedded in circuit boards.

Vandell Norwood, owner of Corona Visions, a recycling company in San Antonio, Texas, remembers when foreign scrap brokers began trolling for electronics to ship to China. Today he opposes the practice, but then it struck him and many other recyclers as a win-win situation. "They said this stuff was all going to get recycled and put back into use," Norwood remembers brokers assuring him. "It seemed environmentally responsible. And it was profitable, because I was getting paid to have it taken off my hands." Huge volumes of scrap electronics were shipped out, and the profits rolled in.

Any illusion of responsibility was shattered in 2002, the year Puckett's group, BAN, released a documentary film that showed the reality of e-waste recycling in China. *Exporting Harm* focused on the town of Guiyu in Guangdong Province, adjacent to Hong Kong. Guiyu had become the dumping ground for massive quantities of electronic junk. BAN documented thousands of people—entire families, from young to old—engaged in dangerous practices like burning computer wire to expose copper, melting circuit boards in pots to extract lead and other metals, or dousing the boards in powerful acid to remove gold.

China had specifically prohibited the import of electronic waste in 2000, but that had not stopped the trade. After the worldwide publicity BAN's film generated, however, the government lengthened the list of forbidden e-wastes and began pushing local governments to enforce the ban in earnest.

On a recent trip to Taizhou, a city in Zhejiang Province south of Shanghai that was another center of e-waste processing, I saw evidence of both the crackdown and its limits. Until a few years ago, the hill country outside Taizhou was the center of a huge but informal electronics disassembly industry that rivaled Guiyu's. But these days, customs officials at the nearby Haimen and Ningbo ports—clearinghouses for massive volumes of metal scrap—are sniffing around incoming shipments for illegal hazardous waste.

High-tech scrap "imports here started in the 1990s and reached a peak in 2003," says a high school teacher whose students tested the environment around Taizhou for toxics from e-waste. He requested anonymity from fear of local recyclers angry about the drop in business. "It has been falling since 2005 and now is hard to find."

Today the salvagers operate in the shadows. Inside the open door of a house in a hillside village, a homeowner uses pliers to rip microchips and metal parts off a computer motherboard. A buyer will burn these pieces to recover copper. The man won't reveal his name. "This business is illegal," he admits, offering a cigarette. In the same village, several men huddle inside a shed, heating circuit boards over a flame to extract metal. Outside the door lies a pile of scorched boards. In another village a few miles away, a woman stacks up bags of circuit boards in her house. She shoos my translator and me away. Continuing through the hills, I see people tearing apart car batteries, alternators, and high-voltage cable for recycling, and others hauling aluminum scrap to an aging smelter. But I find no one else working with electronics. In Taizhou, at least, the e-waste business seems to be waning.

Yet for some people it is likely too late; a cycle of disease or disability is already in motion. In a spate of studies released last year, Chinese scientists documented the environmental plight of Guiyu, the site of the original BAN film. The air near some electronics salvage operations that remain open contains the highest amounts of dioxin measured anywhere in the world. Soils are saturated with the chemical, a probable carcinogen that may disrupt endocrine and immune function. High levels of flame retardants called PBDEs—common in electronics, and potentially damaging to fetal development even at very low levels—turned up in the blood of the electronics workers. The high school teacher in Taizhou says his students found high levels of PBDEs in plants and animals. Humans were also tested, but he was not at liberty to discuss the results.

China may someday succeed in curtailing electronic waste imports. But e-waste flows like water. Shipments that a few years ago might have gone to ports in Guangdong or Zhejiang Provinces can easily be diverted to friendlier environs in Thailand, Pakistan, or elsewhere. "It doesn't help in a global sense for one place like China, or India, to become restrictive," says David N. Pellow, an ethnic studies professor at the University of California, San Diego, who studies electronic waste from a social justice perspective. "The flow simply shifts as it takes the path of least resistance to the bottom."

It is next to impossible to gauge how much e-waste is still being smuggled into China, diverted to other parts of Asia, or—increasingly—dumped in West African countries like Ghana, Nigeria, and Ivory Coast. At ground level, however, one can pick out single threads from this global toxic tapestry and follow them back to their source.

In Accra, Mike Anane, a local environmental journalist, takes me down to the seaport. Guards block us at the gate. But some truck drivers at a nearby gas station point us toward a shipment facility just up the street, where they say computers are often unloaded.

There, in a storage yard, locals are opening a shipping container from Germany. Shoes, clothes, and handbags pour out onto the tarmac. Among the clutter: some battered Pentium 2 and 3 computers and monitors with cracked cases and missing knobs, all sitting in the rain. A man hears us asking questions. "You want computers?" he asks. "How many containers?"

Near the port I enter a garage-like building with a sign over the door: "Importers of British Used Goods." Inside: more age-encrusted PCs, TVs, and audio components. According to the manager, the owner of the facility imports a 40-foot (12 meters) container every week. Working items go up for sale. Broken ones are sold for a pittance to scrap collectors.

All around the city, the sidewalks are choked with used electronics shops. In a suburb called Darkuman, a dim stall is stacked front to back with CRT monitors. These are value-less relics in wealthy countries, particularly hard to dispose of because of their high levels of lead and other toxics. Apparently no one wants them here, either. Some are monochrome, with tiny screens. Boys will soon be smashing them up in a scrap market.

A price tag on one of the monitors bears the label of a chain of Goodwill stores head-quartered in Frederick, Maryland, a 45-minute drive from my house. A lot of people donate their old computers to charity organizations, believing they're doing the right thing. I might well have done the same. I ask the proprietor of the shop where he got the monitors. He tells me his brother in Alexandria, Virginia, sent them. He sees no reason not to give me his brother's phone number.

When his brother Baah finally returns my calls, he turns out not to be some shady character trying to avoid the press, but a maintenance man in an apartment complex, working 15-hour days fixing toilets and lights. To make ends meet, he tells me, he works nights and weekends exporting used computers to Ghana through his brother. A Pentium 3 brings $150 in Accra, and he can sometimes buy the machines for less than $10 on Internet liquidation websites—he favors private ones, but the U.S. General Services Administration runs one as well. Or he buys bulk loads from charity stores. (Managers of the Goodwill store whose monitor ended up in Ghana denied selling large quantities of computers to dealers.) Whatever the source, the profit margin on a working computer is substantial.

The catch: Nothing is guaranteed to work, and companies always try to unload junk. CRT monitors, though useless, are often part of the deal. Baah has neither time nor space to unpack and test his monthly loads. "You take it over there and half of them don't work," he says disgustedly. All you can do then is sell it to scrap people, he says. "What they do with it from that point, I don't know nothing about it."

Baah's little exporting business is just one trickle in the cataract of e-waste flowing out of the U.S. and the rest of the developed world. In the long run, the only way to prevent it from flooding Accra, Taizhou, or a hundred other places is to carve a new, more responsible direction for it to flow in. A Tampa, Florida, company called Creative Recycling Systems has already begun.

The key to the company's business model rumbles away at one end of a warehouse— a building-size machine operating not unlike an assembly line in reverse. "David" was what company president Jon Yob called the more than three-million-dollar investment in machines and processes when they were installed in 2006; Goliath is the towering stockpile of U.S. e-scrap. Today the machine's steel teeth are chomping up audio and video components. Vacuum pressure and filters capture dust from the process. "The air that comes out is cleaner than the ambient air in the building," vice president Joe Yob (Jon's brother) bellows over the roar.

A conveyor belt transports material from the shredder through a series of sorting stations: vibrating screens of varying finenesses, magnets, a device to extract leaded glass, and an eddy current separator—akin to a reverse magnet, Yob says—that propels nonferrous metals like copper and aluminum into a bin, along with precious metals like gold, silver, and palladium. The most valuable product, shredded circuit boards, is shipped to a state-of-the-art smelter in Belgium specializing in precious-metals recycling. According to Yob, a four-foot-square (1.2-meter-square) box of the stuff can be worth as much as $10,000.

In Europe, where the recycling infrastructure is more developed, plant-size recycling machines like David are fairly common. So far, only three other American companies have such equipment. David can handle some 150 million pounds (68 million kilograms) of electronics a year; it wouldn't take many more machines like it to process the entire country's output of high-tech trash. But under current policies, pound for pound it is still more profitable to ship waste abroad than to process it safely at home. "We can't compete economically with people who do it wrong, who ship it overseas," Joe Yob says. Creative Recycling's investment in David thus represents a gamble—one that could pay off if the EPA institutes a certification process for recyclers that would define minimum standards for the industry. Companies that rely mainly on export would have difficulty meeting such standards. The EPA is exploring certification options.

Ultimately, shipping e-waste overseas may be no bargain even for the developed world. In 2006, Jeffrey Weidenhamer, a chemist at Ashland University in Ohio, bought some cheap, Chinese-made jewelry at a local dollar store for his class to analyze. That the jewelry contained high amounts of lead was distressing, but hardly a surprise; Chinese-made leaded jewelry is all too commonly marketed in the U.S. More revealing were the amounts of copper and tin alloyed with the lead. As Weidenhamer and his colleague Michael Clement argued in a scientific paper published this past July, the proportions of these metals in some samples suggest their source was leaded solder used in the manufacture of electronic circuit boards.

"'The U.S. right now is shipping large quantities of leaded materials to China, and China is the world's major manufacturing center," Weidenhamer says. "It's not all that surprising things are coming full circle and now we're getting contaminated products back." In a global economy, out of sight will not stay out of mind for long.

The Real Roots of Darfur

The violence in Darfur is usually attributed to ethnic hatred. But global warming may be primarily to blame.

To truly understand the crisis in Darfur—and it has been profoundly misunderstood—you need to look back to the mid-1980s, before the violence between African and Arab began to simmer. Alex de Waal, now a program director at the Social Science Research Council, was there at that time, as a doctoral candidate doing anthropological fieldwork. Earlier this year, he told me a story that, he says, keeps coming back to him.

De Waal was traveling through the dry scrub of Darfur, studying indigenous reactions to the drought that gripped the region. In a herders' camp near the desert's border, he met with a bedridden and nearly blind Arab sheikh named Hilal Abdalla, who said he was noticing things he had never seen before: Sand blew into fertile land, and the rare rain washed away alluvial soil. Farmers who had once hosted his tribe and his camels were now blocking their migration; the land could no longer support both herder and farmer. Many tribesmen had lost their stock and scratched at millet farming on marginal plots.

The God-given order was broken, the sheikh said, and he feared the future. "The way the world was set up since time immemorial was being disturbed," recalled de Waal. "And it was bewildering, depressing. And the consequences were terrible."

In 2003, another scourge, now infamous, swept across Darfur. Janjaweed fighters in military uniforms, mounted on camels and horses, laid waste to the region. In a campaign of ethnic cleansing targeting Darfur's blacks, the armed militiamen raped women, burned

Stephen Faris, "The Real Roots of Darfur," from *Atlantic Monthly*, April 2007. Copyright © 2007 by Atlantic Monthly Company. Permission to reprint granted by the publisher.

The Real Roots of Darfur | 343

houses, and tortured and killed men of fighting age. Through whole swaths of the region, they left only smoke curling into the sky.

At their head was a 6-foot-4 Arab with an athletic build and a commanding presence. In a conflict the United States would later call genocide, he topped the State Department's list of suspected war criminals. De Waal recognized him: His name was Musa Hilal, and he was the sheikh's son.

The fighting in Darfur is usually described as racially motivated, pitting mounted Arabs against black rebels and civilians. But the fault lines have their origins in another distinction, between settled farmers and nomadic herders fighting over failing lands. The aggression of the warlord Musa Hilal can be traced to the fears of his father, and to how climate change shattered a way of life.

Until the rains began to fail, the sheikh's people lived amicably with the settled farmers. The nomads were welcome passers-through, grazing their camels on the rocky hillsides that separated the fertile plots. The farmers would share their wells, and the herders would feed their stock on the leavings from the harvest. But with the drought, the farmers began to fence off their land—even fallow land—for fear it would be ruined by passing herds. A few tribes drifted elsewhere or took up farming, but the Arab herders stuck to their fraying livelihoods—nomadic herding was central to their cultural identity. (The distinction between "Arab" and "African" in Darfur is defined more by lifestyle than any physical difference: Arabs are generally herders, Africans typically farmers. The two groups are not racially distinct.)

The name *Darfur* means "Land of the Fur" (the largest single tribe of farmers in Darfur), but the vast region holds the tribal lands—the *dars*—of many tribes. In the late 1980s, landless and increasingly desperate Arabs began banding together to wrest their own *dar* from the black farmers. In 1987, they published a manifesto of racial superiority, and clashes broke out between Arabs and Fur. About 3,000 people, mostly Fur, were killed, and hundreds of villages and nomadic camps were burned before a peace agreement was signed in 1989. More fighting in the 1990s entrenched the divisions between Arabs and non-Arabs, pitting the Arab pastoralists against the Fur, Zaghawa, and Massaleit farmers. In these disputes, Sudan's central government, seated in Khartoum, often supported the Arabs politically and sometimes provided arms.

In 2003, a rebellion began in Darfur—a reaction against Khartoum's neglect and political marginalization of the region. And while the rebels initially sought a pan-ethnic front, the schism between those who opposed the government and those who supported it broke largely on ethnic lines. Even so, the conflict was rooted more in land envy than in ethnic hatred. "Interestingly, most of the Arab tribes who have their own land rights did not join the government's fight," says David Mozersky, the International Crisis Group's project director for the Horn of Africa.

Why did Darfur's lands fail? For much of the 1980s and '90s, environmental degradation in Darfur and other parts of the Sahel (the semi-arid region just south of the Sahara) was blamed on the inhabitants. Dramatic declines in rainfall were attributed to mistreatment of the region's vegetation. Imprudent land use, it was argued, exposed more rock and sand, which absorb less sunlight than plants, instead reflecting it back toward space. This cooled the air near the surface, drawing clouds downward and reducing the chance of rain. "Africans were said to be doing it to themselves," says Isaac Held, a senior scientist at the National Oceanic and Atmospheric Administration.

But by the time of the Darfur conflict four years ago, scientists had identified another cause. Climate scientists fed historical sea-surface temperatures into a variety of computer models of atmospheric change. Given the particular pattern of ocean-temperature changes worldwide, the models strongly predicted a disruption in African monsoons. "This was not caused by people cutting trees or overgrazing," says Columbia University's Alessandra Giannini, who led one of the analyses. The roots of the drying of Darfur, she and her colleagues had found, lay in changes to the global climate.

The extent to which those changes can be blamed on human activities remains an open question. Most scientists agree that greenhouse gases have warmed the tropical and southern oceans. But just how much artificial warming—as opposed to natural drifts in oceanic temperatures—contributed to the drought that struck Darfur is as debatable as the relationship between global warming and the destruction of New Orleans. "Nobody can say that Hurricane Katrina was definitely caused by climate change," says Peter Schwartz, the co-author of a 2003 Pentagon report on climate change and national security. "But we can say that climate change means more Katrinas. For any single storm, as with any single drought, it's difficult to say. But we can say we'll get more big storms and more severe droughts."

With countries across the region and around the world suffering similar pressures, some see Darfur as a canary in the coal mine, a foretaste of climate-driven political chaos. Environmental degradation "creates very dry tinder," says de Waal. "So if anyone wants to put a match to it, they can light it up." Combustion might be particularly likely in areas where the political or social geography is already fragile. "Climate change is likely to cause tension all over the world," says Idean Salehyan, a political scientist at the University of North Texas. Whether or not it sparks conflict, he says, depends on the strength, goodwill, and competence of local and national governments. (For more on the economic, political, and military tensions that global warming might create, see "Global Warming: What's in It for You?" by Gregg Easterbrook, on page 52.)

In Darfur itself, recognizing climate change as a player in the conflict means seeking a solution beyond a political treaty between the rebels and the government. "One can see a way of de-escalating the war," says de Waal. "But unless you get at the underlying roots, it'll just spring back." One goal of the internationally sponsored peace process is the eventual return of locals to their land. But what if there's no longer enough decent land to go around?

To create a new status quo, one with the moral authority of the God-given order mourned by Musa Hilal's father, local leaders would have to put aside old agreements and carve out new ones. Lifestyles and agricultural practices would likely need to change to accommodate many tribes on more fragile land. Widespread investment and education would be necessary.

But with Khartoum uncooperative, creating the conditions conducive to these sorts of solutions would probably require not only forceful foreign intervention but also a long-term stay. Environmental degradation means the local authorities have little or no surplus to use for tribal buy-offs, land deals, or coalition building. And fighting makes it nearly impossible to rethink land ownership or management. "The first thing you've got to do is stop the carnage and allow moderates to come to the fore," says Thomas Homer-Dixon, a political scientist at the University of Toronto. Yet even once that happens, he admits, "these processes can take decades."

Among the implications arising from the ecological origin of the Darfur crisis, the most significant may be moral. If the region's collapse was in some part caused by the emissions from our factories, power plants, and automobiles, we bear some responsibility for the dying. "This changes us from the position of Good Samaritans—disinterested, uninvolved people who may feel a moral obligation—to a position where we, unconsciously and without malice, created the conditions that led to this crisis," says Michael Byers, a political scientist at the University of British Columbia. "We cannot stand by and look at it as a situation of discretionary involvement. We are already involved."

This article available online at:

http://www.theatlantic.com/magazine/archive/2007/04/the-real-roots-of-darfur/5701/

The Chad-Cameroon Oil Project
Poverty Reduction or Recipe for Disaster?

Together, we need to demonstrate that petroleum resources can be used to lift people out of deep poverty. The world is watching this experiment closely.[1]

—Callisto Madavo, Vice President
for Sub-Saharan Africa, The World Bank

Life in the world of oil is such that morals will never have a place in it.[2]

—Loic le Froch-Prigent
ex-CEO of Elf Aquitane

I t was mid-July 2003, and a series of press releases had just announced the initial production of oil from the Miandoum field in the Doba basin of Chad. The oil was to traverse a 1070 kilometer (665 mile) pipeline from southern Chad through Cameroon before reaching the Kribi terminal on the Cameroon coast. The project was coming on line early, by as much as six months, according to one report.[3]

This would seem to be good news for the three major oil firms involved, the World Bank, and other financial organizations which had joined in the project, and, perhaps most of all, for the citizens of the two primary countries involved, Chad and Cameroon. Yet a great deal of cynicism and criticism in respect to this largely privately funded $3.7 billion project still existed among a sizeable portion of interested observers, particularly among some of the better-known Non-Governmental Organizations (NGOs). In addi-

M. E. Barrett, "The Chad-Cameroon Oil Project: Poverty Reduction or Recipe for Disaster?" pp. 1–12. Copyright © 2004 by Thunderbird: The Garvin School of International Management. Permission to reprint granted by the publisher.

The Chad-Cameroon Oil Project | 347

tion, the rebel Movement for Democracy and Justice in Chad (MDJT) described the event as "a dark day for the entire Chadian people."[4]

COUNTRY BACKGROUND

A former French colony, Chad was widely viewed as being among the poorest and least-developed countries in the world. Located near the geographic center of the African continent, the borders of this landlocked nation were more than 1000 kilometers (625 miles) from the nearest seaport.

Despite the fact that much of the country is arid and dry, about 90% of its population is involved in agriculture or animal grazing, rendering them subject to the vagaries of both weather and worldwide commodity prices. Through the early 2000s, its primary exports were cotton and beef cattle. The land area of Chad, some 1.284 million square kilometers, is roughly twice the size of Texas (two and one-third times that of France). Population estimates in the early 2000s ranged from 7.6 to 8.6 million people.

A largely rural population (approximately 76%) and only 2.5% of its land classified as arable made the lifestyle of the average Chadian both harsh and challenging. Life expectancy at birth was only 48 years, compared to 78 and 79 in the U.S. and France. One in ten infants perished shortly after birth, with only eight in ten surviving five years. Approximately one-half of the population was 14 years of age or younger. Adult literacy was 44%, with female literacy at 36%.

A pronounced lack of basic, Western-style infrastructure added to the difficulties faced by the local people. While there were as many as 32,000 kilometers (km) of roads in the country (approximately 20,000 miles), almost 80% of them appeared to be slightly improved dirt roads that became unusable in the rainy season. Another 20% or so were improved and usable, but unpaved. Somewhere between 300 and 500 km of paved, all-season roads existed by mid-2003. In addition, electricity was unavailable to all but about 5% of the population, and its cost was three to four times that found in North America or Western Europe. The 2001 gross domestic product (GDP) per capita was $200, or less than six-tenths of 1% that of the United States.[5]

The average annual growth rate in Chad's GDP between 1990 and 2001 was 2.5%, comparing unfavorably to an average population growth rate of 2.7%. By late 2001, however, the GDP growth rate was up to 8.5%, with expectations of even higher rates in 2002 through 2005 as the Chad-Cameroon Oil Project progressed through the construction phase and on to the actual production and sale of crude oil. See Exhibit 1 for additional, and comparative, demographic and economic data.

In general, the country was one of contradictions, complexities, and constraints. It was home to more than 200 ethnic groups, over 100 languages and dialects and three major religious beliefs (Islam, Christianity and Animism). There was a long-standing history of rivalry and enmity between the predominantly nomadic northerners and the primarily agricultural southerners. The ethnic, linguistic, religious and occupational differences were accompanied by mistrust, misunderstandings and, over the past 40 years or so, rather brutal clashes.

Historical Background

Chad historically served as a crossroads area providing a passageway between the largely Islamic regions of the north and the Animist (and later, Christian) regions of the more tropical and agriculturally hospitable regions of southern Chad, Cameroon, and Nigeria. Chad's central-African location also led to its being the site of widespread trade in Black African slaves by Arab traders over the period roughly defined as 1500 to 1900.

The first French military incursions into Chad occurred in the late 1800s. After 20 to 25 years of sporadic battles, the French completed their occupation by moving into northern Chad. Armed clashes, however, continued for many years.

In 1960, Chad became a fully independent nation with Francis Tombalbaye from the French-speaking southern region of the country elected as president. Though originally elected by popular vote, Tombalbaye moved steadily toward dictatorial rule. In response, a number of citizens, predominantly northerners, joined armed opposition groups and a long period of civil war and economic chaos began. In 1975, Tombalbaye was replaced in a military coup by another southerner.

A wide variety of governments existed over the 15 years that followed. Two notable events were the 1982 armed overthrow of a transitional government by forces loyal to a northerner by the name of Hissene Habre and the growing involvement, including militarily, of Libya which continued until the mid-1990s. The emergence of northerners as leaders resulted in the reversal of 20 years of bias against northerners—increasingly substituted with bias against the tribal and ethnic groups from the south. The Libyan involvement (almost always on the side of northerners) led to counter responses on the part of France on several occasions.

In late 1990 with the tacit support of both France and Libya, Idriss Deby, a member of an Islamic minority tribe in northeastern Chad, led a military force which overthrew the existing government. He was elected president in a popular election in 1996 and re-elected in 2001, although serious charges of vote rigging were made by opposition parties in respect to both elections. Governmental instability marked much of the 1990s, with five different prime ministers and 20 different governments existing between 1990 and 1998. Armed resistance of at least some significance continued through mid-2003.

In the midst of the political chaos, a variety of NGOs raised issues of human rights abuse by forces loyal to the central government as well as by those opposed. Amnesty International's 2000, 2001 and 2002 annual reports, for example, all cited a continuing pattern of torture, disappearances, and/or extrajudicial executions.[6] In a June 2001 letter to James Wolfensohn, President of the World Bank, a senior environmental economist from the NGO Environmental Defense cited the example of a former member of parliament from Chad's oil producing region who was beaten with iron bars while in government detention. He was later flown to France for medical treatment.[7] The man in question had been detained by government forces not long after presenting a claim to an international panel requesting an investigation into the Chad-Cameroon Oil and Pipeline project.

Government Operations and Funding

As noted, the decade of the 1990s was a chaotic period in terms of the operational stability of the Chadian government. An earlier case on the Chad-Cameroon Oil Project cited central government finances as being "chaotic" with civil servants often "paid two or three months late."[8]

As an independent country, Chad historically had been dependent on foreign aid, much of which had come from France, although France's contribution had dropped dramatically in the most recent years.

Chad's external debt totaled $1.116 billion in 2000, with $918 million of that from either the International Development Association (IDA) of the World Bank, the International Monetary Fund (IMF) or other multilateral lenders. The country's total debt service in the same year was 11.1% of the value of its exports, a number that would have been much higher without the ongoing debt forgiveness and concessionary interest rates which it had been receiving from its multilateral lenders.

Chad's central government revenue amounted to approximately $112 million (US) in 2000. It had decreased by about 34% (in dollar terms) since 1991. Foreign Direct Investment (FDI) amounted to just $15 million in 2000—and that was a four-fold increase from 1991.

THE WORLD BANK AND THE NGOS

Conceived during World War II in Bretton Woods, New Hampshire, USA, the World Bank was created to provide assistance in the rebuilding of Europe after the war. Its first loan, in the amount of $250 million, was granted to France in 1947 for post-war reconstruction. Over time, the bank both expanded and changed its focus.

Increasingly, the publicly stated overarching goal of the institution became poverty reduction with a worldwide focus. Funding sources for the World Bank (other than interest earned and principal repayments on existing loans) came from a rather large group of donor countries. A Board of Executive Directors, consisting of individuals who represented one or more donor countries, had to approve all lending and investment decisions.

By 2002, the World Bank was involved in more than 100 developing countries. It dispensed more than $19.5 billion that year and encompassed the following overlapping institutions:

- The International Bank for Reconstruction and Development (IBRD)
- The International Development Association (IDA)
- The International Finance Corporation (IFC)
- The Multilateral Investment Guaranty Agency (MIGA)
- The International Center for Settlement of Investment Disputes (ICSID)

Non-Governmental Organizations

Non-Governmental Organizations are non-profit agencies involved in social and developmental activities around the world. Some are large, well-funded and well-known, such as the Red Cross. Others are small, inadequately funded and known only to a few people.

While the exact count of NGOs in existence was an elusive number by the early 2000s, it was abundantly clear that there were a large and growing number of them. By the late 1990s, for example, the UN had granted consultative status to some 1350 such organizations. In addition, there were said to be 50,000 NGOs in South Africa and the Kenya-based *Sunday Nation* newspaper reported that some 240 new NGOs were being formed each year in Kenya alone, where they joined the competition for $1.2 billion in annual donor funding.[9]

It was also clear that NGOs, in total, had a large and growing influence. As early as 1996, as much as $7 billion a year of foreign aid was being channeled through NGOs, with $3.5 billion of that in Africa alone.[10]

As one might imagine, a group of organizations of the size and influence noted was not without critics. Some cited so-called "pocket NGOs" with no known offices or with businesses employing multiple members of the same family.[11] Others noted that "a middle-level NGO worker in Africa" could easily earn five times, or more, what was paid to a typical civil servant in sub-Saharan Africa. This, it was claimed, resulted in draining human resources away from existing government agencies in this region of the world.[12]

Despite such criticism, a combination of donor frustration with the corruption and/or ineffectiveness of the governments of many developing countries and the results of internal audits performed by staff members at institutions such as the World Bank and the Asian Development Bank (ADB)[13] indicated that the role of NGOs in developing nations was likely to grow.

THE CHAD-CAMEROON DEVELOPMENT PROJECT

Attempts to develop oil resources in Chad date back to the late 1960s when Conoco found signs of oil in the south. A combination of poor quality oil, civil strife and lack of infrastructure caused a halt in exploration and Conoco later sold its rights to a group consisting of Exxon, Royal Dutch Shell and Chevron. This group, in turn, negotiated a 30-year concession with the Chadian government in 1988. In 1990, Elf Aquitane of France replaced Chevron in the consortium.

In the 1990s, at least four significant events occurred in the ongoing march toward developing an active oil industry in Chad. First, in the mid 1990s significant oil reserves—amounting to perhaps as much as one billion barrels—were confirmed. Second, in 1996 a bilateral treaty was signed between Chad and Cameroon covering details of the construction and operation of a pipeline through Cameroon. Third, in 1997 an amended agreement between the three-firm oil consortium and the government of Chad was enacted by the Chadian National Assembly. Finally, in 1999, the makeup of the consortium itself was altered as Royal Dutch Shell and Elf Aquitane withdrew. After some negotiation, ExxonMobil was able to convince Petronas (the national oil company of Malaysia) and Chevron (later known as ChevronTexaco) to join the consortium and progress resumed.

The Project

The Chad-Cameroon Petroleum Development and Pipeline Project, as it is formally known, is focused on the development of oil fields in southern Chad with an initial estimate of costs in the neighborhood of US$1.5 billion and on the construction of a 1070 kilometer pipeline and offshore transshipment facilities along Cameroon's coast with an initial estimated cost of US$2.2 billion. It was the largest foreign direct investment in sub-Saharan Africa at the time of its approval by the World Bank in June 2000. See Exhibits 2 and 3 for maps showing the location of both the pipeline and the oil fields.

ExxonMobil, Petronas and ChevronTexaco held, respectively, 40%, 35% and 25% ownership positions in the three-firm oil consortium. By mid-2003, it was projected that the project would result in anywhere from $2.5 billion to $5.0 billion in direct revenues for Chad over the approximately 25 years of the project.[14] These revenues would come from three distinct sources: a 12.5% royalty on the oil produced (in cash or in crude oil), income tax on the consortium's taxable income, and Chad's share of the net income from the joint ventures (TOTCO and COTCO) formed to own and operate the Chadian and Cameroonian sections of the oil pipeline. While the pipeline profit should prove to be reasonably stable, the royalty and income tax payments, which will comprise the bulk of the money involved, will fluctuate in line with both the price of crude oil and the volume of production.

A World Bank publication noted in December 2002 that Cameroon could expect to receive approximately $500 million over the life of the project (or an average of $20 million per year).[15]

By almost any measure, the Chad-Cameroon Project was an immense undertaking. The oilfield development alone included drilling up to 300 wells across three reasonably adjacent oilfields in southern Chad. The pipeline project involved laying 665 miles of 30-inch diameter pipe (along with fiber optic cable to serve as the backbone for the project's telecommunications system) buried one meter in the ground through terrain that was environmentally sensitive and, on occasion, technically challenging.

The offshore marine terminal near the terminus of the pipeline necessitated a 12-km undersea pipeline and a Floating Storage and Offloading (FSO) vessel which was built in Singapore. Advance planning for the overall project involved, in addition to direct discussions and negotiations with the two host governments, 145 meetings with 260 NGOs over the 1993 to 1999 period.

Organizational Aspects

The three-firm oil consortium consisted of an affiliate of ExxonMobil (Esso Exploration and Production Chad, Inc.), Petronas and ChevronTexaco. Esso Chad served as the operator. In addition to the two host countries, there were two joint venture firms formed to own and operate the pipelines, plus the World Bank and some additional international developmental and/or financial institutions and a significant number of NGOs. The pipeline joint venture firms (TOTCO for Chad [Tchad in French] and COTCO for Cameroon) were over 80% owned by the consortium with the Chadian government owning a minority interest in both and the Cameroonian government owning a minority share in COTCO.

Financing

The overwhelming majority (just under 97%) of the financing for the project came from either the consortium or its lenders. In total, approximately 60% came directly from the consortium partners. The World Bank Group and the European Investment Bank provided a loan to the Chad and Cameroon governments which was used by them to fund their equity interests in the two joint venture pipeline firms. These loans, originally envisioned as being at concessionary rates, were granted at market rates after a series of comments and complaints from some NGOs, many of whom were opposed to the overall project.

World Bank Role

In addition to providing a modest amount of direct financing, the World Bank Group played several other roles in the overall project. Its concessionary lending affiliate, the IDA, provided financing in the approximate amount of $48 million to agencies of one or the other of the two host governments. This money was to be used to help build the administrative structure necessary to oversee various aspects of the regulatory and/or environmental issues surrounding the overall project. It also played a key role in both the creation of a Revenue Management Plan and a series of environmental safeguards and initiatives.

Likely Benefits

Apart from the direct effects of the revenues to be received by the national governments of Chad and Cameroon, there were several quite visible areas of indirect benefit.

Due to the remote location of much of the overall project and to the almost pre-industrial stage of the economies of both Chad and Cameroon, a substantial amount of work had to be done in respect to either creating or improving various aspects of the local infrastructure. Many of these improvements had to occur prior to the actual work on the oil fields and the pipeline. On the transportation side, the road from Ngoundai, Cameroon to Komé, Chad was substantially upgraded with new culverts, an improved surface and a new bridge over the M'béré river. In all, improvements to 600 kilometers of roads (including culverts and bridges) were made in the two countries. Cameroon's rail system was also extensively upgraded. In addition, airstrips, work camps and storage or shipping yards were built or improved in both countries. Finally, a variety of educational, medical or water access projects were undertaken.

At the outset, the consortium had planned on 7000 project specific construction jobs and 500 ongoing operations related jobs. The actual peak on the construction side during the fourth quarter of 2002 proved to be around 13,100, with local nationals comprising about 72% of that number. In the first quarter of 2003, some $10 million in wages was paid to local nationals, with about 60% of that going to Chadians. Due to both the use of a lottery system to select villagers for temporary unskilled work in their own region and an acceleration of the work schedule for some facilities, more than 35,000 workers had held jobs with the project at one time or another between October 2000 and March 2003.

Finally, some $612 million ($275 million in Chad) had been spent by the consortium and its contractors on goods and services bought from local contractors through late March 2003. The numbers had begun to decline by then as the construction phase of the project began to wind down. With a multiplier of three, however, the cumulative effect on the Chadian GDP was about $825 million, or the equivalent of six months of annual GDP as of 2001.

ISSUES AND OPPORTUNITIES: WHAT HAS BEEN WROUGHT?

Chad is surrounded by cautionary tales. To the west is Nigeria, where per capita income has dropped 23% since 1975, despite $300 billion earned from oil. To the east is Sudan, with its petroleum-fueled civil war. And to the south is Angola, where international oil companies (including ExxonMobil) have indirectly financed 27 years of ruinous conflict. "Look at Gabon, look at Algeria, look at Equatorial Guinea," says Samuel Nguiffo of the Center for Environment and Development, an

NGO in Cameroon. "You have no example of oil leading to development. How do you believe that things will be different in this case?

—Jerry Useem
Fortune Magazine[16]

The findings of the Panel will lead to improvements in the ongoing implementation of this challenging project, which has enormous potential to bring great benefits to the people of Chad and Cameroon.

—James D. Wolfensohn President,
The World Bank[17]

Despite the substantial progress made to date by the oil consortium and its contractors, both directly on the oil field, pipeline and export infrastructure development and in terms of working relationships with a variety of governmental, developmental and NGO agencies, a significant amount of criticism and cynicism was still present by mid-2003.

The areas of concern, expressed largely by or through NGOs, ranged from outright opposition to any and all public financing for fossil fuel and mining projects to a widely dispersed set of opinions of the Chad-Cameroon Petroleum Development and Pipeline Project.

The International Financial Institutions Programme of Friends of the Earth International asserted publicly that "fossil fuel and mining projects ... do not contribute to poverty alleviation, nor the creation of sustainable societies, as is the stated mission of international financial institutions like the World Bank."[18]

At a slightly less general level, a number of NGOs took issue with the Chad-Cameroon Project due to its tie to national governments in Chad and Cameroon, regimes which they considered to be corrupt, brutal or both. Korinna Horta, writing in the *Harvard Human Rights Journal* asked:

Can the world's most powerful development agency achieve its goal of reducing poverty where political rights are repressed, where freedom of expression and discussion are absent and opposition forces are persecuted?[19]

The article cited above also criticized the World Bank for its (earlier) continuing support of Suharto in Indonesia and Mobuto in Zaire, now the Democratic Republic of Congo, despite what the writer claimed to be widespread evidence that the funds were basically being used to either support armed repression or were "leaking" to cronies of the regime in power. The article, and several others as well, cited alleged instances of Chadian government forces killing hundreds of unarmed civilians in what would become the oil-producing region of Chad in the late 1990s. Finally an "Environmental Justice Case Study" available through the University of Michigan cited a Chadian NGO member as stating:

They say they will kill even women and children, everyone who tried to say they were against the (oil development) program.[20]

Specific to the Chad-Cameroon Project, a substantial level of concern was expressed in respect to how the Chadian national government's share of the overall project revenue was likely to be spent. Critics of the project pointed to countries such as Sudan, Nigeria and Angola as examples of what should not happen. The World Bank and the Oil Consortium, partly in response to such concerns, worked with the government of Chad to create a Revenue Management Plan (RMP) which was adopted by the country's parliament and signed into law by its president in late 1998.

Under the terms of this law, all oil royalties and dividends were to be deposited in an Offshore Sequestered Account with an international financial institution. The funds were not to be commingled with the country's general fund. More interestingly, the funds were to be allocated according to a predetermined set of guidelines as shown below:[21]

- 72% of the funds will be allocated to high priority national programs for public health, education, infrastructure such as roads, agricultural development, environmental improvements and water resources.
- 4.5% of the revenues will be specifically dedicated to development programs for the communities in the oil producing region.
- 10% will be invested in a savings account held in an international financial institution and dedicated to the benefit of future generations, a legacy of long term economic benefit to remain when the project has run out.
- The remaining 13.5% of the oil revenues will fund Chad's operating and investment expenses associated with the development of the oil.

In addition, the use of the revenues from the project was to be monitored by a group of nine individuals, called the committee for Control and Supervision of Oil, which would be drawn from the following sources:[22]

- A judge of the Chadian Supreme Court
- A deputy (member) of the Chadian Parliament
- The National Director of the Bank of the Central African States
- A Senator
- The Director of the Treasury
- A representative of local NGOs
- A representative of Chadian trade unions
- A representative of the Chadian Human Rights Association
- A representative of religious groups (alternates between Catholic, Protestant and Islamic representatives)

Exhibit 1. *Comparative Country-Related Data*

Category	Chad	Cameroon	Angola	Egypt	Nigeria	France	USA	World
Surface Area (000 sq. km)	1,284	475	1,247	1,001	924	552	9,629	133,883
Arable Land (% of total)	2.5	12.7	2.3	2.3	30.6	31.8	20.6	10.2
Population: Amount (millions)	8	15	14	65	130	59	285	6,130
Population: Annual Growth (%; 1980–2001)	2.7	2.6	3.1	2.2	2.9	0.4	1.1	1.5
Population: Urban (%; of total)	24	50	35	43	45	76	77	47
Population: Density (per sq. km)	6	33	11	65	143	108	31	47
Population: Age (%; 0–14 years)	49.6	41.6	47.4	34.7	43.9	18.7	21.2	29.6
Life Expectancy (years)	48	50	47	67	47	79	78	66
Infant Mortality (per 000 live births)	101	76	128	42	84	5	7	54
Illiteracy (%; 15 years & over)	56	23	-44	35	0	0	22	-
HIV Prevalence (% of adults: 1999)	2.69	7.73	2.78	0.02	5.06	0.44	0.61	1.05
GDP: Amount (current $, billions)	1.6	8.5	9.5	98.5	41.4	1,300	10,100	-
GDP: Avg Annual Growth (%; 1990–2001)	2.5	2.1	2.0	4.5	2.5	1.9	3.4	2.7
GDP: Per Capita (Current $)	202	559	703	1,510	319	24,490	35,087	-
Gross FDI** (% of 2001 GDP)	1.0*	1.2	14.2	0.5	2.9	10.4	3.1	5.1
Invest. In Telecom ($; billions; 1996–2001)	.012	.266	.068	2.550	.969	-	-	-
Total Debt/GDP (%)	79.4*	77.3	97.6	28.6	20.4	-	-	-
Value Added: Agriculture (% of 2001 GDP)	38.6	43.9	8.0	16.9	29.5*	-	-	-
Value Added: Industry (% of 2001 GDP)	13.7	20.2	66.8	33.2	46.0*	-	-	-
Value Added: Services (% of 2001 GDP)	47.7	35.9	25.3	50.0	24.5*	-	-	-
Exports: % of 2001 GDP	14.3	31.8	74.0	17.6	45.4	-	-	-
Imports: % of 2001 GDP	52.8	29.2	62.2	22.1	37.8	-	-	-

*2000 data

**FDI = Foreign Direct Investment

Source: 2003 World Development Indicators Database, World Bank; http://devdata.worldbank.org

Despite the unique nature of this program with its clear focus on social and infrastructural aspects of the economy, criticism continued to flow from some prominent NGOs. In particular, it was noted that the RMP gave the President the power to modify the allocation of revenue every five years by decree, without input from Parliament.[23] In addition, it was noted that the RMP covered only revenues from the three existing oil fields, leaving in question those that followed. Finally, a May 2001 article in the *New York Times* included a claim that only three or four of the nine members of the monitoring group were truly independent.[24]

There were also concerns expressed about issues more closely related to the actual construction of the project. As might have been expected of an undertaking of this size, a number of environmental, social, and economic issues arose during the planning and construction phase. The actual construction process, for example, involved the displacement of up to 100 families;[25] the destruction and/or removal of some buildings, trees or agricultural areas; and the temporary inconvenience of a number of people. The consortium arranged for a compensation plan that involved payment in kind as well as in cash to individual land users. Payments had totaled approximately $11 million by the end of the first quarter of 2003.[26]

The commentary about the actual implementation of the compensation plan proved to be mixed. Both the World Bank and the Oil Consortium pointed to an extensive process of consultation, communication, and compensation. In addition, the Secretary General of the Catholic Bishops Conference of Cameroon noted that "the compensation issue would seem to have been the best addressed so far, … (with some modest caveats)."[27]

On the other hand, other comments in various NGO publications asserted a host of problems, including:

- "It is only the Bantus (a specific tribe) who have been compensated (and, no Bagyelis—a Pygmy tribe)."[28]
- "… stealing of compensation by people linked with the authorities."[29]
- "How can one give … money to people without offering training in financial management"[30]

Other commentators expressed concern about issues such as the ethnic composition and the wage-related compensation of the workers, alleged environmental damage, and social issues such as prostitution and AIDS occurring at or near various construction sites. Oil consortium and World Bank spokespersons cited a variety of initiatives that were in place in order to deal with such issues.

Some Final Commentary

Before the project, I was just getting along. But now I have a much better situation.
—An unidentified man who used funds earned as a maintenance worker
on the project to build a house, buy two cows, and pay a dowry[31]

When the villagers heard that a big American company would pay them for their losses, they thought Father Christmas had arrived. They thought they'd get everything they wanted and were disappointed when they only got part.

—Oliver Mokum
Cameroonian Offices of Catholic Relief Services, a U.S.-based NGO[32]

There have been some positives and some negatives, but the changes have not been great. We thought this was going to be a development project, and that is not what has happened.

—Savah,
A villager in Mpango, Chad[33]

There's a need to distinguish between the company's role and the government's role, especially as the government presence has been largely absent.

—Ellen Brown
ExxonMobil Anthropologist[34]

While there was widespread agreement that the Chad-Cameroon Development Project was substantial in size with the potential to change the very nature of the countries involved, particularly so in the case of Chad, there was no shortage of opposing views, even as oil began to flow through the pipeline.

NOTES

1. Onishi, Norimitsu, and Neela Banerjee, "Chad's Wait for its Oil Riches May be Long," *The New York Times on the Web*, May 16, 2001. http://www.nytimes.com/2001/05/16/world/16CHAD.html.

2. Nguiffo, Samuel, and Susanne Breitkopf, *Broken Promises: The Chad-Cameroon Oil and Pipeline Project;Profit at any Cost*, Friends of the Earth International, Amsterdam, June 2001, p. 1.

3. "The Chad-Cameroon Oil Pipeline Comes On Stream," Panafrican News Agency; Yaoundé, Cameroon, July 16, 2003 as quoted by Countrywatch at http://www.countrywatch.com/cw_wire.asp?vCOUNTRY=035&COUNTRYNAME=Chad&UID=881348.

360 | International Relations

4. "Rebel Movement Opposes Extraction of Oil in Chad," Panafrican News Agency, Paris, France, July 16, 2003 as quoted by Countrywatch at http://www.countrywatch.com/cw_wire.asp?vCOUNTRY=035&COUNTRYNAME=chad&UID-881306.

5. On a Purchasing Power Parity basis, the per capita GDP in 2001 was approximately $1,060.

6. See the Amnesty International Reports for 2000, 2001, and 2002 at www.amnesty.org.

7. As cited in a June 13, 2001, letter by Korinna Horta to James D. Wolfensohn, President of the World Bank. The letter is available at http://www.environmentaldefense.org/documents/459_letter%20to%20Mr%20James%20... as accessed on 4/20/2003.

8. Gee, Fransesca and Olivier Cadot; *Chad's Billion-Barrel Oilfield: From Rags to Riches?* (Fontainebleau, France: INSEAD, 1999), page 5.

9. Chege, Sam, "Donors Shift More Aid to NGOs," *Africa Recovery Online: A United Nations Publication,*United Nations, New York City, at http://www.un.org/ecosocdev/geninfo/afrec/vol13no1/aid2ngo.html, as accessed on May 9, 2003.

10. Ibid.

11. Ibid.

12. Ibid.

13. A late 2001 article in the *Financial Times* of London noted both a recent report by the World Bank's internal audit staff that "barely half of its lending operations in the past decade are likely to produce sustainable benefits," and an ADB internal audit that showed "fewer than a third of its projects in recent years are likely to provide lasting social or economic benefits." See Rich, Bruce, and Steve Schwartzman, "OPECD: How to Improve Development: Western Aid All Too Often Ends Up in the Wrong Hands," *Financial Times*(London), November 28, 2001, USA Edition, page 1.

14. "Chad Begins Production, Though Crude Exports Still Several Months Away," *Platt's Oilgram News,*Volume 81, No. 132, Friday, July 11, 2003, pp. 1 and 4.

15. "The Chad-Cameroon Petroleum Development and Pipeline Project: Project Overview," The World Bank Group: Sub-Saharan Africa, last updated December 18, 2002, as accessed on January 22, 2003. See http://www.worldbank.org/afr/ccproj/project/pro_overview.html.

16. Useem, Jerry, "Exxon's African Adventure: How to Build a $3.5 Billion Pipeline with the 'Help' of NGOs,the World Bank, and, Yes, Chicken Sacrifices," *Fortune*, April 15, 2002, page 106.

17. "World Bank Board of Directors Approves Management's Response to Inspection Panel Report on Chad-Cameroon Pipeline Project," DevNews Media Center, The World Bank Group, September 12, 2002 as accessed on April 20, 2003. See http://web.worldbank.org/WBSITE/EXTERNAL/NEWS/Ocontent MDK:20067840~menu.

18. Nguiffo, Samuel, "Traversing Peoples Lives," Friends of the Earth International and Centre Pour L'Environnement et le Developpement (CED) Cameroun, Yaourde, Cameroon, September 2002, page 2.

19. Horta, Korinna, "Rhetoric and Reality: Human Rights and the World Bank." *Harvard Human Rights Journal,* Volume 15 (2002), page 229.

20. Grimes, Kathleen, "Environmental Justice Case Study: The Chad-Cameroon Oil and Pipeline Project," page 4 of 8 at http://umich.edu/~snre492/Jones/pipe.htm, as accessed on May 15, 2003.

21. Chad-Cameroon Development Project: Benefits: Revenue Management Plan, Esso Exploration and Production Chad, Inc. at http://www.essochad.com/Chad/Benefits/Revenue/Chad_Revenue.asp, as accessed on July 24, 2003.

22. Ibid.

23. Rosenblum, Peter, "Analysis of Chad's Revenue Management Law" in *The Chad-Cameroon Oil and Pipeline Project: A Call for Accountability*, Environmental Defense, USA, et al., page 10.

24. Onishi and Banerjee, "Chad's Wait for Its Oil Riches May Be Long."

25. All permanently displaced families were said to be in Chad in the oilfield development areas.

26. Chad Export Project Report #10, 1st Quarter 2003, Esso Exploration and Production Chad, Inc., page 27. Available at http://www.essochad.com.

27. Msgr. Patrick Lafon, "The Concerns of the Church" in *The Chad-Cameroon Oil and Pipeline Project: A Call for Accountability*, page 8.

28. Felix Devalois Ndi Ongbwa, "The Impact of the Pipeline on People and the Environment in Ocean Province," Center for Environment and Development, Lolodorf, Cameroon, *The Chad-Cameroon Oil and Pipeline Project: A Call for Accountability*, page 17.

29. In a January 30, 2002, letter to the International Advisory Group: Chad-Cameroon Petroleum Development and Pipeline Project, by Korinnna Horta of Environmental Defense, U.S. and others.

30. Felix Devalois Ndi Ongbwa, "The Impact of the Pipeline," page 16.

31. Silverstein, Ken, "Pipeline's Profit May Bypass Africans," *Los Angeles Times*, June 17, 2003, page A-1.

32. Ibid.

33. Ibid.

34. Ibid.

Exhibit 2   Pipeline Transportation System

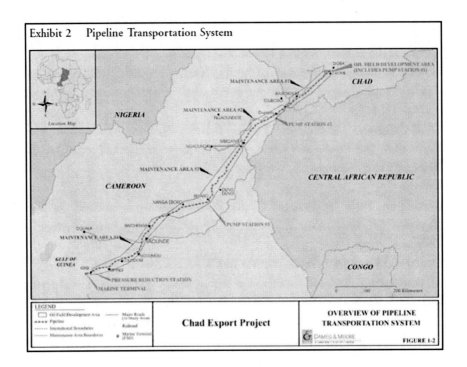

Exhibit 3   Oil Field Project Area

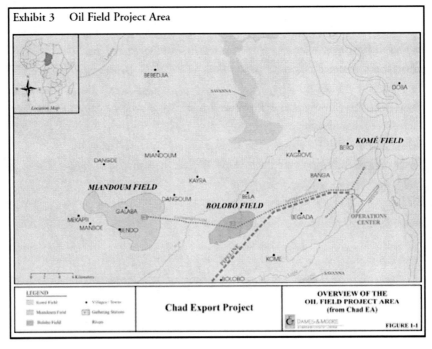

Breinigsville, PA USA
14 December 2010

251365BV00004B/2/P